ArtScroll Series®

Rabbi Nosson Scherman / Rabbi Meir Zlotowitz

General Editors

THE KATZ EDITION

CHOFETZ CHAIM

Published by

Mesorah Publications, ltd

in conjunction with

THE
CHOFETZ CHAIM
HERITAGE
FOUNDATION

Loving Kindness

Daily lessons in the power of giving

Based on the Chofetz Chaim's *Ahavas Chessed*

By Rabbi Fishel Schachter
with Chana Nestlebaum

Reviewed by Rabbi Moshe Mordechai Lowy

FIRST EDITION
First Impression ... March 2003

Published and Distributed by
MESORAH PUBLICATIONS, LTD.
4401 Second Avenue / Brooklyn, N.Y 11232

Distributed in Europe by
LEHMANNS
Unit E, Viking Industrial Park
Rolling Mill Road
Jarrow, Tyne and Wear, NE32 3DP England

Distributed in Israel by
SIFRIATI / A. GITLER
6 Hayarkon Street
Bnei Brak 51127
Israel

Distributed in Australia and New Zealand by
GOLDS WORLD OF JUDAICA
3-13 William Street
Balaclava, Melbourne 3183
Victoria, Australia

Distributed in South Africa by
KOLLEL BOOKSHOP
Shop 8A Norwood Hypermarket
Norwood 2196, Johannesburg,
South Africa

THE ARTSCROLL SERIES®
CHOFETZ CHAIM: LOVING KINDNESS
© *Copyright 2003, by* MESORAH PUBLICATIONS, Ltd.
4401 Second Avenue / Brooklyn, N.Y. 11232 / (718) 921-9000 / www.artscroll.com

A project of
THE CHOFETZ CHAIM HERITAGE FOUNDATION
6 Melnick Drive / Monsey, N.Y. 10952 / (845) 352-3505

Typography by CompuScribe at ArtScroll Studios, Ltd.

Printed in the United States of America by Noble Book Press Corp.
Bound by Sefercraft, Quality Bookbinders, Ltd., Brooklyn N.Y. 11232

מכתב ברכה מאת
הרב ר' שמואל קמנצקי שליט"א
ראש ישיבה, ישיבה דפילאדעלפיא

לטוב יזכר האי גברא יקירא הרב ר' פישל שכטר שליט"א שסידר מחדש הלימודים היום יומיים של הקונטרס הקדוש "אהבת חסד" שחובר ע"י מרן החפץ חיים זצ"ל

הספר החדש יהי' לתועלת הרבים בתור שיעורים יומיים ובוודאי יתחזקו הלומדים על ידי זה.

יתברכו המחזיקים והמסייע במצוה גדולה זו להרבות אהבת חסד וקיומו.

ויהי רצון שבזכות זה יתקיים בנו שאלת תלמידי ר' אלעזר "מה יעשה אדם וינצל מחבלו של משיח? יעסוק בתורה ובגמילות חסדים."

שמואל קמנצקי

מכתב ברכה מאת
האדמו"ר מנאוואמינסק שליט"א

יעקב פרלוב
ביהמ"ד עדת יעקב נאוואמינסק
ברוקלין נ.י.

RABBI YAAKOV PERLOW
1569 • 47TH STREET
BROOKLYN, NY 11219

באתי בזה בדברי הוקרה וברכה ועידוד להמפעל הנשגב של The Chofetz Chaim Heritage Foundation על החיבור החשוב והמועיל *Chofetz Chaim: Loving Kindness* המבוסס על ספרו הקדוש של מרן החפץ חיים זצ"ל — "אהבת חסד", שמתכוננים להוציא לאור ושיהיה בעז"ה ברכה לכל בית ישראל.

אין די מילים להביע התועלת הרבה היוצאת מן התנועה הנ"ל לקיום מצוות שבין אדם לחברו; ויהי רצון שיתעוררו כל בני ישראל להגביר חיילים בדבר זה, ועל ידי כך לטהר את נפשותינו ורוחותינו, לתקן המידות ולקרב פעמי הגאולה.

[חתימה]

יעקב פרלוב

מכתב ברכה מאת
הרב ר' מתתי' סלומון, שליט"א
משגיח רוחני דישיבת בית מדרש גבוה דלייקוואוד

ט"ז אדר ב, תשס"ג לפ"ק
פה לייקווד יצ"ו

שים שלום טובה וברכה חן וחסד ורחמים עלינו ועל כל ישראל עמך
ברכנו אבינו כולנו כאחד באור פניך כי באור פניך נתת לנו ה' אלקינו
תורת חיים ואהבת חסד וכו'. ומבאר החפץ חיים זצ"ל בספרו הבהיר
אהבת חסד חלק ב' סוף פרק א' כי אור פנים זו הי' בשעת מתן תורה
כאשר נגלה ה' כמש"כ אתה הראית לדעת כי ה' הוא האלוקים אין עוד
מלבדו ואז כאשר ראו כולם עד היכן עולם חסד יבנה נכנס בלבם
אהבה עזה למדה זו ולהלך בדרכיו יתברך כדי שיוכלו להתקיים בזה
ובבא ועיין דבריו שם.

בימינו אלה אשר העולם מתמוטט כי עת מלחמה היא וכל מגמתינו
להיות זוכים לעת שלום כמה חשוב ונחוץ לכל ישראל להיות הוגים
בספר הקדוש אהבת חסד אשר כל מטרתה להשכין שלום בעולם בין אדם
לחברו ובין אדם לקונו ועל כן נחזקינא טבא להמוסר הקדוש מורשת
חפץ חיים והמחבר החשוב כמוה"ר פישל שכטר שליט"א על שהוציאו
לאור בשפה המדוברת ספר שלם מיוסד על הספר הקדוש אהבת חסד
כדי לזכות הרבים.

וכמה גדול הזכות מבואר בח"ח שמירת הלשון ח"ב סוף פ' ז' וז"ל שם
כתבו הספרים בשם הזוה"ק דבי כנישתא חדא אם היו שומרים מדת
השלום כדבעי יכולים לזכות לביאת המשיח עכ"ל. אמן כן יה"ר!

ממני הכו"ח לכבוד מזכי הרבים הנ"ל

מתתי' חיים סלומון

This *sefer* is dedicated in memory of
Rabbi Dr. Leon Katz זצ״ל
הרב אליעזר בן הגאון הרב ראובן כ״ץ זצ״ל

arav Eliezer Katz, Rabbi Dr. Leon Katz, was a unique and revered individual. A Rabbi's Rabbi, a noble gentleman, possessing an angelic smile, eloquent and erudite; these were the traits by which he was described by his colleagues, friends and congregants.

Rabbi Katz was born is Steipsk, Poland in 1911. Son of HaRav Reuven Katz, ז״ל, Chief Rabbi of Petach Tikvah, Israel, and Rabbanit Reichel (Maskil-Eitan) Katz, ז״ל, Rabbi Katz studied with Rav Shimon Shkop in Grodno before he came to the United States in 1929 to continue his studies. He received Rabbinic ordination from Rabbi Isser Zalman Meltzer and Rabbi Abba Yaacov Boruchov in Jerusalem as well as from Yeshiva University, where he also received his Bachelor and Doctorate degrees.

In 1938, he took his first and only pulpit, receiving a lifetime contract from Congregation Adas Israel in Passaic, New Jersey, where he remained as the Mara D'asra for 63 years. In 1946, he married his Aishet Chayil, Rivkah, sh'tichye, who remained by his side for 55 years.

He pursued his vision of building Passaic into a hub of modern-orthodox Judaism, establishing its first Hebrew day school, its only kosher hospital and senior citizen center, and a flourishing Jewish community center.

Rabbi Katz dedicated his life to the service of Klal Yisrael. His life spanned almost a century of transition from the Old World of the shtetl to our present technological age. Rabbi Katz's life can be characterized as a bridge from the past to the present. From his base in Passaic, he became one of the leaders of modern-centrist orthodox Judaism, assuming leadership roles in the Orthodox Union, the Rabbinical Council of America, Religious Zionists of America, Yeshiva University and many other Jewish organizations.

Although Rabbi Katz suffered much personal hardship and pain, having endured the premature loss of two children and a grandson, he remained a tower of strength and inspiration; his devotion to the precepts of the Torah never waned. He drew strength from his faith and became even more determined to transmit his wisdom to future generations; to educate the youth in the ways of Torah, G-d's most precious gift. May the publication of this book serve as a further aliyah for his neshamah.

In honor of

Rebbitzen Rivkah Katz, שתחי׳
and
Miriam and Walter Mansky, שתחיו

In loving memory of

Mayer Labe Katz, זצ״ל

Varda Roni Katz Nistar, זצ״ל

Mayer Moshe Nistar, זצ״ל

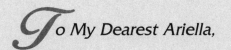

December 26, 2002

o My Dearest Ariella,

Although you may not understand at your young age, as you grow older you will come to realize the depth of my love for you.

I write to you today knowing that I will not always be physically present to partake in the experiences you will have as you grow. My hope is that I can find the words that will inspire you to become everything you can be, and that I can share with you the many lessons life has taught me.

The world around us tells us that there is so much we must have, but in truth, the necessities are very few. These are the irreplaceable things that I hope you will cherish throughout your life.

Over the past few years, I have gone through many trying times. It was only by turning my eyes toward G-d and finding strength in the love of family and friends that I was able to grow through these circumstances. There is nothing in this world that can replace the power of prayer and the love of your family and friends, who will always be there for you.

In the Iggeres HaRamban, the Ramban urges his son to build the traits of humility, respect for others and love for G-d. Striving toward these goals takes a lifetime, but this striving is in itself a way of life. I challenge you to set your standards high and to push yourself to be a leader in everything you do. Life will offer many choices and pull you in many directions; choose carefully.

With all the love in the world,

Your father

להכרת הטוב להאי גברא רבא

הרב אברהם יעקב בן הרב שלמה שיחי'

ואשתו החשובה מרת חיה גיטל בת ר' בצלאל הכהן שתחי'

יהי רצון שיזכו לראות בנים ובני בנים

עוסקים בתורה ובמצות

מתוך שלום ושמחה, עושר וכבוד

Dedicated in loving memory of
G. Leonard Rubin ע״ה

לע״נ ר׳ גרשון ליפא ב״ר ליב עזריאל ז״ל

נפ׳ ט׳ ניסן תשנ״ו

תהא נשמתו צרורה בצרור בחיים

*T*here is no more fitting place for a tribute to our beloved husband, father and grandfather, G. Leonard Rubin, than within the pages of a *sefer* teaching lessons of chesed. Chesed was the defining trait of his life. The needs of other people cried out to him, and in his own unique way, he answered them all — often anonymously. Only Hashem could possibly measure the number of lives he touched, or the number of burdens he lightened throughout his lifetime.

Who else would read in a newspaper about a blind storeowner losing $500 in a robbery, and take it upon himself to replace every penny? Who else would personally and secretly assume the expense of a shul's youth program when the shul board refused to fund it? Who else would buy all of a street vendor's newspapers so he wouldn't have to stand outside in the pouring rain to earn his living that day? Indeed, even we, the closest members of his family, did not learn of some of his acts of chesed until years after his *p'tirah*.

Not only did Lennie Rubin keep the principles of chesed uppermost in his own heart, he also strove to instill them fully in his children and grandchildren. He gave each of his children a copy of *Sefer Ahavas Chesed* to learn and to live. Every Erev Shabbos, he would ask each of his young grandchildren to describe a chesed they had done that week before rewarding them with a candy bar. Pop Pop wanted the mitzvah of chesed to be as sweet to them as it was to him. He would then give them each 36 cents to put in the *pushka*, to train their hands in the art of giving. To him, giving was indeed an art, and he was a master artist. We pray that this *sefer* will spread far and wide the *Ahavas Yisrael* and *Ahavas Chesed* his life exemplified.

Bernice Rogoff Rubin
Baltimore, Maryland

Linda and Michael Elman
Ari and Inbal, Aliza, Dov, and Rena
Baltimore, Maryland

Dale Allison Rubin
Cedarhurst, New York

Pia and Paul Rubin
Elie, Yossi, Tziporah, and Tova
New York, New York

✍ Table of Contents

THE CHOFETZ CHAIM HERITAGE FOUNDATION

*A not-for-profit foundation
dedicated to the teaching of
Jewish ethics & wisdom*

Dear Friend:

We are pleased and privileged to bring you this latest addition to our publications based on the works of the Chofetz Chaim, a Torah luminary whose wisdom continues to guide our generation.

The Chofetz Chaim Heritage Foundation is an organization devoted to disseminating the works of the Chofetz Chaim in order to move *Klal Yisrael* toward the Torah's vision of a united, holy nation. By spreading his teachings on human relations, personal integrity, ethical behavior and proper speech, we hope to strengthen the connection of Jews to each other and to Hashem.

We invite you to join us in building a world worthy of Hashem's Presence by spending some time each day learning from the Chofetz Chaim's works. If each of us can make his teachings part of our lives, together we can move our world forward toward Redemption.

Together, we can get there.

The Chofetz Chaim Heritage Foundation

6 Melnick Drive
Monsey, New York 10952
Tel 845 352-3505
Fax 845 352-3605

✎ *Authors' Acknowledgments*

וכל קרבן מנחתך במלח תמלח (*Vayikra* 2:13)
"You shall salt your every meal offering with salt."

*T*here are many explanations as to why *korbanos* require salt. One of them is that we appease the water that remained below during Creation by using its salt. Rav Yisrael of Chortkov explains that no one ever eats a dish of plain salt. Salt as an independent entity has almost no purpose other than *kashering* meat or melting the snow on the sidewalk. Salt as a food can only be internalized by allowing other foods to absorb it.

When offering a sacrifice and requesting a new chance at life, one's attitude makes all the difference. Even in your service of Hashem, if your approach focuses on "me" as an independent unit, it falls short. If you are willing to commit yourself to others and to *Klal Yisrael* at large by allowing yourself to be absorbed into the lives of the people around you, your sacrifice will "make a difference" and give you a new lease on life.

I would like to thank the entire wonderful staff at the **Chofetz Chaim Heritage Foundation** for giving me the *z'chus* of being a "pinchful of salt" in your dynamic organization. You are all part of a unit that focuses on getting everyone to focus on everyone else, and your sacrifices are truly "אשה ריח ניחוח לה'" a burnt-offering, a fire offering, a satisfying aroma to Hashem."

I would like to express my heartfelt gratitude to:

Mrs. Chana Nestlebaum for masterfully rendering the spoken word into its written form and greatly enhancing its presentation.

Mrs. Shaindy Appelbaum for exhibiting endless patience and perseverance without which deadlines would have never been met and this work would still be on schedule to be completed tomorrow.

"אחרון אחרון חביב," my wonderful family who have accepted as a way of life rearranging their schedules for Tatty to finish his work in the attic, while at the same time creating an abode of chesed down below.

May we all be *zocheh* to "תורת חיים ואהבת חסד ... באור פניך נתת לנו."

Fishel Schachter

Adar II 5763

*W*ords cannot express my gratitude to Hashem Yisborach for giving me the opportunity to take part in the creation of this *sefer*. I can imagine no more uplifting work than spending each day immersed in the world of chesed, the wisdom of the Chofetz Chaim and the illuminating *shiurim* of **Rabbi Fishel Schachter** on *Sefer Ahavas Chesed*.

Throughout the past 14 years, **Mr. Michael Rothschild** and the **Chofetz Chaim Heritage Foundation** have given me countless opportunities to delve into the Torah's depths, to learn, to write and to be an active part of this dynamic organization's inspiring work. I am deeply grateful to Mr. Rothschild for entrusting this project to me.

Abundant thanks go to **Mrs. Shaindy Appelbaum**, my "other half" in this and many other projects. Her sensitive ear for language and nuance has helped me hone each sentence to its sharpest point. Her research and organizational skills have given me the luxury of being able to just sit down and write.

I would also like to thank my parents, **Mr. and Mrs. George and Norma Berman**, and my parents in-law, **Mr. and Mrs. Chaim** ע"ה **and Miriam Nestlebaum**, for showing me what it means to live a life devoted to giving and caring for others. It is because of the values they have imparted that this *sefer* resounds so deeply for me.

I thank my children for heeding the frequent plea, "Please let Mommy work," for being proud of me and for challenging me to set my standards high.

To my husband **Mendel**, whose limitless devotion keeps me afloat, I cannot begin to express my gratitude. His tremendous *mesiras nefesh* on behalf of our family, his delight in a good *S'fas Emes*, the music and *simchah* he brings to others are forever my inspiration. May we merit Hashem's blessings as we raise our children and travel through life together.

Chana Nestlebaum

Adar II 5763

↦ *Acknowledgments*

*O*ur gratitude to Hashem *Yisbarach* is inexpressible for His having permitted us to produce this *sefer* and spread the teachings of the Chofetz Chaim.

We would like to express our deepest gratitude to RABBI MOSHE MORDECHAI LOWY, *shlita*, for his invaluable contribution to the creation of this *sefer*. His passion for accuracy, his wisdom and scholarship have assured that each word of this work is a precise reflection of the Chofetz Chaim's message. The endless hours that he spent poring over each page, researching sources, checking and rechecking, have greatly fortified the foundation upon which this *sefer* rests.

Our success flows from the Torah leaders who map out our path:

THE MANCHESTER ROSH YESHIVAH, HAGAON HARAV YEHUDAH ZEV SEGAL, *ZT"L*, the founding Rabbinic Advisor of our organization, was one of the precious resources of our generation. His love and concern for every Jew can only be compared to that of the Chofetz Chaim himself.

HAGAON HARAV SHMUEL KAMENETSKY, *SHLITA*, is the Chairman of our Rabbinical Board. He is our source of inspiration and guidance, constantly taking time out of his busy schedule to answer our questions, to give us direction and advice and to attend all our board meetings. His *mesiras nefesh* for us is incredible and we are forever indebted to him.

HAGAON HARAV AVRAHAM PAM, *ZT"L*, long provided us with his wisdom and advice as a member of our Rabbinical Board of Advisors.

HAGAON HARAV YAAKOV PERLOW, *SHLITA*, continues to guide and encourage us as a member of our Rabbinical Board of Advisors.

We are deeply grateful to the outstanding people of the Chofetz Chaim Heritage Foundation:

To our board of directors who have been a tremendous help in forging the path of our organization:

RAYMOND BEYDA, ABRAHAM BIDERMAN, ABA CLAMAN, NACHMAN FUTTERMAN, DAVID LOBEL, YITZCHOK MASHITZ, ARI PARNES, GEORGE ROHR, KURT ROTHSCHILD, DAVID SHWEKY, GEDALIAH WEINBERGER AND MOSHE ZAKHEIM.

If you have benefited from any of our programs, productions or publications, it is thanks to the selfless dedication of numerous talented individuals, our superb coordinators and our efficient office staff:

ALAN PROCTOR, ELCHONON SNYDER, BEN WYMORE, SHAINDY APPELBAUM, SHAINDY BRAUN, DRAIZY BRULL, ETTI DEAN, YOCHEVED EISENBACH, BLIMIE FRIEDMAN, BASSIE GUGENHEIM, KAYLA HALPERN, GITTY KALIKSTEIN, ETTI KLEIN, SURI KNOBLOCH, ESTIE KOOT, BLIMIE LESSER, CHAVA'LE LONDINSKI, CHUMI MANDELBAUM, ESTHER MOR, CHANA NESTLEBAUM, YAEL NEUMAN, HEIDY ORT, LEAH OZERI, RUCHIE PERLSTEIN, LEAH SEKULA, CHANA SCHNALL, TZIPPORY STEINMETZ AND CHAVIE TWERSKY.

The Chofetz Chaim Heritage Foundation is forever grateful to RABBI MENDEL KESSIN, whose tapes inspired us to start our organization.

Our organization's success is due to friends around the world who have brought our programs to their *shul*, school or community. To our 450 local coordinators—the *Rabbanim*, principals and lay people who have put their time and energy into uplifting *Klal Yisrael* — thank you so much.

To all of the above, as well as those who support us financially—the major supporters who wish to remain anonymous, the main sponsors of this book, the people who have dedicated a day in this *sefer* and the many others that have supported us—may the great *z'chus* of the Chofetz Chaim stand by you, your families and all of *Klal Yisrael*.

The Chofetz Chaim Heritage Foundation
Adar II 5763

16   □   CHOFETZ CHAIM

❧ Introduction

"Then G-d formed man from the dust of the ground and breathed into his nostrils the spirit of life ..." (*Bereishis* 2:7).

Every human being carries within himself a part of G-d, a Divine essence that was invested in man at the moment G-d breathed life into him. That essence — the soul — is what separates man from the rest of creation. But how does a person activate his soul within himself? How does he open a channel through which his soul can manifest itself in the physical world?

Chesed — kindness — is a vehicle through which a human being expresses the Divine essence in this world. That is because chesed is one of G-d's defining attributes. When a human being performs an act of chesed, he is not just "being nice." He is fulfilling the purpose for which he was created. The Torah commands us to emulate G-d. When we consider G-d's constant, limitless, perpetual act of chesed, we come to understand why doing chesed is a fulfillment of this Torah directive. All G-d does is for the ultimate benefit of His creations. He is the provider of food for millions of species of plant and animal. He concocts the right combination of elements to enable the world to breathe, thrive, reproduce and renew. He designs systems of infinitesimal precision that keep body and brain chemicals in balance, and systems of unimaginable magnitude that keep the universe in balance. He gives us the capacity to be touched by beauty, moved by sadness and awed by grandeur. All of this He projects continually into our world.

G-d's entire existence is expressed through the constant care He lavishes upon His creation. That is how we discern His nature. When we emulate His ways by lavishing care upon our fellow man, we walk in the "footprints" G-d casts upon the world.

Our Need to Give

It is therefore a further kindness that G-d has created a world full of needs for us to fill. Each individual has needs he cannot fill without the help of others. Even the richest person must depend on others for his basic necessities. Without the farmer, the trucker and the grocer, he would not eat. Without the doctor and the pharmacist, he would not recover from illness. Without the plumber, the carpenter and the electrician, his home would fall into neglect.

Hashem could easily have created a world of self-sufficient people. Instead, he created each of us with gaps and deficiencies in our abilities. In doing so, He assured that mankind would be woven together in a fabric of chesed formed of countless interlocking threads of human need and generosity. Through this design, every day of life presents a vast array of opportunities to touch the G-dliness within ourselves. Man requires chesed to keep his soul vital and expressive. Without it, his greatness remains shrouded.

When a wealthy person encounters a poor man who needs his help, his perception is that the poor man is the taker, and he is the giver. He believes that the poor man needs him. The real beneficiary, however, is the wealthy man, for he has been given an opportunity to live up to his potential as a G-dly being. In reality the poor man is the giver — the wealthy man, the taker.

Transforming Everyday Life

One might think it necessary to find the poor, the hungry or the ill in order to activate this G-dly attribute within ourselves. In reality, however, the opportunities are around us every day. Opening the door for a person encumbered by bundles is chesed. Loaning a neighbor a few dollars in an emergency is chesed. Loaning one's lawn mower or vacuum cleaner, giving someone a ride, caring for our own families, offering some advice or a few encouraging words — these are everyday acts that can rise to the level of G-dliness if we simply perform them with that intent. People laboring over mundane household chores can define themselves in two ways: Without an awareness of the chesed in their tasks, they are physical beings performing physical tasks. With that awareness, they are G-dly beings bringing cleanliness and order to their family's corner of the universe.

How You See It

Even in the work we do for a livelihood, chesed plays a major role. Each professional, businessman, craftsman and laborer is helping others through his efforts.

The Chofetz Chaim once stopped at an inn with a fellow traveler. The Chofetz Chaim lauded the innkeeper for the tremendous chesed he was doing by providing hospitality. "But Rebbe," the fellow traveler protested, "he does it for money."

"If he didn't charge money, how would he be able to keep the inn running?" the Chofetz Chaim replied.

"But he makes a profit!" the companion exclaimed.

"And if he didn't, how would he feed his family?" the Chofetz Chaim responded.

The fact that the man made a livelihood from his chesed did not diminish it in any way in the Chofetz Chaim's eyes. The innkeeper was providing shelter, a warm bed and nourishing food to travelers. In seeing to their comfort, his work was also his chesed, but only if he performed it with that intent. We, too, can transform our work into chesed with a simple change in perspective.

The Essence of the World

The Torah teaches that G-d built the world on a foundation of chesed. In the times of Noah, the powers of greed and corruption — the precise antithesis of chesed — eroded this foundation, and G-d brought the flood to wash away the perverse remnant of humanity. G-d's chesed formed the world, and therefore, He had to refine it back down to that essence in order to have a sound foundation upon which to rebuild.

Noah's ark was that refined essence. Rabbi Eliyahu Dessler (*Michtav M'Eliyahu* Vol. II) explains that for the entire time during which Noah, his wife, three sons and daughters-in-law were confined to this miraculous vessel, they worked nonstop to care for the thousands of animals they had taken on board. Each species was fed according to its natural schedule — diurnal animals in the daytime and nocturnal creatures at night. Each was fed its preferred food. Caring for the needs of their charges occupied every moment of the family's day and night. At that moment, the ark was essentially the whole world, and it was a world entirely consumed with chesed. Through it, G-d told the generations to come that chesed is the basis of the world's existence.

Training the Heart

Acts of chesed are the physical manifestation of *Ahavas Yisrael* — love of our fellow man. They are what transform "lip service" concern for others' welfare into real service to others. On its face, the Torah's directive to "love your fellow as yourself" might seem like an impossible demand. Every human being knows that it is nearly impossible to force oneself to feel love. By performing acts of chesed, however, one fulfills the mitzvah. Rav Dessler explains that giving is the very basis of love. The Hebrew word for love, *"ahavah,"* comes from the root word *"hav,"* which means give. But the connection is more than etymological. It is a deeply felt reality in human relations. The more one invests oneself in another person, the more one comes to love that person. The ultimate example of this principle is the parent-child relationship. No relationship calls for a higher level of giving, and no love is as pure as that of a parent for a child.

As a person continues to perform acts of chesed, he gradually strengthens his capacity for love. He learns to look outward toward the rest of the world, see the needs that are there and be the one to respond. *Ahavas Yisrael* expresses itself through chesed, and acts of chesed in turn nurture the constant growth of *Ahavas Yisrael* within a person's heart.

Pursuit of Happiness

Giving is a key to a fulfilling life. Through the Torah's concept of chesed, we come to understand that this sense of fulfillment springs from the soul's joy in expressing its G-dliness. Chesed feels good. Countless people have risen from despair all the way to true happiness by thrusting themselves into the role of giver, even as they waded through their own great personal challenges. The act of giving fortifies the person who is struggling, allowing him to access the light that lies within him, even as darkness surrounds him.

A Protective Shield

Beyond the benefits to the individual, chesed is the generator of powerful protective merit for the Jewish people. The years during which the

Chofetz Chaim wrote *Ahavas Chesed* were times of great travail for the Jews. World War I had taken a terrible toll and the unfathomable nightmare of World War II awaited in the wings. The Chofetz Chaim urged his generation and every generation onward to gather under the protective shelter of chesed to weather history's storms.

The Torah instructs us that when strict justice is raining down from Heaven, we have the power to mitigate its force by showing compassion to each other, for our compassion draws G-d's compassion. A simple allegory elucidates the dynamics at work: War is raging across Europe and Jewish children are being led like lambs to the slaughter. There is one possibility of escape for Reuven's 10-year-old son — a secret transport that will bring him to Sweden, where a non-Jewish family will keep him safe. Reuven looks at the innocence and fear on his son's face — the face he has kissed, the eyes he has dried, the hair he has tousled. He sees his son's spindly arms and legs and wonders if they will serve him through all the dangers that lie ahead. But there is no choice. The child must be sent forth into danger.

How would Reuven feel if he knew that as soon as his son left his embrace, he would be guided and helped every step of the way by a kindhearted man who took pity on the child? His gratitude would know no bounds. He would do anything within his power to reward this man's kindness.

G-d is our Father, and the pure souls He sends into this world are His children. Each soul is dispatched into our flawed and dangerous world to complete its own unique mission. G-d cherishes those who help His children in their time of need. When they, in turn, arrive at their time of need, G-d responds with overflowing mercy and compassion, protecting them just as they protected His children.

Surviving Upheaval

Our Torah leaders leave no doubt that the tremendous upheavals the world is now experiencing are the throes of the "birth pangs of Moshiach," the chaos and uncertainty that will precede the Final Redemption. The imperative for *Klal Yisrael* to prepare itself is becoming ever clearer.

"What should a person do to save himself from the birth pangs of Moshiach?" asks the Talmud. It answers: "He should occupy himself with Torah and acts of kindness."

Now, as in the Chofetz Chaim's time, we feel the frightening tremors of the ground shifting beneath our feet. Through *Sefer Ahavas Chesed*, the Chofetz Chaim offers us a mooring. He urges *Klal Yisrael* to grab hold of this mitzvah and never let go. His work was a gift to a generation facing troubled times — an inheritance that our own generation is impelled to dust off and examine anew under the light of breaking dawn.

Learning Kindness

The Torah's guidelines for chesed are the essential underpinning that assures that our kindness actually does good and serves G-d's purposes. In contrast, free-floating kindness rides like a helium balloon on the winds of individual emotions and the cultural currents of the times. The format of this volume allows each person to slowly infuse his life, day by day, with the Torah's chesed — a path of kindness that truly rises to its definition as an emulation of G-d.

The title of the Chofetz Chaim's volume is not simply *"Chesed,"* but *"Ahavas Chesed,"* the love of kindness. The Chofetz Chaim seeks to inspire us not only to help each other, but to develop a love of helping. He builds this love within us by revealing the vast, unseen value of every kind act we do. Every favor we do for a neighbor, every chore we perform for our household, every penny we loan or give stands as an eloquent advocate for us in Heaven and fills our earthly lives with satisfaction and goodness.

May the learning and future chesed engendered in this book, as well as the Jewish people's countless daily acts of kindness great and small, bring G-d's boundless mercy upon His children and usher in the Final Redemption with sweetness and joy.

A Note to the Reader:

The Chofetz Chaim's original work, *Sefer Ahavas Chesed*, is divided into three sections. The first section, which is not included in this book, deals with the specific laws governing loans, collateral, proper wages and payment terms for workers. The second section explores the benefits of performing acts of chesed and methods of nurturing within oneself a love for this mitzvah. The final section details various categories of chesed and the requirements entailed in each one. As this book is not meant to render halachic decisions, the first section of *Sefer Ahavas Chesed* is not included in Loving Kindness.

Appearing beneath the title of each segment in Loving Kindness is its source in *Sefer Ahavas Chesed*. These sources indicate the corresponding chapter and paragraph(s) in the Hebrew work (e.g. *Sefer Ahavas Chesed*, Part II, Chapter XII).

Some terms which are repeated throughout the book are translated below for easy reference:

Ahavas Chesed — Love of kindness

Beis HaMikdash — Holy Temple

Chesed — Kindness

Halachah — Laws that set the standards for proper performance of religious duties

Hashem — G-d

Klal Yisrael — The Jewish People

Mitzvah — Torah commandment

Chofetz Chaim

Loving Kindness

א תשרי
1 TISHREI / CYCLE 1

September 27, 2003
September 16, 2004
October 4, 2005
September 23, 2006
September 13, 2007
September 30, 2008
September 19, 2009

א ניסן
1 NISSAN / CYCLE 2

April 3, 2003
March 23, 2004
April 10, 2005
March 30, 2006
March 20, 2007
April 6, 2008
March 26, 2009
March 16, 2010

✑ *Fueling Chesed's Flight*

SEFER AHAVAS CHESED — **Part II Chapter I**

"*He* has told you, man, what is good. What does Hashem require of you but to do justice, to love kindness and to walk humbly with your G-d?" (*Micah* 6:8).

The Chofetz Chaim teaches that the world is built upon the foundation of chesed. All Jews are linked to each other by their ability to give and their occasional need to take, a dynamic that weaves the Jewish people together in a fabric of compassion. Chesed, in and of itself, is obviously a concept of immeasurable intrinsic value.

Nevertheless, the words of the prophet Micah teach that chesed alone is not the ultimate goal for a Jew. There is an added element — *ahavas chesed* — the love of chesed, that takes this already powerful vehicle for serving Hashem and fuels its launch into the Heavens.

The Chofetz Chaim explains the difference between performing chesed and loving chesed. One can discern this difference for oneself by examining the thoughts and attitudes that accompany an act of chesed. For instance, when the charity collector knocks on the door, a person may experience a momentary sinking feeling. He may think, "I haven't got time for this," or "I haven't got money to give away." He knows he would much prefer the collector bypass his house. The contribution he gives will be chesed, but there is no *ahavas chesed* in this act.

Contrast this with another scenario: There is a family that advertises itself in the local Jewish newspaper as the place for out-of-town charity collectors to come for free room and board. This family considers it a triumph when they hear that knock on the door. They feel just as enthusiastic about the time and money they put into this venture as they might feel about putting the same time and money into a family vacation. In another example, a man commutes from a suburb each day to a major city an hour and a half away. He constantly asks those with relatives or business in that city, "Do you need a ride? Do you need anything delivered?" He looks for his chesed "customers" as aggressively as he would for paying customers.

The simplest way to identify the feeling of *ahavas chesed* is to think about the way one feels expending time or effort on one's own family. One wants his son's bar mitzvah suit to be the very best he can afford — a perfect fit, of good quality and comfortable. One takes pride in seeing his son wear the suit. The parent doesn't feel that he has lost money in this endeavor; he feels only a sense of gratitude and joy at having been able to give.

This is the attitude Hashem wants each Jew to develop toward chesed. Performing this mitzvah with love and enthusiasm provides it with its ultimate power, far beyond the already potent force of chesed performed out of a sense of obligation.

Step by **Step**

Today, when an opportunity for chesed comes my way, I will try to think of the recipient as a beloved member of my family.

1 Tishrei — Mendel Rosenblum זצ"ל לע"נ ר' מנחם בן פנחס
Dedicated by his children

1 Nissan — Rivky Piller תש"ס לע"נ רבקה אסתר ע"ה בת ר' דוד משה נ"י, יבלחט"ט, שנפטרה א' ניסן
Dedicated by her friends and classmates at Bais Yaakov High School

ב תשרי
2 TISHREI / CYCLE 1

September 28, 2003
September 17, 2004
October 5, 2005
September 24, 2006
September 14, 2007
October 1, 2008
September 20, 2009

ב ניסן
2 NISSAN / CYCLE 2

April 4, 2003
March 24, 2004
April 11, 2005
March 31, 2006
March 21, 2007
April 7, 2008
March 27, 2009
March 17, 2010

✎ *Mining the Heart*

SEFER AHAVAS CHESED — **Part II Chapter I**

A person with enough self-discipline and persistence can force himself to perform an act of chesed, even if he has no real desire to do it. A more difficult task is to force oneself to love chesed when the feeling doesn't seem to be present in one's heart. This is a far greater challenge, but it cannot be an impossibility, simply because the Torah never commands the impossible. Therefore, one must assume that within each Jew dwells the capacity to love chesed, even if a person must dig deeply within himself to search for the emotion.

Such a search, conducted by a simple Jew, provided a lifetime of inspiration for the chassidic rebbe, Rabbi Bunim of Pshis'che. Rabbi Bunim spent his early years as a businessman. In his constant business travels, he used every interaction as a means to bring Jews closer to Hashem. On one such journey, he stopped at an inn on a cold, stormy night. The Jewish innkeeper found in Rabbi Bunim a sympathetic ear for his tale of a failing business. The peasants no longer came to him, vats of liquor sat untouched in the basement and the landlord was growing impatient for the rent. Rabbi Bunim spoke with the man for awhile, and then sat down to learn.

In the middle of the night, there was a loud knock on the door. A traveler, drenched and freezing, begged the innkeeper to admit him, even though he had no money with which to pay. The innkeeper sighed at his misfortune — he finally had a customer, but even this wouldn't bring him any money. Nevertheless, he helped the traveler. He let him in, gave him a change of clothing and a room for the night. The traveler, however, was still shivering. "Could you bring me some vodka, please?" he asked. "I don't have any money, but I'm so cold."

The innkeeper went to the basement to tap into his vodka supply for the first time in weeks — once again, for no profit. He didn't notice that Rabbi Bunim was there, watching him. What the rabbi saw, however, struck him so powerfully that he told of the scene for the rest of his life. The innkeeper poured a cup of vodka, then shook his head firmly and smashed the cup to the floor. Once, twice, three times, four times he repeated this procedure, oblivious to the sin of wastefulness he was committing. Finally, upon pouring the fifth cup, he happily proclaimed, "Now!" and brought the vodka to his guest.

Rabbi Bunim asked the innkeeper to explain his strange behavior. The explanation was touchingly simple. He couldn't serve the guest a drink he had poured with disappointment and resentment in his heart. He knew he had been handed a golden mitzvah — a chance to revive a shivering, hungry, poor man, yet his financial worries were clouding his ability to appreciate this gift. He tried and tried again, until he reached the vein of *ahavas chesed* that was within him. Then, satisfied that he was doing his act of kindness with a full heart, he brought the man his drink.

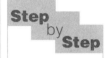

Today, I will think of a method to invoke enthusiasm for a chesed I regularly do that sometimes causes me annoyance.

2 Tishrei — Donna Bazelon Miller ה"ע לע"נ דני' בת גדול
Dedicated in loving memory by her children, Todd and Terry Miller, and her grandchildren

2 Nissan — Joseph Saltzman ז"ל לע"נ יוסף נח בן יצחק אייזיק
Dedicated by Harold and Gilla Saltzman and family, Silver Spring, MD

DAY 3

ג תשרי

3 TISHREI / CYCLE 1

September 29, 2003
September 18, 2004
October 6, 2005
September 25, 2006
September 15, 2007
October 2, 2008
September 21, 2009

ג ניסן

3 NISSAN / CYCLE 2

April 5, 2003
March 25, 2004
April 12, 2005
April 1, 2006
March 22, 2007
April 8, 2008
March 28, 2009
March 18, 2010

❧ *Supporting Creation*

SEFER AHAVAS CHESED — Part II Chapter I

A Jew never has to wonder why the world was created, because this mystery that troubles mankind was revealed to the Jewish people in one flashing moment at Mount Sinai. What was learned there is expressed in the final blessing of *Shemoneh Esrei*, which acts as a summary of all the blessings that are included in this definitive prayer. The final blessing says, in part, "through the light that emanates from You, You have given us, Hashem, the Living Torah and a love of chesed." The "light" of which this blessing speaks is interpreted by the Chofetz Chaim as the light that shone upon the Jews when they stood at Mount Sinai. It was a light of revelation — a peek behind the curtains of the Heavens — that had never shone before and will never shine again until the time of the Final Redemption.

Hashem had a purpose in affording the people of Israel this glimpse of the hidden; they were to glean from it a fundamental understanding of Hashem, His Creation and mankind's place within it. What was the lasting impact of this light? What did the Jews see at Mount Sinai that prepared them for their mission of carrying Torah into the world? The blessing from the *Shemoneh Esrei* explains: Within the light of Hashem, they saw the Living Torah and the love of chesed. They saw that the Torah is the blueprint for the world — the purpose of Creation. They understood that without the Torah, Creation would return to the void and emptiness that preceded it. This principle is stated in the Talmud (*Shabbos* 88a), where Hashem tells all of Creation, "If the people of Israel accept My Torah, all is well. If not, I will make you revert to void and nothingness."

The light did not, however, illuminate only one foundation of the Creation. Joined to the "Living Torah" is the "love of chesed." On equal footing with the Torah is the ardent pursuit of kindness toward others. The Torah provides the blueprint, but *ahavas chesed* provides the script for what is to transpire within the realm of the Creation. Hashem's people learned that they must not only perform acts of kindness, but develop a love for this trait that will assure that it never fades, for without loving kindness, Creation cannot stand.

In doing a kind act, no matter how small, today I will focus on the fact that this small gesture is an essential support for the world.

DAY 4

ד תשרי
4 TISHREI / CYCLE 1

September 30, 2003
September 19, 2004
October 7, 2005
September 26, 2006
September 16, 2007
October 3, 2008
September 22, 2009

ד ניסן
4 NISSAN / CYCLE 2

April 6, 2003
March 26, 2004
April 13, 2005
April 2, 2006
March 23, 2007
April 9, 2008
March 29, 2009
March 19, 2010

A Matter of Survival

SEFER AHAVAS CHESED — **Part II Chapter I**

Do right, and one is rewarded. Do wrong, and one is punished. The world of perfect justice is a simple world with no surprises; neither is there any room for human error. On first glance, it would seem that such a world would function quite well — a model of consistency that would guarantee mankind's best behavior.

There are two factors, however, that throw this model off kilter. First of all, human beings are subject to too many temptations and misjudgments to always "do right," even when they have the best intentions. Thus, in a world of strict judgment, nobody could stand before Hashem free of guilt. This leads to the second problem: Hashem's desire is to reward and sustain man, even when strict judgment would dictate that he deserves no such reward. Therefore, Hashem infuses this world with chesed. Only through the attribute of chesed can Hashem fulfill His desire to bestow a livelihood, food, clothing, sunlight, water and all manner of good upon fallible, flawed human beings. Without chesed to temper Hashem's judgment, no one can survive; the world cannot survive.

The Chofetz Chaim, citing the *Midrash Socher Tov* on *Tehillim*, describes a world without chesed as a four-legged chair that wobbles and threatens to overturn. To make the chair usable, a person places some small object — a pebble or piece of wood — under the shaky leg. The chair is thereby firmly set in its place, able to support a man's weight. This is the mechanism referred to in the verse: "The Throne will then be established with kindness" (*Yeshayah* 16:5). The *Midrash* on this verse says that Hashem's Throne of Glory can be compared to this shaky chair: "It was shaking. It wasn't complete, until Hashem supported it from underneath. With what did Hashem support it? He supported it with chesed."

This is the structure of the earthly sphere in which man lives. Through this trait of chesed, Hashem expresses His infinite patience with humanity's flaws, bestowing upon man far more than he deserves. By displaying this attribute, Hashem also teaches His people what they are expected to emulate. The more one strives to emulate Hashem's chesed, the more one becomes worthy of receiving it himself. In pursuing chesed, one is in reality lavishing love and care upon the mechanism that allows his own life, and the world, to keep ticking.

As I extend kindness to someone else today, I will keep in mind that I am helping to evoke Hashem's compassion.

"ישיש עליך אלוקיך כמשוש חתן על כלה" — **4 Tishrei**
Dedicated by E.F.

4 Nissan — Hillel Shaffren נ"י לזכות הלל שמחה יחזקאל בן הענדל צירל נ"י
Lovingly dedicated by his family

ה תשרי
5 TISHREI / CYCLE 1

October 1, 2003
September 20, 2004
October 8, 2005
September 27, 2006
September 17, 2007
October 4, 2008
September 23, 2009

ה ניסן
5 NISSAN / CYCLE 2

April 7, 2003
March 27, 2004
April 14, 2005
April 3, 2006
March 24, 2007
April 10, 2008
March 30, 2009
March 20, 2010

❧ G-dliness in the Mirror

SEFER AHAVAS CHESED — Part II Chapter II

*M*an was put on earth with a difficult mission — to emulate G-d. "To walk in His ways and to cleave to Him" (*Devarim* 11:22), the Torah commands. Upon no other creature in Creation does this grand expectation rest. Only man must strive for G-dliness, because he alone is equipped to do so. Only man was created in the image of Hashem. The challenge each person faces in his life is to seek out this element of G-dliness in himself and strengthen it by emulating Hashem's ways. Acts of chesed are the means to that end.

To emulate Hashem, a person must comprehend His nature. Man's knowledge of Hashem is limited to what he sees of Him in this world; He is the Creator, the Healer, the Protector, the Comforter, the Giver, the Sustainer of all life. "He gives bread to all flesh," says *Tehillim* 136:25. Every creature in Creation is sustained by Hashem's giving hand; there is a form of nourishment and shelter provided for everything from the ameba to the elephant. Therefore, the most effective way for a person to emulate Hashem is for him to give to and care for others. The more he expresses his desire to do kindness, the more precisely he reflects the image of Hashem.

Someone who deludes himself into believing that chesed is an "extra," something to be avoided if possible, obscures Hashem's image in himself. He takes himself down from the pedestal upon which Hashem placed mankind — the only creation made in His own image — and sets himself instead among the masses of creatures that roam the earth. Not only does he lose sight of Hashem's image in himself, he fails to see it in others as well. One who sees other people as a reflection of Hashem naturally feels love and respect for them, and this, in turn, naturally expresses itself in a desire to help others. The person who loves chesed is the person who understands the true greatness of man and the Source from which this greatness flows.

Step by **Step**

As I do something for someone else today, I will remind myself that I am acting in a G-dly way.

5 Tishrei — Moshe Schwartz ז"ל לע"נ ר' משה ראובן בן יוסף ז"ל
Dedicated by his family
5 Nissan — לזכות לנו ולכל ישראל לבוב"ב עוסקים בתוי"ש ומקדשים שם שמים

ו תשרי
6 TISHREI / CYCLE 1

October 2, 2003
September 21, 2004
October 9, 2005
September 28, 2006
September 18, 2007
October 5, 2008
September 24, 2009

ו ניסן
6 NISSAN / CYCLE 2

April 8, 2003
March 28, 2004
April 15, 2005
April 4, 2006
March 25, 2007
April 11, 2008
March 31, 2009
March 21, 2010

❧ *Give and Take*

SEFER AHAVAS CHESED — Part II Chapter II

*T*he population of the world is not neatly divided between the needy and the well-off. In Hashem's design, those two categories merge and change moment by moment. All are needy at some time, in some way, and all have something to give. The Chofetz Chaim offers an example of how even the richest man needs the kindness of others: He makes an elegant wedding for his beloved daughter, sparing no expense, but the guests do not come to share his joy, to share in the feasting and dancing. Without the presence of others, the beautiful wedding is transformed into a depressing disaster.

So life goes throughout its duration. If a person becomes ill, he requires others to tend to his needs and show their concern. When the time comes for his mother or father to pass into the Next World, he needs others to visit and comfort him. Finally, when his own last day arrives, he needs others to see to his burial.

Life's milestones are not the only occasions for give-and-take; this dynamic is woven into the fabric of everyday existence. The world is designed in a way that constantly reminds each person that he cannot exist without the good will of others. Some of these everyday acts of chesed have remarkable, long-lasting impact. In particular, the Chofetz Chaim points out that giving someone an opportunity to work goes beyond the mitzvah of chesed, fulfilling the commandment to "strengthen your friend; allow him to live among you." In this way and many others, people's lives are intertwined with those around them. Loans, advice, job referrals, introductions, a second pair of hands, a second perspective — all of these forms of chesed play a vital role in every person's life.

Wealth, health and intelligence in no way mitigate one's neediness. Even the most expensive car can break down on a lonely, dark road. Even a luxurious mansion can have trouble with wiring or plumbing, necessitating the services of a reliable, honest and capable person. Even the strongest, healthiest man on earth needs a door held open as he struggles with too many packages. Even a brilliant physicist needs advice on raising his children.

This integration of chesed into the structure of everyday life presents yet another facet of Hashem's own chesed. First, He illustrates, through His bountiful kindness, exactly what chesed is. Then, He instructs man to emulate this attribute, showering infinite reward upon those who do. Finally, as if to insure that man will come to reap these rewards, He structures the world so that the opportunity to perform chesed is before man always. There is no way for a person to cut himself off from his fellow man. He will inevitably need to take, and he will inevitably have opportunities to give.

Today, I will acknowledge someone who performs a service for me, because this service — even if it is a paid service — helps my life function smoothly.

6 Tishrei — Chana Perel Gensler ע"ה לע"נ חנה פערל בת יעקב שמשון ע"ה הונצח על ידי משפחת דאן

6 Nissan — לע"נ מרת חיה שטערנא ע"ה בת ר' נחום יבלחט"א, נלב"ע י"א ניסן תשנ"א

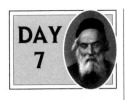

ז תשרי
7 TISHREI / CYCLE 1

October 3, 2003
September 22, 2004
October 10, 2005
September 29, 2006
September 19, 2007
October 6, 2008
September 25, 2009

ז ניסן
7 NISSAN / CYCLE 2

April 9, 2003
March 29, 2004
April 16, 2005
April 5, 2006
March 26, 2007
April 12, 2008
April 1, 2009
March 22, 2010

◈ *A Sure Investment*

SEFER AHAVAS CHESED — **Part II Chapter II**

A worker will not work if he doesn't know what his pay will be. He wants to know precisely what his investment of time and effort will yield, and based on this, he determines whether a job is worthwhile. Chesed is a "job" that, the Sages teach, pays plentiful dividends in this world, while the vast bulk of the payment — the principal — awaits in the World to Come. The nature of the Heavenly payment, however, is a mystery to mortal man. It is only alluded to, only allegorically described, and yet, a Jew is commanded to dedicate his life to performing the task that earns this reward. How does a person assure himself of a healthy "principal" in the Next World when he has no real idea of what that principal comprises?

The Sages offer a hint as to the nature of the soul's experience in the Next World; it is a feeling of constant, never-ending pleasure. Contrasted with the pleasures of this world, Heavenly pleasure has no saturation point. One can absorb it forever and never tire of it. It is a delight that time does not diminish in the slightest. The source of this joy, the Sages teach, is the "light of Hashem's presence." The meaning of this, too, is obscure, but the description leaves no doubt that one's connection to Hashem is, in some way, the key to this eternal pleasure.

The connection with Hashem does not commence upon arrival in Heaven. It begins when one enters this world, and is fortified throughout one's life by every mitzvah performed, every bit of Torah learned, every prayer uttered. Chesed, by its very nature, is a powerful means to strengthen this connection, for chesed is an actual emulation of Hashem — a straightforward, undiluted means of coming close to Him. A Jew understands that Hashem sustains Creation with His goodness, and therefore he must sustain those around him to the best of his ability. He offers help whenever he sees a need. He alleviates suffering, provides comfort, companionship and support, just as Hashem does. The more chesed one performs during one's lifetime, the broader, deeper and stronger will be his bond with Hashem. Arriving in the Next World, such a person will be positioned to bask fully in the radiance that awaits those who do Hashem's work in this world.

Today, I will pay attention to the "good feeling" I get when I help someone else, realizing that this is the feeling of coming closer to Hashem.

7 Tishrei — May today's learning be a זכות for כלל ישראל.
Dedicated by the Hoffman family

7 Nissan — לע"נ אליעזר גרשון בן אברהם דוד ז"ל
Dedicated by his family

ח תשרי
8 TISHREI / CYCLE 1

October 4, 2003
September 23, 2004
October 11, 2005
September 30, 2006
September 20, 2007
October 7, 2008
September 26, 2009

ח ניסן
8 NISSAN / CYCLE 2

April 10, 2003
March 30, 2004
April 17, 2005
April 6, 2006
March 27, 2007
April 13, 2008
April 2, 2009
March 23, 2010

~ Setting Mercy in Motion

SEFER AHAVAS CHESED — Part II Chapter III

*M*ost people are keenly aware that they are not perfect. One may exert great effort at fulfilling mitzvos, serving Hashem and dealing properly with others, but little that a human being does is done without flaw. Prayer may lack complete concentration. A mitzvah may fall short on some halachic requirement. Interactions with others may be hampered by temper, fatigue or misunderstanding. How, then, does one acquire enough merit to earn a favorable judgment in the Heavenly Court?

If one cannot count on the perfection of his deeds, he must instead count on the mercy of the Court. He must hope that his foibles and flaws are viewed with understanding, and that he receives credit for his efforts, despite the fact that they failed to bear unblemished fruit. In fact, this is how Hashem wants to judge His people. His nature is to do good, and He seeks ways to express His goodness. For this reason, Hashem provided an alternative principle to strict judgment; He allowed His attribute of mercy to enter into the proceedings.

This attribute, however, is not applied in every case. There are those who are judged according to the strict letter of the law, with no allowances for the failings of human nature. The reason they are subject to this form of justice is that they, themselves, judged others in this manner throughout their lives. They carefully weighed the merits of those who crossed their path, and gave them precisely their due and no more. In Heaven, such people receive the same unyielding treatment.

The decision as to which attribute — that of strictness or that of mercy — will be applied in any given case is determined completely by the defendant. The Chofetz Chaim informs us that each individual has the power to guarantee that, when the time comes for him to be judged, the attribute of mercy will be forthcoming. One creates this climate of compassion for oneself by cultivating a life of *ahavas chesed*, loving kindness. A person who teaches himself to love chesed gives without weighing and measuring each beneficiary's merits. He doesn't scrutinize his mental ledger to make sure that this person deserves his help; he simply gives it, because giving is an opportunity not to be missed. In return for that benevolence, the Heavenly Court judges him with benevolence. It does not scrutinize each sin; it looks with favor upon his efforts, despite his shortcomings.

Each person has the opportunity every day to lay the groundwork for his Heavenly defense, simply by opening his eyes and heart to the needs of others. These are acts that are often simple in nature — shoveling off the neighbor's portion of the sidewalk because he doesn't get home until late; helping a spouse with a task that he or she typically performs, because the help is needed; taking over someone else's turn with the carpool, even though he can't repay the favor; calling a friend, even though she is rarely the one to initiate contact. Piece by piece, each of these small acts accumulates into an unimpeachable defense, a glowing testimony to carry into the World to Come.

Step by **Step**

Today, when I perform an act of kindness, I will try to emulate Hashem's compassion by giving without measuring what the person deserves.

ט תשרי
9 TISHREI / CYCLE 1

October 5, 2003
September 24, 2004
October 12, 2005
October 1, 2006
September 21, 2007
October 8, 2008
September 27, 2009

ט ניסן
9 NISSAN / CYCLE 2

April 11, 2003
March 31, 2004
April 18, 2005
April 7, 2006
March 28, 2007
April 14, 2008
April 3, 2009
March 24, 2010

✑ *Merit Without Limit*

SEFER AHAVAS CHESED — Part II Chapter IV

*I*f one earns a dollar and spends it, the dollar is gone. Even a million dollars accumulated over a lifetime can disappear in a few fleeting moments, for almost anything one earns in this world is consumed eventually. There is, however, an exception to this rule; the reward for certain mitzvos can be dispersed again and again, yet remain completely undiminished, both in this world and in the World to Come. Chesed is such a mitzvah. According to the Jerusalem Talmud, an act of chesed stands as a credit forever, reaping even greater rewards than simple charitable giving. The merit of the charity one gives accrues to his children and his children's children — three generations. The merit of an act of chesed has no statute of limitations. The rewards one receives for it in this world are considered "dividends." They can be enjoyed throughout a lifetime without diminishing in any way the "principal," which is the reward awaiting in the World to Come.

An act of chesed is also an impenetrable shield against troubles; it renders protection that even the learning of Torah cannot match. In the Talmud's Tractate *Avodah Zarah*, a conversation takes place between R' Elazar ben Prata and R' Chanina ben Tradyon, both of whom were captured by the Romans. R' Elazar says, "How fortunate are you. Even though the Romans have filed five different charges against you, I know that you will be freed. And woe is me. I was arrested on one charge, but I know that I will not go free, for you engaged in acts of Torah learning and chesed, and I only engaged in acts of Torah learning." R' Elazar did in fact perform chesed; he was the trustee of a charity fund. Nevertheless, he expresses an awareness that more was expected of a man of his stature.

The ultimate protective power against troubles in this world and the Next World, says the Chofetz Chaim, comes from the combination of Torah learning and chesed. A person with this dual merit claims the rewards of both Issachar and Joseph. His learning earns him Issachar's deep level of understanding and wisdom. His chesed earns him the complete protection from harm that was granted to Joseph, whose "enemies fell before him." Joseph stands as an exemplar of chesed because he fed the world during a time of famine, and he performed the altruistic act, at great personal risk, of seeing that his father Jacob's remains were removed from Egypt and buried in the land of Israel, as Jacob had requested.

The Chofetz Chaim urges each Jew to carefully examine the nature of chesed's rewards. When one understands the great protective power of an act of chesed, and appreciates the everlasting, constantly renewing nature of its merits, one understands why this is a mitzvah to pursue relentlessly throughout one's life.

Step by **Step**

I will take one act of chesed I do today, and remind myself that I am creating a merit that stands forever, and a shield against life's difficulties.

9 Tishrei — Yitzchok Eisik Feig ז"ל לע"נ ר' יצחק אייזיק בן ר' יוסף צבי
Dedicated by Mrs. Bertha Feig, Mr. and Mrs. Israel Press and Mr. and Mrs. Mordechai Feig

9 Nissan — Joel Green ז"ל לע"נ יואל בן אהרן יוסף
Dedicated by Ann and Aaron Green

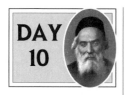

י תשרי
10 TISHREI / CYCLE 1

October 6, 2003
September 25, 2004
October 13, 2005
October 2, 2006
September 22, 2007
October 9, 2008
September 28, 2009

י ניסן
10 NISSAN / CYCLE 2

April 12, 2003
April 1, 2004
April 19, 2005
April 8, 2006
March 29, 2007
April 15, 2008
April 4, 2009
March 25, 2010

❧ *The Generous Boss*

SEFER AHAVAS CHESED — Part II Chapter IV
footnotes

A quick glance at the sky, the backyard, even the palm of a person's hand, is enough to testify to Hashem's kindness. If a Jew is to emulate Hashem's kindness, however, he must comprehend more than the fact of its existence. He must understand its true nature. The Chofetz Chaim illustrates the dynamics of Hashem's chesed through the following parable:

A family contracts with a craftsman to take their young son as an apprentice for a period of five years. During that time, the boy will learn the trade and help the craftsman to the extent that he is able. The family will pay the craftsman 25 rubles, and the craftsman will supply the boy with room and board, as well as training. After five years, the boy will be expected to have mastered the trade sufficiently to be of real help to the craftsman. He will still reside in the craftsman's house, but now, instead of the family paying the craftsman, the craftsman will pay the boy a token amount — a half ruble — for his labor.

The arrangement works out as planned. In five years, the boy is a capable craftsman, and his mentor is doing a booming business. To alleviate his workload, the mentor sends out some work to local subcontractors. He pays them four rubles each for their work. The apprentice becomes disgruntled and complains to his boss: "I do just as good a job as they do. Why do you pay them four rubles when I only get a half ruble?" The craftsman is incredulous: "I taught you everything you know! You use my tools and my shop. You live in my house and eat my food. And you want to get paid what they get? They use their own tools and materials. They pay for their own food and shelter. Everything you have comes from me!"

This is the "kindness" of man. He weighs and measures and takes each credit and debit into careful account, then gives what he construes as the total due. Yet this method also seems to apply to the kindness of Hashem, as the Chofetz Chaim explains in a notation on the verse from *Tehillim* 62:13: "And Yours, Hashem, is kindness, for You repay each man according to his deeds." This definition appears to contradict the idea of chesed as the granting of more than is deserved, but the contradiction is quickly resolved by focusing upon the vast difference in attitude between the craftsman in the parable, and Hashem.

Every mitzvah one performs for Hashem is achieved using materials Hashem has provided. His food provides the energy. The hand that touches the *mezuzah*, the tongue that speaks the *tefillos*, the mind that absorbs the Torah learning, the feet that carry one to the synagogue or to the side of someone in need — Hashem enables every act, provides the materials and instructions. Even so, the verse tells us, He pays "each man according to his deeds." The full value of each mitzvah accrues to the doer; there's no deduction for room and board, no tuition fee. Hashem's kindness comes not in a measured trickle, but in a gushing stream to those who do His work.

Today, when I do something for someone else, I will consciously overlook any debts that person might already owe me.

10 Tishrei — Harold Engelstein לזכות מנשה צבי בן אסתר נ"י
Dedicated by Simeon, Sharon, Jason, Zachary and Nicole Wohlberg

10 Nissan — לע"נ שיינא רות בת חיים אהרון ע"ה
In loving memory of Janet Freedland, by her son and husband

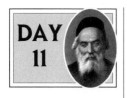

יא תשרי

11 TISHREI / CYCLE 1

October 7, 2003
September 26, 2004
October 14, 2005
October 3, 2006
September 23, 2007
October 10, 2008
September 29, 2009

יא ניסן

11 NISSAN / CYCLE 2

April 13, 2003
April 2, 2004
April 20, 2005
April 9, 2006
March 30, 2007
April 16, 2008
April 5, 2009
March 26, 2010

✑ *The Judge's Prerogative*

SEFER AHAVAS CHESED — Part II Chapter IV
footnotes

A defendant being brought to justice must sometimes make a pivotal decision before the trial begins: Would he rather be tried by the judge or the jury? Since the outcome rests upon that choice, he would want to know whether the judge is compassionate. In Heaven, the same choice exists; one can be judged by Hashem alone, or by the Heavenly Tribunal. In that venue, however, the character of the judge is well known. Compassion is His very essence.

Unlike the Heavenly Tribunal, Hashem the Judge has the prerogative to overlook incriminating evidence. He can place great weight on the weakest of mitigating circumstances. He can suspend the sentence.

This, the Chofetz Chaim says, is another meaning of the verse discussed earlier: "And Yours, Hashem, is kindness, for You repay each man according to his deeds" (*Tehillim* 62:13). Hashem's chesed is in the fact that He chooses to judge the case himself, giving the defendant every possible benefit. Hashem's merciful brand of judgment, however, is extended only to those who have been kind and merciful in their dealings with others.

Wherever Hashem deals directly with man, chesed is the underlying force. Hashem's direct hand in dispensing the necessities of life expresses itself eloquently in the prayer of *Ashrei*. After many verses of third-person praise, the prayer turns directly to Hashem to say: "The eyes of all look to You with hope and You give them their food in its proper time."

Hashem alone holds the key to sustenance and therefore, it comes through the channel of chesed.

The Chofetz Chaim cites a passage in the Talmud that reveals that Hashem retains three "keys" for His exclusive use; no messenger may use them. One of these is the key to sustenance, so that Hashem can freely reward a livelihood, even to those who currently lack the merit. The prayer of *Ashrei* says that Hashem "gives food to all living things," a line that is followed immediately by the words "Righteous is Hashem in all His ways, and magnanimous in all His deeds." The juxtaposition of these lines expresses the tight link between Hashem's care and His kindness; He gives to man not because man is deserving, but because He is compassionate.

The *Shemoneh Esrei* acknowledges the other two keys Hashem holds. "You provide life through chesed," the prayer says. This refers to the key of childbirth, and indicates that the ability to bring children into the world relies entirely upon Hashem's kindness. The very next words are "You revive the dead in Your abundant mercy." In mentioning the revival of the dead, the Sages are not only referring to the extraordinary events awaiting in the days of the Messiah; they refer to the "ordinary" event of awaking each morning with one's soul restored to one's body. Each night the soul must account for its day's work; Hashem redeems it from harsh judgment and returns it, every night of a person's life, to revive the body for another day.

There are three essentials that make it possible for people to live their lives in this world: birth, sustenance and the body's continuing viability. By keeping these three functions under His own personal jurisdiction, Hashem makes certain that chesed will be the principal

(Continued on page 382)

Step by **Step**

Today, I will acknowledge one of the ways in which I am the recipient of Hashem's chesed.

11 Tishrei — Henry Borger לע"נ יחזקאל מרדכי בן אברהם יעקב ז"ל
Dedicated by Chaim and Yehudis Frenkel and family

11 Nissan — In honor of the Lubavitcher Rebbe
Dedicated by the Storch family of Hillside, New Jersey

Loving Kindness □ 47

יב תשרי
◊ 12 TISHREI / CYCLE 1

October 8, 2003
September 27, 2004
October 15, 2005
October 4, 2006
September 24, 2007
October 11, 2008
September 30, 2009

יב ניסן
12 NISSAN / CYCLE 2

April 14, 2003
April 3, 2004
April 21, 2005
April 10, 2006
March 31, 2007
April 17, 2008
April 6, 2009
March 27, 2010

✑ *Replenishing the Account*

SEFER AHAVAS CHESED — Part II Chapter V

*A*braham, Isaac and Jacob left their children history's greatest bequest — an account so filled with merit that the Jewish people still, today, draw upon it for protection. However, that account has been called upon by generation upon generation, so that now, the balance hovers at a dangerously low point. Nonetheless, this source of merit is still desperately needed to stand by the Jewish people in times of trouble. The account needs to be replenished, and acts of chesed are the only means to replenish it.

The initial "deposit" in this account arose from the forefathers' dedication of their entire beings to laying a foundation of faith and service to Hashem. Through the tests they withstood, through the prayers they said on behalf of their children, they created a protective cocoon around the Jewish people. Within that cocoon, a nation was able to take form, grow and take its place in the world, then to endure the miseries of slavery, the wandering in the wilderness and the settling of the land of Israel. The fathers' merit was ample enough to shield their children throughout all the exiles, persecutions, wars and troubles that followed. However, all those "withdrawals" have added up.

In the Talmud, R' Yudan bar Chanan says in the name of R' Berechya: "Hashem said to the people of Israel, if you see that the merits of your fathers and the merits of your great mothers have been diminished due to the many things charged against it, then go and attach yourself to the virtue of kindness." Kindness is the answer, the verse explains, because if the people act toward each other with kindness, then "My kindness shall not be removed from you" (*Yeshayah* 54:10).

Chazal, our Sages of blessed memory, credit the forefathers with bringing Hashem's presence, step-by-step, into the realm of man, where it could be at least fleetingly perceived. Abraham began the process by personifying the trait of kindness. Through this, mankind got its first glimpse of Hashem's nature. Each forefather continued the process, which culminated at Mount Sinai when Hashem communicated directly with the entire Jewish people. The good that the forefathers brought into the world was immense, long lasting and powerful enough to sustain the Jewish people through centuries of struggle. Each Jew has the opportunity to replenish this merit for present and future generations whenever he performs a simple act of kindness.

Today, I will utilize an opportunity for chesed as a means to create merit to help my community and the Jewish people as a whole in a time of need.

12 Tishrei — May today's learning be a זכות for our children and grandchildren
Dedicated by Yaakov and Rachel Devorah Klappholz

12 Nissan — Cesia Fleischer לע"נ צביה בת אברהם לייב ז"ל
Dedicated in loving memory by Mendel and Judy Fleischer

יג תשרי
13 TISHREI / CYCLE 1

October 9, 2003
September 28, 2004
October 16, 2005
October 5, 2006
September 25, 2007
October 12, 2008
October 1, 2009

יג ניסן
13 NISSAN / CYCLE 2

April 15, 2003
April 4, 2004
April 22, 2005
April 11, 2006
April 1, 2007
April 18, 2008
April 7, 2009
March 28, 2010

❧ *The Redeeming Value*

SEFER AHAVAS CHESED — Part II Chapter V
footnotes

*O*nly Hashem can make miracles, but the Jewish people — by keeping Hashem's Presence before them — can elicit miracles. The way to make Hashem an active presence in one's life is through acts of chesed. The Chofetz Chaim relates that chesed is the currency with which the Jewish people acquire redemption. Chesed was the catalyst for the redemption from Egypt, and it will set in motion the process of the Final Redemption as well.

In Egypt, under harsh circumstances that could easily have stripped the Jewish slaves of their humanity, they remained humane and caring toward each other. The Sages relate, "They made a covenant among themselves to do chesed with one another." Even in their state of exhaustion and despair, they would periodically gather to reinforce for each other the legacy of Abraham, Isaac and Jacob. They never lost sight of their obligation to serve Hashem and help each other in any way possible. On the surface, the Exodus appears to have been brought about by the plagues Hashem brought upon the Egyptians and the miracles he performed for the Jews. Beneath the surface, however, chesed was the operating force that set the redemption in motion. The Jews' compassion for one another brought Hashem into their presence. Because they kept Hashem in the picture, Hashem could use His supernatural power on their behalf.

In the jubilant song, *"Az Yashir,"* that the Jews sang upon the splitting of the Red Sea, the primacy of chesed comes to the forefront. "You have guided us through mercy. You have redeemed this people," the song exclaims. The Chofetz Chaim teaches that the Sages find further meaning in the verse "With Your kindness You guided this people that You redeemed." Hashem's guiding hand was activated not only by His own trait of mercy, but by the compassion the Jews showed to one another. Through chesed they kept Hashem before them, and therefore, He was there to guide them.

This dynamic opened the channels of miracles and wonders for the Jews in Egypt, and it has remained in force throughout every exile. As chesed strengthens among the Jewish people, Hashem's Presence strengthens as well. Ultimately, through this means, Hashem will be present in full force once again to guide His people, fight their battles and lead them to the Final Redemption.

Step by **Step**

I will dedicate one act of chesed today to the goal of bringing redemption to someone I know who is in need of Hashem's help.

DAY 14

יד תשרי
14 TISHREI / CYCLE 1

October 10, 2003
September 29, 2004
October 17, 2005
October 6, 2006
September 26, 2007
October 13, 2008
October 2, 2009

יד ניסן
14 NISSAN / CYCLE 2

April 16, 2003
April 5, 2004
April 23, 2005
April 12, 2006
April 2, 2007
April 19, 2008
April 8, 2009
March 29, 2010

❧ *Perpetual Protection*

SEFER AHAVAS CHESED — Part II Chapter V

*C*hesed is a unique form of life insurance. Not only does it protect the doer, but it safeguards his offspring in ways that sometimes — as in the following story — become abundantly clear.

The story takes place in a small Hungarian town, several decades before World War II. The townspeople employed a rebbi to teach their boys, but they were unable to pay him any money. Instead, the parents took turns providing meals for him and his family. After many years, the rebbi's wife died, his children moved away and he was left alone. No longer able to teach, he was replaced by a new rebbi. Those who had brought meals to the old rebbi turned their attention to the new one. Only one woman felt a continued obligation to support the man who had taught her children so well, albeit many years ago. For five years, until the end of the rebbi's life, she repeated her daily climb of the stairs to his small apartment to bring him his lunch.

Time passed, and the war quickly crushed the small Jewish community's tenuous existence. The woman, however, was saved from witnessing the worst of the destruction; she died of natural causes. Most of the townspeople were herded away to their deaths, but this woman's grandchildren somehow found help. They were led to a small apartment, where a brave gentile woman risked her life to hide them behind a false wall that she built for them. She provided their meals, each day weaving a tortuous path among the shops to purchase only small portions that would attract no suspicion. Her apartment sustained several raids and searches, but her "fugitives" were never discovered.

When they emerged from hiding, the children learned that their refuge had once belonged to a different tenant — the old rebbi their grandmother had fed. The same stairs the gentile woman climbed, bearing their provisions, had born their grandmother upward as well, on a mission of chesed that, decades later, saved their lives.

Today I will remember, as I help someone else, that my actions also help to protect those I love.

14 Tishrei — לע"נ יצחק בן חיים צבי ז"ל
Dedicated by the Mark family

14 Nissan — May today's learning be a זכות for our משפחה.
Dedicated by Zalman Robinson and family, Brooklyn, NY

טו תשרי

15 TISHREI / CYCLE 1

October 11, 2003
September 30, 2004
October 18, 2005
October 7, 2006
September 27, 2007
October 14, 2008
October 3, 2009

טו ניסן

15 NISSAN / CYCLE 2

April 17, 2003
April 6, 2004
April 24, 2005
April 13, 2006
April 3, 2007
April 20, 2008
April 9, 2009
March 30, 2010

✌ *Extra Mileage*

SEFER AHAVAS CHESED — Part II Chapter V

*O*ne may go far spiritually, but sometimes, one goes only so far. The fuel that takes a person above and beyond his existing limitations and into the realm of greatness is chesed. The story of Ruth and Boaz, canonized for all generations to study, exists specifically to teach this lesson. The Chofetz Chaim relates that in the *Midrash Rus*, Rabbi Zeira says that the Megillah was written for no other reason than to teach the value of chesed. The text of the Megillah provides the basis for no halachos; it has no practical application. It is a simple narrative of human kindness and the great rewards it brings.

The Megillah describes Boaz' discovery of a woebegone young woman searching for leftover grain in his fields. Ruth was a foreigner, out of place and out of money, while Boaz was a well-respected leader of the community. Nonetheless, Boaz felt compassion for her. He befriended her and married her, lifting her out of her poverty and isolation. In doing so, he rose from an important man of his times to a great man for all time—the forebear of King David and the dynasty that will ultimately yield the Messiah.

The Chofetz Chaim adds that in the here and now, in three specific areas, chesed brings a bonus of blessing into one's life. The first of these blessings is rain, which comes into the world because of chesed. The Jerusalem Talmud (*Ta'anis* 14b; 3:3,) explains that rain refers to more than the water that falls from the sky; it refers to all sustenance in general. The food on a person's table is the direct result of his chesed. The second blessing is redemption from death (*Tanchuma Parshas Kedoshim, Mishpatim* 15). One for whom death has been decreed in Heaven, G-d forbid, can at times reverse that decree through acts of kindness. The third blessing is protection from the Evil Inclination (*Avodah Zarah* 5B). The Talmud declares: "Fortunate are the people of Israel, for they are involved in the study of Torah and acts of kindness." Occupied with these pursuits, they are in control of the Evil Inclination, rather than the opposite.

The Chofetz Chaim explains exactly how this works. When the Evil Inclination gains a foothold in a person's mind, it refuses to withdraw. It insinuates itself into his thoughts, voicing cynicism and doubts, raising wrong-headed ideas and temptations that become an obsession. Eventually, the thoughts invade the body, and he is obliged to act upon them. When one studies Torah, however, his mind is pervaded with purity and holiness. These, too, create an inner "obsession," which also invades one's physical being. The obsession must be satisfied, and it is — through acts of kindness. One steeped in Torah does chesed; he can't help it.

Like all human beings, there are areas of my life in which I would like to strengthen my self-control. Today I will use the acts of kindness that I do as a way to earn Hashem's help in these areas.

טז תשרי
16 TISHREI / CYCLE 1

October 12, 2003
October 1, 2004
October 19, 2005
October 8, 2006
September 28, 2007
October 15, 2008
October 4, 2009

טז ניסן
16 NISSAN / CYCLE 2

April 18, 2003
April 7, 2004
April 25, 2005
April 14, 2006
April 4, 2007
April 21, 2008
April 10, 2009
March 31, 2010

✑ *A Parent's Wish*

SEFER AHAVAS CHESED — **Part II Chapter V**
footnotes

*C*hildren who grow up to possess wisdom; children who grow up to merit wealth; children from whose mouths sweet words of Torah flow and bring others close to Hashem — these are a parent's fondest wishes. A parent need not just wish, however. He can make chesed an integral part of his life, and such children will be his reward, says the Chofetz Chaim.

If one looks closely at this promise, he says, one realizes that it rests on the assumption that the doer of chesed will merit having children. One cannot have wise children, after all, unless he first has children. The many people who desperately pursue expensive and difficult means to bring children into the world should not overlook the power of acts of kindness, the Chofetz Chaim advises. By this, he does not mean occasional good deeds. He means establishing consistent, active vehicles of chesed — setting up a free-loan fund, seeking out families in need of financial help, children in need of education, people in need of a connection to Torah. These are investments of time, money and effort whose only observable reward is often stress and frustration. Beneath the surface, however, the continual daily infusion of chesed can transform both the person and his situation. "Many people in our times have done this and have been successful," the Chofetz Chaim states.

Before there can be wise and wealthy children, there must be healthy, surviving children; chesed has the power to accomplish that. The Chofetz Chaim tells of one desperate man who sought out a wise man's advice because his children, one after another, were dying. The wise man counseled him to establish a free-loan fund. The man followed the advice, and as the fund grew and thrived, so did his family. Many years later, the fund had grown so large that the burden of running it became exhausting. The man returned to his adviser and asked if, perhaps, he might turn over the management of the fund to another person. The wise man advised against letting go of the chesed that had been his salvation, but the man insisted that the work had become overwhelming for him. He turned the fund over to a manager. The next day, he was back at the wise man's door, choked with grief; one of his children had died.

In his personal memoirs, the Chofetz Chaim's son reveals that the "wise man" was the Chofetz Chaim himself. The story he tells illustrates the Chofetz Chaim's deep desire to make every Jew aware that only those who run toward, rather than away from opportunities to perform chesed will reap its richest rewards.

Today I will begin to think about an organized, ongoing chesed that is needed in my community, and how I might help to get it started.

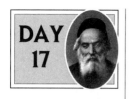

DAY 17

יז תשרי
17 TISHREI / CYCLE 1

October 13, 2003
October 2, 2004
October 20, 2005
October 9, 2006
September 29, 2007
October 16, 2008
October 5, 2009

יז ניסן
17 NISSAN / CYCLE 2

April 19, 2003
April 8, 2004
April 26, 2005
April 15, 2006
April 5, 2007
April 22, 2008
April 11, 2009
April 1, 2010

❧ *Children of Kindness*

SEFER AHAVAS CHESED — **Part II Chapter V**
footnotes

*T*here are those who, despite unending prayers and untiring efforts, live out their lives in this world having never been blessed with children. They may believe that, when their time comes to go on to the Next World, they will leave nothing behind. The Chofetz Chaim tells a tale of the Baal Shem Tov that illustrates how acts of kindness done during one's lifetime can create for a person the largest, most loving family imaginable.

A childless couple came for help to the Baal Shem Tov, and he invited them to accompany him to a village far away. There, he questioned child after child, "What is your name?" Nearly all the boys were called Moshe, and nearly all the girls were Devorah Leah. "Let me tell you how this came to be," the Baal Shem Tov said, and he told this story:

A couple from the village — Moshe and Devorah Leah — were childless. In passing by the *beis midrash* one day, Moshe heard a passage that said that when one teaches a child Torah, it is as if he gave birth to the child.

Moshe ran to his wife with an idea. In their village, there was no reliable source of Torah education for the children. The parents made do with whatever rebbis would agree to teach, and often the haphazard methods did more harm than good. Therefore, Moshe proposed that he and his wife set up a system to teach the village's children Torah properly. They found the best *melamdim* they could and paid them well. They kept their system well financed and supplied, and extended this education to every child in the village.

Now that every child was "their" child, they saw to other needs as well. For some families, they provided money for household expenses, money for weddings — everything a parent would give for his children. It wasn't long before the town began to recognize the beauty of the generation this couple was nurturing. In the children's love of Torah, their refined character and intelligence, they shone brighter than the children of any other town in the region.

As Moshe and his wife approached their final years, they wrote a will leaving money to their relatives, setting up a home for the poor and donating all the rest of their wealth to the upkeep of the children's education. When their time came to go on to the Next World, the great affection and high esteem in which the townspeople held Moshe and Devorah Leah poured out in a very special way. Almost every child born in those years was named after these "honorary grandparents," who with endless love and concern brought the town's children into a life of Torah and mitzvos.

"Now, let me ask you," said the Baal Shem Tov. "Was this couple childless, or did they have more children than anyone else?"

Step by Step

Like the story's Moshe, who was inspired by words he heard in passing, today I will try to hear and heed signs around me that call for an act of chesed.

17 Tishrei — Solomon Kann לע"נ שלמה בן דניאל ז"ל
Dedicated in loving memory by his family

17 Nissan — R' Chaim Boruch Olshin לע"נ ר' חיים ברוך בן ר' שמואל אבא ז"ל
Dedicated by his children, grandchildren, nephews and nieces

יח תשרי
18 TISHREI / CYCLE 1

October 14, 2003
October 3, 2004
October 21, 2005
October 10, 2006
September 30, 2007
October 17, 2008
October 6, 2009

יח ניסן
18 NISSAN / CYCLE 2

April 20, 2003
April 9, 2004
April 27, 2005
April 16, 2006
April 6, 2007
April 23, 2008
April 12, 2009
April 2, 2010

❧ *Creative Accounting*

SEFER AHAVAS CHESED — Part II Chapter VI

*H*ere in this world, the reward for work is calculated according to a very simple system. The auto mechanic gets his $65 an hour. Even though the repair might have enabled a man to get to his job, enabling him to earn his salary, enabling his family to eat, the mechanic doesn't collect a penny for all these extremely valuable results. The doctor gets paid for his medical treatment, not the future accomplishments of the person whose life he is saving. The waiter gets paid for serving the food, not for restoring his customer's strength and spirits. In repaying the chesed one does, however, Heaven uses a calculation that awards the maximum benefit to the doer of the kind act, a benefit based on an all-encompassing view of everything the act will ever accomplish. One who loans a dollar gets back not just a dollar, but perhaps his entire life, or the life of someone he loves.

In rewarding a kind act, Hashem doesn't only reward one's outlay of time, effort or money. He rewards the good that even a small outlay can produce. Perhaps a person comes to the door to ask for money to marry off his child. He may be embarrassed, depressed, or crushed by his situation. At one house, however, he gets an invitation to come in and have a cup of hot coffee. The donor cannot pay for the wedding, but the few dollars he gives are given with graciousness and genuine concern. The man leaves with his heart restored, with strength to continue his quest and go on for yet another day. In tangible terms, the donor has given nothing more than a few dollars, a cup of coffee and a few kind words. In Heaven, however, the true measure of his act is recorded — he has given someone back his strength, perhaps even his health or his life. Therefore, if the time comes when there is a threat against the donor's health or life, he will collect his true reward.

The Chofetz Chaim draws this concept from a *Midrash* (*Tanchuma Mishpatim* 15) which expounds on a verse that says that a person who performs an act of kindness "He (Hashem) will repay him his reward" (*Mishlei* 19:17). It doesn't mean, as it would seem, that if someone gives a penny to a poor person, Hashem gives him back the penny. Rather, the Creator says, "The soul of the poor person was trembling to depart, and you gave him the sustenance he needed at that moment. You gave him life; I will give you life." The action that earns a person this reward of "life" may be nothing more than a few phone calls to arrange a job interview for someone who is unemployed. Even a half-hour of time and a sympathetic ear can rise to the level of restoring someone else's life.

One should not defer these opportunities to help, the Chofetz Chaim warns. There is bound to come a time in each person's life when he is in need of help and encouragement. Even someone who, today, is blessed with an adequate income, good health, a family and a home may at some time in the future suffer a reversal of fortunes. Businesses go bad, health fails, family life hits rough spots. For the one who has spent his life reaching out for opportunities to help others, the help he needs will always be there.

Step by **Step**

As I do a favor today, I will think about its ripple effect on the life of the person I am helping.

לע"נ דבורה בת הרב זוסמאן ע"ה — **18 Tishrei**
Dedicated by Rabbi & Mrs. Y. Sorkin and family

18 Nissan — Raymond Glezerman לזכות רפאל בן ריבא נ"י
Dedicated by his children

DAY 19

יט תשרי
19 TISHREI / CYCLE 1

October 15, 2003
October 4, 2004
October 22, 2005
October 11, 2006
October 1, 2007
October 18, 2008
October 7, 2009

יט ניסן
19 NISSAN / CYCLE 2

April 21, 2003
April 10, 2004
April 28, 2005
April 17, 2006
April 7, 2007
April 24, 2008
April 13, 2009
April 3, 2010

✎ Infinite Reach

SEFER AHAVAS CHESED — **Part II Chapter VI**

*T*he average person living the average life does not think of himself as a world leader able to influence destiny with his every action. Most people are content if they can just keep their own small corner of the universe in order. The Chofetz Chaim urges each Jew to rethink that assessment and realize that every act, and every failure to act, sets in motion forces that can envelop hundreds — even thousands — of lives.

For example, perhaps a man is on the verge of bankruptcy. His friend is in a position to help the man reestablish his business on a firmer footing. The friend debates with himself: Should he provide a loan and take a chance on losing his money, or should he let his friend try to find some other way out? Finally, the man decides to take the risk and help his friend.

The business survives. The 150 workers the business employs remain employed. They are saved from the grim prospect of coming home to announce they've lost a job. The marital stress that job loss might have caused in some homes never comes to pass. One worker who was on the verge of buying a house is able to close the deal and resettle his family in a safe, clean neighborhood where his children thrive. Another is able to afford a home-care aide for his elderly mother. The restaurant across the street from the business maintains its steady lunch-time clientele, as does the newspaper vendor, the drugstore and the candy shop. The friend who made the loan reaps the reward for all of this, and the further, nearly infinite ways in which his good deed reverberates into the future.

A decision not to help would also have vast repercussions, for which the friend would bear some responsibility. Perhaps the business would have collapsed and the workers would have been dismissed. In many households, this would have meant a terrible rise in the level of tension. Perhaps some marriages would have disintegrated amid fighting and rancor. Perhaps a child would have fled from the turmoil and turned to unsavory friends for companionship. Some of the workers would almost certainly have suffered health problems as a result of the strain — maybe serious or fatal problems. The employee on the verge of buying a house would have had to scuttle his plans, leaving his family in an unsafe, crime-ridden neighborhood. The man who hired the aide for his mother would have had to put his mother into a nursing home — a move she was loath to make. All these people's miseries would have landed, at least in part, upon the lap of the man who could have helped, but didn't.

In tracing the trajectory of the friend's actions in the above example, the Chofetz Chaim illustrates that there really is no such thing as a private individual, living his own, quiet life. Each person is actually an important public figure. His every deed and decision has the potential to light up the worlds of people he may never even contemplate, and his reward in Heaven takes every spark of that light into careful account.

Step by **Step**

Today, I will find some kind act to do that will set positive forces in motion.

19 Tishrei — Fay Kasmer Broome לע״נ צפורה ע״ה בת משה דוד יבלח״ט
Dedicated by Bernard H. Broome

19 Nissan — שיזכו לזווגים הגונים

כ תשרי
20 TISHREI / CYCLE 1

October 16, 2003
October 5, 2004
October 23, 2005
October 12, 2006
October 2, 2007
October 19, 2008
October 8, 2009

כ ניסן
20 NISSAN / CYCLE 2

April 22, 2003
April 11, 2004
April 29, 2005
April 18, 2006
April 8, 2007
April 25, 2008
April 14, 2009
April 4, 2010

❧ *Beyond Reckoning*

SEFER AHAVAS CHESED — Part II Chapter VI

*K*nowing where an act of chesed will lead is impossible. One cannot possibly trace its progress through the world as it spreads goodness through the many lives intertwined in the fabric of humanity. No one can see what Hashem sees as the effects of one kind act mount higher and higher. No one, therefore, can imagine the immeasurable reward he earns for his act of kindness. A person can only know that the good he has done is no doubt far greater than the good he thinks he has done.

The Chofetz Chaim extracts this message from an account of a famine in the times of King David. King David turns to Hashem for help, and Hashem explains the reason behind the great suffering: "It is because Shaul killed the Givonim" (*Shmuel II* 21:1). The Talmud (*Bava Kamma* 119a) notes that there is no mention anywhere of King Shaul killing the people known as the Givonim. The Givonim were a branch of local Canaanite people who, during the times of Yehoshua, pretended to be foreigners seeking refuge among the people of Israel. Yehoshua took them in and relegated them to work as woodchoppers and water-carriers. The Kohanim took upon themselves the task of feeding them. Many years later, King Shaul became enraged at the Kohanim in the city of Nov, for reasons completely unrelated to their care of the Givonim. Shaul had the Kohanim killed, and in the process, cut off the Givonim's source of support. In Hashem's eyes, King Shaul's removal of the Givonim's sustenance — even though it was a completely unintended result — made Shaul directly responsible for their demise. For this, a famine was sent to ravage the Jewish people.

Through this account, the Chofetz Chaim emphasizes how great is a person's responsibility for every result his acts set in motion. The point, however, is not only to ponder the guilt one might be forced to bear for his unkind act. It is to understand that, as the Torah teaches (*Tosefta Sotah* 4:1), "The reward is always greater than the punishment." Any commandment that carries with it a punishment also carries a reward which is far more powerful. By looking squarely upon the devastation Shaul brought by disregarding the well-being of others, one can catch a glimpse of the radiance bestowed upon one who makes other people's welfare his own constant concern.

Today I will try to appreciate the importance of the small, seemingly insignificant acts of kindness I do.

כא תשרי
21 TISHREI / CYCLE 1

October 17, 2003
October 6, 2004
October 24, 2005
October 13, 2006
October 3, 2007
October 20, 2008
October 9, 2009

כא ניסן
21 NISSAN / CYCLE 2

April 23, 2003
April 12, 2004
April 30, 2005
April 19, 2006
April 9, 2007
April 26, 2008
April 15, 2009
April 5, 2010

✑ *Staking a Claim*

SEFER AHAVAS CHESED — Part II Chapter VI

A person prays for what he needs. He turns to Hashem for his sustenance, hoping that Hashem will take care of him. It would seem, then, that the efficacy of the prayers rests with Hashem, but that is not an accurate picture. It is the petitioner who determines the extent to which his prayers are answered. Commensurate with the degree to which he takes care of others, Hashem will answer his prayers and take care of him. The Chofetz Chaim cites *Midrash Shocher Tov* (*Parashah* 65) that relates the formula for having one's prayers answered: In the words of R' Ben Azai and R' Akiva, "Of one who is engaged in acts of kindness, let it be known that his prayers are answered. Plant your charity and you will reap it according to kindness," says Hoshea (10:12). The verse continues: "Now is the time to seek of Hashem and you will be answered," in proportion to the kindness shown toward others. Thus, one who wishes to stake a claim on Hashem's loving care can do so; if he puts chesed into the world, he can draw chesed from Heaven.

The claim one stakes through kindness is even greater if the recipient is one who is occupied with Torah learning or his own acts of chesed. The Chofetz Chaim explains that when one helps such a person, he enables him to continue his occupation. The vast merit the recipient earns through his learning and his chesed becomes a credit for the person who helped him.

Ultimately, this person will have enough merit to claim a seat in the Heavenly Academy in the company of scholars and sages — not on the basis of his own learning, but on the basis of his chesed, which smoothed the way for the scholars and sages to fulfill their roles. He will bask in the same Divine glow that bathes these exalted figures, simply because he provided a Torah scholar with the support he needed to continue learning. The reason he earns this great status, according to the Talmud (*Pesachim* 53b), is that "in the shadow of wisdom is the shadow of money" (*Koheles* 7:12). This is interpreted to mean that someone who utilizes his money for the proper purpose is rewarded like someone who uses his intellect for the proper purpose.

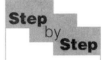

Today I will donate some time or money to supporting Torah scholarship.

One who gives support to a Torah scholar actually forms an association with the Divine Presence — a force far too powerful for a human to even approach. "For Hashem, your G-d, is a consuming fire," says *Devarim* (4:24). Even so, the fire does not consume one who draws close in order to stoke the blaze of a Torah scholar's learning. The Talmud (*Kesubos* 111b) relates that a connection with the Divine Presence comes from marrying one's daughter to a scholar, which also encompasses any support one provides from his family or assets to bring the scholar the peace of mind he needs to immerse himself in study. The answer to prayers, the Heavenly company of sages and scholars, a connection to the Divine Presence itself — all are rewards the average person may fear he will never merit. Nonetheless, one who dedicates his life to chesed can claim them as his own.

21 Tishrei — Dr. Naftali H. Bursztyn לע"נ ר' נפתלי הערצל בן אברהם משה ז"ל
Lovingly dedicated by his wife, Esther Bursztyn and all the children

21 Nissan — May today's learning be a זכות for כלל ישראל.
Dedicated by the Storch family

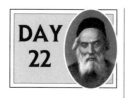
כב תשרי
22 TISHREI / CYCLE 1

October 18, 2003
October 7, 2004
October 25, 2005
October 14, 2006
October 4, 2007
October 21, 2008
October 10, 2009

כב ניסן
22 NISSAN / CYCLE 2

April 24, 2003
April 13, 2004
May 1, 2005
April 20, 2006
April 10, 2007
April 27, 2008
April 16, 2009
April 6, 2010

ᕽ *Preventing Tarnish*

SEFER AHAVAS CHESED — Part II Chapter VII

*W*hen one refuses to do a chesed, he may believe that he is doing nothing wrong. Rather, he may think he is simply bypassing the opportunity to do something right. There is, however, a designation for such a person that denotes just how wrong his omission is. The Chofetz Chaim quotes the verse in *Devarim* (15:8) that calls someone who averts his eyes from the needs of the poor a *"bli-al."* This, says the Chofetz Chaim, is a true badge of shame, a nametag no one should wish to wear. A *"bli-al,"* directly translated, is a person "without a yoke." This is someone who has squirmed out from under the yoke of Torah to live a life dedicated to his own personal gains. It is someone others cannot trust, for he does not bind himself to the Torah's definition of right and wrong. He is not perceived as a basically good person making a mistake; he is actively vilified. The Torah urges a Jew to stay away from such a person (*Gittin* 36a).

Furthermore, the Chofetz Chaim urges a Jew to stay away from becoming such a person and to understand just how low a character this *"bli-al"* is seen to be. He traces the Torah's disdain to the verse from the Talmud (*Kesubos* 68a) that equates the person who turns away from chesed with an idol worshipper: "The person who hides his eyes from the opportunity to give *tzedakah*, it is as if he serves idols."

One must stay away from those who do not wish to lend money. This applies especially to the time preceding the Sabbatical year, for in that year, all debts are forgiven. The "bli-al" cynic, at a time when the communal responsibility to provide support is heaviest, will find reasons to ignore others' needs to protect his own capital. Having done that, the verse continues, he will go out among the people and convince them to worship idols. The connection between evading the obligation to do chesed and inciting idol worship is explored in depth later; at this juncture, the Chofetz Chaim focuses a harsh spotlight on the Torah's contempt for the evader.

Obviously, no Jew wants to fall into a category the Torah deems worthy of ostracism. No one wants his reputation tarnished with the dishonorable title of "bli-al." Nonetheless, there are those who find chesed an inconvenient intrusion into their real agenda, and to them, the Chofetz Chaim is sending a message: If the agenda doesn't list chesed as its first priority, the yoke of Torah is not being properly worn, for chesed is the purpose of a Jew's existence.

Step by **Step**

Today I will begin gearing myself to say "yes" to any favor I can reasonably do.

22 Tishrei — Mollie Schechter Weinstock לע"נ מלכה נטי-ה בת משה ע"ה
Dedicated by the Rappaport, Gluck, Teicher and Wachberg families

22 Nissan — לע"נ צבי בן חיים ז"ל
Dedicated by the Kalish, Smith and Shapiro families

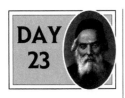

DAY 23

כג תשרי
23 TISHREI / CYCLE 1

October 19, 2003
October 8, 2004
October 26, 2005
October 15, 2006
October 5, 2007
October 22, 2008
October 11, 2009

כג ניסן
23 NISSAN / CYCLE 2

April 25, 2003
April 14, 2004
May 2, 2005
April 21, 2006
April 11, 2007
April 28, 2008
April 17, 2009
April 7, 2010

✍ *False Security*

SEFER AHAVAS CHESED — Part II Chapter VII

*O*ne of the classic philosophical questions, pondered by the simplest and most sophisticated minds alike, is this: Why do unkind people seem to amass so much of the world's riches? Why do so many of them lead apparently untroubled, satisfying lives? The Talmud (*Temurah* 16a) bursts the illusion that one can prosper by withholding chesed. "When a poor person goes to the head of an established household for help, if the man helps him, he had done what he should." However, if he doesn't help him, Hashem Who made one poor and the other rich may reverse their stations. This conclusion is based on the verse in *Mishlei* (22:2), "The rich man and the poor man meet; Hashem is the Maker of them all."

In the Talmud's scenario, there is a poor man, desperate to meet his barest requirements. There is a rich man, settled, satisfied and comfortable. The two come together, and what transpires has an inevitable impact on both of their futures. If the wealthy man takes care of the poor man to the best of his ability, fulfilling his responsibility with care and kindness, his status rises. He has kept Hashem's trust, and therefore, Hashem will allow his wealth to remain with him. If, on the other hand, he turns his back on the poor man, he will at some point discover that the roles of rich and poor are temporary and easily reversed. It may not happen immediately — the rich man may even have decades of good fortune ahead of him. In the end, however, his seemingly substantial fortune can dissipate like smoke into the air.

The Chofetz Chaim himself witnessed the unfolding of just such a story. A recently widowed woman with young children was unable to pay her rent. The landlord pressed to evict her, while the community begged him to be patient and allow them to organize some help for her. The landlord would not wait; neither, however, could he find anyone willing to physically remove the family from the house. In his mind, this was a situation that called for desperate measures. He hired a crane to come and remove the roof from the house. "Let it rain on them. Let it snow on them. They'll be out soon enough," he thought. The family was indeed forced out into the street, and the landlord seemed to live on with impunity. His properties increased; his fortunes doubled and tripled.

The Chofetz Chaim, however, warned the man that he would receive his recompense in full measure. Thirty years later, a plague hit the region. The landlord was stricken by the disease, but no doctor would help him for fear of contagion. He died alone in the street. Because his body carried the dreaded plague, it remained untended for many days. No one was willing to risk illness for the sake of his dignity. It rained on him, it snowed on him and, ultimately, his frail, elderly father came to claim the son's disgraced remains and lay him in a shallow grave.

A person with the means and the opportunity to help someone else may believe he has an option before him. As this story illustrates, however, there is really only one choice for one who wishes to protect the blessings he has. That is, to look at the poor person standing in the doorway or living down the block and think, "What can I do to help?" and then, to do it.

If there is something I could have done for someone recently, but didn't, today I will try to rectify the situation.

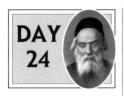

DAY 24

כד תשרי
24 TISHREI / CYCLE 1

October 20, 2003
October 9, 2004
October 27, 2005
October 16, 2006
October 6, 2007
October 23, 2008
October 12, 2009

כד ניסן
24 NISSAN / CYCLE 2

April 26, 2003
April 15, 2004
May 3, 2005
April 22, 2006
April 12, 2007
April 29, 2008
April 18, 2009
April 8, 2010

ᴥ *Passing the Test*

SEFER AHAVAS CHESED — Part II Chapter VII
footnotes

Schoolchildren share a common habit. As the teacher launches into a new subject, students' hands shoot into the air to ask the question, "Is there going to be a test on this?" The prospect of a test influences how closely they will pay attention. The Chofetz Chaim lets every Jew know that in life, there are indeed going to be tests. Careful attention must be paid to the criteria for those tests, for the results go on a record that is not only permanent, it is eternal.

The Chofetz Chaim cites a *Midrash* (*Shemos Rabbah*, *Parashah* 31:3) that says, "There is no one Hashem doesn't test." A rosh yeshivah once counseled a man who had run into difficult times in the later years of his life. He told the man that life is like school; a person is tested, first at an easy level, and then at increasingly more difficult levels as he progresses through his "courses." Even when he reaches graduation, there can be further tests — perhaps the most difficult of his life. If he passes them, he reaps the benefits forever.

Wealth and poverty are tests, the *Midrash* continues. With poverty, the test is simple to recognize. Deprivation and suffering clearly try a person's faith and strength. Those who pass this test, who accept their lot without resentment, lack for nothing in the World to Come. The test of wealth is more subtle, for wealth is also a very recognizable blessing. A rich person passes his test by keeping his hand open to the poor. Through his treatment of the poor, he earns the right to keep his money and enjoy it in this world as a dividend, while the principal, the true reward, remains intact for him in the world to come.

Tehillim (41:2) further clarifies the test of wealth: "Fortunate is the one who deals wisely with the poor. On the day of evil, Hashem will save him." The rich man is required to deal wisely with the poor — to care for him in a way that is appropriate and dignified. By doing so, he will acquire the best possible insurance; Hashem will save him from Gehinnom on "the day of evil," his Day of Judgment.

In the final analysis, one's wealth is defined not by what one has, but by what one has given away. In the times of Baron Rothschild, the king demanded to know exactly how much the Rothschilds' assets were worth. The baron brought the king a ledger, in which a figure was tallied. "This is a large amount," said the king. "But I know you are worth much more. Give me a true figure."

"This is a list of my charities," the baron explained. "You asked to know how much I'm worth, and this is all I really own. The rest is up in the air."

Step by **Step**

Whether my current "course" is in wealth or need, today I will take stock of how well I am scoring.

24 Tishrei — May today's learning be a זכות for our משפחה.
Dedicated by Tzvi Kramer and family

24 Nissan — Mrs. Suri Weissman שתחי״ לזכות חי׳ שרה בת פערל שתחי״
Dedicated by Yehuda and Chaya Levin

כה תשרי
25 TISHREI / CYCLE 1

October 21, 2003
October 10, 2004
October 28, 2005
October 17, 2006
October 7, 2007
October 24, 2008
October 13, 2009

כה ניסן
25 NISSAN / CYCLE 2

April 27, 2003
April 16, 2004
May 4, 2005
April 23, 2006
April 13, 2007
April 30, 2008
April 19, 2009
April 9, 2010

❧ *A Winning Proposition*

SEFER AHAVAS CHESED — Part II Chapter VII

*T*here is nothing to be gained, and everything to be lost, when one attempts to hold onto what one should give. On the other hand, fulfilling one's obligations toward others is an ironclad guarantee that hard-won gains will never be ripped from one's hands. The results of failing to give when the opportunity presents itself are spelled out in a discussion in the *Midrash* (*Tanna D'Vei Eliyahu Zuta* 16) regarding verses of admonition in the Torah (*Devarim* 28:47).

The Torah verse warns: "Because you did not serve Hashem, your G-d, with joy and goodness of heart ... So you will serve your enemies ... in hunger and in thirst, in nakedness and without anything."

The *Midrash* comments on this verse, "Define hunger." It then answers, hunger is "when the poor person comes and he asks of the rich person, 'Give me a drop of beer to drink,' or 'Give me a little bit vinegar,' and the rich person says, 'Don't bother me now. I have my customers to tend to.'" The rich man's negligence earns its due. Eventually, soldiers burst through his doors and demand his best wines. Thus, he loses the few swallows of beer he had tried to withhold, along with his most valuable inventory. This, the Chofetz Chaim explains, is the sequence of events that can be expected by one who has the means to give, but doesn't. He will lose that which he thought he could hoard, and many times more than that.

The Talmud (*Kesubos* 66b-67a) illustrates this point with the story of Nakdimon ben Gurion. Rav Yochanan ben Zakkai came upon Nakdimon's daughter in a field, picking grains of barley from animal dung. He asked her how her family, one of the richest in Jerusalem, had fallen into such a dire situation. "Charity is the salt of money," she replied, explaining that her father had failed to "salt" — to preserve — his fortune by giving sufficient charity. Even her father-in-law's fortune, which had become mixed with Nakdimon's, had evaporated.

The Talmud does, however, record many instances of great philanthropy on Nakdimon's part. His mistake, concludes one opinion, was that he should have given much more. Even if he gave a constant stream of charity, it was lacking if, according to his means, it should have flowed in rivers.

Whenever a person incurs a loss, he should examine his own dealings in his search for the cause. The Chofetz Chaim was once approached by a wagon driver who had lost his horse. "Why did it happen?" the Chofetz Chaim asked. The driver thought of some practical mistakes he might have made in caring for the horse. But the Chofetz Chaim probed further: "Did you ever let it graze in someone else's field? Did you cause some damage you didn't make whole?" he inquired. The wagon driver countered, "But Rebbe, I drove you somewhere once and you lost your coat. Surely your horse didn't graze in someone else's fields!"

The Chofetz Chaim assured the man, "I hold myself to the exact same standard. I sell books. Perhaps a buyer paid full price for a book with a faulty binding. Perhaps he was embarrassed to ask for a refund and he hasn't forgiven me. I am accountable."

The wealth put into a Jew's hand is a volatile substance. Only when it is acquired with purity and dispersed with *ahavas chesed* does it remain useful and whole.

Step by **Step**

If I haven't given serious consideration to exactly what assets I have to give, today I will begin to do so.

25 Tishrei — Israel Weiss ז"ל לע"נ ר' ישראל בן ר' דוד וייס ז"ל
Dedicated by Judy Leichtberg, USA and Dr. David Weiss, Israel

25 Nissan — May today's learning be a זכות for our dear son ערן ניסים בן ארלי נ"י
Dedicated by his parents, Orly and Mordechai

כו תשרי
26 TISHREI / CYCLE 1
October 22, 2003
October 11, 2004
October 29, 2005
October 18, 2006
October 8, 2007
October 25, 2008
October 14, 2009

כו ניסן
26 NISSAN / CYCLE 2
April 28, 2003
April 17, 2004
May 5, 2005
April 24, 2006
April 14, 2007
May 1, 2008
April 20, 2009
April 10, 2010

✒ *Perfecting the Performance*

SEFER AHAVAS CHESED — Part II Chapter VII
footnotes

*T*he test of wealth is seldom administered in a calm, quiet place where one can carefully think through his response. A person is tested at precisely the most difficult moments. He is rushing out the door when the phone rings; it's his lonely, old aunt in the mood for a rambling chat. He is dashing around the catering hall checking the last details for his daughter's wedding when a ragged man halts his progress with his tale of woe. He has just laid out a fortune for a car repair when a letter arrives about a family teetering on the edge of poverty. His response to these situations can determine whether he remains in his well-heeled position, or is unceremoniously thrust into the needy man's shoes.

One of the countless tales that illustrates this principle is the story of Reb Yaakov, a luckless man who failed to provide for himself and his bitter, critical wife. As Erev Yom Kippur arrived, the couple could not even scrape together a meal that would sate their hunger. Reb Yaakov's wife soundly berated him yet again, and he set out for the synagogue, his stomach empty, his spirit crushed. Upon arriving, he noticed Reb Menashe, sitting by the eastern wall of the synagogue with the other wealthy, prominent men. He thought of Reb Menashe's silver snuffbox. "Maybe he'll let me have just a pinch of snuff," thought Yaakov. "At least that will sustain me for a little while."

He approached Reb Menashe and quietly made his request. "I'm standing here preparing to confess my sins and pray for my life, and all you can think about is snuff?" the outraged Menashe snapped. Reb Yaakov drifted back to his place, with yet another blow throbbing in his heart.

That Yom Kippur marked a year unlike any seen before in the town. The notoriously unlucky Reb Yaakov began slowly amassing some wealth. Meanwhile, Reb Menashe's fortunes went into a rapid free fall. One day, Rabbi Levi Yitzchak of Berditchev came to town, and Reb Menashe ran to him for counsel. Under Rabbi Levi Yitzchak's questioning, Menashe recognized the moment on Yom Kippur that had set off his disaster. "You must go to Reb Yaakov and ask him for snuff," advised the Rebbe. "If he treats you the way you treated him, the roles will be reversed once more."

Fortunately, Reb Yaakov's daughter was being married that very night. Reb Menashe waited until the height of the proceedings under the *chuppah*, and then brusquely pushed his way to Yaakov and demanded a bit of snuff. "Please stop for a minute," Yaakov told the celebrants. "Here, Reb Menashe, please take what you need."

Menashe was crushed. After the wedding, he tearfully explained to Reb Yaakov what he was trying to accomplish, and Yaakov was saddened that his success had ridden upon Menashe's downfall. The two went back to Rabbi Levi Yitzchak. An agreement was made to split Reb Yaakov's fortune between them, and equilibrium was restored.

Hashem gives some people the role of "giver," and some the role of "taker." As the story illustrates, the only way to retain one's giving role is to perform it well.

Step by **Step**

When someone interrupts me at a busy moment, today I will slow down and attend carefully to the person's needs.

---

26 Tishrei — Sidney Broome לע"נ ישראל יצחק בן ר' אברהם שלמה ז"ל
Dedicated by Bernard H. Broome

26 Nissan — Salamon Mandel לע"נ מרדכי שלמה בן בנימין אליעזר ז"ל
Dedicated in loving memory by his wife, children and grandchildren

כז תשרי
27 TISHREI / CYCLE 1

October 23, 2003
October 12, 2004
October 30, 2005
October 19, 2006
October 9, 2007
October 26, 2008
October 15, 2009

כז ניסן
27 NISSAN / CYCLE 2

April 29, 2003
April 18, 2004
May 6, 2005
April 25, 2006
April 15, 2007
May 2, 2008
April 21, 2009
April 11, 2010

❧ *National Identity*

SEFER AHAVAS CHESED — **Part II Chapter VII**

*T*o a Jew, compassion for others is not just a trait. It is an identity. Chesed is one of the fundamental components of the Jewish heart, and if a heart is devoid of this component, its connection to the people of Abraham is considered questionable. So essential is this trait that the Torah protects it from dilution by setting a limit on who is permitted to join the Jewish people as a convert. Two nations in particular are excluded: Ammon and Moab. A verse in the Torah (*Devarim* 24:5) explains that members of these tribes may not convert because as the people of Israel were passing by on their way out of Egypt, Ammon and Moab neglected to bring them bread and water.

The *Midrash* (*Vayikra Rabbah*, *Parashah* 34:8) inquires into this explanation. Rav Simone in the name of Rav Elazar asks: Why did the Jews need bread and water? They were fed by manna, provided water from a well that traveled with them through the desert and protected by the Clouds of Glory. Furthermore, the other nations knew of these miracles; they knew the Jewish people were well cared for. What, then, was the crime of these tribes? The answer is that they simply failed to display common courtesy toward these travelers. They revealed a coldness of heart that disqualified them forever from becoming part of a people whose essence is chesed.

Even someone who is ostensibly a Jew calls his lineage into question by displaying cold-heartedness. The Talmud (*Beitzah* 32b) tells of wealthy Jews in

Babylon who refused to give charity. So abhorrent was this trait that the only way they could achieve atonement was to undergo the purification of Gehinnom. The Talmud further relates the story of a man named Shabsai, who came to a town and asked the townspeople to invest in a business with him — an enterprise that would have profited both Shabsai and the local people. They refused. He was then forced to lower himself and ask them outright for some food. Again they refused. In explaining the townspeoples' behavior, Shabsai suggests that they were not really Jews at all, but descendants of the *erev rav*, the Egyptian rabble that followed the Jews into the desert. In other words, if a person is without mercy, he loses his Jewish identity.

The Sages declare that whoever has mercy on G-d's Creation bears the sign that he is a descendant of Abraham, and all who do not have mercy demonstrate that they are not from Abraham's seed. Thus, performing an act of chesed bestows yet one more benefit upon the doer; it secures his position within the compassionate brotherhood of the Jewish people.

Today I will offer help to someone, even if it seems they may not need it.

לע"נ הרב אברהם דוד בן הרב שלמה יוסף ז"ל — **27 Tishrei**

27 Nissan — HaRav Avigdor Miller זצוק"ל לע"נ הגאון הצדיק הרב אביגדור בן ישראל
Dedicated by Mr. & Mrs. Robbi Newman and family

כח תשרי
28 TISHREI / CYCLE 1

October 24, 2003
October 13, 2004
October 31, 2005
October 20, 2006
October 10, 2007
October 27, 2008
October 16, 2009

כח ניסן
28 NISSAN / CYCLE 2

April 30, 2003
April 19, 2004
May 7, 2005
April 26, 2006
April 16, 2007
May 3, 2008
April 22, 2009
April 12, 2010

✒ *Undeniable*

SEFER AHAVAS CHESED — **Part II Chapter VII**

*T*he Torah delivers the ultimate indictment against the lack of chesed, equating it with the cardinal sin of idol worship. There is, however, a way to steer clear of guilt on this account as one negotiates the ebb and flow of daily life. That is by keeping one's thoughts from straying into the dangerous mind-set of "denial." The *Midrash* (*Koheles Rabbah*, *Parashah* 7,4), in its indictment of the chesed evader, says: "If someone denies chesed, it is as if he denies Hashem Himself." The use of the word "deny" is unusual. Chesed is either done or not done; what is there to deny? The Chofetz Chaim explains: The denier of chesed is denying the value of chesed. In doing so, he denies the basis upon which Hashem has built the world. "Even though chesed is Your very essence, it's nothing to me," he tells Hashem through his thoughts and actions.

This attitude rises to the level of idol worship. The Talmud (*Kesubos* 68a) states the equation clearly: "Whoever averts his eyes from giving *tzedakah*, it is as if he is an idol worshipper." The verse describes a person who looks away, who gets busy, who suddenly must leave the room when the needy person is spotted approaching. Such a response could never emanate from a heart that comprehends chesed as the purpose of existence.

One who downplays the importance of chesed in his mind is guaranteed to stumble upon the dire consequences delineated in earlier chapters. Each opportunity to help will present a new stumbling block. This individual will constantly place his own convenience and comfort ahead of another person's needs. He will convince himself that the other person doesn't really require or deserve his help. He will fail life's tests again and again.

Therefore, says the Chofetz Chaim, one should "distance himself from these bad thoughts" and seek instead to emulate Hashem by doing good for others. Usually, the term "bad thoughts" refers to heresy, temptation or lust, but here it refers to the thought that chesed is not a matter of importance or value. The Chofetz Chaim doesn't just warn against failing to perform acts of kindness or give charity; he takes the warning a step further. One must not even allow oneself to entertain the thoughts that inevitably will lead to these lapses.

Instead, a person must work on internalizing the Torah's perspective: the more one gives, the more one receives. In that light, every request for help becomes an opportunity. Every favor, every dollar given or loaned, is seen as a sure-fire investment — a penny stock guaranteed to earn a million times its initial worth.

The righteous Jew of generations past — and still today — prefaced his night's sleep with the question, "What act of kindness did I do for a fellow Jew today?" If he could not recall an instance of chesed, he would commit himself to helping someone the next day. Only then could he fall asleep. To such a person, the lack of chesed is a tangible feeling, a breach in the *neshamah* that must be repaired. One who trains himself in this way of thinking earns himself full-fledged membership in the Jewish people, the human race and the world Hashem created.

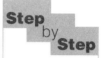

Today I will initiate the practice of recounting each night an act of kindness I have done during the day, and planning a chesed I can accomplish tomorrow.

28 Tishrei — לע"נ יעקב בן שלמה שטרנברג ז"ל
ואשתו רחל בת הרב יצחק אייזנברג ע"ה

28 Nissan — Beverly Bielory לזכות בתי' ברייגדל בת חי' שרה שתחי"
Dedicated by the Berkowitz and Weissman families

כט תשרי

29 TISHREI / CYCLE 1

October 25, 2003
October 14, 2004
November 1, 2005
October 21, 2006
October 11, 2007
October 28, 2008
October 17, 2009

כט ניסן

29 NISSAN / CYCLE 2

May 1, 2003
April 20, 2004
May 8, 2005
April 27, 2006
April 17, 2007
May 4, 2008
April 23, 2009
April 13, 2010

✑ *Risk Analysis*

SEFER AHAVAS CHESED — Part II Chapter VIII

*N*o one is required to destroy his own financial situation to help someone else. For some people, this principle serves as a convenient basis for refusing to help others. Such people do not refuse out of an outright lack of compassion; they have what they believe to be sound reasons. They cannot spare the cash. The borrower is a poor credit risk. The money is earmarked for a lucrative investment.

The Chofetz Chaim offers an acronym that defines the overall problem afflicting the reluctant giver. The acronym states: *"Yehi petza atzeil,"* which means "The lazy one shall be wounded." The Chofetz Chaim observes that laziness is an underlying reason for withholding one's help. Laziness is a devastating wound; because of it, not one limb of the body performs at its full capacity. Thus incapacitated, the lazy man cannot fulfill his purpose in life.

Laziness is one of many traits that manifest themselves in negative attitudes toward chesed. The Chofetz Chaim reveals these many manifestations through his acronym. The Hebrew letter *"yud,"* which starts the word *"yehi,"* stands for *"yirah,"* which represents fear of the risks involved in a loan. The second letters are *"hei"* and another *"yud,"* which stand for *"helam yidiyah,"* a lack of knowledge regarding the obligations of chesed. The next letter, *"pei,"* represents *"patur,"* meaning exempt. This refers to an individual who assumes that he is exempt from obligation. The letters *"tzaddik"* and *"ayin"* represent the words *"tzar ayin,"* an expression for stinginess.

The Chofetz Chaim first examines the faulty reasoning of one who sees chesed as too high a risk. A person may have ample means to provide a loan that will allow someone to stay in business, yet he fears that the debtor may be slow in repaying or default altogether. These hurdles are far higher in the lender's mind than they are in reality. Even if the money is slow to return, the lender has already established that this is money he can do without. If the money never comes back, it becomes outright charity, which in any event the lender is obliged to give.

More likely, the Chofetz Chaim says, the problem is that the individual being tapped for a loan does not want the trouble of becoming involved. His fears reflect a desire to be left alone, free of worry about the loan and its return. If fear of loss were his real concern, he could ask for collateral, but the "lazy" lender sees this as even more trouble: How would he redeem the collateral? What if he incurs the debtor's wrath? These problems can also be solved if there is a will to put in the necessary effort.

The final blow to the "fear of loss" rationalization is an assessment of the risks one is willing to take to make money. Many people are willing to make high-stakes, high-risk investments in the stock market. They know they can lose everything, but the promise of a big pay off is enough to bolster their courage. Chesed offers the biggest pay off of all. It is true that one can lose money, but in chesed, the real return is guaranteed, and it is infinitely greater than the dollars invested.

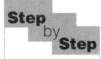

Today I will compare the amounts of money I risk on investments to the amounts I "risk" on chesed.

ל תשרי
30 TISHREI / CYCLE 1

October 26, 2003
October 15, 2004
November 2, 2005
October 22, 2006
October 12, 2007
October 29, 2008
October 18, 2009

ל ניסן
30 NISSAN / CYCLE 2

May 2, 2003
April 21, 2004
May 9, 2005
April 28, 2006
April 18, 2007
May 5, 2008
April 24, 2009
April 14, 2010

❧ *Reality Check*

SEFER AHAVAS CHESED — Part II Chapter VIII

*T*he rich man may realize that his blessings are G-d given. Nevertheless, he may harbor the inner belief that Hashem gave these gifts to the right person—himself—a whirling vortex of energy who achieves success by virtue of his ceaseless effort. The poor man, in the view of some successful people, does not have what it takes. He fails to go out there and "grab the bull by the horns," and therefore, he has not achieved success. Furthermore, even if the rich man loans him money, his rationale goes, the poor man will still be incapable of making it. To this, the Chofetz Chaim answers: Be aware that Hashem invested the rich man with his strengths, and Hashem formed the poor man with his weaknesses. Isn't a poor man who is without talent and drive even more worthy of mercy?

The rich man should instead examine his own flaw— his willingness to say, "I can't give," when the reality is "I don't want to trouble myself to give." In the previous day's lesson, the Chofetz Chaim provided an acronym representing the justifications that people use to avoid chesed. The first letter of the acronym, *"yud,"* and the *"yirah"* — fear — that it represents, is now explored in yet another form. This is the fear of one who tells himself that he cannot give because he may need the money. He fears that he will miss some golden opportunity at just the moment that the money leaves his hands.

To some extent, this fear is reasonable. The Torah teaches that a person's own welfare takes priority over that of his friend. If one has a real need for the money

— one is saving for his first house, trying to start a business or has other pressing needs — he has the right to politely decline to make the loan. Often, however, these needs are not the ones being anticipated by the man fearful of lending. Instead, his mind is abuzz with "maybes." Maybe his stockbroker will call with a fantastic opportunity. Maybe his boss will offer to sell him an interest in the business. These are dreams the person may have harbored for years; only because someone is asking for the money do they suddenly seem like real possibilities. Chances are, they will remain dreams, even if the person keeps his money. If he loans the money to someone who needs it, however, something concrete is achieved. The borrower has the money he needs, and the lender has the merit of an act of chesed.

The "what if" justification rings even more hollow when voiced by someone wealthy and well established. One who already owns dozens of properties, already has widespread investments and business interests, is still liable to think that he must have all his money accessible. After all, how did he get to his current station in life if not by taking advantage of every opportunity? In fact, his concern is unfounded, because one more investment or purchase will not significantly alter his status. On the other hand, that same money could put another person on a whole new footing. It might get him started in business, get him out of debt, or pay his children's tuition.

The successful man must realize, says the Chofetz Chaim, that if the possibility of making another million keeps him from lending, he is ultimately impoverishing himself. He may make every penny there is to be made in this world, but he will arrive empty-handed in the World to Come.

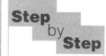

Today I will begin a fund (even if it is in a shoebox) that I can eventually use to provide substantial help to someone in need.

30 Tishrei — Rav Heshy Chapler ז"ל לע"נ הרב צבי הערש בן הרב אליהו יחזקאל ז"ל
May he be a מליץ יושר for כלל ישראל.

30 Nissan — לזכות רחל לאה בת עזריאל שתחי"
For Bauby Rochel, a tireless advocate of Sh'mirat Halashon

א חשון
I CHESHVAN / CYCLE 1

October 27, 2003
October 16, 2004
November 3, 2005
October 23, 2006
October 13, 2007
October 30, 2008
October 19, 2009

א אייר
II YAR / CYCLE 2

May 3, 2003
April 22, 2004
May 10, 2005
April 29, 2006
April 19, 2007
May 6, 2008
April 25, 2009
April 15, 2010

✌ *Fame and Fortune*

SEFER AHAVAS CHESED — **Part II Chapter VIII**

*W*hile many would find great pleasure in being known as a great philanthropist, there are those who would much rather keep their financial status under wraps. The Chofetz Chaim introduces this type of person under another subdivision of the category of "fear." These are people who fear that word of their generosity will spread, and they will be accosted by representatives of every charitable cause that exists. Such a person translates the $10,000 he loans today into tomorrow's request for money to repair the *mikveh*, build an addition to the yeshivah and dedicate a new wing for the hospital. He can afford the $10,000, but not the hundreds of thousands he believes will ensue. Therefore, he refuses the first $10,000.

Once again, there is a failure of reasoning behind this "reason." The basic flaw is in believing that by giving, one loses. The Chofetz Chaim cites the promise in *Tanna D'Vei Eliyahu Zuta* (*Perek* 4): "If you gave charity, you will merit money. If you merited money, then give charity with it." When one has money to give, one has the opportunity to create a permanent asset. Hashem is giving the person a chance to make an investment that earns principal and dividends in this world and the World to Come. By giving the money, one cannot lose. "You shall surely give him, and let your heart not feel bad when you give him, for in return for this matter, Hashem, your G-d, will bless you in all your deeds and in your every undertaking," says *Devarim* (15:10). Even if word of the $10,000 loan brings the lender a long line of supplicants, each is yet another opportunity. If he has more to give, he can give it, and earn yet more of the same blessing and merit.

The matter becomes much clearer when the chesed perspective is compared to the business perspective. For instance, one can imagine a scenario in which a real estate broker calls a wealthy man and says, "I have a major office building that is being offered at a fire-sale price. You need to come up with a half-million-dollar down payment tomorrow, but you'll be making millions a year from this building." It would be almost unthinkable that the man would say, "I'm going to pass this one up. I don't want anyone to know that I have a half-million to invest. The next thing you know, everyone will be offering me deals."

As foolish as this response sounds, it precisely mirrors the response of the man who is afraid to give. Because more people might ask him for money, he turns his back on the opportunity to place himself under Hashem's Wing, to connect to the Divine Presence, to bring protection and blessing to his family. Moreover, if this fear of fame is truly the only barrier to giving, the Chofetz Chaim provides a simple solution. The man can give the money to a third party, who can then make the loan. The third party gets the fame, while the real lender gets the fortune.

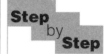

When I give time or money to chesed today, I will focus on eliminating the sense that I am losing something, and bolster my awareness of what I am gaining.

1 Cheshvan — Rabbi Heshy Chapler ל"צ יחזקאל אליהו הרב בן הערש צבי הרב נ"לע
Dedicated by Mrs. Suzie Chapler, children and grandchildren

1 Iyar —

ב חשון
2 CHESHVAN / CYCLE 1

October 28, 2003
October 17, 2004
November 4, 2005
October 24, 2006
October 14, 2007
October 31, 2008
October 20, 2009

ב אייר
2 IYAR / CYCLE 2

May 4, 2003
April 23, 2004
May 11, 2005
April 30, 2006
April 20, 2007
May 7, 2008
April 26, 2009
April 16, 2010

✑ *Enjoy!*

SEFER AHAVAS CHESED — Part II Chapter IX

*R*euven walks down the street, preoccupied with his mountain of financial woes. "If someone could just loan me a thousand dollars ..." he thinks.

Shimon, a prominent businessman, is walking up the street. As the two men approach each other, Reuven lifts his gaze from the concrete and recognizes his old friend. An inspiration suddenly lightens his heart: "Maybe Shimon would help me out."

At this moment, Shimon has the opportunity to perform a direct commandment of the Torah. "When you lend money to My people, to the poor person who is with you, do not act toward him as a creditor; do not lay interest upon him," says *Shemos* (22:24). Just as the Torah commands a Jew to hang a *mezuzah* on his doorpost, or bless a *lulav* and *esrog* or eat matzah, it mandates the loaning of money to those in need. The mitzvah is a gift — a means Hashem has given mortal man to serve Him and earn the eternal rewards that it brings.

One might think, then, that Shimon would pull out his checkbook with a joyous smile and write a check on the spot. It would seem that his heart should be as full and proud at it is when he writes a $300 check for a choice *esrog*. He doesn't grumble about the expense then; he relishes it.

The mitzvah of loaning money, however, elicits no joy from Shimon, and that is because he falls within the next of the Chofetz Chaim's categories in the verse: "The lazy one shall be wounded." The next letters, *"hei"* and *"yud,"* represent *"helem yediah,"* an absence of knowledge. This person rests upon the belief that giving is a "nice thing" for nice people to do but certainly not an obligation. If he finds a loan request inconvenient or uncomfortable, he feels free to exempt himself, something he would never do if the same obstacles were to come between him and a "real mitzvah."

Such a person might say, "I don't have any cash on me today. Why don't you come by my office tomorrow and I'll see what I can do." He thereby leaves the person to wallow in his troubles, unsure of how much help he will receive, certain only that he must make yet another humiliating appearance, yet another request.

If Shimon understood the nature of his obligation, he would greet Reuven as the bearer of a wonderful opportunity. He would feel an urgency to do the mitzvah, no matter what the logistical problems might be. Rather than delivering an excuse, he would act as if Erev Succos had arrived and he needed to buy *s'chach* at the only outlet in town, which was about to close. There's no doubt that, in that case, Shimon would run to the store: "Can you stay open for just another half-hour while I get some money out of the bank?" He would race to the bank, race back to the store and bring the *s'chach* home with the mien of a conquering hero.

Someone who sees chesed in its true light, who does not fall victim to "*helem yediah*," offers his help with just such energy and focus. His climb over the logistical obstacles is not draining, but revitalizing. In his drive to get the job done, he finds joy and purpose. The Chofetz Chaim cites *Mishlei* (21:21), which makes the case: "One who pursues *tzedakah* and chesed will find life ..."

> **Step by Step**
>
> *As I do an act of chesed today, I will think of it as the fulfillment of a mitzvah and do it as completely and joyfully as I can.*

2 Cheshvan — Mrs. Ann Lopin ע"ה לע"נ חנה בת ר' אהרן יעקב ע"ה
Dedicated by her grandchildren and great-grandchildren

לע"נ שרה ע"ה בת שלמה זלמן זצ"ל — **2 Iyar**

ג חשון
3 CHESHVAN / CYCLE 1

October 29, 2003
October 18, 2004
November 5, 2005
October 25, 2006
October 15, 2007
November 1, 2008
October 21, 2009

ג אייר
3 IYAR / CYCLE 2

May 5, 2003
April 24, 2004
May 12, 2005
May 1, 2006
April 21, 2007
May 8, 2008
April 27, 2009
April 17, 2010

❧ *With Open Eyes*

SEFER AHAVAS CHESED — **Part II Chapter IX**
footnotes

*W*herever the potential is greatest for a Jew's *neshamah* to fully blossom, the *yetzer hara* is there, planting spiritual weeds to undermine its growth. Since chesed is the *neshamah's* ultimate nourishment, chesed is the *yetzer hara's* prime target: "You don't have to do this. It's not a requirement. Leave it to someone better prepared, better equipped."

The Sages, to protect the Jewish people from succumbing to these false ideas, point out the unambiguous commandment of chesed in the Torah, along with the many relevant halachos, which apply to every Jew. It is not only the wealthy or the wise who are commanded to help; it is every person, according to the assets Hashem has granted him.

The *yetzer hara*, however, does not surrender in the face of this clear rebuttal. It simply plants one more virulent weed to drain the life out of the Sages' logic: "You're better off not learning. That way, if you fail to do the mitzvah correctly, it will be out of ignorance rather than defiance."

The Chofetz Chaim presents an allegory that paints a pathetic, yet accurate picture, of the folly in this reasoning: A traveler embarks upon a road that is pocked with gaping holes. Another man stops him and warns: "I wouldn't walk that way if I were you. It's very dangerous. You could fall into one of those holes and be seriously injured."

"Oh, no problem!" the traveler confidently replies. "You see, I have a handkerchief."

"A handkerchief? How is that going to help?" the man inquires.

"I'll just put it over my eyes, and that way, I won't see the holes. You see, if I fall in with my eyes open, people will laugh at me. But if I fall in with my eyes covered, they will realize that I couldn't help myself because I couldn't see."

The traveler is unaware that he will be the object of even worse derision, because as foolish as it may be to fall into a hole, how much more foolish is it to cover one's eyes? This, the Chofetz Chaim says, is the reasoning of one who chooses not to know.

In advising or reprimanding others, he acknowledges, there is a principle that favors allowing someone the bliss of his ignorance. This arises when a person would be unable or unwilling to accept the halachah. In that case, one is told to refrain from informing that person so that his sins may remain in the category of the unintentional. However, when one is dealing with oneself, no such allowance exists. Each person has the obligation to learn all he can and do all he can to comply with the Torah's laws.

"What you don't know won't hurt you" is the *yetzer hara's* fraudulent advertising slogan. The truth, as told in *Bava Metzia* (33b), is that "The lack of learning ultimately results in willful neglect." Only the person who seeks the Torah's guidance understands the imperative of chesed — an understanding that leads inevitably to a life of giving, a life of blessing.

Step by **Step**

If there is an aspect of my obligation in chesed about which I am not sure, today I will seek a definitive answer.

ד חשון
4 CHESHVAN / CYCLE 1

October 30, 2003
October 19, 2004
November 6, 2005
October 26, 2006
October 16, 2007
November 2, 2008
October 22, 2009

ד אייר
4 IYAR / CYCLE 2

May 6, 2003
April 25, 2004
May 13, 2005
May 2, 2006
April 22, 2007
May 9, 2008
April 28, 2009
April 18, 2010

✎ *Mine Alone*

SEFER AHAVAS CHESED — **Part II Chapter IX**

*T*here is a man who appears to have ample financial resources around him. In fact, he is surrounded by wealth. His parents own a well-established business. His in-laws are known for their philanthropy. When he needs a loan, however, he goes to his next-door neighbor, the owner of a just-making-it bakery. The baker may wonder, "Why me? Surely there are other people in town that have more money to loan. I'm struggling with my own bills. I'm sure he can get a loan from his father or his in-laws. And certainly they have much more of an obligation to help him than I do."

In Jewish law, charity begins at home. One's responsibilities rest first with one's immediate family, then with the extended family and then outward toward one's community and the rest of the Jewish people. Thus, the baker's assumption would be a reasonable one; the man's close relatives should be taking care of his needs, especially if they are well off. Nonetheless, the baker is in danger of falling into the next category in the Chofetz Chaim's acronym — "*patur*," represented by the letter "*pei*." The word "*patur*" means "exempt." This is the person who believes that someone else bears the responsibility to step forward for a particular act of chesed, and that he, himself, has no obligation.

The danger in this assessment, the Chofetz Chaim points out, is that even if there are other parties who bear a greater responsibility for the person's welfare, those parties may not be fulfilling their role. He may have asked and been refused. He may have exhausted their good will. The "rich" relatives may be having problems of their own. There may be any number of reasons why this individual, surrounded though he is with wealth, cannot access it when he needs it. In some dire cases, the refusal to help him could lead him into deeper trouble, perhaps even destroying his health.

The Ridbaz poses this question: Is the fact that a person has wealthy relatives a capital crime? Should a person lose his health, perhaps even his life, because others leave his welfare to those they feel are better positioned to provide for him? The idea of exemption, when closely examined, is often based on unwarranted assumptions. A request for help — even from a millionaire's cousin or brother-in-law — is still an opportunity to perform an act of kindness. No one who truly comprehends the value of this mitzvah would wish to be exempt from it, any more than a man would wish to be *"patur"* from wearing *tefillin*, or a woman from lighting Shabbos candles. Like these beloved mitzvos, chesed is a Jew's glory.

Step by **Step**

The next time my mind defaults to the thought, "Someone else will probably take care of it," I will motivate myself to be that "someone else."

4 Cheshvan — Helen Kirshenbaum ע"ה לע"נ חיה לאה בת ליבא וחיים ע"ה
Dedicated by Les and Ruchie Kirshenbaum and family

4 Iyar — In memory of our dear grandparents
Dedicated by Shmuel and Leah Wieder

ה חשון
5 CHESHVAN / CYCLE 1

October 31, 2003
October 20, 2004
November 7, 2005
October 27, 2006
October 17, 2007
November 3, 2008
October 23, 2009

ה אייר
5 IYAR / CYCLE 2

May 7, 2003
April 26, 2004
May 14, 2005
May 3, 2006
April 23, 2007
May 10, 2008
April 29, 2009
April 19, 2010

✑ *Close Calls*

SEFER AHAVAS CHESED — Part II Chapter IX

*M*ost people envision charity as something one gives to strangers. It seems especially laudable to share one's money with people outside one's circle of family and friends. Certainly, supporting charitable causes wins the giver a great deal of appreciation and admiration. The Chofetz Chaim points out, however, that charity should first be directed toward immediate relatives and then the extended family. Only after their needs are met should one pursue outside philanthropies.

In recent times, this point was illustrated most graphically by the Kapishnitzer Rebbe. One morning, he called a prominent member of his community at his business office in Manhattan. He explained that he would like to visit the man to discuss an opportunity to give *tzedakah*. The man, out of respect for the Rebbe, insisted that he would go to Brooklyn rather than cause the Rebbe to take the subway to Manhattan. "No," the Rebbe replied. "I want to come to your office, and I want you to set aside a few moments for me to talk to you."

He arrived. The man cut off all phone calls, barred any interruptions, and left customers sitting in the waiting room. He invited the Rebbe into his office. There, the Rebbe detailed the dire financial situation of a family with many children. The breadwinner had lost his job, his health was suffering and financial pressures were crushing the family's spirits. Something needed to be done immediately.

The man didn't hesitate for a moment. "I'll write a check for a thousand dollars right now," the man said. "But I still don't understand why you had to trouble yourself to come all the way here for this." Pen poised above his checkbook, the man asked, "For whom is the check?" The Rebbe stared at the floor for a few long moments, then answered, "For your brother."

The "charity" due one's own family is not always money. A young man once visited the Steipler Rav and complained bitterly, "I don't know which way to turn. My house is in a constant state of chaos. I come home Erev Shabbos to find diapers on the floor, dishes in the sink. My wife is just not managing. I can't live like this anymore."

"You don't know where to turn?" asked the Rav. "I'll tell you. Turn to the closet and take out a broom. Has it occurred to you to help?"

While it is unlikely to win anyone a plaque of recognition or a spot on the board of directors, the chesed one does for one's family is uniquely altruistic. There is no honor, sometimes there is not even an adequate thank-you, but there's a message in this kindness. It says that one's giving is not for display only; it is an integral part of one's true, private, inner nature.

Today I will do a chesed — outside the realm of what I usually do — for a member of my family.

ו חשון
6 CHESHVAN / CYCLE 1

November 1, 2003
October 21, 2004
November 8, 2005
October 28, 2006
October 18, 2007
November 4, 2008
October 24, 2009

ו אייר
6 IYAR / CYCLE 2

May 8, 2003
April 27, 2004
May 15, 2005
May 4, 2006
April 24, 2007
May 11, 2008
April 30, 2009
April 20, 2010

❧ *Taking the Gamble*

SEFER AHAVAS CHESED — Part II Chapter IX

*T*he realm of *"patur"* — the belief that one is exempt from the obligation of giving — rests on many supports, most of them wobbly. Among these faulty supports is the idea that one who has been "burned" giving a loan has the right to refuse to take that risk again. While in some instances this assumption may be correct, in many instances it is not. The Chofetz Chaim emphasizes the need to examine each situation individually to determine the likelihood of another default.

Neglecting or refusing to repay a loan when one is capable of making payment is a grave matter. In *Tehillim* (37:21) King David refers to such a person as "the wicked one (who) borrows but repays not." The term *"rasha,"* wicked person, is applied in only the most extreme circumstances; it is a separate category, a person others are allowed — in fact, encouraged — to despise. Even if that term were aptly applied to a person who failed to repay a debt, every other Jew in need of help should not be forced to bear his guilt. The one who refused to repay may indeed be a *"rasha"* and a person may truly be exempt from a requirement to help that one person. Nonetheless, the next person to request a loan cannot be painted with the same brush. He must still be treated as a fellow Jew, to whom the obligation of chesed applies.

Even one who fails to repay a debt does not usually fall within the category of *"rasha."* The average person will pay if he can. If he fails to repay, it is simply because he lacks the means. This person's imperfect credit history does not disqualify him from deserving the kindness of his fellow Jews. In such a situation, the lender might protect himself by taking some form of collateral. In that way, if the borrower is unable to return the money, the lender's loss is mitigated.

There are, however, people who will not pay back, will not turn over collateral if it becomes due and will feel no compunctions about causing misery to the person who attempted to help them in a time of need. If one knows that the potential borrower is such a person, and one knows that collateral will ultimately be of no practical use, one is permitted to refuse to make the loan.

"*Patur*," as the Chofetz Chaim explains, does have a legitimate place in the realm of chesed, but only under very limited circumstances. Having lost money once, twice, or even a dozen times does not, in itself, exempt the lender from ever opening his checkbook again. One's orientation must be toward wanting to give, hoping to have assets to give and looking for ways to make even a risky situation suitable for giving. If a person's heart is inclined toward finding opportunities to give, he will not see before him a long line of exemptions; he will see a fellow Jew in need of his generosity.

If there is someone for whom I've been unwilling to take on the risk of loaning a car, money or other valuable asset, today I will consider ways in which I could undertake this chesed.

לע"נ מרת מינדל בת ר' יעקב ע"ה — **6 Cheshvan**
Dedicated by Rabbi and Mrs. Eliezer Hamburger

לע"נ ברוך וורגוץ בן ר' הלל ז"ל — **6 Iyar**
Dedicated by his daughter and family in Bnei Brak

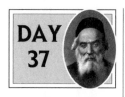
❧ *Narrow Straits*

SEFER AHAVAS CHESED — **Part II Chapter X**

*U*ntil now, the rationales represented by the Chofetz Chaim's acronym, "The lazy one shall be wounded," bear a degree of sophistication. A person might fear loss, misunderstand his obligations or find reasons to consider himself exempt from chesed. These are all excuses, but at least they acknowledge that a refusal to give requires an excuse. At this point, the Chofetz Chaim comes to an excuse that is more accurately a character flaw, a failure to move beyond the possessiveness of a small child. The acronym has reached the letters *"tzaddik"* and *"ayin"* in the word *"petza."* This represents *"tzar ayin,"* an idiom that, literally translated, means a narrow eye.

"Tzar" means tightness, narrowness — a passage through which one must push and squeeze. This describes the *"tzar ayin"* dynamic of giving. If such a person gives at all, it is only with great reluctance, so tight is his hold on his possessions.

This attitude, especially if it should afflict an entire community, can have deadly results. The Sages in the Talmud (*Sotah* 37b) implicate this trait of stinginess in an explanation of the procedure followed when a corpse is found alone on the road. A *beis din* of rabbis from the neighboring cities must convene at the site and state: "Our hands did not spill this blood; our eyes did not see who did this."

The Sages then explain why these respected figures must undergo the humiliating process of "pleading innocent" to a base murder. It is because the death is blamed on a failure of the townspeople to provide for the wayfarer. Perhaps they did not give him lodgings or provisions for the road; perhaps they did not treat him respectfully or escort him on his way. One or more of these omissions, it is assumed, caused his demise. The rabbis, who are responsible for instructing their followers, must bear some of the blame for allowing "*tzar ayin*" to take root.

So damaging a trait is "*tzar ayin*" that *Mishlei* (23:6-7) warns that one should not enter the house or eat the food of a person who fits this description. The Chofetz Chaim, however, advises looking within for signs of this trait. The symptoms are not difficult to spot: Any object being requested is always being used, being repaired, or otherwise not available. Any favor being asked always comes at an inconvenient time. Money is loaned in the minimal possible amounts, or not at all. Just as a narrowing of the arteries prevents the heart from functioning, this narrowness prevents the spiritual heart from functioning. Kindness simply cannot pass through these tight channels.

The Chofetz Chaim describes this unfortunate person's fate: "One overeager for wealth has an evil eye; he does not know that want will befall him" (*Mishlei* 28:22). The Sages apply this verse particularly to someone who lends money on interest without meeting the halachic requirements. Afflicted with "*tzar ayin*," a person's vision is narrowed to the point of blindness. Like one who is blind, he cannot see the dangers along the road on which he is traveling. Neither can he see the radiant beauty of a world alive with chesed.

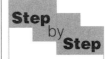

Today I will check my own inner workings for symptoms of "tzar ayin."

7 Cheshvan — Rabbi Simon Burnstein לע"נ הרב יהושע בן הרב מנחם מענדל ז"ל
Dedicated by the Burnstein, Goldstone, Preis, Schmuckler and Steinberg families

7 Iyar — Rebbetzin Ethel Adler ע"ה לע"נ האשה החשובה מרת עטל בת ישראל שלמה
Dedicated in loving memory by her family — .ת.נ.צ.ב.ה

DAY 38

ח חשון
8 CHESHVAN / CYCLE 1

November 3, 2003
October 23, 2004
November 10, 2005
October 30, 2006
October 20, 2007
November 6, 2008
October 26, 2009

ח אייר
8 IYAR / CYCLE 2

May 10, 2003
April 29, 2004
May 17, 2005
May 6, 2006
April 26, 2007
May 13, 2008
May 2, 2009
April 22, 2010

✑ *Your Worst Enemy*

SEFER AHAVAS CHESED — Part II Chapter X

*W*ho would destroy his own house? The rational people of the world do all they can to build up their own house, and would never consider causing its destruction. Ironically, however, the person afflicted with *"tzar ayin"* pours relentless effort into destroying the home and possessions he ardently seeks to protect. This individual's vision is so narrow that he cannot see a reason to give anything he owns to someone else. He justifies his tight-fisted grasp on his belongings with excuses: Someone might break my lawnmower, misplace my cuff links, crash my car, lose my money.

In this person's view, his domain is his alone. Admitting others means allowing them access to his belongings: They can then eat his food, break his crystal, see an item they want to borrow, see his wealth, or perhaps his miserliness.

The paradigm for his tragically misdirected energy is found in the Torah's account of the type of *"tzaraas,"* leprosy, that afflicts the walls of a house. The Chofetz Chaim relates that one of the sins for which a house is stricken with leprosy is *"tzar ayin."* The measure-for-measure justice in such a case is clear. When a house exhibits discoloration characteristic of *"tzaraas,"* a Kohen must be called in to investigate. In some cases, the house is declared impure, and it must be dismantled. All the belongings must be removed and the walls brought down. The possessions the person had sought to keep under his own roof are then on display for all to see; the roof itself is gone.

The Torah specifies (*Vayikra* 14:35) that the owner of the house must come before the Kohen to declare that his house might be afflicted. The Chofetz Chaim explains that the owner's grasping sense of possession has caused his problem, and therefore, he alone must answer for it. In his dealings with those in need, he has said, in effect, "This house and all that is in it are mine, mine, mine." The Torah forces him to reconfirm that ownership and accept its consequence.

Tzaraas of the type the Torah discusses does not exist today. Nevertheless, as the Chofetz Chaim points out, there are many ways to bring one's own house down. He speaks of a wealthy man who refused to utilize his assets to do chesed and thereby honor Hashem. As a consequence of his *"tzar ayin,"* the man went insane, burned his house, smashed his barrels of fine wine and oil, and cast his gold and silver into the ocean. Even without certifiable insanity, one can quickly destroy oneself. In a few short moments, an otherwise conservative person can decide to take a major risk in business or on a stock. He can succumb to the temporary insanity that makes people believe they cannot lose — but they can, and do, because *"tzar ayin"* makes them susceptible to such disastrous misjudgment.

The Chofetz Chaim shows a dark picture of the grief and doom that hangs over the head of the person afflicted with *"tzar ayin,"* but the most sorrowful aspect of the picture is that this person has painted it himself. He can, however, brighten the palette, by opening his narrowed eyes to the real value of his assets and what they can accomplish in the world.

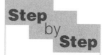

Today I will think about an asset of which I am particularly possessive, and consider some ways it can be used to help someone else.

8 Cheshvan — David Rubin לע״נ דוד בן אברהם ז״ל
Dedicated in loving memory by his children

8 Iyar — לע״נ מלך בן אברהם חיים ז״ל — נפטר ח׳ אייר תשס״א
הונצח על ידי משפחתו

ט חשון
9 CHESHVAN / CYCLE 1

November 4, 2003
October 24, 2004
November 11, 2005
October 31, 2006
October 21, 2007
November 7, 2008
October 27, 2009

ט אייר
9 IYAR / CYCLE 2

May 11, 2003
April 30, 2004
May 18, 2005
May 7, 2006
April 27, 2007
May 14, 2008
May 3, 2009
April 23, 2010

❧ *The Right G-d*

SEFER AHAVAS CHESED — Part II Chapter X

*H*ashem is the protector of His people. The Torah (*Shemos* 20:20) prohibits a Jew from turning to "gods of silver and gods of gold," and there is probably no one walking the earth today who could say he has ever seen a Jew worship such a god. To modern minds, it is almost inconceivable that one could ascribe any protective power to a golden idol.

When one looks beneath the surface, however, one sees gold-and-silver worship alive and well. It is present in the person who consults his online banking system every night before bed. Balances growing, investments paying off, dividends accruing, he feels he can sleep soundly. In his mind, the gold and silver have the power to protect him from troubles.

Rather than acting as his protector, however, his gold is in reality a test. "The test of a rich person is greater than that of a poor person," says (*Chovas Halevavos Shaar Hachniah* 4). As wealth increases, so does the necessity for compassion. The more one is able to help others, the more he must train himself to see and tend to their needs. For one whose outlook is based on *"tzar ayin,"* the test is impossible to pass, and the consequences of failure can be dire.

The lack of compassion is a greater sin than theft, as is illustrated in an encounter between King David and the prophet Nathan. The prophet wished to reprimand the king regarding his callousness. He conveyed his point with a parable: There was a poor man who had nothing but one lamb. With great difficulty, he managed to raise it, and by shearing a little bit of wool, he could earn enough to avoid starvation. Someone stole the lamb from him and slaughtered it.

David ruled that, as punishment for the theft, the thief had to pay the owner four times the value of the lamb. That was not all, however. "The one who did this deserves death," he declared, "because he had no mercy on another person."

Even one who generally has a giving nature can fall into "tzar ayin" when difficulties in his own life mount. He may express his tension by slamming the door on other people's needs, telling himself, "I've got my own problems right now." For the person who is selfish by nature, these justifications arise at every occasion in which help is requested. Often his own abhorrence of giving leads him to discourage others from chesed as well. He may mock those who make pledges at a fundraising event, or denigrate the cause to which they are giving. In turning others away from chesed, he becomes a "rasha," a wicked person (Avos 5:16). Ultimately, his closed fist deprives not only those in need, but himself and his own household. Parting with the money becomes so difficult that he can no longer even enjoy what he has.

The Chofetz Chaim illustrates that the gold worshipper has chosen a god that will quickly lure him onto a path of spiritual poverty and worldly poverty as well. Only when the idol is smashed does the gold regain its value and luster, because then it can be utilized for its real purpose. As an instrument of chesed, it can buy true joy in this world, and true security in the World to Come.

Step by **Step**

The next time a charity solicitation comes while I am in an angry or depressed mood, I will turn my focus away from my grievance and onto the other person's need.

9 Cheshvan — לרפו"ש חיה רייזל בת מינטשא שתחי' בתושח"י
Dedicated by Toby Shachar

9 Iyar — Chaya Raizy Markowitz לע"נ חי' רייזל בת ר' יהושע ע"ה
Dedicated by Shia and Shoshana Markowitz

DAY 40

י חשון
10 CHESHVAN / CYCLE 1

November 5, 2003
October 25, 2004
November 12, 2005
November 1, 2006
October 22, 2007
November 8, 2008
October 28, 2009

י אייר
10 IYAR / CYCLE 2

May 12, 2003
May 1, 2004
May 19, 2005
May 8, 2006
April 28, 2007
May 15, 2008
May 4, 2009
April 24, 2010

✎ *Healthy Wealth*

SEFER AHAVAS CHESED — **Part II Chapter X**

*G*ood health allows a person to use his faculties to their fullest. His limbs, organs and senses all operate at peak capacity, allowing him to accomplish all he can. Without his health, he may have all the same limbs, organs and senses, but they cannot fulfill their potential. In exactly the same way, a person can become "sick" with his wealth so that all his assets have no power to help him.

In *Koheles* (5:12), King Solomon says, "There is an evil sickness that I have seen under the sun." This terrible malady is evident when "riches are hoarded by their owner to his misfortune." The *Zohar* explains why this particular illness is defined with the word "evil" — a word that would seem to apply to any sickness; it reveals that there are tangible forces in this world that insinuate themselves into a person's nature. They manifest themselves as a deep-seated fear of letting go of money. A person controlled by these forces is not even generous with himself; he won't make a purchase today, because he might need the money for something else tomorrow. He won't give to one poor man, because perhaps tomorrow there will be someone who needs the money more. It is as if he is paralyzed in regard to using his money. His wealth is like the body of a terribly sick person; it lies there, unable to accomplish anything.

The most tragic element of this malady is that the victim brings it upon himself. Just as physical illnesses attack where immunity is compromised, the forces about which the *Zohar* speaks are also opportunistic. They vest themselves where an opening has been provided for them, in the heart of someone who sees his wealth as his alone, to use solely for his own personal benefit. Heaven helps him along the path he has chosen, making him so watchful of his money that he cannot even enjoy spending it on himself. Wealth accomplishes nothing positive for this person, and eventually, he passes into the Next World, leaving his carefully guarded treasure behind.

Ultimately, his wealth goes to others — people who will allow it to be utilized as an active, positive force. These are people who will loan the money, donate the money, offer their home, their time and other assets to those in need of help. They are able to rally the inner strength to overcome the evil illness King Solomon described. They become masters over the money, rather than slaves to it. The Chofetz Chaim urges every Jew to build this strength within himself. If one's wealth is to lead to blessing rather than ruin, one must bend in the opposite direction of *"tzar ayin."* One can and should consciously train oneself in the art of giving, until it becomes a way of life.

Step by **Step**

Today I will select one small, manageable chesed that I will do regularly as a means of inclining myself away from "tzar ayin."

10 Cheshvan — Chaim Nestlebaum לע"נ ר' חיים ישראל בן ר' יהודה אריה הכהן נעסטלבוים ז"ל
Dedicated by his wife and the Nestlebaums, Racers, Benvenistis and Shaffrens

10 Iyar —

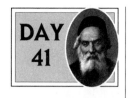

י"א חשון
11 CHESHVAN / CYCLE 1

November 6, 2003
October 26, 2004
November 13, 2005
November 2, 2006
October 23, 2007
November 9, 2008
October 29, 2009

י"א אייר
11 IYAR / CYCLE 2

May 13, 2003
May 2, 2004
May 20, 2005
May 9, 2006
April 29, 2007
May 16, 2008
May 5, 2009
April 25, 2010

✌ *Thinking Straight*

SEFER AHAVAS CHESED — Part II Chapter X
footnotes

*P*eople with a normal sense of decency would never wish to be the cause of an innocent person's downfall. They would never want to think of themselves as having caused someone's suffering. The Chofetz Chaim warns, however, that one can bear a tremendous burden of guilt for another person's suffering, and not even be aware of the sin. A person may only become aware of his guilt upon arriving in the Next World, when it is too late to atone. The only way to avoid such an inadvertent tragedy is to develop a love for chesed, for then, one's enthusiasm for helping others will assure that all who cross one's path are treated with compassion.

The Chofetz Chaim offers a view of the scene in the Next World. A newcomer arrives, serene in the knowledge that he has lived according to Hashem's will. He is given a Torah scroll, and each mitzvah within it is methodically reviewed to ascertain the person's merits. The review reaches the commandment (*Vayikra* 25:35): "If your brother becomes impoverished and his means falter... you shall strengthen him." The person stands tall, claiming credit for having helped many people. Then, he is shown a scene from his life. He sits with his family at the dinner table. There is a knock on the door. The man is annoyed at the disturbance and the appearance of yet another *tzedakah* collector. "Look, it's our dinnertime and you're the third person to come to the door tonight. Come back tomorrow and I'll see what I can do."

The *tzedakah* collector walks away, and the man thinks of him no more. On the other side of the door, however, is a crushed human being. He had walked up and down the block for fifteen minutes before finding the courage to knock. He fought to overcome his embarrassment, finally telling himself that there was simply no other choice. His wife had insisted he try this house, where a prominent businessman resided. She was worn and ill from worrying, and the electricity would be cut off tomorrow without a payment. Should he come back tomorrow? Should he have come earlier? Later? Should he try somewhere else? He enters his home to see his wife's expectant face, but she knows instantly that the mission has been a failure.

The Heavenly recording of this scene of despair comes as a terrible awakening to the man, who had considered himself a kind-hearted person. "How could I have known?" he pleads. The Chofetz Chaim answers: He couldn't have known. He could, however, have given the collector his serious attention, allowed himself to feel the man's plight, and realized that, by virtue of the knock on the door, the obligation to help had fallen upon him. By thinking the right thoughts, he would have made the right choice.

Step by **Step**

When someone comes to me for help, I will sincerely listen to his plight.

לע"נ הרבנית הדס ריזל בת ר' יעקב מרדכי ע"ה וואסיליסקי — **11 Cheshvan**
הונצח על ידי משפחה

לע"נ שמחה הערש בן ר' בערל הלוי **11 Iyar** — Sam Krugman
In loving memory of our father and grandfather, by the Krugman family

DAY 42

יב חשון
12 CHESHVAN / CYCLE 1

November 7, 2003
October 27, 2004
November 14, 2005
November 3, 2006
October 24, 2007
November 10, 2008
October 30, 2009

יב אייר
12 IYAR / CYCLE 2

May 14, 2003
May 3, 2004
May 21, 2005
May 10, 2006
April 30, 2007
May 17, 2008
May 6, 2009
April 26, 2010

◆ *Today's Mission*

SEFER AHAVAS CHESED — Part II
Chapter XI/XI footnotes

*T*here are kind-hearted, generous people who are perfectly happy to share their wealth. They are not prepared, however, to invest it in chesed. The money is not the issue; their obstacle is the effort involved in making the loan, arranging repayment terms and collecting the money.

Such people consider themselves far too busy to be occupied with such matters — or any religious obligation that threatens to usurp productive time. Yet such people do not expressly state, "I will never loan money to a needy person." Instead, they tell themselves, "Next time around, I'll help out. There's no time for it right now. I'm in the middle of a busy period." The concept of "tomorrow" is what preserves their self-image as righteous men; they feel like doers, even as they sit back and do nothing. The tomorrows mount, until at last they run out. In the end, all that remains is a swath of empty yesterdays.

Time and time again, the Torah emphasizes the concept of acting today, now. "And now, Israel, what does Hashem your G-d ask of you?" (*Devarim* 10:12). "Now," the Chofetz Chaim observes, "is the relevant word. What one does for Hashem, one must do at the earliest possible moment. "This day, Hashem your G-d commands you to perform His laws and statutes," says the Torah (*Devarim* 26:16). The present is the only relevant moment, the Sages teach, because the future is never certain.

To comprehend the urgency of acting today on whatever can be accomplished today, one must understand that the entire world depends upon it. Hashem places before each person the tasks that only that person can accomplish. Each person is required to look at the situation before him and ask himself, "What does Hashem ask of me?" The answer that he perceives must then become, in his mind, the only task in the universe that commands his effort at that moment. The inclination to see service to Hashem as a futile, intractable burden is then defeated. He has only this one deed to perform — whether it is to learn Torah, to pray, to help another person, to earn money for his family, to say a word of encouragement — and only he can perform it, for it lies before him alone.

In the prayer "*Shema Yisrael*," one says the words: "And these things which I command you this day." Every day, the small things Hashem commands each Jew, individually, are arrayed before him. Each person has his own private commandments assigned to him on "this day." They are his, and his alone.

Step by **Step**

Today I will ask myself, at least once, "What does Hashem want of me right now?"

12 Cheshvan — In honor of our dear parents, Rabbi and Mrs. Eli Friedman of Montreal, Canada
Dedicated by their children

12 Iyar — Marvin J. Rauzin ז"ל לע"נ משה בן יואל ז"ל
Dedicated in loving memory by Alan and Erica Rauzin

יג חשון
13 CHESHVAN / CYCLE 1

November 8, 2003
October 28, 2004
November 15, 2005
November 4, 2006
October 25, 2007
November 11, 2008
October 31, 2009

יג אייר
13 IYAR / CYCLE 2

May 15, 2003
May 4, 2004
May 22, 2005
May 11, 2006
May 1, 2007
May 18, 2008
May 7, 2009
April 27, 2010

✑ *Growing*

SEFER AHAVAS CHESED — **Part II Chapter XI**

*W*hen a person owns a fertile tract of land, he may seem to have the key to bounty in his hand. Soil alone, however, will not produce anything of value. King Solomon described a field he observed, which bore all the indications of the laziness of its owner. It was covered not with ripening crops, but with rocks, thistle and weeds. Its potential was gradually diminishing as it became increasingly matted with stubborn undergrowth.

Why did this field produce nothing of value? The Chofetz Chaim explains that a field must be plowed and planted; only then does the soil produce life. Life grows from the carefully prepared soil, and still more life is sustained from the produce it yields. Once a person plows and plants, he must protect his field with a fence so that wild animals will not intrude and destroy what his work has produced. In contrast, the lazy person's field — this potential spawning ground of life — lies in ruins, covered in thorns and weeds.

The lazy man might one day look around and say to himself, "This is such a waste. I'm going to plant this field." By that time, however, his task will be enormous. He will have to cut through the deeply embedded roots, remove the rocks, turn the soil, rebuild the gate. His energy will be drained before he even begins to plant.

This scenario, says the Chofetz Chaim, describes one who puts off Torah learning, self-improvement and kind deeds to another day. His effort to catch up will be hobbled by the thick tangles of unholiness that, through neglect, have taken root. Learning and kind acts are the means by which one plows the field to ready it for spiritual growth. By grasping each day's opportunities to serve Hashem, a person builds a fence around his field that keeps the opportunistic, life-draining weeds away. Within this protected field, wisdom, fine character traits and inner beauty can sprout and blossom. Ultimately, once a person has put in his effort, Hashem takes over the work, blessing the field with the ability to grow on its own.

The Chofetz Chaim quotes the Talmud (*Berachos* 32b) which states that there are four areas in which one needs constant strengthening: learning Torah, performing kind acts, praying and treating others with respect. The ability to do good does not sprout on its own; it requires training and effort. Laziness is the normal "default" mode of human nature. If a person allows himself to drift into that mode, he will fail to cultivate good deeds, and he will be unable to reap their merit. At some later time when that merit is needed, the storehouse will be empty. The Talmud (*Berachos* 63a) explains that this principle affects not only individual lives, but the Jewish people as a whole. In times of crisis, Hashem's agents of compassion scour the world for kind acts in order to bolster the cause of mercy. By refusing to put off chesed for tomorrow, each person has the ability to assure that Hashem will be powerfully moved by the myriad kind acts, small and large, that blossom forth continually from each Jewish home.

Today I will compel myself at least once to act immediately on a thought of a chesed I want to do.

13 Cheshvan — William Pearlman ז"ל לע"נ חיים וועלוול בן ברוך ז"ל
Dedicated in loving memory by his sons, Moshe, Avrohom and Dovid Pearlman

13 Iyar — Margit Baldinger ע"ה לע"נ פרומט בת לוי הלוי ע"ה
Dedicated by Dr. and Mrs. Levi Moshe Baldinger and family

יד חשון
14 CHESHVAN / CYCLE 1

November 9, 2003
October 29, 2004
November 16, 2005
November 5, 2006
October 26, 2007
November 12, 2008
November 1, 2009

יד אייר
14 IYAR / CYCLE 2

May 16, 2003
May 5, 2004
May 23, 2005
May 12, 2006
May 2, 2007
May 19, 2008
May 8, 2009
April 28, 2010

❧ *Staying in Business*

SEFER AHAVAS CHESED — Part II Chapter XI

*E*very customer that comes into a store creates work for the storekeeper. He must show the customer the merchandise, keep adequate supplies on hand, replace what is purchased, keep the shelves orderly and keep track of the sales and expenses. Despite all this, no storekeeper would complain of having too much business. Time, effort and capital outlay are the instruments that create his profit.

The Chofetz Chaim says this paradigm reflects perfectly what a person's attitude should be toward the time, effort and money invested in chesed. The more "business" one is able to do, the more profit one will earn. If there are setbacks, the storekeeper will analyze his mistakes and forge ahead. He will not give up his source of livelihood simply because he has endured a disappointment or difficulty. The same must hold true of a person engaging in chesed. If he endures difficulty, he must nonetheless persist, for there is no other source of merit that can replace chesed. It is, in effect, his livelihood.

This is especially true of the task of collecting money that has been loaned. In this area, one's laziness can easily be mistaken for one's higher instincts. Rather than go through the trouble of calling a debtor repeatedly to recoup the money, a person may tell himself, "I'll forgive the loan. I'll give him a break and forget about the whole thing." This, the Chofetz Chaim says, is counterproductive, because the money will no longer be available for further chesed.

Furthermore, the lender might use his loss as justification for refusing future requests for loans.

In this area, especially, a person must consider himself a businessman. He must "stay in business" even if some of his customers are slow at paying. He must make his best effort — within the confines of halachah — to collect his loan so that the money can be reinvested, earning more profit and more merit for his life's crucial enterprise. In fact, every time he calls the debtor to remind him of his obligation — every time he endures the embarrassment and discomfort this entails — he increases the merit he has earned for this act of chesed. His effort is meritorious because its goal is to ensure that there will be enough money to perform further acts of chesed in the future. The storekeeper exerts himself to collect money due to him, even though he earns not one additional penny for his trouble, and even though his profits are the temporal riches of this world. For the eternal riches earned through chesed — even through pursuing repayment of a loan — one should be at least as zealous.

Today I will find out what the Torah's guidelines are regarding collection of a loan from a fellow Jew.

14 Cheshvan — לע"נ ר' בנציון גבריאל בן ר' אליעזר ז"ל
Dedicated by Rabbi and Mrs. Eliezer Hamburger

14 Iyar — לע"נ יענטא בת משה ע"ה

טו חשון
15 CHESHVAN / CYCLE 1

November 10, 2003
October 30, 2004
November 17, 2005
November 6, 2006
October 27, 2007
November 13, 2008
November 2, 2009

טו אייר
15 IYAR / CYCLE 2

May 17, 2003
May 6, 2004
May 24, 2005
May 13, 2006
May 3, 2007
May 20, 2008
May 9, 2009
April 29, 2010

✑ *Required Dosage*

SEFER AHAVAS CHESED — Part II Chapter XII

*O*ne who needs a certain daily dose of medicine to stay alive does not leave the dosage to chance. It's too important. He does whatever is necessary to remember the medication and to keep a strict account of it. He cannot countenance a situation in which, at the end of the day, he must wrack his brain to remember whether he took the day's dose.

Chesed is the *neshamah's* life-sustaining medicine, yet the dosage is often left to chance. On some days, opportunities to help arise and are seized. On some days, opportunities are bypassed, and on some days, no one asks for help. The Chofetz Chaim sees this as a dangerously haphazard system for conducting one's life. It is comparable to a diabetic saying, "Some days I take my insulin. Some days I remember it but I don't bother with it. And then, some days I just don't feel I need it."

Chesed is too important to one's life in this world and the next to be handled in such a manner. The Chofetz Chaim therefore urges each person to pursue chesed on a consistent, daily basis. The best way for a person to be sure he is not "forgetting to take his medicine" is to keep a daily log in which he records acts he has performed that have helped another person. By reviewing the day from this perspective, the person trains himself to see chesed as a crucial element in every day. He assures himself that he has gotten his "daily dosage" of this life-sustaining mitzvah, and his nightly self-review subtly alters the way he approaches his days.

The Chofetz Chaim quotes from the *Shaar HaKedushah* by R' Chaim Vital, the great student of the Arizal, that a person should feel bereft if he finds that his day has been void of chesed and learning. Many Torah scholars follow the practice of keeping a daily log, and the standard they set for themselves — that no day pass without doing some act of chesed — is one that almost any Jew can aspire to. The log need not feature daily feats of greatness and self-sacrifice. Even simple favors and acts of kindness count. A person may only have given a compliment that lifted someone's spirits, or lent someone the use of a cell phone or a fax machine, or bought some raffle tickets to support a local institution. Perhaps the person gave up some precious time to advise a friend. Anything one has done that day that benefits another person has a place in one's log. Keeping track of chesed in this way elevates it in one's mind, and one's life, to its rightful place of importance.

Tonight I will start a log in which I will record at least one act of chesed I have done during the day. If there is nothing to record, I will commit myself to a specific act for the next day.

15 Cheshvan — May today's learning be a זכות for כלל ישראל for רפואות וישועות.

15 Iyar — In memory of Flora and Nathan Englander
Dedicated by their grandchildren and great-grandchildren

טו חשון
16 CHESHVAN / CYCLE 1

November 11, 2003
October 31, 2004
November 18, 2005
November 7, 2006
October 28, 2007
November 14, 2008
November 3, 2009

טו אייר
16 IYAR / CYCLE 2

May 18, 2003
May 7, 2004
May 25, 2005
May 14, 2006
May 4, 2007
May 21, 2008
May 10, 2009
April 30, 2010

✎ *Open Access*

SEFER AHAVAS CHESED — Part II Chapter XII

*H*ashem has given the Jewish people three pathways to holiness. One is the study of Torah, the second is *"avodah,"* service, which encompasses prayer, and the third is chesed. The second pathway, prayer, is in reality a detour route, a necessary alternative to the primary *"avodah,"* which is the service in the *Beis HaMikdash*. With the destruction of the *Beis HaMikdash*, the Jews' access to the earth's most concentrated source of holiness was closed off. The remaining pathways — prayer, study of Torah and acts of kindness — are therefore all the more vital to the *neshamah's* earthly journey.

The Chofetz Chaim illustrates that acts of kindness possess the power to achieve, at least in part, what the *Beis HaMikdash* achieved for the Jewish people. He sites the Talmud (*Berachos* 5b) discussing the verse in *Mishlei* (16:6), "Through kindness and truth iniquity will be forgiven." Kindness, says the Talmud, refers to one who pursues opportunities to give charity and help others; truth refers to the Torah.

A scene depicted in *Midrash Yelamdeinu* strengthens the link between chesed and atonement: Rabbi Yehoshua ben Chananyah is walking with Rabbi Yochanan ben Zakkai past the ruined Temple Mount. Rabbi Yehoshua says, "Woe is to us! The Temple, the source of forgiveness for our sins, has been destroyed." Rabbi Yochanan ben Zakkai replies, "My son, don't despair. We have another source of atonement, and that is acts of kindness." Another verse

(*Hoshea* 6:6) goes even further, declaring that Hashem says, "For I desire kindness, not a sacrifice."

It is clear from these verses that, although the absence of the *Beis HaMikdash* cuts off a crucial "express route" to holiness, acts of kindness can take a Jew to the same spiritual destination.

One must realize, however, that for kindness to have a power parallel to that of the *Beis HaMikdash*, one must adhere to standards that are parallel to those of the *Beis HaMikdash*. There, the fire of the altar burned constantly. The Kohanim brought sacrifices constantly because sin is a constant in the world, and the atonement the sacrifices afforded was always needed. For chesed to achieve the same level of power to bring forgiveness, it too must be a constant.

Torah, service to Hashem and acts of kindness are the only three real nutrients for a Jew's *neshamah*. They provide its nourishment, its energy and its protection from corrupting forces. With one of these three essential elements compromised, the only way to stay in "good health" is to absorb more nourishment from those that remain. Even with the *Beis HaMikdash* in ruins, forgiveness and kindness still rule Hashem's world.

Today I will commit myself to a concrete plan to make kindness more of a "constant" in my life.

יז חשון
17 CHESHVAN / CYCLE 1

November 12, 2003
November 1, 2004
November 19, 2005
November 8, 2006
October 29, 2007
November 15, 2008
November 4, 2009

יז אייר
17 IYAR / CYCLE 2

May 19, 2003
May 8, 2004
May 26, 2005
May 15, 2006
May 5, 2007
May 22, 2008
May 11, 2009
May 1, 2010

≈ *Today's Story*

SEFER AHAVAS CHESED — Part II Chapter XII

*L*ife is not as fleeting as one may imagine, for the deeds of each day live on in eternity. It is in each person's hands to define the eternity in which he, and his deeds, will live. The Chofetz Chaim turns to the *Zohar* to explain how every person must account for his usage of the days he was allotted. Each day testifies, as if to say, "This is how you used me." Heaven records a person's every activity, and the recording forever plays and replays a day that the person thought was long forgotten. Each day one lives is a spiritual, eternal reality, a creation of one's own hands, heart and mind. No day is insignificant.

How does one live a worthwhile day? The Chofetz Chaim prescribes a substantial amount of Torah study, for this leads to love of Hashem and fulfillment of His commandments. It inculcates a person with an awe of Hashem which inspires him to do all that is within his ability to emulate His ways. This leads naturally to an active form of goodness, a desire to find ways to help others. To the person whose days are rooted in Torah and chesed, Hashem promises, "Your light will shine even in the darkness, and your deepest gloom will be like the noon" (*Yeshayah* 58:10).

When the Sages discuss what is required to reach the loftiest levels of spirituality, they speak of one who is an *"osek"* in Torah and kind acts. The word *"osek"* denotes a commitment far stronger than simply learning Torah and performing deeds of kindness. It denotes someone to whom these activities are life's enterprise. Just as one would put all the time and effort possible into running a business, one who is "osek" in chesed stretches himself to the limits of his ability to help others. To him, chesed provides the greatest satisfaction, the greatest joy in life.

The Chofetz Chaim expounds on this concept because, he says, many people erroneously believe that the obligation of chesed can be fulfilled on a "once-in-a-while" basis. They believe that, if they loaned somebody money yesterday, they do not need to provide someone else a loan today. If they did their next-door neighbor a favor last week, they are not expected to do him another favor this week. Such a philosophy misses the point. It fails to understand that chesed is not an episode; it is a perspective that informs every day of one's life. Living with that perspective, one creates days that will bring joy and elation when they testify in Heaven, "This is how you used me."

The next time I think to myself "I've done enough" for a certain person or cause, I will reassess and consider if, perhaps, I really do have more I could reasonably give.

לע"נ יהודה אהרן בן משה ישראל ז"ל — **17 Cheshvan**
Dedicated by the Leibov family

לזכות ניסעם אלעד, ומרדכי חביב — **17 Iyar**

יח חשון
18 CHESHVAN / CYCLE 1

November 13, 2003
November 2, 2004
November 20, 2005
November 9, 2006
October 30, 2007
November 16, 2008
November 5, 2009

יח אייר
18 IYAR / CYCLE 2

May 20, 2003
May 9, 2004
May 27, 2005
May 16, 2006
May 6, 2007
May 23, 2008
May 12, 2009
May 2, 2010

❧ *The Chesed Primer*

SEFER AHAVAS CHESED — Part II Chapter XII

*E*lectricity is a powerful, complex force. One perceives it only in its final manifestation; it can light up a city, make factory machinery hum, empower vast computer networks or just shed a little light on the dinner table. If one wants to understand how electricity really works, one must study the physics, the scientific formulas that express what is really happening within the wires. Chesed is the most powerful force of all. It is the force that runs the world, and like any mighty force, it contains within it many unseen dimensions. The Chofetz Chaim provides a formula that unlocks the mysteries of chesed, revealing its inner dynamics. That key is the *alef-beis*.

The Talmud (*Shabbos* 104a) introduces this formula. It relates that small children came into the study hall and introduced concepts so deep that even in the days of Joshua ben Nun — in the generation that directly followed the giving of the Torah — such ideas were not taught. One might wonder what profound wisdom these small children had to teach. Their wisdom, the Talmud says, was precisely the wisdom of little children. They taught the *alef-beis*: " '*Alef-beis*' stands for '*alef binah*,' " they said. "*Alef*" means learning, and "*binah*" means understanding. This refers to the study of Torah.

The next letters in their "lecture" were "*gimmel*" and "*daled*," which stand for "*gemol dalim*," meaning "help the poor." Parenthetically, the Chofetz Chaim explains that this phrase does not mean one should not help a wealthy person in need. It merely recognizes that the poor are more often in need of help, and have fewer resources to turn to. Looking more closely at the "gimmel," there is a further message. The letter is formed with a "foot" that extends to the right, toward the "daled." In "gemol dalim," the help — the "gemol" — is extended toward the poor — the "dalim." One whose desire is to help the poor will extend himself toward them, seeking out those who need his help rather than waiting for them to appear on his doorstep.

The next two letters of the alef-beis — "hei" and "vav" — represent Hashem's name. The Chofetz Chaim explains this segment of Talmud by referring to another segment (Bava Basra 75b), which says that a time will come when the righteous are called by Hashem's name; the righteous will overflow with such G-dliness that they will actually bear Hashem's name.

This, says the Chofetz Chaim, explains the sequence of alef-beis that the children expounded. "Alef binah," if a person commits himself to learning Torah; and "gemol dalim," if he helps the poor; then he arrives at "hei" and "vav." Hashem will pronounce His name upon him.

As the Talmud relates, the interpretation given by these small children came as an awakening to those who heard them. "Why didn't we ever realize this?" they wondered. The Sages explain that the words of children — even when they do not understand completely what they are saying — are sometimes a medium of prophecy. Hashem provided this channel to mitigate the loss of the full power of prophecy, which He removed from His people. By listening carefully to the words of these children, one can comprehend the formula that makes kindness the moving force in Hashem's Creation.

Step by **Step**

Any Torah learning that I do today I will complement with an act of kindness.

18 Cheshvan — Mrs. N. Yoselovsky לע"נ נחמה בת ר' מאיר הכהן ע"ה
Dedicated by the Yoselovsky family, Lakewood, NJ

18 Iyar — Barry Lampel לע"נ ברוך בן צבי ליפא ז"ל
Dedicated by Zvi and Blima Lampel and Josh and Barbara Gertelman

יט חשון
19 CHESHVAN / CYCLE 1

November 14, 2003
November 3, 2004
November 21, 2005
November 10, 2006
October 31, 2007
November 17, 2008
November 6, 2009

יט אייר
19 IYAR / CYCLE 2

May 21, 2003
May 10, 2004
May 28, 2005
May 17, 2006
May 7, 2007
May 24, 2008
May 13, 2009
May 3, 2010

❧ *Good Directions*

SEFER AHAVAS CHESED — Part II Chapter XII

*A*lef-beis, *gimmel-daled*; these are road-signs that orient one's path in life. One takes the first step with *alef-beis*, learning Torah. One's feet are then automatically pointed in the direction of *gimmel-daled*, helping others. Rabbi Moshe Feinstein, whose advice and halachic decisions guided the last generation and continue to resound today, provided a paradigm for this steady, upward progress. In one instance, the secular court wished to consult Rav Moshe regarding a case before it. A court officer visited Rav Moshe and asked him the relevant questions. When the official part of the interview was concluded, the officer had a personal question to ask: "I understand that you are one of the greatest rabbis and your opinions in Jewish law are widely respected. How does one reach this status? Why do people listen to you? Are you elected?"

Rav Moshe explained: "Someone once came to me with a question, and he liked the answer I gave him. Then someone else came, and he also liked my answer. People soon heard that I gave good answers and sound advice, so more and more people began to come." That was the simplistic explanation, geared to a secular understanding. On the spiritual level, Rav Moshe was actually explaining the link between Torah learning and chesed. He spent his days in learning, and therefore, he merited Divine assistance in his efforts to alleviate the problems of others. His guidance was golden because it shone with truth of Torah.

Rav Moshe's learning laid the foundation of his greatness, but he reached his highest state when he turned that learning into a vehicle for helping others. At that point, Hashem rested His presence upon him.

When one's days are oriented in this direction, the success of one's life's journey is virtually assured.

The *alef-beis* lays out a sequence, a path toward constant spiritual growth, and the Chofetz Chaim urges every Jew to follow it. A person must first learn and understand, which will lead him to help others. Hashem will then bestow His presence upon the person and his faith in Hashem will grow stronger. This will lead to more learning, which will bring a greater ability to help and a greater sense of joy and purpose in life. Every step along the path leads upward, in an ascent that has no limit.

Step by **Step**

Today, if someone asks me for advice, I will try to make sure my answer is drawn from valid Torah concepts.

כ חשון
20 CHESHVAN / CYCLE 1

November 15, 2003
November 4, 2004
November 22, 2005
November 11, 2006
November 1, 2007
November 18, 2008
November 7, 2009

כ אייר
20 IYAR / CYCLE 2

May 22, 2003
May 11, 2004
May 29, 2005
May 18, 2006
May 8, 2007
May 25, 2008
May 14, 2009
May 4, 2010

☙ *Hashem's Payroll*

SEFER AHAVAS CHESED — Part II Chapter XII

ollowing the directions set by the first six letters in the *alef-beis*, one could still be left with a major question: If Torah study and acts of kindness are to be the primary activities of a Jew's life, how does one find time to earn an income? The Torah is, after all, for this world, and in this world, one needs a livelihood. This question leads the Chofetz Chaim to the next letter expounded upon by the children in the Talmud's story. The letter *"zayin"* represents *"zan,"* which means to provide sustenance. The *alef-beis* sequence already explored leads directly to *"zan."* If one learns and helps others, if one merits Hashem's presence in his life, then one lands upon the promise of *"zayin,"* that Hashem will provide. Sustenance is the next element in the chesed formula.

The Chofetz Chaim warns that a person must not think that acts of charity and kindness will take one penny off the bottom line of his wealth. The same is true of studying Torah, If one follows the path paved by the *alef-beis*, he loses nothing; instead, he gains Hashem's promise of sustenance. Obviously, one must shoulder his financial responsibilities to the best of his ability, but in doing so, he should understand on the deepest level that the more he helps others, the more his efforts are going to yield. "Take off your 10 percent, and as a result you will have more," says *Shabbos* 119a. The Chofetz Chaim makes clear that this promise pertains not just to charity, but to physical help and time that one gives others. Equally, it applies to the time one commits to studying Torah.

Trusting in Hashem's providing hand calls for faith, but this faith is built upon tangible reality. During the time that manna fell in the wilderness, Hashem instructed the Jews to preserve some of this miraculous substance in a jar. The manna was passed down through the generations, until the times of the prophet Jeremiah. He exhibited the jar of manna to the Jews, providing them with living proof that Hashem can provide for everyone, even when they take time from pursuing their livelihoods to study Torah.

Today, the manna is no longer there to awaken people to the true source of their livelihood. Sustenance hides behind the veil of nature, apparently governed by the laws of cause and effect. If one looks, one can see behind this veil, however. One need only consider the debit side of the Jewish ledger: large families to support, weekly Sabbaths and yearly Yomim Tovim during which business cannot be conducted, *succos* to build, *tefillin* to buy, charity to give. Somehow, most Jews find a way to cover these extraordinary expenses day after day, year after year.

Behind the veil, one can clearly see that the manna is still falling. Hashem is providing, and He is the "employer" one most needs to please. In that light, the idea that chesed leads to sustenance makes perfect sense. A person who delights in doing chesed makes himself Hashem's valuable agent in this world. He earns his pay directly from the only real Source of wealth.

The next time I feel hesitant to donate money, I will remember that chesed is an integral part of my livelihood.

20 Cheshvan — Gary and Cindi Singer שיחי"ו לזכות יהודה יוסף וטובה סינגר
Dedicated by Michael, Jeff and Jessica

20 Iyar — May today's learning be a זכות for our משפחה.
Dedicated by Raphael and Malka Waldman, Baltimore, MD

כא חשון
21 CHESHVAN / CYCLE 1

November 16, 2003
November 5, 2004
November 23, 2005
November 12, 2006
November 2, 2007
November 19, 2008
November 8, 2009

כא אייר
21 IYAR / CYCLE 2

May 23, 2003
May 12, 2004
May 30, 2005
May 19, 2006
May 9, 2007
May 26, 2008
May 15, 2009
May 5, 2010

❧ *Beloved*

SEFER AHAVAS CHESED — Part II Chapter XII

*H*eaven holds a blessing that everyone wants, yet it is possibly the most elusive of blessings. If a person wishes to have the blessing of wealth, he can enter a profession or start a business to open up a channel through which money can flow. If a person wishes to become a scholar, he can put his time into learning. If he wants the blessing of children, he can get married and establish a household. There is almost always some groundwork a person can lay to draw a blessing into his life. One exception to this is the blessing of *"chein,"* which means "grace." A person with *"chein"* has a pleasantness about him that makes him likable. People respond to him with warmth. They enjoy his presence and seek his company. *"Chein"* turns a person's life into a long series of wonderful, happy encounters, yet one cannot bring this attribute upon oneself. In fact, it is often the case that the harder a person tries to curry favor with others, the less he is liked.

This precious quality of *"chein"* is represented by the letter *"ches,"* the next letter in the Talmud's review of the *alef-beis*. It is the next step in the sequence set in motion by Torah study and acts of kindness. From the previous letter, *"zayin"* for *"zan,"* one learns that Hashem takes care of the material needs of those who study Torah and help the needy. Now, through the letter *"ches,"* one is assured that emotional needs will also be met. Unlike *"zan,"* which might mistakenly be thought to emanate from man's efforts, *"chein"* is clearly a gift of Heaven.

The person blessed with *"chein"* experiences life completely differently from one who lacks this blessing. His life is filled with joy and friendship rather than loneliness and strife, yet it is almost impossible to define what this person has that others do not. Rabbi Samson Raphael Hirsch points out that the root of the word *"chein"* is also the root for the word *"chinam,"* which means "nothing." Often there is no clear reason why a person is liked, except that he has received a special Divine blessing. While it is true that a person cannot force others to like him, he can increase his own allotment of *"chein,"* through the proper mix of Torah study and acts of kindness.

Even among small children, it becomes immediately apparent that some of them have "got it" and others do not. One 6-year-old child marveled that his friend, the most popular boy in his class, went on to become the most popular boy in day camp as well, even among a completely different group of children. "Nobody told them that they were supposed to like him," the child told his father. "They just did." In truth, however, Hashem "told them" to like the child. Whether child, adolescent, adult or elder, the warmth and friendship of others is a life-sustaining gift and it need not be elusive. One can reach for this gift, grasp it and enjoy it for a lifetime, simply by embracing the trait of kindness.

If friction with others is a problem in my life, today I will commit to an ongoing chesed with the goal of meriting the blessing of "chein."

כב חשון
22 CHESHVAN / CYCLE 1

November 17, 2003
November 6, 2004
November 24, 2005
November 13, 2006
November 3, 2007
November 20, 2008
November 9, 2009

כב אייר
22 IYAR / CYCLE 2

May 24, 2003
May 13, 2004
May 31, 2005
May 20, 2006
May 10, 2007
May 27, 2008
May 16, 2009
May 6, 2010

❧ *The Crowning Touch*

SEFER AHAVAS CHESED — Part II Chapter XII

A recurring theme in fairy-tale fantasies is the granting of three wishes. Inevitably, the hero stalls on wish number three; it is his last opportunity to get anything he wants, and he knows he needs wisdom to perceive what, in the long run, will do him good. For a Jew, however, the solution would be clear. One would ask Hashem, "Do good for me," leaving the details of "good" to the only One Who can accurately perceive it. The Chofetz Chaim relates that for those who follow the Talmud's *"alef-beis"* sequence of life, the next letter, *"tes,"* grants exactly this wish for *"tov,"* for Hashem's good.

The two letters that follow elaborate on some of that good. The letter *"yud"* represents *"yerushah,"* an inheritance. The unique element of this blessing is that an inheritance comes to a person simply because of who he is. The heir does not have to toil for his assets; they are bestowed upon him. To further define the nature of this inheritance, the Chofetz Chaim cites the Talmud (*Bava Kamma* 17a): "All who dedicate themselves to Torah and kind acts merit the inheritance of Issachar." The tribe of Issachar had a magnificent inheritance. It was the tribe that dwelled closest to Moses, and therefore absorbed the largest share of his attributes. From this tribe emerged the Sanhedrin — judges who possessed the wisdom to read the stars and moon to calculate the calendar. Issachar enjoyed the special blessing of a wisdom that flowed from one generation to the next.

The next letter, "*kof*," represents the "*kesser*," which is a crown. Besides all that Hashem does in this world for one who clings to Torah and the trait of kindness, He "ties a crown" for him in the World to Come. The image evoked in this phrase is one of profound love as Hashem Himself sets a crown on the person's head. The Chofetz Chaim underscores the emotions this image conveys with an analogy: A mother's beloved only child is about to go out the door, but before he leaves, his mother gently wipes a last bit of dirt off his face, adjusts his coat and hat for warmth and gives him a good-bye kiss. Through her personal attention, she fills the child's heart with a sense of her love and care. It wasn't a maid who tended to him, but his mother's own loving hands. The scene offers a glimpse of what a Jew will feel when Hashem Himself places the crown upon his head.

The intensity of this love can be understood further, says the Chofetz Chaim, through the principle that states: "The reward is greater than the punishment" (*Sotah* 11a). The punishment for one who fails to respond to the needs of others is that Hashem then fails to respond to that person's needs. For those who do show love and concern to their fellow man, the reward comes multiplied a thousandfold. In this world and the World to Come, they bathe in the glow of the profound love that Hashem showers upon His cherished children.

If I am feeling burdened by helping my child, parent or spouse, today I will try to find motivation in the fact that my effort is being rewarded with Hashem's loving care.

22 Cheshvan — L'zichron Olam, Robert Louis Breslow לע״נ יהודה בן אליעזר הלוי ז״ל
Dedicated with love by the Breslow, Kruman and Moldovsky families

22 Iyar — Ada Blecher לע״נ איידע בת ר׳ יצחק הלוי ז״ל
Dedicated by her great-grandson, Shaul Ginsberg

DAY 53

כג חשון
23 CHESHVAN / CYCLE 1

November 18, 2003
November 7, 2004
November 25, 2005
November 14, 2006
November 4, 2007
November 21, 2008
November 10, 2009

כג אייר
23 IYAR / CYCLE 2

May 25, 2003
May 14, 2004
June 1, 2005
May 21, 2006
May 11, 2007
May 28, 2008
May 17, 2009
May 7, 2010

✑ *Ready, Willing and Able*

SEFER AHAVAS CHESED — Part II Chapter XIII

*E*very dollar has thousands of potential destinations. Nevertheless, one has an obligation to make sure that a certain percentage of those dollars reach the hands of the needy. The Chofetz Chaim offers practical advice to prevent money destined for chesed from being waylaid on its voyage to do good. He points out that the *yetzer hara* puts great effort into convincing a person that his money belongs elsewhere, and that any given opportunity for chesed is best deferred until after a particular expense is covered or a particular deal is completed. One must have a defense against these arguments, for they may be temporarily overcome in some instances, but they are never completely defeated.

The best defense, the Chofetz Chaim suggests, is the preemptive strike. One with the means to do so should set aside a certain amount of money for chesed. This permanent loan fund should be established before anyone even asks for money. In setting the money aside, a person is stating to himself, his family and anyone who might have input into his spending decisions: "This is the money I have available to loan. That is the purpose of this money."

With that declaration, a person has taken out of his hands the on-the-spot decision-making that gives the *yetzer hara* its golden opportunity to destroy good intentions. The money has no other purpose than chesed. It is not available for a business deal or a household expense, therefore those arguments are defeated before they are even voiced. The major question that a request for a loan provokes — "Do I have money available to make the loan, and if so, how much?" — is answered automatically.

One might believe that it is preferable to take an equivalent amount of money and donate it to an established loan fund that assists established businesses. That type of contribution provides a sense that the money will be secure and wisely disbursed. The Chofetz Chaim, however, states a clear preference for keeping the money in a personal loan fund. By having the money on hand, ready for use, one can respond generously to those who appear at one's doorstep seeking help. The money is there for a neighbor or relative in need, or an out-of-luck stranger hoping to tap the compassion of a fellow Jew. A person who awakens each day ready and willing to help others, says the Chofetz Chaim, is a person who understands how to turn his love and fear of Hashem into a concrete, everyday reality.

Step by **Step**

If I have the means to do so, today I will set aside a certain amount of money to be used exclusively to provide loans. (One can also set aside objects — taped Torah lectures, baby furnishings, table centerpieces — for loan.)

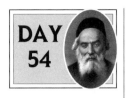
כד חשון
24 CHESHVAN / CYCLE 1

November 19, 2003
November 8, 2004
November 26, 2005
November 15, 2006
November 5, 2007
November 22, 2008
November 11, 2009

כד אייר
24 IYAR / CYCLE 2

May 26, 2003
May 15, 2004
June 2, 2005
May 22, 2006
May 12, 2007
May 29, 2008
May 18, 2009
May 8, 2010

❧ *Maximum Return*

SEFER AHAVAS CHESED — Part II Chapter XIII

*O*ne person takes $5,000 once a year and donates it to a large organization that provides free business loans to community enterprises. The organization thanks him profusely for his generosity, and quickly dispenses the money to the many places in which it is needed. One month later, the $5,000 is long gone. The donor has shifted his focus to other concerns; he will not be giving the community's needs another thought until the time arrives for the next year's donation.

Another person gives $50 a week to a small fund that helps the poor. Some weeks, his money buys a Shabbos meal for a widow and her children. Some weeks, it pays for simple weekday dinners for an elderly man living alone. Before the Yomim Tovim, it buys a few new dresses for girls who would otherwise be attired in worn hand-me-downs. The man's heart aches for the plight of the families the organization helps. Sometimes he helps deliver meals to the families. Sometimes he travels around town collecting contributions from the donation boxes.

Each of these two men is giving what he is required, according to his income, to give. The Chofetz Chaim examines this scenario and reveals that the second man — the one who gives smaller amounts more frequently — will benefit far more from his investment in charity than the first man will benefit from his large, one-shot donation. The first man may be giving the correct amount, but he has nothing left to offer when a poor man arrives at his doorstep. Even as he fulfills his obligation to donate 10 percent of his income, he renders himself unable to fulfill the mitzvah of caring for the poor.

On the other hand, the second man is a frequent investor in chesed. The Chofetz Chaim explains that chesed operates under the same principles as business investment. A person who invests smaller amounts regularly usually earns far more interest than one who invests large amounts infrequently. The frequent investor's continual, systematic involvement in the market allows him to weather its ups and downs. Similarly, systematic involvement in chesed provides one with continual opportunities to help others; some may be more successful, some less successful, but there are always more opportunities ahead. Dollar for dollar, the frequent investor in chesed will usually have a far higher rate of return than the lump-sum investor.

The most important benefit of frequent giving is that it transforms one into a giver. By continually giving, one develops the habit of looking outward, perceiving other people's needs and acting to help them. One's heart is touched and one's hand is opened far more easily when one is in the habit of giving. In contrast, the person who gives only occasionally — even if the donation is very substantial — must by necessity train himself in hard-heartedness. There is no doubt that, if he is a person who has the means for an occasional large donation, people will be coming to him for help throughout the year. For him to hold to the course he has set for himself, he must learn to remain unmoved by their appeals and say "no" to their requests.

(Continued on page 382)

Step by **Step**

Today I will establish an ongoing, regular system of giving charity or doing chesed.

כה חשון
25 CHESHVAN / CYCLE 1

November 20, 2003
November 9, 2004
November 27, 2005
November 16, 2006
November 6, 2007
November 23, 2008
November 12, 2009

כה אייר
25 IYAR / CYCLE 2

May 27, 2003
May 16, 2004
June 3, 2005
May 23, 2006
May 13, 2007
May 30, 2008
May 19, 2009
May 9, 2010

✤ Tipping the Balance

SEFER AHAVAS CHESED — Part II Chapter XIII

In mitzvos, quantity counts. "The world is judged," says the Mishnah (*Avos* 3:14), "and it all depends on the majority of the actions." According to the Rambam, the choice of words in this statement reveals an important lesson. The Mishnah does not state that the world is judged according to the greatness of actions; it uses the word *"rov,"* meaning majority. This means that Hashem weighs the quantity of good deeds being done in the world against the quantity of bad, selfish, hurtful deeds.

One might understand this concept from the perspective of a classroom teacher. If the teacher has 25 students, and 23 of them are disruptive and disinterested, the atmosphere of the classroom will be miserable, even if the remaining two students are pure sterling. If, on the other hand, she has 23 students who participate in a positive way with her lessons and with each other, the atmosphere will be pleasant and productive, even if there are two disruptive students, and even if none of the 23 good students is pure sterling. Hashem wants to see a world in which good deeds are the common currency, used every day in every interaction.

This principle should guide a person in making a choice between doing one major good deed or performing smaller acts of kindness whenever he can. The steady flow of kind acts adds to the quantity of good deeds done in the world, mounting a far more powerful counterforce to the negative elements than could be achieved by one grand gesture. The one great deed might bring the person immense merit, but in Hashem's accounting as He judges the world, it is still just one deed.

Mitzvos come to man as a means of elevation. Each mitzvah a person performs provides the fuel for ascent up the ladder of holiness and closeness to Hashem. It makes sense, therefore, that a person who performs 100 small acts of kindness a day will have a smoother and more rapid ascent than the person who saves his chesed for special occasions.

These acts are often simple, yet difficult. For instance, a businessman is attempting to complete his morning prayers and get a busy workday underway, but is accosted by one after another individual, each with a hard-luck story. One person has a daughter to marry off. One needs an expensive operation for his mother. One is trying to prop up a struggling yeshivah in South America. Each time the businessman stems the tide of annoyance that begins to rise, reaches into his pocket and gives with a smile and a word of encouragement, he has climbed. He has helped the world by tipping the balance of deeds toward good, and he has helped himself by strengthening the spiritual muscles that expedite his climb, ensuring that ultimately, he will reach the summit.

Step by **Step**

Today I will try to keep track of every instance of chesed in my day. At the end of the day, I will assess whether chesed is present in "quantity" in my life.

25 Cheshvan — Mrs. Chana Weisz ע"ה לע"נ מרת חנה בת ר' שלמה ע"ה
Dedicated by her family: Basch, Bernfeld, Berger and Rubin families

25 Iyar — May today's learning be a זכות for our children,
Kopel Yosef, Avrohom Michoel and Yocheved.

כו חשון
26 CHESHVAN / CYCLE 1

November 21, 2003
November 10, 2004
November 28, 2005
November 17, 2006
November 7, 2007
November 24, 2008
November 13, 2009

כו אייר
26 IYAR / CYCLE 2

May 28, 2003
May 17, 2004
June 4, 2005
May 24, 2006
May 14, 2007
May 31, 2008
May 20, 2009
May 10, 2010

✒ *Clothed in Kindness*

SEFER AHAVAS CHESED — Part II Chapter XIII

*O*ne who lets chesed take him rung by rung up the ladder of holiness can literally brush with Heaven. The story of a charity-fund administrator — a *"gabbai"* — in a small Polish town illustrates the upper reaches of a lifelong ascent. The story begins 150 years after the *gabbai's* death. Polish authorities were commencing work on a highway that would traverse a Jewish cemetery, and the Jews were permitted to rebury their forefathers in another location. Upon opening the *gabbai's* grave, an inexplicable sight was beheld. There he lay, perfectly whole, in beard and *peyos*, clothed in priest's garments.

Those who saw him scoured the town until they found an elder who knew the *gabbai's* story: As a *gabbai*, this man was inundated each day with the troubles and plights of others, yet his dedication to their welfare never flagged. One day, after an arduous round of collections, he came home ill and went to bed.

That night, two desperate individuals, one after another, came to his door begging him to accompany them on a circuit of door-to-door collections. The *gabbai* knew that each subsequent circuit would become more difficult as the hour grew later and the townspeople became impatient with the constant requests. Nonetheless, he climbed out of his sickbed both times to lend his assistance.

Upon concluding his second round, his rest was interrupted once more, this time by a man who had borrowed money from criminals. If he did not produce a payment by the morning, he cried, anything could happen to him. The *gabbai* resisted: It was 3 a.m., there was no one awake and nothing to be gained from another circuit around town. The frantic debtor had a suggestion: "Come with me to the tavern. There's still plenty of life there." The *gabbai* knew the tavern would be filled with the lowest elements of the town. Who would give even a penny?

Nonetheless, the *gabbai* went with the debtor to the tavern. There, he stood on a stool and stated his cause. The crowd roared with laughter, until one of the tavern's patrons silenced them. "I'll pay off the debt," he vowed to the *gabbai*. "But here's what you have to do. Walk through town carrying two candles and wearing priest's clothing. Lead us in a procession through the Jewish neighborhood, just as everyone is waking up."

Even this, the *gabbai* did. His neighbors beheld what they thought was a blasphemous scene, and showed their outrage with a hail of rotten potatoes and garbage. The debtor got his money, and the *gabbai* finally got his much-needed rest.

In the weeks that followed, the saintly Sanzer *Rav* visited the town. As he passed the *gabbai's* home, he was drawn by the scent of the Garden of Eden. He knocked on the door, and the *gabbai* greeted him. He followed the scent to the closet, and there, he found the origin of the Heavenly aroma. It came from the priest's garments. The *gabbai* then told the Sanzer *Rav* the story behind the strange item in his closet. "Because of this incident, you will go directly to the Garden of Eden," the *rav* told him. "Instruct your family that when you die, you are to be buried in these clothes. The angels of destruction will not dare touch you."

Step by **Step**

Every day I make sacrifices to care for others in my life. Today I will be aware of those moments, and the elevation that comes from them.

26 Cheshvan — Efraim Goren ז"ל לע"נ אפרים בן אברהם ז"ל
Dedicated by Eliyahu and Chaia Frishman

26 Iyar — Avraham Y. Zola ז"ל לע"נ ר' אברהם יהודה בן ר' יצחק דוב ז"ל
Dedicated by his family

כ״ז חשון
27 CHESHVAN / CYCLE 1

November 22, 2003
November 11, 2004
November 29, 2005
November 18, 2006
November 8, 2007
November 25, 2008
November 14, 2009

כ״ז אייר
27 IYAR / CYCLE 2

May 29, 2003
May 18, 2004
June 5, 2005
May 25, 2006
May 15, 2007
June 1, 2008
May 21, 2009
May 11, 2010

❧ *Family Foundation*

SEFER AHAVAS CHESED — Part II Chapter XIII

*T*hink like a tycoon, the Chofetz Chaim advises. Owning one's own charity fund is within the reach of many people who believe that such ventures are for millionaires only. They mistakenly believe that one must have thousands of dollars tucked away for loans and donations before one can conceive of starting a fund. The Chofetz Chaim, however, teaches that an envelope stuffed with single-dollar bills can also serve as a family foundation, if that is the amount one can afford to set aside and one keeps the money flowing from the envelope out to those who need it. The key element is not the dollar amount one gives, but the consistency and open-handedness with which it is given.

To make sure that there is always money in the house available to give, the Chofetz Chaim recommends having a special fund for that purpose. As mentioned earlier, the designation of the money for chesed avoids much of the decision-making process ignited by a request for a donation or loan. If a person has set aside a fund, he knows how much money is available to give. He need not weigh the chesed against other purposes the money might fulfill, because the decision has already been made to reserve this money for chesed only. The stage is set for an act of kindness; all that is missing is the needy person. When he arrives, as he inevitably will, the act of chesed can be performed without a second thought.

The result of following the Chofetz Chaim's advice is that chesed becomes a regular feature of family life. A person can use his fund to give small loans or donations to many people over the course of time. As he replenishes the fund and distributes further money, $30, $50 or $100 can become the instrument of hundreds of acts of chesed. There is a story of a yeshivah student who took a $20 bill and put it aside as a fund for fellow students, who were often caught short of the bus fare they needed to go home for a Shabbos or Yom Tov. The students would repay the money on returning to the yeshivah, enabling the boy to loan it again and again. His $20 investment worked for years, bringing the boy the merit of countless acts of chesed.

A family that keeps a supply of money at the ready for those who come knocking is equipping itself to make chesed an integral part of the household. There never comes a time when a needy person must be turned away because the spouse in charge of the family finances is not home, or there is no cash on hand. Family members have the opportunity to practice day after day the fine art of hearing another person's plight and doing something to alleviate it. As a person practices this art, he perfects it; at the same time, it perfects him.

Today, with my family, I will designate a certain amount of money for chesed, and a certain place for its safekeeping.

כ״ח חשון
28 CHESHVAN / CYCLE 1

November 23, 2003
November 12, 2004
November 30, 2005
November 19, 2006
November 9, 2007
November 26, 2008
November 15, 2009

כ״ח אייר
28 IYAR / CYCLE 2

May 30, 2003
May 19, 2004
June 6, 2005
May 26, 2006
May 16, 2007
June 2, 2008
May 22, 2009
May 12, 2010

﹌ *A Good Name*

SEFER AHAVAS CHESED — Part II Chapter XIII

*O*f all the assets one can acquire in this world, a good name is perhaps the most valuable. Unlike other valuable assets, however, it is not beyond the average person's reach. Chesed is the currency by which it is procured. The Mishnah in *Avos* (4:13) teaches that there are three crowns: the crown of Torah, the crown of priesthood and the crown of kingship. There is one other crown said to "stand above them all," and that is the crown of a good name.

What makes a good name so precious? A good name is an asset with great value in Heaven, because one who bears this crown upon his head is one whose deeds and character bring glory to Hashem. The beauty of his presence inspires others. They try to emulate him, and in doing so, they increase their own measure of goodness. All these positive effects are credited to the person who inspired them, and therefore, the Sages say: "Who is destined for the Garden of Eden? One about whom you hear people saying as he passes, 'That is the way. Go in it' " (*Shabbos* 153a).

The Chofetz Chaim cites further proof of a good name's priceless value: "More choice is a good name than great riches" (*Mishlei* 22:1). The person who is known as the one to turn to in times of trouble, as one always willing to lend a hand, is the person with the good name. The Chofetz Chaim points out that all the money in a wealthy man's account is worthless if he is not willing to use it to help others. It accomplishes nothing of value in this world. In fact, his money actually works to his detriment, for he will be required to answer in Heaven for his refusal to properly invest the money Hashem entrusted to him.

The fact that a person possesses more than he needs to live is proof, says the Chofetz Chaim, that he bears the responsibility to take care of others. He illustrates this principle through an allegory of the Alshich: A father has several sons, all of whom he loves dearly. In his old age, he wishes to turn his money over to his children to administer. One son, he knows, is far more responsible and business minded than the others; therefore, he gives that son the money. He does this not so that one son should have everything and the others nothing, but so that all the sons will be well provided for. The son who receives the money is a trustee; he would be greatly misinterpreting his father's intentions if he kept all the money for himself.

The Alshich says this concept is reflected in the verse (*Shemos* 22:24), "When you lend money to My people, the poor person with you," meaning what the poor person needs is with you, in your possession. It is for that purpose alone that the wealthy person has been given his money.

One who wisely administers his Father's estate to the benefit of all His children is a person others love, respect and admire. His name is golden, thus, he wears the crown.

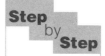

There are people I know who I would describe as wearing the "crown of a good name." Today I will think about one such person's attributes, and resolve to emulate that person in some way.

28 Cheshvan — Florence Rupp ע"ה לע"נ פריידא בת ר' יעקב בן ציון ע"ה
הונצח על ידי משפחתה — נלב"ע כ"ח חשון

28 Iyar — Isadore Pastor לע"נ יצחק יעקב בן יהודה
Dedicated by his wife, Helen, and children: Lerhaupt, Kestenbaum and Solganik families

DAY 59

כ חשון*
29 CHESHVAN / CYCLE 1

November 24, 2003
November 13, 2004
December 1, 2005
November 20, 2006
November 10, 2007
November 27, 2008
November 16, 2009

כ אייר
29 IYAR / CYCLE 2

May 31, 2003
May 20, 2004
June 7, 2005
May 27, 2006
May 17, 2007
June 3, 2008
May 23, 2009
May 13, 2010

** When this month has
only 29 days, the lesson
for 30 Cheshvan should
also be studied today.*

✑ Write-off

SEFER AHAVAS CHESED — Part II
Chapter XIII/XIII footnotes

*C*redit is an essential in business. It enables businessmen to purchase inventory even when the coffers are empty, with the understanding that once the goods are sold, the creditor will receive his payment. Most businesses could not survive without this system, and even though there are occasional defaults, the practice of extending credit persists. People are willing to take the risks because they are far outweighed by the benefits. This reasoning, the Chofetz Chaim says, should extend to chesed as well. There are indeed loans that are not repaid. There are losses. The benefits, however, far outweigh the risks.

Following the example of business, the Chofetz Chaim says one should anticipate a certain amount of loss. When a bank projects its budget for the coming year, it anticipates a certain number of loan defaults. As long as the losses stay within the expected number, the bank sees the year as a success. A manufacturer might send inventory on credit to 200 customers, knowing that of the 200, only 100 will pay on time, 85 will pay late and perhaps up to 15 will not be able to pay at all. He anticipates the loss, but it is more than offset by the 185 profitable sales he will have made — none of which would have been made without his offer of credit.

In chesed, the exact same principles apply. The profits — the immense merit of chesed, its value in protecting one's family, protecting one's assets, bringing one closer to others and to Hashem — far out-weigh the occasional loss. An unpaid debt is simply a business expense in a Jew's lifelong enterprise. [See Day 120 for the borrower's responsibilities.]

The Chofetz Chaim observes a phenomenon in his times which certainly holds true in current times: Wealth is often temporary. At the peak of a person's prosperity, right after he has moved into his mansion with its antique furniture and floor-to-ceiling windows, rumors begin making their way around town. People hear that the man has been forced to take out a second mortgage to cover his first mortgage, his investments are failing, his assets are dwindling. In turning the wheel so dramatically, Hashem is making a statement: "I am giving you this gift for a limited time, to see what you will do with it." To extend the duration of this gift of wealth, the Chofetz Chaim says, one must prove himself to be a worthy trustee.

Today I will honestly calculate the amount I can afford to lose in unpaid debts.

ל חשון*
30 CHESHVAN / CYCLE 1

November 25, 2003
November 21, 2006
November 17, 2009

א סיון
1 SIVAN / CYCLE 2

June 1, 2003
May 21, 2004
June 8, 2005
May 28, 2006
May 18, 2007
June 4, 2008
May 24, 2009
May 14, 2010

❧ *Tithing Time*

SEFER AHAVAS CHESED — Part II Chapter XIII

*M*odern life is a cluttered affair. Telephones ring late into the night. Laptops and cell phones make work possible in venues that were once reserved exclusively for quiet contemplation. Beepers, once the domain of physicians and emergency personnel, now reside in the pockets of high school students, housewives and commuters. Everyone is on 24-hour call.

Under such circumstances, a person might well be more reluctant to share his "spare time" with others than he is to share his money. Nonetheless, the investment of time is a crucial element in chesed, because time can accomplish much that money cannot. Only an investment of time can bring warm companionship to an elderly Jew alone in a nursing home. It takes time to forge a connection with a troubled teenager, make a telephone call to a sick relative, reach out to an unaffiliated Jew, listen to a friend's troubles, take in a neighbor's children in an emergency, sit with a frightened patient in a hospital room. One cannot buy these simple acts of kindness. Even if one were to pay others to do them, they would lack the vital ingredients of love and concern, which are at the heart of giving one's time.

Today, when most families are under-rested and over-scheduled, finding the time for these activities is truly difficult. Rabbi Moshe Feinstein in *Iggros Moshe* (*Even Haezer* Volume 4 Chapter 26:4) taught that just as one must tithe money, one must tithe time. Initially,

*When this month has only 29 days, the lesson for 30 Cheshvan should be learned together with 29 Cheshvan.

many people believe they do not have an income substantial enough to give away 10 percent. They assess their income, assess their expenses and determine that there is nothing left to give. In most circumstances, however, people find the required 10 percent to give to charity, just as they will somehow find money to buy *shmurah matzah* or an *esrog*. For these expenses, one will pinch a bit from this account and a bit from that account to meet one's obligations.

The same can be done with time. If one carefully examines the agenda of each day, one often finds that there is some small amount of time that can be "pinched" off the clock to accommodate chesed. The same systematic accounting that goes into meeting the monetary obligation should go into meeting the obligation of giving time. Perhaps the "donation" might be ten minutes a day to call someone in need of attention. "Tithed time," used in a systematic way, can accomplish great things. In Israel, it has provided the manpower for a massive outreach movement that has brought thousands of Jewish children to yeshivos. One need not necessarily undertake a major project, however. If one can donate one or two full hours during the week, one might be able to help a local chesed organization, or visit a hospital or nursing home. Without even adding to one's schedule, one can transform a commute into a chesed by taking along a passenger or a package that needs to get to the same destination. When a person becomes aware of the obligation to give of his time, he becomes aware of ways in which the minutes can be fruitfully utilized.

The fear that some people harbor about giving away their money — that they will be left with nothing

(Continued on page 382)

Today I will find a way to commit some portion of my time to a specific act of kindness.

DAY 61

א כסלו
1 KISLEV / CYCLE 1

November 26, 2003
November 14, 2004
December 2, 2005
November 22, 2006
November 11, 2007
November 28, 2008
November 18, 2009

ב סיון
21 SIVAN / CYCLE 2

June 2, 2003
May 22, 2004
June 9, 2005
May 29, 2006
May 19, 2007
June 5, 2008
May 25, 2009
May 15, 2010

❧ *Down to the Penny*

SEFER AHAVAS CHESED — Part II Chapter XIII

For every Jew, there is one annual "salary review." That is Rosh Hashanah, when one's wealth for the coming year is determined. Income is not the only item under review, however; expenses for the year are also determined at that time. The Chofetz Chaim cites a verse in the Talmud (*Bava Basra* 10a) that states the concept: "Just as a man's sustenance is determined on Rosh Hashanah, so man's losses are determined on Rosh Hashanah." On the very first day of the year, Hashem decides what that year will cost each person. Hashem decides upon the amount of the expenditure, but man has a hand in deciding how the money will be spent. If he spends it on chesed and *tzedakah*, he will receive the vast dividends derived from those mitzvos. Otherwise, he may well find himself spending it on his automobile transmission or his termite problem.

A story is told in the Talmud (*Bava Basra* 10a) of Rabbi Yochanan ben Zakkai, which illustrates down to the penny the precision of Hashem's accounting. Rabbi Yochanan saw in a dream that his sister's children were destined that year to lose the tremendous sum of 700 dinarim. To help them mitigate their loss, Rabbi Yochanan repeatedly approached his nephew for contributions to various charitable causes. He never told them the reason for his requests, and he never specified that he needed 700 dinarim. After an entire year of piecemeal contributions, the nephew's total came to 683 dinarim.

When Erev Yom Kippur of the next year arrived, the nephews were arrested and imprisoned. Rabbi

Yochanan visited them and reassured them, "Don't worry. For another 17 dinarim you are going to be released." Later that day, the officials came to demand 17 dinarim, and the family was released in time for Yom Kippur.

Understandably, the nephews were perplexed as to how their uncle knew the exact amount that would save them. When he told them about his dream, they protested that they certainly would have given the 700 dinarim had they known that was the amount required. Rabbi Yochanan replied that the dream could not have been disclosed, for then the nephew's contributions would have been ransom, not charity. His chesed would have been for his own sake, not the sake of Heaven.

Furthermore, had the family known that 700 dinarim would save them from trouble, they would not have been exercising faith in Hashem each time they provided money for Rabbi Yochanan's charities. They were spared 683 dinarim worth of difficulty because each of the 683 dinarim they gave away demonstrated their trust that Hashem would provide for them.

Even so, they were left with their 17dinarim worth of difficulty. This illustrates a principle upon which a Jew lives. When troubles strike, a person must not believe that his giving has failed to protect him. He must recognize that all he has given has gone toward mitigating his current losses — losses that were etched into the year from the day it dawned. His charity has indeed protected him from the 683-dinar trial, even if he still has a 17-dinar obstacle to overcome. Every dollar he has expended was destined to leave his grasp. If he was wise in his spending, he has gained even from his loss.

Step by **Step**

If I have not done so already, I will find out exactly how much money I am obligated to give to charity based on my personal situation. I will consult a learned person to determine how to arrive at the correct amount.

1 Kislev — Devora Gottlieb לע"נ אמנו היקרה דבורה רחל בת דוד ע"ה
Dedicated by her daughters, Sara Grosman and Pearl Abrahamson

2 Sivan — Irving Resnick לע"נ ישראל בן ירחמיאל ז"ל
Dedicated in loving memory by his children and grandchildren, David and Rina Resnick and family

ב כסלו
2 KISLEV / CYCLE 1

November 27, 2003
November 15, 2004
December 3, 2005
November 23, 2006
November 12, 2007
November 29, 2008
November 19, 2009

ג סיון
3 SIVAN / CYCLE 2

June 3, 2003
May 23, 2004
June 10, 2005
May 30, 2006
May 20, 2007
June 6, 2008
May 26, 2009
May 16, 2010

✑ *The Minus Side*

SEFER AHAVAS CHESED — Part II Chapter XIII

*I*t is human nature to believe that when money comes into a person's hand, it is his. When it leaves his hand, therefore, he experiences a sense of loss. The Chofetz Chaim observes that this sense of loss is based on a fallacy; he refers once again to the verse in the Talmud: "Just as man's sustenance is determined on Rosh Hashanah, his losses are determined on Rosh Hashanah." The person's real due for the year can only be calculated by subtracting the predetermined losses from the predetermined gains. If he earns $50,000 and expends $40,000, he arrives at the amount that is really his for that year — $10,000.

Viewing one's income in this context, the broken cars, unforeseen tax bills, leaky roofs and lost luggage are not taking one's money out of one's hand. They are simply balancing the books, leaving a person with the amount he is destined to have. If a storekeeper receives $10,000 in a day's sales, and he spends $5,000 the next day on inventory, he does not think to himself, "I had $10,000 and now I've lost half of it." He recognizes that he had only earned $5,000 in the first place. One who believes that his wealth is determined on Rosh Hashanah experiences life's expenses in the same way that the storekeeper experiences his expenditures.

This explanation still leaves a question. What does Hashem accomplish by giving a person money and then taking it away? Why not simply give him his due and no more? The answer is that the money is not given with the intent to remove it. Hashem uses these expenses as a means of allowing us to make amends — relatively painlessly — for our sins.

The prophet Elijah said, "Every day of a person's life, he is sold as a slave, and every day he is redeemed" (*Tanna D'Vei Eliyahu*). The frustrations that beset people in daily life are, in effect, redemption. They upset one's mind, jangle one's nerves, challenge one's patience, and then, they are over and the sins they atoned for are forgiven. Rather than raising one's fist to the Heavens and wondering why one should be subject to such frustration, one should raise one's eyes to Heaven and give thanks. The irritations that beset a person pay a price that is due. For instance, a man may lose his wallet. He may spend hours searching for it, all the while worrying about canceling credit cards, losing his money and getting a new driver's license. The wallet is eventually redeemed, but all the upset the man had experienced was not a futile exercise, for through it, he himself was redeemed.

A verse in *Tehillim* (31:6) says: "In Your hand I entrust my spirit; You redeemed me, Hashem." Each night while a person sleeps, a portion of his soul ascends to Heaven, where his day's activities are judged. Nobody ascends unencumbered by some sin, yet Hashem does not wish to invoke the full weight of justice. In His mercy, He allows the minor irritations of life to act as atonement. When a criminal goes to court and the judge metes out a minor punishment, it is referred to as a "slap on the wrist," and perceived as a merciful act. The frustrations and expenses one endures every day are Hashem's "slap on the wrist," which, seen in context, are truly expressions of His love.

Step by **Step**

The next time I incur an unexpected expense, I will keep in mind that the money I must expend was not mine to keep.

2 Kislev — Chagit Firestone חגית בת רות שתחי' לאריכת ימים ולרפואה שלמה בתושח"י
Dedicated by Ezra and Miriam Firestone

3 Sivan — Surina Nojovitz ע"ה לע"נ שרה בת יעקב ע"ה
Dedicated in loving memory by her grandchildren, Rabbi Avigdor and Rochel Slatus

ג כסלו
3 KISLEV / CYCLE 1

November 28, 2003
November 16, 2004
December 4, 2005
November 24, 2006
November 13, 2007
November 30, 2008
November 20, 2009

ד סיון
4 SIVAN / CYCLE 2

June 4, 2003
May 24, 2004
June 11, 2005
May 31, 2006
May 21, 2007
June 7, 2008
May 27, 2009
May 17, 2010

❧ All Good

SEFER AHAVAS CHESED — Part II Chapter XIII

*I*n perspective, the Chofetz Chaim has shown, the losses one incurs in daily life are actually gains. Money lost is atonement gained. The Heavenly books are thus balanced, and each person ends the year having amassed exactly as much wealth as had been determined on Rosh Hashanah. Losing money, however, is not the only way to balance the books. The far more pleasant and rewarding way is to put one's money into charity and acts of kindness.

A person who pays his debts through the mitzvah of giving charity, says the Chofetz Chaim, has "traded inferior grain for beautiful diamonds." Any mitzvah that exacts a cost also earns great rewards. This is especially true of charity, which is rewarded not only because it requires self-sacrifice, but because the mitzvah itself invokes a vast sea of blessings. A person's heart should not ache when he gives charity, the Torah says (*Devarim* 15: 10). His heart should soar, because Hashem will bless this person and all he does. He has gained on all fronts. The money with which he has parted already was destined to leave his hands. By giving it to charity, the person has essentially paid off his debt with money that will go directly back into his own account and earn interest into eternity.

Faith is a key component in this formula. One does not see one's reward the day after the money is given; if that were the case, the payment would not be real *tzedakah*. Hashem works according to His own timetable. A person might struggle for years to make money at a business, and then finally find his fortune from an entirely different source. Ultimately, says the Chofetz Chaim, a person will act correctly if he truly believes that he will have what he is meant to have — no more and no less.

Giving money toward chesed is an opportunity to preempt life's expensive frustrations and troubles with a great source of blessing. When such an opportunity arises, one should grasp it, actively making a choice as to how one's debt will be paid. "A house that is not open to poor people is open to doctors," say the Sages (*Shir Hashirim Rabbah* 6:17). Money that should be given, but is not, will be taken. A wise person knows that when someone comes to him for help, he is being given a firsthand view of a difficulty that could have been his own, that perhaps should have been his own. He knows that he has been given a gift — the ability to fulfill his obligations by helping the needy person instead of having to endure that person's misfortune. The Chofetz Chaim offers a blessing to those who instill this perspective into their hearts: There will be no second thoughts, no lingering doubts. "It will be good from every angle."

Today I will look back over the past six months and tally the unexpected expenses I have had to meet. Now I will ask myself a question: Would I have thought that I had that much money to give away?

3 Kislev — לע"נ יהודה אריה ליב בן ר' נחמי' הכהן ז"ל
Dedicated by the Isbee families and Weinrib family

4 Sivan — Shimon Spira לע"נ שמעון אלתר בן ר' ישראל ארי' ז"ל
Dedicated by his wife, children, grandchildren and great-grandchildren

ד כסלו
4 KISLEV / CYCLE 1

November 29, 2003
November 17, 2004
December 5, 2005
November 25, 2006
November 14, 2007
December 1, 2008
November 21, 2009

ה סיון
5 SIVAN / CYCLE 2

June 5, 2003
May 25, 2004
June 12, 2005
June 1, 2006
May 22, 2007
June 8, 2008
May 28, 2009
May 18, 2010

✑ *The Smart Money*

SEFER AHAVAS CHESED — **Part II Chapter XIV**

To some degree, most people struggle for their livelihood, albeit on different levels. For one person the struggle is putting food on the table. For another, food is not a problem, but tuition is. Still another covers his routine expenses with ease, but struggles when an unforeseen repair or medical bill arises. Even those with plenty of money to spend and to give may have to struggle with their businesses and investment decisions. It is the rare person, therefore, who thinks of himself as a philanthropist. Chesed, in many people's view, is for the rich man — the one who does not have to struggle for and worry about his money.

When one engages in this line of thinking, the Chofetz Chaim says, one does himself harm. He disqualifies himself from a way of life that could bring him untold reward, believing that he is not wealthy enough to engage meaningful chesed.   He has declared his own ineligibility, and thereby clapped an iron lid on his own spiritual and material potential.

There is a certain absurdity to leaving chesed to those one believes to be richer and more savvy. This absurdity becomes obvious when one remembers that chesed is an investment with an enormous return. If a broker were to approach this same individual — the one who believes he is not in the giving class — and offer him a chance to buy a lucrative business for a very minimum price, surely the man would not say, "Lucrative businesses are for the rich, not for me. I'm just a struggling middle-class man."

He would grab the opportunity, hoping that it would change his entire lifestyle.

For the person who seeks to follow the lead of those he sees as savvy, the Chofetz Chaim offers two role models – our forefather Abraham and King Solomon. Both were financially successful, both were as wise as human beings can be, and both continually pursued opportunities to give charity and help others. Following their lead does not necessarily require large amounts of money. One can channel one's kindness into deeds, like teaching people and bringing people close to Hashem, as Abraham did. Much chesed can also be accomplished with small amounts of money, helping to provide loans, food or clothing to others. Opportunities present themselves to each person, suited to that person's talents and abilities.

King Solomon (*Mishlei* 21:21) says that one who pursues charity and acts of kindness will find life, charity and honor. That is the investment advice of the world's wealthiest man. The middle-class man is not expected to donate half of the new *mikveh*, but he can give his share or help raise the money. His part of the chesed cannot be passed along to the rich man to do. If he wishes to walk the path paved by history's "smart money," he must grasp each opportunity that presents itself to him. It is his.

The next time I receive a request for a chesed that seems beyond my means, I will consider whether there is a way, within my ability, to help this cause.

לע"נ ר' ישראל אליעזר בן משה מיכאל זצ"ל — נלב"ע ג' כסלו — **4 Kislev**
Dedicated in loving memory by his grandchildren and great-grandchildren, St. Louis, MO

5 Sivan — May today's learning be a זכות for our משפחה.
Dedicated by Yehuda Aryeh Link, Brooklyn, NY

ה כסלו
5 KISLEV / CYCLE 1

November 30, 2003
November 18, 2004
December 6, 2005
November 26, 2006
November 15, 2007
December 2, 2008
November 22, 2009

ו סיון
6 SIVAN / CYCLE 2

June 6, 2003
May 26, 2004
June 13, 2005
June 2, 2006
May 23, 2007
June 9, 2008
May 29, 2009
May 19, 2010

❧ *An Enduring Legacy*

SEFER AHAVAS CHESED — Part II Chapter XIV

*A*ny parent would be happy to achieve a strong, lifetime bond with his child. In a home of chesed, the bond between parent and child extends far beyond the parent's lifetime, into eternity. When deeds of kindness are a constant occupation in the home, the children naturally inherit a concern for their fellow Jew; they carry on a family tradition that connects them to their parents long after their parents have left this world.

Hashem acknowledges the hereditary quality of chesed when He makes His decision to share with Abraham His plans to destroy Sodom. Abraham merits this revelation especially because he has imbued his household with the trait of loving kindness and raised his children to continue down that path: "Because he commands his children and his household after him that they keep the way of Hashem, doing charity and justice" (*Bereishis* 18:19).

The hereditary nature of chesed is born out in thousands of ways each day throughout the Jewish world. For instance, there is one large family in which every sibling — all of whom have already raised families of their own — is immersed in hundreds of kind acts, large and small. They help others in ways most people would not even think of. Their capacity for kindness is understandable, however, when one examines the household in which they were raised.

The family lived in Williamsburg, Brooklyn, during World War II. As European refugees began pouring into their neighborhood, the family informally turned their small apartment into a shelter. The father's meager salary was stretched to feed the endless influx of guests, help them find homes and start their own businesses. The mother, besides caring for the household and her own large family, would go from apartment to apartment cleaning and caring for those refugees too weak to care for themselves. This couple's legacy is a high-powered international chesed enterprise — a network of siblings, living in communities throughout the world, generating oceans of kindness.

This, says the Chofetz Chaim, is an inheritance that will never dry up. Had this Williamsburg family taken the money they spent on chesed and instead saved it for their children's inheritance, it may well have caused harm rather than the limitless good it is causing still today. The children may have argued over the money. The money may have been misspent. Even if it was invested and transformed into a fortune, the pleasure money can buy is of a limited nature. One quickly becomes bored and restless, yearning for the next purchase.

Regarding the pleasure one experiences in Heaven, however, there is no saturation point. It is a joy that can increase endlessly. The acts of chesed one's children perform, especially if they perform them because "this is what my mother and father would have done," bring the parents' souls an ever-flowing source of enrichment. Rabbi Abraham Pam once noted that the saying of Kaddish for one's parents is like a "postcard" to them in Heaven. If a person learns Torah as a merit for the parent, he is sending a "letter."

(Continued on page 382)

> **Step by Step**
>
> *Today I will find a meaningful, pleasant way to involve a child in my family in a chesed that I already do.*

ו כסלו
6 KISLEV / CYCLE 1

December 1, 2003
November 19, 2004
December 7, 2005
November 27, 2006
November 16, 2007
December 3, 2008
November 23, 2009

ז סיון
7 SIVAN / CYCLE 2

June 7, 2003
May 27, 2004
June 14, 2005
June 3, 2006
May 24, 2007
June 10, 2008
May 30, 2009
May 20, 2010

❧ *Real Estate*

SEFER AHAVAS CHESED — Part II Chapter XIV

*O*ne who has never climbed a mountain cannot understand the majesty of the view from the top. Likewise, one who has never pushed himself to a higher level of chesed cannot comprehend the exultation he would feel if he were to view the world from "up there." A person cannot appreciate the vista until he sees it for himself, but all too often, he is reluctant to undertake the climb. Sometimes, however, circumstances force the person to tread this upward trail. He may complain all the way, until he finally gets to see with his own eyes this whole new view of the world. A story in the *Meseches Kallah* (1:2) illustrates this dynamic at work.

In the story, there was a grievance in Heaven against the Sage, Rabbi Tarfon. He was accused of failing to give enough charity in relation to his exalted spiritual level and his immense personal wealth. Rabbi Akiva set out to remedy the situation. He came to Rabbi Tarfon and said, "Rebbi, I would like to purchase for you a city or two." Rabbi Tarfon's wealth was apparently ample enough to make this proposition realistic. Rabbi Tarfon agreed to let Rabbi Akiva conduct the transaction on his behalf, and handed him a fortune in gold dinarim to accomplish the purchase. Rabbi Akiva distributed the money to the poor.

After several days, Rabbi Tarfon met Rabbi Akiva, "Where are the cities that you bought me? Can you give me a map? Can you show me where they are?"

Rabbi Akiva took Rabbi Tarfon by the hand, brought him to the study hall, and took out a *Sefer*

Tehillim. Together they recited *Tehillim*, until they came to the verse: "He distributed widely to the destitute, his charity endures forever" (*Tehillim* 112:9). Rabbi Akiva pointed to those words and said, "This is the city that I bought you." Rabbi Tarfon stood up, kissed him on the head and exclaimed, "You are my teacher and my general," and gave him additional money to distribute.

That he would call Rabbi Akiva his teacher is understandable. The word conveys acknowledgment of Rabbi Akiva's keen intelligence, understanding of the Torah and ability to convey its concepts. The term "general," however, requires explanation. Here, Rabbi Tarfon was saying that in matters of conduct in this world, Rabbi Akiva acted as his leader. A general orders his soldiers to march through rough terrain that they would prefer to avoid. Only when they conclude the march do they understand why this is what they had to do in order to achieve victory. Rabbi Tarfon would have preferred to avoid giving away such a large fortune, but Rabbi Akiva forced his hand. Only when the mitzvah had been fulfilled could Rabbi Tarfon perceive the heights to which Rabbi Akiva had "marched" him.

The Chofetz Chaim further explains that Rabbi Akiva was not dealing falsely with Rabbi Tarfon when he offered to purchase cities for him. The Heavenly real estate one acquires through the mitzvah of *tzedakah* is also referred to as a "city." By acting as Rabbi Tarfon's "real estate agent," Rabbi Akiva helped him acquire countless radiant Heavenly cities — cities to which Rabbi Tarfon would forever hold the key.

Step by **Step**

Today I will focus on gently stretching my capacity for chesed, going one step beyond what I perceive my obligation to be.

ז כסלו
7 KISLEV / CYCLE 1

December 2, 2003
November 20, 2004
December 8, 2005
November 28, 2006
November 17, 2007
December 4, 2008
November 24, 2009

ח סיון
8 SIVAN / CYCLE 2

June 8, 2003
May 28, 2004
June 15, 2005
June 4, 2006
May 25, 2007
June 11, 2008
May 31, 2009
May 21, 2010

❧ *Your Share*

SEFER AHAVAS CHESED — **Part II Chapter XIV**

A loving parent works throughout his life with two goals in mind: to give his family a good life, and to leave something behind for his children. In his unselfish desire to provide for his children in this world, however, he may rob himself of the one and only asset that will sustain him in the Next World — the money given to charity and chesed.

The Chofetz Chaim illustrates with a parable just how illogical it is to skimp on charity in order to fatten one's children's inheritance: A man is taken away to prison and told that he has the choice of turning over his entire estate or being tortured with hot coals. In such a situation, the man would give every penny, with no concern for his legacy, to escape physical pain. Nobody would think of advising him, "Accept the torture. Think of your children."

In the Next World, the charity a person has given during his lifetime serves to save him from the torment of Gehinnom. Of one who deals sensitively with the poor, *Tehillim* (41:2) says, "On the day of evil, Hashem will rescue him." The word for evil, *"raah,"* refers to Gehinnom, explains the Chofetz Chaim. A person's charity and kindness literally stand between him and Divine punishment, thus, it is simple self-preservation to make sure that there is enough money flowing into that all-important account during one's lifetime.

The Torah teaches that the obligation for charity starts with those closest to a person — his immediate family, then his extended family, then his neighbors and community. The source of this teaching is the verse (*Yeshayahu* 58:7): "From your own flesh do not turn away." The Chofetz Chaim argues that here, "your own flesh" is oneself. A person must be kind to himself, building his own estate in the Next World by properly fulfilling his obligation of charity.

On the other hand, the Chofetz Chaim does not deny or belittle the need to leave an inheritance for one's children. He cites the Ramban, who says that when children take their father's inheritance and conduct themselves properly in regard to it, they are keeping their father's essence alive in the world. The challenge is to arrive at the proper balance between giving and saving, and this is an issue that a person must explore with the help of a rabbi. The Chofetz Chaim's point is not that one should drain one's estate. Rather, he urges a proper perspective. The wealth one leaves one's children holds its value for a maximum of 120 years. The money one dedicates to charity and acts of kindness during one's lifetime provides Heavenly "social security," protecting and sustaining one's soul forever.

Today I will review my strategy for providing for my heirs and see if it is properly balanced against my obligations for chesed.

ח כסלו
8 KISLEV / CYCLE 1

December 3, 2003
November 21, 2004
December 9, 2005
November 29, 2006
November 18, 2007
December 5, 2008
November 25, 2009

ט סיון
9 SIVAN / CYCLE 2

June 9, 2003
May 29, 2004
June 16, 2005
June 5, 2006
May 26, 2007
June 12, 2008
June 1, 2009
May 22, 2010

❧ *For the Road*

SEFER AHAVAS CHESED — Part II Chapter XIV
footnotes

*T*here was a large family that traveled each summer from New York to Boston to visit grandparents. On the day the family would prepare for their return trip, the grandmother would always produce a daunting array of sandwiches, fruit, drinks and snacks, stuffed into oversized shopping bags lined with ice packs.

"It's only a five-hour drive," her daughter would say. "There are places to stop on the highway. We don't need so much."

"You never know," her mother replied. "It's a long trip and you might as well be prepared."

The Chofetz Chaim would have each Jew consider the long return journey to the World of Truth in the same light. A person naturally thinks first of his children when he arranges his affairs for his ultimate departure from this world. The Talmudic Sage, Mar Ukva, however, teaches that one's legacy is not for the benefit of one's children alone. It is also the best available means to provide for one's own unfathomable journey into the Next World. Mar Ukva is cited throughout the Talmud as a paragon of charity. He and his wife, throughout their lifetimes, poured every ounce of energy into attending to the needs and dignity of the less fortunate. (An extraordinary story of Mar Ukva and his wife is told in detail on Day 88.) With all the tremendous merit earned in his lifetime, Mar Ukva still designated an immense portion of his wealth to be distributed to charity after his death. "It is a long trip, and I do not have enough food for the way," Mar Ukva explains (*Kesubos* 67a).

In one's lifetime, contributions to charity are limited by halachah to a maximum of 20 percent of one's income. That limitation does not apply, however, to the amount one leaves behind. Mar Ukva understood that there is no way to know what rigors the *neshamah* must undergo before it comes to its final reward in the Next World. By leaving as much as he could to charity, he "packed" as much sustenance as possible for the journey. "Charity will walk before him [in front of his *neshamah*]" (*Tehillim* 85:14), to protect him from Heavenly accusations.

In previous lessons, the Chofetz Chaim has clearly stated the primacy of providing for one's own family. One who leaves his estate to charity and leaves his children in dire straits is performing no great act of chesed. Mar Ukva's statement of needing "food for the journey" is not cited as a basis for taking wealth away from one's children, but rather as a motivation for making adequate preparations — while there is time — for the final journey. In fact, the thought and care one gives to making proper arrangements for one's passing is considered an omen for a long life. A person who takes time now to discuss his legacy with a learned person — a rabbi, *rosh yeshivah*, rebbe — is helping to insure that he will have the maximum time possible in this world to earn even greater merit "for the road."

If I have not done so already, today I will designate a time-frame and a person to guide me in apportioning my estate.

8 Kislev — Mrs. Dina Halberstam לע"נ דינה בת ר' מיכא' יהודא ע"ה
Dedicated by the Halberstam and Kopel families

9 Sivan — May today's learning be a זכות for the Reiss family.

ט כסלו
9 KISLEV / CYCLE 1

December 4, 2003
November 22, 2004
December 10, 2005
November 30, 2006
November 19, 2007
December 6, 2008
November 26, 2009

י סיון
10 SIVAN / CYCLE 2

June 10, 2003
May 30, 2004
June 17, 2005
June 6, 2006
May 27, 2007
June 13, 2008
June 2, 2009
May 23, 2010

✑ *Directions*

SEFER AHAVAS CHESED — **Part II Chapter XIV**

A wealthy, childless man was coming to the end of his life. The Chofetz Chaim saw this man's wealth as a potential source of good for the many charities and yeshivos in the community. In helping these causes, the man could also acquire the merit he was sorely lacking for his passage into the Next World. The man himself, however, had never entertained any such thoughts. Nonetheless, the Chofetz Chaim sent emissaries to him, who patiently explained the community's needs — the yeshivah students struggling against poverty, the sick in need of financial support, the hungry, the homeless. The man's heart was impervious to their pleas and insensible to his own desperate need for some powerful merit to fill his empty coffers in the World to Come. He died, leaving his entire estate to a hospital that researched canine diseases.

How, the Chofetz Chaim's students asked, could a person make so misguided a decision as his last act on earth? The Chofetz Chaim explained: "On the path a man wants to go, he is sent" (*Makkos* 10b). If a person has worked throughout his life to understand what is truly good and important, and to incline himself in that direction, Hashem will lead him toward good decisions. His instincts will be right. On the other hand, a person who has lived solely for himself will be abandoned to the vortex of his own selfishness.

This principle is the final explanation of why people fail to grasp the chance to do good. Essentially, they do not want to look beyond their own immediate desires. Their own will escorts them to the edge of a spiral that draws them deeper and deeper into nothingness, and Hashem, in accordance with their own will, leaves them to its power. At the last moment of their lives, when they could make a decision that would save them, they are left to their own misguided rationalizations.

Even rationalizations that appear rational can sometimes be the fruit of this misguided thinking. The Chofetz Chaim cites in particular the case of the person who feels he does not have enough time to distribute charity. If a person was to understand that chesed is a Jew's most profitable business enterprise, he would approach this situation in the same manner as he would approach a growing business. A person whose business becomes too big for him to handle alone hires others to help him. The same can be done for a charitable fund; a person can hire an agent to distribute and manage the money. If a person cannot afford to pay someone to perform this task, he might find a person who has time, but not money, to give to chesed. In tandem, the two can perform the mitzvah efficiently, each reaping the benefits.

Excusing oneself from performing chesed is, overall, a line of thinking fraught with pitfalls. The difficulty lies in separating valid reasons from invalid excuses. The key to avoiding self-deception is to develop a true love of chesed, built upon an understanding of its priceless value in this world and the Next World. When a person's will is to do good, Hashem steers him away from the pitfalls and lovingly guides him toward a life of bounty and blessing.

Today I will perform an "excuse" inventory on myself. When I refuse to do a chesed, what are my usual reasons? How valid are these reasons? Are there ways of overcoming some of them?

י כסלו
10 KISLEV / CYCLE 1

December 5, 2003
November 23, 2004
December 11, 2005
December 1, 2006
November 20, 2007
December 7, 2008
November 27, 2009

יא סיון
11 SIVAN / CYCLE 2

June 11, 2003
May 31, 2004
June 18, 2005
June 7, 2006
May 28, 2007
June 14, 2008
June 3, 2009
May 24, 2010

✌ *Piece in the Puzzle*

SEFER AHAVAS CHESED — Part II Chapter XIV

A Jew is commanded to loan money. If he fulfills this commandment, he is promised limitless reward. Could it be that this commandment of the Torah — one that carries such rich rewards — is reserved for the wealthy alone? Emphatically, the Chofetz Chaim answers, "No." This mitzvah and its rewards are for every Jew. If a person is self-disciplined about taking a regular amount off of his income — whatever he can spare — and putting it aside in an account strictly reserved for loans, he can have a part in this mitzvah, and not just a small, secondary part, but a primary part — his part, the part he is here to play.

One man has $100,000 to give to a yeshivah's building campaign; the new wing is named for his beloved, departed father and the impact of his contribution is clear for all to see. Another man has $100 that he uses to clear up his neighbor's past-due grocery bill. His role is to relieve this family's stress and help reenergize them for their climb out of debt. Hashem put him, not the wealthy yeshivah supporter, in a position to know of the family's difficulties; it is his role to help them, and because he has set aside this $100, he can fulfill it. Had he left this mitzvah to "the rich guys," it may well have never been performed.

The Chofetz Chaim sees the mitzvah of chesed as something far more powerful than an isolated commandment. If chesed is implanted within each and every Jewish household, it has the power to transform the Jewish people into a wellspring of goodness that would overflow and fill every corner of the world: "How good it would be if only this idea would pass from person to person and take hold among all the Jewish people. The entire world would be full of chesed and all the travails and troubles would dissolve. They will cease to exist, because there is only a certain amount of space in this world for either trouble or good. If it is filled with good, there is no place for troubles."

The key to this transformation is the totality of the Jewish people's involvement in chesed. No one group, any one economical or social class must say, "Chesed is for someone else, not for me."

The Chofetz Chaim cites the *Tanna D'Vei Eliyahu* (23:9), who sees this all-inclusive principle at work when the Jews enslaved in Egypt made a pact to help each other. The verse says, "They made a pact together." "Together," according to this commentary, means that everyone from the lowest to the most privileged was included in the pact, each promising to help in whatever way he could. The contributions of each fit together to form a whole, beautifully rendered picture of G-dliness. Moved by that picture, Hashem delivered their redemption.

If I have exempted myself from establishing a loan fund, believing I would not be able to offer significant help, I will start one today, even if I can only set aside one dollar a day.

יא כסלו
11 KISLEV / CYCLE 1

December 6, 2003
November 24, 2004
December 12, 2005
December 2, 2006
November 21, 2007
December 8, 2008
November 28, 2009

יב סיון
12 SIVAN / CYCLE 2

June 12, 2003
June 1, 2004
June 19, 2005
June 8, 2006
May 29, 2007
June 15, 2008
June 4, 2009
May 25, 2010

✑ *Opening Doors*

SEFER AHAVAS CHESED — Part II Chapter XIV

To the Chofetz Chaim, a Jew who turns away from chesed is like someone who sees the key to Heaven's gate dangling before him, and simply refuses to grab it. Hashem has given His people chesed as a means to find favor for their prayers and open the channels of blessing. The Chofetz Chaim pleads with each Jew to take the key: "Hashem in His mercy has strengthened us in this holy trait and we should merit through this all the goodness in this world and the World to Come."

The merit of doing a simple favor for someone else is a necessary ingredient even for those dwelling in the upper stratospheres of holiness. The Tzemach Tzedek was of such an elevated status that when he needed clarification in his learning, he would obtain it from the Baal HaTanya, his revered, departed grandfather, whom he would consult in his dreams. The grandfather and grandson learned together on a regular basis, until one day, the contact ceased.

After a period of time, the Tzemach Tzedek decided to undertake an especially intense period of prayer to try to regain the spiritual level from which he seemed to have slipped. He prepared throughout the prior evening and the morning, doing all he could to assure that his prayers would resound with intense concentration. On his way to the synagogue that morning, he was approached by a poor Jew. "Could you loan me 30 rubles until tonight?" the man requested. "Today is market day, and I'm sure if I could just buy some inventory I would be able to sell it and pay you right back."

The Tzemach Tzedek told the man, "I'm on my way to synagogue right now and I don't have the 30 rubles on me. Come to me after prayers and I will help you."

As he donned his *tallis* and *tefillin* in the synagogue, he began thinking: The long, intense prayers on which he intended to embark would no doubt overlap the opening of the market place. The man would have nothing to sell for several hours. The Tzemach Tzedek could not leave the situation as it stood. He removed his *tallis* and *tefillin*, ran home, took 50 rubles and threaded his way through the teeming market place looking for the man. At last he found him, standing dejectedly before an empty table.

"Here, take these 50 rubles and buy some inventory," the Tzemach Tzedek told him.

Upon returning to synagogue, he once again donned his *tallis* and *tefillin* and immediately saw before him the shining visage of the Baal HaTanya, who answered all his questions. As the grandfather explained to his grandson, there is nothing as effective for opening the gates of Heaven as a wholehearted act of kindness for another Jew.

Each day I will precede my prayers with an act of kindness or charity.

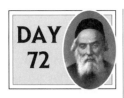

DAY 72

יב כסלו
12 KISLEV / CYCLE 1

December 7, 2003
November 25, 2004
December 13, 2005
December 3, 2006
November 22, 2007
December 9, 2008
November 29, 2009

יג סיון
13 SIVAN / CYCLE 2

June 13, 2003
June 2, 2004
June 20, 2005
June 9, 2006
May 30, 2007
June 16, 2008
June 5, 2009
May 26, 2010

✄ *One and All*

SEFER AHAVAS CHESED — Part II
Chapter XIV footnotes /XV

A person who cannot afford to purchase a *tallis* is exempt from the requirement of wearing one — but who would take advantage of this exemption? What man would want to arrive in the synagogue on Shabbos morning devoid of this distinctive garment? Even a poor person would find the means to buy himself a *tallis* and have his share in the mitzvah.

A person who cannot afford to give charity is also exempt. Until he is able to meet his family's expenses and debts, he is not required to take a penny away from his income to provide for anyone else's needs. Unlike the exemption for the *tallis*, however, this is an exemption many people have little regret about claiming. The Chofetz Chaim sees this as proof of a terribly skewed perspective, for they are exempting themselves from the source of forgiveness and blessing.

Anyone who understands what chesed does for the doer will struggle to find a means to perform this mitzvah in some form. It is not, as the Chofetz Chaim repeatedly emphasizes, the exclusive domain of the rich. The middle class and the poor have an equal right to the rewards charity and kind acts bring. Furthermore, these mitzvos themselves bring a promise of greater wealth — a reward all the more valuable to those struggling financially. "Tithe so that you will become wealthy," the Talmud (*Taanis* 9a) says. This verse refers specifically to tithing crops, but it is interpreted to apply equally to income.

The Chofetz Chaim stresses that every person should set aside whatever he can for a chesed fund. If a person has only a little, he should take a portion of that small amount and set it aside to help someone else. There will be a role for his small fund to fill, and his reward will be as great as that of one who takes a larger amount from a larger income.

In an earlier chapter, the role of chesed was compared to the role played by the *Beis HaMikdash* when it stood in Jerusalem. The Chofetz Chaim now carries the comparison further. When one imagines life in the days of the *Beis HaMikdash*, one assumes that every single Jew would try to make the journey to Jerusalem at least once in his life. It seems inconceivable that a person could be content to live out his life never having sought this exalted spiritual experience. If the opportunity existed to bring a sacrifice, purify his soul, achieve complete forgiveness and closeness to Hashem, he could not simply throw up his hands and say, "It's too expensive a trip." Even if others were to tell him, "This is not for someone of your limited means," he would reject their opinion and insist on his right as a Jew to bask in the holiness of the *Beis HaMikdash*.

It is every Jew's right to bask in the blessings, forgiveness and closeness to Hashem that are the rewards for acts of kindness.

Today I will reconsider areas of chesed in which I have considered myself exempt, either for lack of time or lack of funds.

12 Kislev — Lena Caplan ע"ה לע"נ לינא בת שמריהו ע"ה
Dedicated by her children

13 Sivan — L'Zecher Nishmas Shraga Favish Krywat ben Menashe ז"ל
Dedicated by his children, Lillian, Cyril and Perry

DAY 73

יג כסלו
13 KISLEV / CYCLE 1

December 8, 2003
November 26, 2004
December 14, 2005
December 4, 2006
November 23, 2007
December 10, 2008
November 30, 2009

יד סיון
14 SIVAN / CYCLE 2

June 14, 2003
June 3, 2004
June 21, 2005
June 10, 2006
May 31, 2007
June 17, 2008
June 6, 2009
May 27, 2010

❧ A Market Niche

SEFER AHAVAS CHESED — Part II Chapter XV

*I*f chesed were an elixir, guaranteed to cleanse the soul and lift the spirits, there is no doubt that every person would scrape together the means to keep a steady supply on hand. Nobody would wish to muddle through life without this miracle drug. As the Chofetz Chaim relates in an earlier chapter, chesed is in fact a powerful agent for cleansing the soul. He bases this conclusion on a conversation (*Avos D'Rabbi Nosson* 4:4) between Rabbi Yochanan ben Zakkai and Rabbi Yehoshua as they walk past the ruins of the *Beis HaMikdash*. Rabbi Yehoshua exclaims in despair that Israel's source of forgiveness has been destroyed, to which Rabbi Yochanan ben Zakkai answers: "My son, do not despair. We have another source of atonement and that is acts of kindness."

Just as the atonement afforded by the sacrifices was available to every Jew, so is the atonement afforded by chesed. In the days of the *Beis HaMikdash*, people living outside Jerusalem had to make an arduous journey to gain access to this atonement. In these times, attaining forgiveness also requires sacrifice — the time, effort and money involved in helping other people. In both cases, with the rewards so immense, it is difficult to imagine circumstances in which a healthy, able person would neglect to make the effort. The perception persists, however, that charitable endeavors are for the wealthy alone. If this perception were true, it would mean that the middle and lower classes are barred from the most effective means of atonement.

Hashem equips each individual with some way in which to access the rewards chesed offers. In vibrant Jewish communities, this concept comes to life in a plethora of *"gemachs,"* free-loan enterprises. Some may involve a large group of individuals, and some are just one household. In Lakewood, New Jersey, a community built around the venerable Beth Medrash Govoha, a directory of *gemachs* lists 128 offerings including: locksmith, translated volumes of Talmud, baby swings, school uniforms, *bris* pillows, cell phones, cars for emergencies, *challah* covers, children's wedding dresses, driver's manuals, wedding gifts, folding beds, gardening equipment, guest accommodations, herbal remedies, high chairs, house cleaning, leaf blowers, pitchers, porta-cribs, *mezuzos,* notary services, *pidyon haben* coins, liquor for bar mitzvahs and weddings, plumbing snakes, Torah tapes, *tefillin, tefillin* for left-handed men, tools, wheelchairs and walkers. In addition, there are 72 small, privately administered financial funds available to the community.

Every person is a potential chesed entrepreneur. Once a person takes stock of what "inventory" he has to offer and finds an effective way to offer it, he is on his way to making his first million, in a currency that forever keeps its value.

Today I will discuss with my family what type of "gemach" we could offer and take a step toward setting it in motion.

יד כסלו
14 KISLEV / CYCLE 1

December 9, 2003
November 27, 2004
December 15, 2005
December 5, 2006
November 24, 2007
December 11, 2008
December 1, 2009

טו סיון
15 SIVAN / CYCLE 2

June 15, 2003
June 4, 2004
June 22, 2005
June 11, 2006
June 1, 2007
June 18, 2008
June 7, 2009
May 28, 2010

✑ *A Dangerous Business*

***SEFER AHAVAS CHESED* — Part II Chapter XV**

A person about to loan someone money might ask himself, "What is the worst that could happen?" His answer, no doubt, would be that the borrower fails to repay. The Chofetz Chaim, however, reveals an even worse scenario. That is, that the borrower does repay — with interest. Charging interest on a loan is considered so grave a matter that it can disqualify a person from being revived from death in the times of the Messiah. This was demonstrated by the prophet Ezekiel (*Yalkut Yechezkel, remez* 375), who was given temporarily the power to revive the dead. Before the prophet's eyes, bones grew new flesh and the bodies came to life. Ezekiel was not able to arouse all of the dead, however. The one who did not return to life, he was told, was the person who had transgressed the prohibition against charging interest.

Most observant Jews are aware of this prohibition, and most would be loath to violate it outright. The Chofetz Chaim notes, however, that there are many who stay within the law technically, but utilize a permissible exception in a way that violates the spirit of the law. The spirit that animates the commandment to loan money is the spirit of kindness. Jews are urged to loan each other money out of concern for the other person, not the desire to compound their own wealth.

The technicality used to dodge this obligation is that of the *heter iska* — a permitted business transaction — which allows one to create a contractual partnership arrangement in which the partner investing the money is permitted to earn interest on his investment. The Chofetz Chaim acknowledges that such an arrangement is perfectly acceptable if it meets halachic requirements and a legitimate business partnership is actually being forged. If, however, the lender can easily make an interest-free loan, the preference should be to do chesed, rather than earn interest.

Acts of kindness are essential to the functioning of Hashem's world, and any strategy designed to sidestep chesed has a destructive effect. In fact, the Chofetz Chaim blames the rampant poverty of his times on the people's reluctance to lend money interest-free. Since chesed is the "salt" that preserves one's wealth, a paucity of chesed allows it to decay. In the generation previous to the Chofetz Chaim, most loans were given with the intention of helping someone else; therefore, Hashem provided that generation with the ample wealth. In the Chofetz Chaim's generation, loans that could have been given as chesed were executed as business partnerships instead, and a great quantity of chesed evaporated from the world. Therefore, the Chofetz Chaim says, the Jewish people's wealth was diminished. They diminished it themselves.

The "heter iska," in the Chofetz Chaim's view, is a tightrope. Those who traverse it may be able to avoid the dire consequences of charging interest, but they are far from safe. Their rejection of the opportunity to help someone creates a situation in which eventual losses are almost assured. Even the interest-paying borrower may not repay, and if he does, the money gained may be lost in thousands of other ways. The wise investor knows that the best way to make sure he does well with his money is to do good with it.

Step by **Step**

If I have utilized a "heter iska" in the past, today I will examine the circumstances and consider whether free loans could have been given instead.

✧ *The Price of Money*

SEFER AHAVAS CHESED — **Part II Chapter XV**

A farmer looks at the soil, seeds and sun, and he sees money. If one were to ask him to give away a bag of seeds, his sacrifice would not be, in his calculation, the price of the seeds. It would be the eventual yield of those seeds and the money it would bring. A $10 bag of seeds to the farmer might mean hundreds of dollars worth of corn.

This concept explains why loaning money is particularly difficult for someone whose business is investing money. He is not just giving away $1,000. He is giving away the $9,000 that first $1,000 might yield. One who is in the business of investing may feel that free loans are simply impossible for him to consider; he would be giving away what he sells for a living. The Chofetz Chaim, while finding no exemption for a person in this line of business, does acknowledge the difficulties and offer advice to avoid the pitfalls.

First of all, there is the issue of interest. One who invests for a living must be certain to become well versed in the laws of *"iska,"* the partnership arrangements discussed earlier, under which interest payment is permitted. Even when all the details of the law are adhered to fully, a professional investor still has a problem; he is in a line of business that removes him from helping people financially just for the sake of the mitzvah. There may be many people with whom he has formed legitimate partnerships who would, under other circumstances, be ideal candidates for a free loan from this same individual.

To compensate for these problems that are inherent in the business of finance, the Chofetz Chaim recommends setting aside money out of investment profits. This money should be placed in a separate account designated strictly for chesed. The loans made from the account should be simple, outright, no-strings-attached loans given to people in need. They may be other businessmen struggling against financial problems, friends or relatives facing unforeseen expenses, or indigent people trying to pay bills and feed families. The key is to put aside the money and actively seek ways of putting it to use. This has the effect of augmenting the amount of chesed flowing into the world, which offsets the amount of chesed lost when the businessman makes his loans under a *"heter iska."*

The financier's bottom line, says the Chofetz Chaim, is ultimately the same as everyone else's. He, too, needs the rewards chesed brings. His business interest in money creates a certain set of challenges for him, but it provides him with a major advantage as well. Many people may wish they could help; he can.

Step by **Step**

Today I will examine the ways in which my business interests and obligation of chesed are intertwined.

לע"נ אהרן שמואל אליהו ז"ל בן חיים יצחק ישראל ז"ל ושיינע רייזל תבלח"ט — **15 Kislev**
Dedicated in loving memory of my son, by Shirley Heller

16 Sivan — Avrum Teichman ז"ל בן שמואל בן אברהם לע"נ
Dedicated by Lillian Teichman and the Teichman, Lieber and Kornfeld families

DAY 76

טז כסלו,
16 KISLEV / CYCLE 1

December 11, 2003
November 29, 2004
December 17, 2005
December 7, 2006
November 26, 2007
December 13, 2008
December 3, 2009

יז סיון
17 SIVAN / CYCLE 2

June 17, 2003
June 6, 2004
June 24, 2005
June 13, 2006
June 3, 2007
June 20, 2008
June 9, 2009
May 30, 2010

❧ *A Monumental Act*

SEFER AHAVAS CHESED — Part II Chapter XV
footnotes

*W*hen parents pass into the Next World, the child's ability to honor and serve them does not disappear. Especially in the week and month following a parent's passing — a time during which the soul undergoes intense scrutiny — the parent needs the child's help more than ever. The type of help needed at this time, and forever after, can only be delivered through the child's acts of kindness.

The Chofetz Chaim observes that many children, moved to display their regard for the departed parent, spend elaborately on a monument fit for a prince. While a respectable monument is indeed a matter of importance, the Chofetz Chaim sees this excessive expenditure as a misguided form of honor. The additional money spent on the deluxe monument is far better utilized for donating books to a synagogue or establishing a loan fund for the poor. Done in the name of one's parent, or perhaps for a relative that left no children, these acts of generosity shower true honor upon the soul in the World to Come.

No matter how great a parent was in his life, he needs these merits. The son of the Shelah HaKadosh wrote that a person's acts of kindness, charity and support of Torah not only save his parent from troubles in the World of Judgment, they can carry him right through the gates of the Garden of Eden. These are precious gifts a child can send his parents long after they have left this world — gifts that every soul needs and appreciates. " For there is no man so wholly righteous on earth that he (always) does good and never sins" (*Koheles* 7:20). Every soul arrives in Heaven with deeds it must answer for; time wasted, opportunities squandered, hurtful words spoken, mitzvos overlooked. A child who undertakes some form of chesed as a merit for his parent helps to mitigate these sins at a time when the parent can no longer help himself.

When a child is feeling his loss most intensely — during the *shivah* week and the first month of the mourning period — the parent's soul is also enduring its greatest tribulation under the harsh light of judgment. The child's yearning for his departed parent can then become a powerful motivation for undertaking a chesed. In this way, the child can still connect with his parent and provide comfort and merit for his soul. Until the time when Hashem wipes away all tears and removes the concept of death from the world, these acts of kindness in a parent's name can illuminate times of sadness with a small flame of joy.

Today I will undertake a chesed as a merit for a departed loved one.

יז כסלו
17 KISLEV / CYCLE 1

December 12, 2003
November 30, 2004
December 18, 2005
December 8, 2006
November 27, 2007
December 14, 2008
December 4, 2009

יח סיון
18 SIVAN / CYCLE 2

June 18, 2003
June 7, 2004
June 25, 2005
June 14, 2006
June 4, 2007
June 21, 2008
June 10, 2009
May 31, 2010

◆ﾟ *Sense of Security*

SEFER AHAVAS CHESED — Part II
Chapter XVI/XVI footnotes

*O*ne man can constitute his own free-loan society, as the Chofetz Chaim has shown. A man with some cash in an envelope, a neighbor with a leaf-blower to loan, a family with a swimming pool others can enjoy — each of these constitutes a standing offer to help. As laudable as these individual enterprises are, the Chofetz Chaim now turns his attention to the need for a community loan fund. The advantage of a combined effort is that it can create a reliable resource for those in need. Throughout history, Jewish communities have supported such funds; they were and continue to be an eloquent illustration of the Torah's ideals put into practice.

The Chofetz Chaim emphasizes that community funds must establish a clear set of bylaws to which they consistently adhere. The first step is to determine a maximum amount of money that can be borrowed from the fund by any one borrower, and the maximum duration of the loans. The fund administrators must calculate these factors based on how much money is available and how much need exists in the community.

Another cardinal rule, says the Chofetz Chaim, is to make sure all loans are secured. This means demanding collateral or a co-signer who will take responsibility should the borrower default. This is a rule that should be followed in every case, no matter how desperate a situation a would-be borrower presents. The reason for the Chofetz Chaim's insistence is simple: the bylaws assure that the money will be there to serve its purpose. A keen student of human nature, the Chofetz Chaim reflects in these rules his certainty that through unsecured loans, the fund would soon disappear.

Those administering a community fund must exercise great caution, for they are acting on behalf of others. While people are naturally careful about loaning their own money, they may feel freer with a fund's anonymous money.

On the borrower's side, the unsecured loan creates great temptation to place repayment at the bottom of the priority list. Without clear repayment terms and security, the borrower can put off repayment forever, telling himself that he will make the payment as soon as he is able.

Finally, having strict, consistent rules in force prevents personal strain on the fund's treasurer. If an exception is made for one individual, in a short time there will be many other individuals pleading to be the next exception. Some may even be the treasurer's relatives or neighbors. His personal integrity and relationships are bound to suffer unless he maintains an objective standard applicable to all. If a particularly heartbreaking case arises and the person cannot find a co-signer in time, the treasurer has the option of providing the loan personally, or finding someone who will, the Chofetz Chaim suggests.

Throughout this discussion, it becomes clear that developing and running a community charity fund sometimes opens an unwelcome window on the darker side of human nature. In the face of these pitfalls, the Jewish people's embrace of this mitzvah is all the more inspiring.

Step by **Step**

Today I will find out about free-loan funds available in my community and either contribute to one in existence, or consider starting one.

יח כסלו
18 KISLEV / CYCLE 1

December 13, 2003
December 1, 2004
December 19, 2005
December 9, 2006
November 28, 2007
December 15, 2008
December 5, 2009

יט סיון
19 SIVAN / CYCLE 2

June 19, 2003
June 8, 2004
June 26, 2005
June 15, 2006
June 5, 2007
June 22, 2008
June 11, 2009
June 1, 2010

✑ *Extra Credit*

SEFER AHAVAS CHESED — Part II
Chapter XVI/XVI footnotes

A community loan fund operates according to an unusual type of mathematics. For example, if a person donates $1,000 to the fund, and ten people take loans from it, one would think that the donor has, in effect, given out ten $100 loans. To the donor, this might seem rather unimpressive. His grand donation has been fractured into several far-less-grand amounts. He might imagine that the impact of his chesed in Heaven has likewise been fractured and diminished.

The Chofetz Chaim counters this line of reasoning. Each person who donates to the fund creates the conditions that allow the fund to exist and function at a certain level. The size of the fund determines how much each borrower will be allowed to take and how long each will be given to repay. The more generous the terms of the loans, the more people can be helped. The $1,000 is not just ten $100 loans; it is an essential piece of the fund's foundation, as is every other donation comprised within the fund. Without each of those donations, the fund would not exist in its present form, or perhaps at all. Hashem therefore credits each donor with each loan in its entirety.

One who is involved in creating a fund helps to removes the guilt that the entire community would bear if it did nothing to care for the needy in its midst. The Chofetz Chaim warns that a person who lives in a community devoid of chesed will be required to account for his choice. The complaint of the neglected poor rises up against the community; each is responsible individually for what all failed to do collectively. One cannot excuse oneself by saying, "There was no fund." If that is the case, one has the obligation to try to create a fund, or at least tend to the poor on one's own to the extent that is possible.

The Chofetz Chaim turns to the laws of Shabbos observance to illustrate the principle of receiving full credit for an act for which one is only partly responsible. He examines the prohibition against carrying, and relates the law that if two people together carry an item from a private to a public domain, neither is held responsible for violating the prohibition. However, if an item is so heavy that one person cannot carry it alone — for example, a large boulder — and two people unite their efforts to carry it, each is guilty individually for the entire act. The reasoning is that, since one person could not have carried the boulder alone, each made the transgression possible for them both. The responsibility of each is total and complete.

The other side of that coin is a situation, such as a community loan fund, in which each person's participation makes possible a mitzvah that none could have performed on his own. Without one person's $50 and another person's $1,000, the fund would not exist in the form it does, and would not be able to help those it helps. Each contributor makes the mitzvah possible for them all. The reward for each is total and complete.

The next time I make a contribution to a community fund, I will remember that the amount I give, no matter what the size, is an integral part of the fund's success.

יט כסלו
19 KISLEV / CYCLE 1

December 14, 2003
December 2, 2004
December 20, 2005
December 10, 2006
November 29, 2007
December 16, 2008
December 6, 2009

כ סיון
20 SIVAN / CYCLE 2

June 20, 2003
June 9, 2004
June 27, 2005
June 16, 2006
June 6, 2007
June 23, 2008
June 12, 2009
June 2, 2010

❧ *Stepping Up, Opting Out*

SEFER AHAVAS CHESED — **Part II Chapter XVI**
footnotes

The captain asks a lineup of 30 soldiers for a volunteer to step forward for a dangerous mission. Twenty-nine soldiers take one step backward, leaving one hapless soldier in the "forward" position. It is an old comedy routine, but one that accurately depicts the means by which some people attempt to avoid the monetary sacrifice involved in chesed. The Chofetz Chaim observes that stepping backward comes with its own cost — a weakening of one's grasp on holiness and closeness to Hashem. He discusses specifically those who attempt to evade requests for contributions to their synagogue by creating alternative *minyanim* at opportune moments, or leaving the premises for a chat while fundraising is underway.

Many synagogues pay for some of their expenses through member pledges. One person might offer to cover the fuel expenses, one the electricity, one the salary of the caretaker — each makes an investment in the continued functioning of the synagogue. Those who opt out of this activity reason that their contribution is not necessary. The synagogue will not close its doors for the lack of their participation. The yeshivah will not go bankrupt because one person's tuition is late, nor will the local *gemach* dissolve because one person did not contribute.

That reasoning misses the point of participating, says the Chofetz Chaim. One who is invested in the community reaps dividends unavailable to those who take the step backward. There is a different quality to the prayer of one who gives something of himself to keep the synagogue running. Because he has drawn close to Hashem by offering a sacrifice of his possessions, Hashem repays him with a closeness unavailable to the person who opts out. Such a person understands that Hashem has set him in a certain place at a certain time because he has something unique to offer those who share this setting with him.

There was a couple living in Williamsburg, Brooklyn, after World War II. Although they had little money to help the incoming European refugees, they took upon themselves one mitzvah — to help the young, orphaned couples who were bravely trying to start families and reassert the Jewish people's presence in the land of the living. The couple would go to the new mother's house after the baby was born and take care of the household and family. The man would cook, and the wife would mop the floors and care for the other children, just as if it were their own child who had given birth.

Their kindness imprinted an indelible message on these lonely refugees: They were not alone; their fellow Jews stood behind them, beside them, all around them.

One cannot calibrate how this couple's efforts have resounded into the future, but there is no doubt that many of these shattered young people might have been lost to Torah without the couple's loving embrace. Now, in Heaven, the voices of generations of children — their learning and prayer — rise to praise the couple whose kindness paved the path on which they travel. Those sounds will echo into eternity, with each new generation bringing new radiance and joy to those two holy *neshamos*.

Step by **Step**

Today I will think about the institutions with which my life intersects, and take on an act of chesed on behalf of one of them.

---

19 Kislev — Leon Wenter ז"ל לע"נ לייבל בן יהודה ז"ל
Dedicated by Yaakov and Shira Molotsky and family

20 Sivan —

DAY 80

כ כסלו
20 KISLEV / CYCLE 1

December 15, 2003
December 3, 2004
December 21, 2005
December 11, 2006
November 30, 2007
December 17, 2008
December 7, 2009

כא סיון
21 SIVAN / CYCLE 2

June 21, 2003
June 10, 2004
June 28, 2005
June 17, 2006
June 7, 2007
June 24, 2008
June 13, 2009
June 3, 2010

❧ *On Commission*

SEFER AHAVAS CHESED — **Part II Chapter XVI**

*E*veryone knows this person. In sixth grade he organizes a class carnival to earn money for charity. In high school he starts a tutoring program for elementary-school boys. As a newlywed, he solicits money for his synagogue's building campaign. Five years later, he raises money for his son's yeshivah. When he is around, everyone in his periphery gets pulled into his orbit. They suddenly find themselves writing checks for his causes and working on his projects, all because of his gentle, persistent tug.

When a person becomes involved in community chesed organizations, he does not just earn his own reward for his own kind act. He earns a "commission," a piece of the credit for the many people he spurs onto their own acts of chesed. The *Midrash Tanchuma* states that if a person, as a result of sin, is liable for a severe punishment, there are actions he can take to avert the consequence. One of these actions is to take upon himself the responsibility of collecting for a chesed fund, for "One who pursues charity and kindness will find life, righteousness and honor" (*Mishlei* 21:21).

Giving what one can certainly evokes Heaven's mercy, but a person can go far beyond the limits of his own financial capabilities by taking on the task of encouraging others to give. He then receives credit for the mitzvos he has encouraged.

This principle is illustrated in the Torah (*Shemos* 17:5) when Hashem instructs Moses: "And in your hand take your staff with which you struck the river." The episode to which Hashem is referring did not happen. Moses never struck the river; he followed Hashem's command to instruct Aaron to strike the river. The stick and the miracles for which it was the agent are attributed to Moses because it was he who caused Aaron to utilize it for its miraculous purpose. The person who causes others to use their assets for their Heavenly purpose shares ownership of their achievements. Their "stick" is also his.

In collecting money for charity, a person can be certain to experience rejection, sometimes even humiliation. He will not, however, come to sin through this endeavor, as the Mishnah in *Avos* (5:18) promises: "One who causes merit to accrue to the masses, no sin comes through his hand." The Talmud (*Bava Basra* 9a) goes further, saying in the name of Rabbi Elazar that one who causes others to give is even greater than one who gives himself. The source of his greatness lies in the difficulty of his endeavor. The Chofetz Chaim says that if a person has amassed a thousand rubles for a charitable fund, he has undoubtedly undergone considerable emotional and perhaps physical hardship in the process.

It is because of this involvement of body and soul in the act of collecting that the rewards are so great. All the good that the money does earns perpetual rewards for those who reached into their own pockets, and it earns still more reward for the one who reached into each of their hearts.

Step by **Step**

The next time someone needs help collecting for a charitable cause, I will try to find time to take part in collecting.

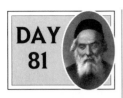

DAY 81

כא כסלו
21 KISLEV / CYCLE 1

December 16, 2003
December 4, 2004
December 22, 2005
December 12, 2006
December 1, 2007
December 18, 2008
December 8, 2009

כב סיון
22 SIVAN / CYCLE 2

June 22, 2003
June 11, 2004
June 29, 2005
June 18, 2006
June 8, 2007
June 25, 2008
June 14, 2009
June 4, 2010

❧ Saying it Aloud

SEFER AHAVAS CHESED — Part II Chapter XVI

"*T*alk is cheap," says the world. When that talk is a pledge to charity, however, it is far from cheap. It is almost as valuable as the act of giving itself. The Chofetz Chaim relates that when a person makes a pledge, he receives the same reward as he receives for actually tendering the money. When he fulfills the pledge, he is rewarded yet again. Just taking one step in the direction of giving brings upon a Jew a new level of holiness; his heart is turned toward the needs of others, and that alone elicits a reward.

There are many reasons that people prefer not to make public pledges. Some feel there is something immodest about publicly indicating that they have the means to give a large amount of money. The Chofetz Chaim answers that the benefit far outweighs whatever show of pride might be involved. The benefit is that a pledge — especially a higher one — sets a level of expectation that pushes others to give more. It tells everyone present that this is an important cause, which has attracted serious support from members of their community. Pride, a powerful motivator, can be pressed into service to promote a mitzvah. The person who makes the pledge receives credit for all those who are spurred by his verbal commitment to make or increase a pledge of their own.

Other people avoid making pledges because they fear they may be unable to fulfill them. To avoid the liabilities that accompany the making of a vow, one need only say the words "*b'li neder*," meaning "without a vow." That

186 ☐ CHOFETZ CHAIM

phrase puts the pledge into the category of an intention one plans to fulfill, but for which one need not make any formal disavowal if fulfillment becomes impossible. Even without the pressure of a holy vow, however, stating an intention in public does put pressure on a person to uphold his word. The sacrifice involved in putting oneself under such pressure is another factor in the reward earned by making a pledge.

There are, of course, unexpected circumstances that truly do render one unable to fulfill a pledge. People undergo unexpected losses or expenses, and suddenly the money they counted on is needed for other urgent matters, or perhaps it is altogether gone. One might think that in such a situation, having made a pledge would seem in retrospect like a disastrous move. The Chofetz Chaim reveals that just the opposite is true. The person is rewarded for his intention, just as if he had fulfilled it.

A person's reward is in no way diminished if he gives without having made a public commitment. He still receives all the blessings that come with the act of giving. He cheats himself, however, out of the double portion that accrues to one who announces his intentions in public. Furthermore, if events develop that prevent him from giving, he does not have the pledge to bring him reward even in the absence of an actual donation.

The benefits of public pledges are even greater on the communal level, for in coming together to publicly support Jewish institutions, communities create an identity for themselves of caring people who work together for the common good. It is an identity that lifts each individual in the community, and everyone who lives within it.

The next time a pledge is requested for a cause I support, I will come forward with a pledge I can reasonably expect to fulfill.

21 Kislev — May today's learning be a זכות for our family.
Dedicated by Dafna and Elliot Prince

22 Sivan — Isfried Stern לע"נ יצחק יעקב בן מרים ז"ל
Dedicated by Anne Littwin in loving memory of my grandfather

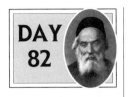

כב כסלו
22 KISLEV / CYCLE I

December 17, 2003
December 5, 2004
December 23, 2005
December 13, 2006
December 2, 2007
December 19, 2008
December 9, 2009

כג סיון
23 SIVAN / CYCLE 2

June 23, 2003
June 12, 2004
June 30, 2005
June 19, 2006
June 9, 2007
June 26, 2008
June 15, 2009
June 5, 2010

✒ *The Hard Sell*

SEFER AHAVAS CHESED — Part II Chapter XVI

*O*ne may have to beg, argue and plead, but it is all worthwhile, says the Chofetz Chaim, if in the end one can convince others to give. One who gives and convinces others to give has performed the mitzvah of *tzedakah* at its highest level, according to *Pirkei Avos* (5:13). The idea that generosity would be rewarded is common sense, but one might wonder why getting others to give — even at the risk of annoying them — is deemed so highly praiseworthy. The suffering of the person doing the cajoling is the basis of the reward. Because the mitzvah exacts a price, Hashem repays the person who performs it.

The Talmud (*Bava Basra* 9a) demonstrates that willingly undergoing this kind of suffering reduces other types of suffering in one's life. The people of the city of Mechuza come to Rava and complain about heavy taxes and oppressive laws that the government has imposed upon them. Rava advises them to create institutions of chesed. He further instructs them to involve community members in the running of these institutions. Rava knew that this was the cure, because the community's chesed institutions would be sure to create pressure and strain for all those involved. The Heavenly ration of stress assigned to the people of Mechuza would be filled from this source, rather than from the government. As Rava predicted, when the people followed his instructions, the government's oppression subsided.

As Rava's advice reflected, stress and aggravation are Divinely apportioned, much as money is. A person will receive his due; either from positive and rewarding sources like chesed, or from any of the thousands of negative sources that flow into people's lives. Taking on the aggravation of collecting and distributing charitable funds is a preemptive strike against the negative sources of stress.

Embarrassment usually goes hand in hand with asking people to give money. Distributing charity is not always emotionally gratifying either. Recipients may feel they have been dealt with unfairly. They may be hostile or embarrassed. The *Shulchan Aruch* (*Yoreh De'ah*, 257:7) states that one who does his best to distribute funds sensitively and fairly yet still arouses anger receives an even greater reward as compensation for his own suffering.

The Torah (*Devarim* 15:11) states: "Therefore I command you, to say, 'You shall surely open your hand to your brother, to your poor and to your destitute in your land.'" The Chofetz Chaim sees the Hebrew word *leimor*, to say, as a reference to opening one's own hand, and then speaking to others— getting others to open their hands. Influencing others to give can have earthshaking consequences, as the following story illustrates:

Prior to World War II, Rabbi Elchanan Wasserman came to America, where he met a young man who was an active force in his *minyan*. He gave him one piece of advice: "Commit yourself completely to helping people." These words guided the future of the young man, Elimelech Gavriel Tress, leading him to step off the corporate ladder and dedicate himself to his fellow

(Continued on page 382)

Step by **Step**

The next time I become involved in a chesed, I will try to convince one or more friends or family members to join me.

22 Kislev — Rabbi Jonah E. Caplan לע"נ הרב יונה אפרים בן שלמה חיים ז"ל
Dedicated by his children

23 Sivan —

כג כסלו
23 KISLEV / CYCLE 1

December 18, 2003
December 6, 2004
December 24, 2005
December 14, 2006
December 3, 2007
December 20, 2008
December 10, 2009

כד סיון
24 SIVAN / CYCLE 2

June 24, 2003
June 13, 2004
July 1, 2005
June 20, 2006
June 10, 2007
June 27, 2008
June 16, 2009
June 6, 2010

≈ *Choosing Both*

SEFER AHAVAS CHESED — Part II Chapter XVII

*I*f a doctor makes the right diagnosis but prescribes the wrong medicine, he will fail to ameliorate the problem. He may even make it worse. The Chofetz Chaim observes that in the case of a person in need of help, the benefactor must understand which "medicine" to apply. In some cases, chesed — a loan — is the answer. In others, charity is the best way to ease the person's pain.

To a certain extent, chesed is viewed as the greater mitzvah. The Talmud (*Succah* 49b) offers three reasons that this is so. First, charity involves only one's assets, but chesed often calls for physical involvement as well. A person who visits someone who is ill or helps marry someone off may be shouldering some financial burden from these deeds, but his physical involvement is at least as important. Secondly, acts of kindness may be performed for both poor and wealthy people; charity is needed only by the poor. Finally, charity is of use only to those living in this world. An act of kindness can be offered to the living as well as those in the World to Come.

Despite these advantages, charity, too, has its greatness. Certainly one must wage a tougher battle with the *yetzer hara* in order to open one's hand for charity, because money donated is not going to be returned by the recipient. To win this battle, one must cling to a firm faith that Hashem returns this money twofold.

True greatness lies neither in chesed alone, nor charity alone. It lies in knowing which one to offer, and in the flexibility to respond appropriately to a given situation. Some people would rather give money outright than become enmeshed in a loan agreement. If the would-be recipient is an established businessman who merely needs to regain his footing, charity would be the wrong medicine. It could even do harm; it could cause embarrassment or indicate a lack of confidence in his ability to recover his former stature.

On the other hand, if a ragged man bangs on the door and presents a pile of letters detailing the dire straits of his family, this is no time to sit down and negotiate a loan. The man needs simple, no-strings-attached charity.

According to *Pirkei D'Rabbi Eliezer*, Heaven has two great chambers. One is for those who have done acts of kindness throughout their lives; the other is for those who have given charity. The prophet Elijah stands between the chambers and directs the people to the chamber in which their reward awaits. The prophet Samuel objects to losing access to one or the other chamber, and states that he will learn the criteria for each mitzvah, so that he may reap the reward for both.

To this, Hashem replies, "You stood between these two paths, and said you will not satisfy yourself with any one of them, but will take both for yourself. On your life I will give you three great presents." These are the three gifts promised in *Mishlei* (21:21) to the person who commits himself to both *tzedakah* and chesed: life, charity and honor.

The next time someone in need approaches me for a loan, I will consider whether the situation is better suited to an outright donation.

23 Kislev — May today's learning be a זכות for our משפחה.
Dedicated by David Miller and family, Toronto, Ontario

24 Sivan — לע"נ ר' אברהם יצחק בן ר' דוד ז"ל
לע"נ ר' מאיר שלמה בן ר' אליהו ז"ל

כד כסלו
24 KISLEV / CYCLE 1

December 19, 2003
December 7, 2004
December 25, 2005
December 15, 2006
December 4, 2007
December 21, 2008
December 11, 2009

כה סיון
25 SIVAN / CYCLE 2

June 25, 2003
June 14, 2004
July 2, 2005
June 21, 2006
June 11, 2007
June 28, 2008
June 17, 2009
June 7, 2010

❧ *Locked Doors*

SEFER AHAVAS CHESED — Part II Chapter XVII
footnotes

*D*oublethink is a word coined to describe the process of convincing oneself that something is exactly the opposite of what it really is. With the *yetzer hara's* able assistance, an entire town can convince itself that kindness lies in a policy of turning all charity collectors away from the door. The logic runs thus: A town in which residents are known to be generous will attract an ever-growing pool of solicitors. Ultimately, the residents will be overwhelmed and unable to give any meaningful assistance to anyone, even their own community members.

The Chofetz Chaim cuts through this logic with one deft slice. It is a terrible mistake, he says, to slam the door on the poor. It is so antithetical to the Torah's viewpoint that even the design of one's home must take the poor into account. An opinion in the Talmud (*Bava Basra* 7b) prohibits constructing the type of gate in front of one's house that will block the sound of knocking.

In one town in Europe, there lived a simple Jew whose house was always open to the poor. One day, this man went to his Rebbe and received a blessing that he would become wealthy. Soon, the man's fortunes rose dramatically. His humble abode was replaced by an exquisite mansion. Although the old wooden door had always been open, the new, carved 10-foot doors were locked tight. The man had been willing to let passersby trod across his old floor; his Oriental rugs were another story. He had been comfortable sharing his bread and cheese with the simple folk who came through, but it seemed absurd to seat them at his grand table to feast on delicacies.

One day, the man's Rebbe paid him a visit. Upon entering the mansion, the Rebbe said nothing. He merely stared at the great arched windows opening to the outside. The man filled the Rebbe in on the windows' origins in Italy and their stratospheric value. After awhile, the Rebbe shifted his gaze to the immense, gilt-framed mirror on the wall. Again the man supplied the pedigree to his purchase.

Finally, the Rebbe spoke: "What is the difference between a mirror and a window?" he asked.

The man answered that the mirror is backed by a bit of crushed silver, resulting in the appearance of a reflection. "Ah," the Rebbe said, "so you have one window where you look out and see the entire world, and you have another window where there's just a little bit of silver placed on it, and suddenly all you see is yourself." With those words the Rebbe left the house, and soon the great, carved doors were opened to the poor.

Today, especially in America, Jewish communities do not usually propagate community-wide policies about giving charity. The Chofetz Chaim's detailed treatment of this subject is still relevant, however, since each of these discussions illuminates deep insights into the dynamics of giving. These are concepts every person must understand, whether acting as part of a community, or simply as part of the Jewish people.

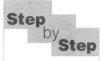

Step by **Step**

Today I will commit myself to graciously greet and give something to all legitimate charity collectors who come to my door.

כה כסלו
25 KISLEV / CYCLE 1

December 20, 2003
December 8, 2004
December 26, 2005
December 16, 2006
December 5, 2007
December 22, 2008
December 12, 2009

כו סיון
26 SIVAN / CYCLE 2

June 26, 2003
June 15, 2004
July 3, 2005
June 22, 2006
June 12, 2007
June 29, 2008
June 18, 2009
June 8, 2010

❧ *The Chesed of Sodom*

SEFER AHAVAS CHESED — Part II Chapter XVII
footnotes

*M*ost of the time, an organized approach is better than a scattershot approach. Most of the time, a one-stop errand is preferable to a long itinerary of stops. Both of those generalizations, however, do not hold true when the issue is charity. Jewish communities in the Chofetz Chaim's day sometimes took it upon themselves to bring charitable giving under one umbrella, eliminating the need for solicitors to go door to door, while at the same time saving the townspeople the trouble of having to open their doors to strangers. This plan, the Chofetz Chaim insisted, was wrong headed and harmful; locking one's doors to the poor — even if one directs them to where help is available — is not what the Torah envisions for the Jewish people.

While it is true that a person's priorities for charity are those closest to him, this does not negate the necessity of keeping doors open to the poor from other communities. Furthermore, if a poor person is denied the opportunity to go door to door, he is denied the chance to find a sympathetic ear. Perhaps one or two people he encounters will be willing to offer him a greater level of assistance than the general fund would allow. If he cannot get past the door, he has no opportunity to state his case to someone who might feel for his particular plight. For instance, someone who has had an ill child might be inclined to give a generous amount to a man collecting for his own child's surgery.

The Chofetz Chaim was not alone in his objections to removing charity from the realm of the private home. A story told about Rabbi Levi Yitzchak of Berditchev graphically defines the essence of this type of system. As a great leader of his generation, Rabbi Levi Yitzchak was constantly being summoned to communal meetings. In his older years, he decided that he wanted to spend more time learning and counseling those who came to him. He instructed the elders of Berditchev to make communal decisions among themselves, and summon him only when some new enactment was being considered.

One day, he was summoned. The elders were debating the idea of shifting all the community's charitable giving into a central fund that would be administered by a treasurer. They sought the Rabbi's consent. "I don't understand why you called for me," the Rabbi said. "I told you only to summon me when you were instituting something new. This is old. It was done first in Sodom and Gomorrah."

"Sodom?" the elders exclaimed. "But those were evil, selfish people. Our idea is to make it easier for the poor people themselves."

The Rabbi would not be swayed. "Do you think the people of Sodom told themselves they were wicked? They had reasons. They had rationalizations as to why they were right to refuse to give. No matter how you explain it, the final result is that doors are closed to the poor. I'll have nothing to do with it."

A central fund has its place. Indeed, it can be a lifeline for people in need of help. The vision Hashem has for his people, however, is not a vision of institutionalized kindness. It is a vision of eyes meeting, hearts responding, hands giving, one into the other.

Step by **Step**

If I have tended to confine my significant giving to organized charities, today I will consider putting more into the money I give at the door.

25 Kislev — לע"נ גרשן בן ישראל ז"ל
Dedicated by Nigel and Rachel Collins

26 Sivan —

כו כסלו
26 KISLEV / CYCLE 1

December 1, 2002
December 21, 2003
December 9, 2004
December 27, 2005
December 17, 2006
December 6, 2007
December 23, 2008
December 13, 2009

כז סיון
27 SIVAN / CYCLE 2

June 27, 2003
June 16, 2004
July 4, 2005
June 23, 2006
June 13, 2007
June 30, 2008
June 19, 2009
June 9, 2010

❧ *It Bears Repeating*

SEFER AHAVAS CHESED — Part II Chapter XVII
footnotes

*W*hat a person does ultimately determines what a person becomes. Giving *tzedakah* on a regular, frequent basis turns one into a charitable person. The Chofetz Chaim offers this as the first of eight reasons to resist any plan that would shift giving from the private to the institutional domain. A person who gives a thousand dollars once a year cannot compare to one who puts his hand into his pocket one thousand times a year — just as he is rushing off to work or synagogue, just as he is about to settle down for the night, just as he begins helping his child with homework — to hand a dollar to a man in need. The constant repetition of the act of giving turns a person into an *"ish* chesed," a person of kindness, a person for whom all the rewards of this world and the Next World are in store.

In a famous parable, a king took the most misanthropic, sour-faced man in the kingdom and appointed him head of an orphanage. He was the one who had to pour the milk for the little children, soothe their hurts, calm their crying and read them their bedtime stories. The king required the man not only to fulfill this role, but to win the children's hearts. If he failed, he would be doomed.

The man did as he was ordered, at first with terrible resentment. Little by little, however, the kindness he was forced to perform began making small inroads into his heart. He began to appreciate the children's smiles and take pride in his ability to care for them. He became what he did. He became a giver.

The benefits accrue not only to the individual, but to the Jewish people as a whole, with each act of kindness performed. As was explained in Day 55's lesson, the world is judged on the quantity of kind acts performed. The thousand donations of one dollar are a thousand merits for the Jewish people. The one donation of a thousand dollars is one merit. Each person who trains himself to give on a consistent basis, as a day-to-day part of his life, helps tip the Heavenly balance, drawing Hashem's mercy and blessing down to this world. This factor alone, the Chofetz Chaim says, should be enough to dispose of any thoughts of closing off the route of private giving. Such a plan denies the Jewish people the most effective training program there is for becoming a paradigm of caring and kindness — a true, real-life representation of Hashem in this world.

Today I will begin to give to a charity on a daily basis. This might be through a collection box at home or synagogue, or some other accessible means.

26 Kislev — Rav Shmuel Kalusziner לע״נ הרב שמואל בן חיים הלוי ז״ל
Dedicated in loving memory by his wife, children, grandchildren and great-grandchildren

27 Sivan — In honor of our grandparents, Suri and Gerald Goldfeder and Gussie and David Rosenberg

כז כסלו
27 KISLEV / CYCLE 1

December 2, 2002
December 22, 2003
December 10, 2004
December 28, 2005
December 18, 2006
December 7, 2007
December 24, 2008
December 14, 2009

כח סיון
28 SIVAN / CYCLE 2

June 28, 2003
June 17, 2004
July 5, 2005
June 24, 2006
June 14, 2007
July 1, 2008
June 20, 2009
June 10, 2010

❧ Scattering Charity

SEFER AHAVAS CHESED — Part II Chapter XVII
footnotes

*W*hen a community decides to centralize all of its charity under one agency, there is often a cost analysis behind the decision. The Chofetz Chaim analyzes this analysis, and shows it to be a losing proposition — another reason to avoid such plans. The logic is that if community members contribute a set amount each month or each year, their costs of giving charity will be contained. They will not be subject to the rising and falling tides of solicitors coming through town. Instead of having no one knock at the door one day, and ten requests the next day, each person would know that he must give his $50 a month.

The Chofetz Chaim looks upon this logic and sees a great gap in understanding.

When homes are open to the poor, the interaction between the needy and the giver creates an occasion to which the giver has an opportunity to rise. He thereby has the chance to give another person his time, money, sympathy and perhaps some food or drink. If, however, the town's official policy is that solicitors are received only by a charitable agency, all of that disappears. The community members may believe they are saving money, but that belief defies all the Torah teaches about *tzedakah*. The Chofetz Chaim cites the *Midrash* (*Mishlei*, Chapter 11): "If you see a person scattering his money for charity, you know he is going to have more." That element of "scattering" the money — handing it out generously, out of compassion for another's plight — cannot co-exist with institutional giving.

The fact that a giver will prosper from his giving is proven by the words the Chofetz Chaim quotes from *Bava Basra* (9b): "All who pursue *tzedakah,* Hashem will make available to them money with which to do *tzedakah.*" When a person performs a mitzvah, Hashem creates a situation for him that will allow him to do more. Based upon that concept, when a person gives *tzedakah*, Hashem provides him with the wealth to give more. A community policy that limits a person's giving to a set amount at set periods also limits, in equal measure, his potential wealth. The more he clings to his assets, the thinner they become.

A further objection to relying exclusively upon a community fund is the strong likelihood that this policy will drive people away from performing a mitzvah. Theoretically, everyone in the community would satisfy his charitable obligations by paying a set amount to the fund each year. There will be households, however, that cannot afford the amount. Discouraged or embarrassed, they will opt out of participation. They would gladly hand out a dollar or two to someone at the door, but the doorbell will no longer ring, thanks to the policies of the community's leaders. Likewise, someone with a job to offer, or a cup of hot coffee or a few encouraging words, will also lose his chance to help. Those who cause this situation to take shape are liable for leading the masses away from mitzvos, a liability few souls can withstand. By simply allowing the doors of each home to remain open, the community can instead reap the immeasurable benefits of kindness allowed to flow freely from the heart.

The next time someone comes to my door in need of help, I will seriously consider his need, and what unique help I might have to offer in this specific situation.

כח כסלו
28 KISLEV / CYCLE 1

December 3, 2002
December 23, 2003
December 11, 2004
December 29, 2005
December 19, 2006
December 8, 2007
December 25, 2008
December 15, 2009

כט סיון
29 SIVAN / CYCLE 2

June 29, 2003
June 18, 2004
July 6, 2005
June 25, 2006
June 15, 2007
July 2, 2008
June 21, 2009
June 11, 2010

✍ *On the Spot*

SEFER AHAVAS CHESED — Part II Chapter XVII
footnotes

*W*hen a person needs help, he does not wish to wait. "Please leave a message" or "Please submit the following documents" are not the phrases he wishes to hear. "Here, take this. This is what you need." These are the magic words. For this reason, the Chofetz Chaim offers another objection to a community-fund-only scheme: It limits the needy person's opportunity to obtain an immediate response to his solicitation. Instead of the satisfaction of knocking on a door and having his problem heard, he is redirected. He must go through proper channels and await a decision.

The value the Torah places on the immediacy of a helpful response is illustrated in the story of Mar Ukva and his wife. The Talmud (*Kesubos* 67b) describes how this couple delivered Shabbos food to needy townspeople. They performed their mission with the utmost discretion, making sure that the source of the food would never be discovered by the beneficiaries, thereby causing them shame. One such recipient, however, was desperate to know the identity of his benefactor. He waited, out of sight, until the couple made the week's delivery, and then stepped out in time to catch sight of Mar Ukva and his wife heading away from his home. He pursued them, eager to know the identity of these people who had been supplying him with Shabbos food so many months.

The couple knew, however, that the recipient would be embarrassed if he were to discover who they were. As they passed by a bakery, they saw a hiding place; they jumped into a hot oven to escape detection. They emerged safely, a miracle which the Sages credit to the merit of their enormous chesed. The soles of Mar Ukva's feet, however, were slightly singed, whereas his wife was completely unscathed. The Sages proclaim that Hashem's complete protection of the wife was evidence that she possessed more merit than her husband, and this extra measure of merit accrued to her because she put food directly into the hands of the poor; her brand of help was immediate and complete. Mar Ukva gave them money with which they bought food; this was one step removed from direct help.

Notwithstanding the fact that there are times when money is more helpful than food, and there are people who are more embarrassed to take food than they are to take money, the point of the story is that the more direct the benefit, the more valuable the mitzvah. That does not mean, however, that indirect help is bad. The Chofetz Chaim reiterates that creating a community fund is not, by any means, a negative act. It can provide much-needed assistance to a large number of people. It gives the poor a place where they know they can go, where they need not worry about doors being slammed in their faces. Such a fund only becomes a negative when it is established with the purpose of replacing private charity. The community fund should never be the only door open to the poor. It should be one of many.

Today I will consider whether there are more direct ways for me to help any of those to whom I give tzedakah.

DAY 89

כט כסלו*

29 KISLEV / CYCLE 1

December 4, 2002
December 24, 2003
December 12, 2004
December 30, 2005
December 20, 2006
December 9, 2007
December 26, 2008
December 16, 2009

ל סיון

30 SIVAN / CYCLE 2

June 30, 2003
June 19, 2004
July 7, 2005
June 26, 2006
June 16, 2007
July 3, 2008
June 22, 2009
June 12, 2010

*When this month has only 29 days, the lesson for 30 Kislev should also be studied today.

❧ *Staying in Character*

SEFER AHAVAS CHESED — **Part II Chapter XVII**
footnotes

*A*s the weekly Torah reading arrives at the story of Abraham, an arts-and-crafts phenomenon occurs in Jewish pre-schools around the world. With oaktag, crayons and glue, the children create tents furnished with four open doors. Abraham, the original Jew, epitomized the trait of hospitality by making sure that, coming from any direction, travelers would see his open door. Hospitality has been a hallmark of the Jewish people ever since.

The open door is yet one more casualty of a policy to confine charity to a community agency; this is the basis for another of the Chofetz Chaim's objections to such a system.

The locked door endangers not only the needy person, but the person barricaded behind it as well. *Maseches Derech Eretz Zuta* (Chapter 9) states that a person should take care when he sits down to eat that his doors are not locked, because locked doors can bring poverty into the home. The Talmud (*Taanis* 20b) relates that before Rabbi Huna would sit down to break bread, he would post a message at his door inviting in anyone who wanted to join him for his meal.

Because hospitality is so integral to the Jewish people, two nations that were inherently lacking in this trait were barred by the Torah from converting to Judaism. As was explained in detail on Day 27, Ammon and Moab were forever excluded from the ranks of the Jewish people because they failed to bring food and drink to the Jews as they wandered through the wilderness. This dire proclamation came about only because they lacked courtesy; the Jews were not even in need of food or drink, for Hashem satisfied all their needs. From here, one can project the heavy burden of guilt borne by one who withholds help from those who really are tired and hungry.

Locked doors also eliminate interaction between the needy and the giver. The Sages (*Kesubos* 111b) convey the value in these interactions with the statement that it is a greater mitzvah to show one's "white teeth" to the poor person than to "feed him milk." Offering an encouraging smile is said to bring upon a person eleven separate blessings. If a person limits his giving to a central committee, which distributes it with bureaucratic sterility, those eleven blessings are lost. Lost is the giver's opportunity to grasp the greatness attained by giving another human being encouragement. This is yet one more objection to barring the poor from soliciting at the door.

Any action that closes off one's home to the poor — even if it is not intended for that purpose — violates the spirit of the Jewish home. The Talmud (*Shabbos* 63a) states that if a person keeps an attack dog in his house, he is judged as someone who eschews chesed, because fear of his dog will keep poor people away. In this case, a person is held accountable for rejecting the poor when it is only an incidental result of his actions. The liability is certainly far heavier for purposely creating an atmosphere in which the poor are officially barred. All the security felt by those who live where the poor dare not come is illusory, the Chofetz Chaim illustrates. The blessings of real security — the security of Hashem's love and protection — can only be found within open doors.

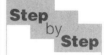

Where I feel it is appropriate and safe, I will offer more actual hospitality — a cup of coffee, a chance to rest — to solicitors who come to my door.

ל כסלו*
30 KISLEV / CYCLE 1

December 5, 2002
December 25, 2003
December 31, 2005
December 21, 2006
December 27, 2008
December 17, 2009

א תמוז
1 TAMMUZ / CYCLE 2

July 1, 2003
June 20, 2004
July 8, 2005
June 27, 2006
June 17, 2007
July 4, 2008
June 23, 2009
June 13, 2010

✑ *Gratitude Knocking*

SEFER AHAVAS CHESED — **Part II Chapter XVII**
footnotes

*J*ust as the bill for summer camp arrives, setting off frenzied calculations as to how to cover limitless expenses with limited income, there is a knock on the door. Standing on the other side of the door, one might instantly conclude, is another expense; a man with a story, carrying a laminated letter signed by several roshei yeshivah. He lives in Israel and needs money to bring his gravely ill, youngest child to America for an operation. If the homeowner were living in a community where all solicitors were pointed in the direction of a central fund, this solicitor would certainly be sent on his way, leaving the homeowner to return to his summer-camp dilemma. If, however, the would-be donor felt obligated to reach into his own pocket, a transformation would now have a chance to occur. He could come to the stark realization that camp expenses were in fact a good thing, indicative of a healthy child. He could come to bless this burdensome bill, as he scraped together what he could to help the other man save his child's life.

Gratitude, says the Chofetz Chaim, is yet another treasure buried by the policy of sending all solicitors to a central fund. In a further objection to this policy, he points out that when the needy arrive at the door, and their story is sincere, a person is being given an opportunity to refocus his attention upon the good in his own life. He sees in front of him the challenges Hashem has set before another person, and realizes his good fortune in being spared such difficulties. When one loses exposure to other people's difficulties, one loses a chance to build gratitude, a precious asset upon which life's happiness and contentment rests.

The value of seeing others' plight is illustrated in the story of Rabbi Akiva's life (*Nedarim* 50a). Rachel, the daughter of one of Israel's wealthiest families, wanted to marry Rabbi Akiva, who was then a completely uneducated man, far beneath her station. Rachel's father objected to the union and refused to provide the couple with any support. So that her husband could pursue Torah learning, Rachel willingly lived with him in abject poverty. The couple did not even own mattresses; they slept each night on a bed of straw. One morning, a distraught man came to their house. He begged for a bit of straw, because a baby had been born to his wife, and he had nothing on which to lay the child. The Talmud relates that the distraught man was the prophet Elijah, who had come to bring the couple encouragement in facing their hardships. They were able to take heart, because at least they had straw.

To derive this benefit from greeting and helping those who come to the door, a person must focus on the other man's problem. He must listen with concern and sincerity. If he listens, he will hear. He will hear that Hashem has been kind to him, that he has been spared many of life's miseries, and that he is far more fortunate than he may have thought he was, just a few minutes ago.

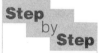

The next time someone comes to my door seeking help, I will pay attention to his story and seek within it some reasons to be grateful.

א טבת
1 TEVES / CYCLE 1

December 6, 2002
December 26, 2003
December 13, 2004
January 1, 2006
December 22, 2006
December 10, 2007
December 28, 2008
December 18, 2009

ב תמוז
2 TAMMUZ / CYCLE 2

July 2, 2003
June 21, 2004
July 9, 2005
June 28, 2006
June 18, 2007
July 5, 2008
June 24, 2009
June 14, 2010

✑ *The Orphan's Cry*

SEFER AHAVAS CHESED — **Part II Chapter XVII**
footnotes

*T*here are treatments that do more harm than the disease they treat. In the Chofetz Chaim's view, the treatment — centralizing all charity — can cause far more damage than the problems it purports to solve. One of the gravest side effects of this "treatment" is the high probability that enforcing the rule will cause pain to the poor. This is the final objection the Chofetz Chaim raises against the policy of limiting solicitors to a community fund.

Inevitably, towns that propagate rules are zealous in enforcing them. Equally as inevitable is the fact that the poor will take their chances going door to door, despite the edict. At that point, the town might summon enforcers to shoo the poor away or physically remove them from the street. The embarrassment of these needy people constitutes a terrible indictment in Heaven against the community.

A town quick to enforce a closed-door policy toward the poor is ignoring the lessons Sodom and Gomorrah were supposed to have taught humanity for all time. Even though the intention is not to shut out the poor altogether, the rule relies upon the principle of locking doors and turning people away. Furthermore, it can evolve into a situation in which the poor are shamed and abused. At the very least, it deprives the poor of the small light of hope that behind one of these doors, there is help.

Among the poor being "bounced" from the town's doorways are bound to be orphans and widows.

These are individuals whom Hashem Himself shelters and comforts, and whose wounds Hashem Himself avenges. The Chofetz Chaim cites Rambam's description of the great sensitivity with which orphans and widows must be treated: Harming or taking advantage of them in any way transgresses an entirely separate prohibition beyond those involved in hurting people in general.

Of those who harm the widow and the orphan, Hashem says (*Shemos* 22:23), "My wrath shall blaze," and warns of a punishment of death by sword. This applies to the wealthy and the poor widow and orphan equally, for both carry a pain in their hearts that makes them especially vulnerable. The Chofetz Chaim stresses that if such dire consequences can befall someone who cheats a wealthy widow, the results of harming a widow struggling for survival are certainly too devastating to risk.

At the core, the reluctance to deal with solicitors one at a time in a personal, direct way is a fear that the demand to give will become overwhelming. The simple rebuttal to that fear is the belief that giving is actually gaining, "because a mitzvah is a candle" (*Mishlei* 6:23). One candle can light a thousand others. Not only does its light remain undiminished; it creates a thousand new sources of light for the world.

When a widow or orphan comes to me for help, I will treat the request with special consideration.

DAY 92

ב טבת
2 TEVES / CYCLE 1

December 7, 2002
December 27, 2003
December 14, 2004
January 2, 2006
December 23, 2006
December 11, 2007
December 29, 2008
December 19, 2009

ג תמוז
3 TAMMUZ / CYCLE 2

July 3, 2003
June 22, 2004
July 10, 2005
June 29, 2006
June 19, 2007
July 6, 2008
June 25, 2009
June 15, 2010

❧ *Dangerous Assumptions*

SEFER AHAVAS CHESED — Part II Chapter XVII
footnotes

*N*o one wants to waste money, and charity given to someone who is not truly needy is, to most people's minds, money wasted. The solicitor who arrives at the door often arouses the scrutiny of the would-be donor, who wonders, "Is he for real? Is his story legitimate?" The homeowner scans the block to see if there is a late-model car standing by for this "pauper." He wonders why welfare or unemployment benefits have not answered the man's needs. There are those who assume all solicitations are a ruse, and flatly refuse to help anyone at the door.

Their indictment would not be made so quickly, nor applied so generally, were they to realize that those who are truly needy come to the door accompanied by an advocate. Hashem Himself endorses their plea, essentially saying: "This is My friend. Please take care of him." One who assumes the worst about every solicitor, therefore, will inevitably come to a time when he slams the door in Hashem's face.

The Sanzer *Rav* was so devoted to the needs of the poor that each day he would distribute every penny he had to give; he would not go to bed until the task was complete. He once rebuked a man who refused to give out of belief that some solicitors were not honest: "Do you know the difference between you and me?" he asked. "I'm willing to give to a thousand poor people, even if 999 are dishonest, just to help the one who really needs it. You are willing to turn down 999 valid requests just to protect yourself from the one who is taking advantage of you."

A poor man once came to the Sanzer *Rav* for help buying a *tallis* for his soon-to-be son-in-law. Just as the transaction was about to occur, the Rav's son interjected: "How can you tell such a lie? I saw you in the store yesterday buying a *tallis*!" The man ran off, humiliated. The *Rav* reprimanded his son, explaining that the man might have needed some other legitimate item for the wedding — a dress for his wife, perhaps — which he was embarrassed to request.

The son ran after the man to apologize, but the man would not forgive him. They went back to the *Rav*, and the man asked, "Should I forgive your son?"

"Only on one condition," said the *Rav*. "That he pay for the entire wedding."

Hashem does not overlook the pain of a poor person. One who causes such pain can know with certainty that at some time in the future, in this world or the Next World, his insensitivity will be repaid.

The plight of the poor is their lack of power. They were not placed in that position, however, so that the cruel and insensitive people of the world would have them to oppress. Rather, they were permanently woven into the fabric of the Jewish people so that a clear, vivid pattern of compassion and generosity would be able to emerge. Their lack of power is an illusion of this world, for in reality, Hashem cares for them like a doting Father, attuned to their every cry.

Step by **Step**

When solicitors come to my door, I will try to keep in mind the concept of Hashem standing by their side, observing my interactions with them.

2 Teves — In loving memory לע"נ יהודית בת שמואל לייב ויעקב בן דוב ז"ל

3 Tammuz — Harvey Wax לע"נ חיים בן מנחם ז"ל
Dedicated by the Wax family

ג טבת
3 TEVES / CYCLE 1

December 8, 2002
December 28, 2003
December 15, 2004
January 3, 2006
December 24, 2006
December 12, 2007
December 30, 2008
December 20, 2009

ד תמוז
4 TAMMUZ / CYCLE 2

July 4, 2003
June 23, 2004
July 11, 2005
June 30, 2006
June 20, 2007
July 7, 2008
June 26, 2009
June 16, 2010

✑ *Sage Advice*

SEFER AHAVAS CHESED — **Part II Chapter XVII**

A G-d-fearing Jew keeps the Next World in sight as he lives his life in this world. The word "G-d-fearing" means what it says; such a person does not make the smug assumption that the pleasures of Paradise surely await him. He recognizes that he has sins to account for, and strives to do all he can to outweigh them. Toward that goal, the Chofetz Chaim points out, chesed and charity are the ultimate tools. Throughout the Talmud, the Sages reiterate the principle that one who treats others with compassion will be treated with compassion in the Next World.

Taken together, these many citations paint a powerful picture of how chesed and *tzedakah* given in this world create a person's reality in the World to Come. The *Tanna D'Vei Eliyahu Zuta,* Chapter 1, quotes the prophet Elijah, who cites some of the proofs of this principle: "How great is charity! From the day that the world was created until now, the world stands on *tzedakah*. If you give an abundance of charity, you are praised. One who gives charity saves himself from the judgment of Gehinnom, as it is said, '(I shall) banish anger from your heart and remove evil from your flesh' (*Koheles* 11:10). And it is said, 'Praiseworthy is he who deals wisely with the needy. On the day of evil, Hashem will save him' (*Tehillim* 41:2)."

One might misinterpret this concept as a recommendation that a person "pay off" the Judge by giving charity. It is not the money a person gives that helps his case, however. It is the compassionate nature the person builds through his dedication to charity that saves him. That is because the Heavenly system of justice essentially allows each person to judge himself. A person who has lived a life of kindness and concern for others, therefore, is judged in the light of kindness and concern. A person who has been unforgiving of others' faults and uncaring about others' needs will be judged in the light of that harshness. As a person lives his life in this world, he writes the script for his appearance before the Heavenly Tribunal.

In view of these facts, one clearly is not going to gain in the long run by greeting requests for charity with a shrewd, cynical, "you-can't-fool-me" perspective. Even if a person calls the situation correctly 95 percent of the time, even if he is the only one on the block not taken in by a scam, his talent for sharp scrutiny will bring him nothing but grief when it turns upon him. His weaknesses will be unforgiven, his excuses rejected. Rather than seeing the good in his heart, the Heavenly Court will "see through" his story.

On the other side of the balance is the person to whom kindness, rather than shrewdness, is life's top priority. He may lose money occasionally to the unscrupulous imposter, but his gains will be eternal. The kindness he radiates in this world will shine back upon him, vastly magnified in its brightness, for all time.

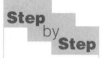

The next time I am suspicious of a poor person's claims, I will consider the value of giving him the benefit of the doubt.

ד טבת
4 TEVES / CYCLE 1

December 9, 2002
December 29, 2003
December 16, 2004
January 4, 2006
December 25, 2006
December 13, 2007
December 31, 2008
December 21, 2009

ה תמוז
5 TAMMUZ / CYCLE 2

July 5, 2003
June 24, 2004
July 12, 2005
July 1, 2006
June 21, 2007
July 8, 2008
June 27, 2009
June 17, 2010

❧ All Types

SEFER AHAVAS CHESED — Part II Chapter XVII

*O*ne person's strength is his intelligence. Another possesses outstanding self-discipline. Still another is blessed with a wide-open heart. It might seem that the third person — the one who exudes kindness and friendliness wherever he goes — would be the one to enjoy the greatest rewards from Heaven. He is, after all, the one most clearly predisposed toward chesed, and therefore the one most likely to earn the vast rewards this mitzvah brings.

The route to chesed's rewards, however, is open equally to all, and all paths of spiritual greatness lead to chesed. The Chofetz Chaim cites extensively *Tanna D'Vei Eliyahu Zuta*, who poses a question: "Why did our forefathers merit this world, the days of the Messiah and the World to Come?" The reward of the forefathers — the glory of their names — holds its value throughout all these phases of their souls' journey. *Eliyahu Zuta* explains that this is because each of them — Abraham, Isaac, Jacob, Moshe, Aaron, David and Solomon — is credited with greatness in his devotion to charity. It might seem that this reward should be reserved for Abraham, as he is the only one among them who is specifically characterized by chesed; it is his hallmark and legacy to the Jewish people. The other forefathers are known for other strengths, other contributions, yet all of them earned their greatest reward through chesed.

Throughout the Torah, the chesed of the forefathers emerges. Isaac's merit is expressed in a verse that relates that he "planted in the land a hundred-fold" (*Bereishis* 26:12). Planting refers to giving charity, for like planting, giving charity does not yield immediate results. When a person plants a seed, he expends tremendous effort only to look out upon a seemingly vacant plot of land. All his work is buried. The seed itself must partially decay before it germinates and sprouts. Like planting, giving charity is a supreme act of faith whose fruits may remain beneath the surface for months or years. Eventually, however, they emerge, lush and plentiful.

For each of the forefathers, *Eliyahu Zuta* cites references to a lifelong endeavor in charity and kindness. Finally, he relates that Hashem praises His own Heavenly Throne because it is built upon charity. "Righteousness and justice are His throne's foundation" (*Tehillim* 97:2).

"Charity saves from death" (*Mishlei* 11:4) because the person who applies his strength and resources to reviving the poor sets in motion the dynamics that bring him renewed life as well. For any Jew, no matter what his strengths or personality traits, charity is the key that unlocks the forces of life.

If I have an image of myself as someone not especially attuned to chesed, I will not allow that to limit my future involvement in charitable endeavors.

ה טבת
5 TEVES / CYCLE 1

December 10, 2002
December 30, 2003
December 17, 2004
January 5, 2006
December 26, 2006
December 14, 2007
January 1, 2009
December 22, 2009

ו תמוז
6 TAMMUZ / CYCLE 2

July 6, 2003
June 25, 2004
July 13, 2005
July 2, 2006
June 22, 2007
July 9, 2008
June 28, 2009
June 18, 2010

✃ *Adding Life*

SEFER AHAVAS CHESED — **Part II Chapter XVII**
footnotes

*M*ost people live on the giving side of the chesed equation. While everyone needs help sometimes, usually they can manage on their own. There comes a time in almost everyone's life, however, when the giver must, of necessity, become the taker. That time is in old age. For most people, advancing years means receding physical ability. Suddenly, the parent who always took care of everyone else needs a ride to the doctor, some help around the house, someone to pay the bills, do the shopping, cook the meals.

Without the help and concern of those around them, the Chofetz Chaim observes, elderly people lose years of their lives. One who cares for an older person, therefore, is adding days, or perhaps years, to his life, and his reward is commensurate with the greatness of this chesed. The Sages (*Sanhedrin* 37a) state that "if you sustain one Jewish life, it is as if you have sustained the entire world." That statement applies to every second of additional life one's intervention brings. A person who brings an elderly person practical help, or makes him feel needed and appreciated, is credited with sustaining the world, even if it is just for an hour.

The challenge in caring for the elderly is that the task requires great patience. While one might naturally accept limitations and irrational behavior in a small child, these factors in an adult are often more difficult to bear. A person must forearm himself with a calm, respectful, loving attitude, whether he is dealing with his own relative or a neighbor in need of help. The effort is well worthwhile, because in a very real sense, the beneficiary of all this tender, patient care is oneself.

This reality is reflected starkly in a famous story. A young child once observed his father throw his grandfather out of the house because the grandfather was unable to keep himself or his surroundings clean. Shaken as the child was, he could not deny the cruelty he had witnessed. Later, he met his grandfather wandering on the street. The grandfather asked the child to bring him a coat, so that at least he could avoid freezing in his homeless state. The child returned to his father and asked him it he could have a coat for the grandfather.

"Go up to the attic," said the father. "There's an old coat up there that he can have."

When the child returned from the attic, he was holding half of a coat. "What happened to the coat?" the father asked. "Why has it been cut?"

"I did it for you," said the child, "so that when you grow old, you can have the other half."

In Yiddish, there is a saying: "What you think you are doing for someone else, you are really doing for yourself." For most acts of chesed, the reward is bestowed by Heaven, but in the case of caring for the elderly, a person actually prepares the reward for himself. He teaches his children — who may one day care for him — giving, at its genuine, selfless best.

If there is an elderly person in my life, I will find a way to give him or her help, time or attention on a regular basis.

5 Teves — Miriam Schlisselfeld לע"נ מרים בת ר' אליעזר ע"ה
Dedicated by the Schlisselfeld family

6 Tammuz — לע"נ בינה מחלה בת יהודה ברוך ע"ה
Dedicated by the Bina Machla Tzedakah Fund

Loving Kindness ☐ 215

ו טבת
6 TEVES / CYCLE 1

December 11, 2002
December 31, 2003
December 18, 2004
January 6, 2006
December 27, 2006
December 15, 2007
January 2, 2009
December 23, 2009

ז תמוז
7 TAMMUZ / CYCLE 2

July 7, 2003
June 26, 2004
July 14, 2005
July 3, 2006
June 23, 2007
July 10, 2008
June 29, 2009
June 19, 2010

✌ *Fortunate*

SEFER AHAVAS CHESED — **Part II Chapter XVII**

The promise of long life — the reward to those who give charity — can be seen as a gift of indeterminate value. A long life is a blessing, after all, only if it is lived well. The Sages therefore phrase this blessing in a way that promises not only a long life, but a good life: "Great is charity, for it extends the days and years of man" (*Tanna D'Vei Eliyahu Zuta* Chapter 1). The expression, long days and years — seen often in the Talmud — seems redundant. If one has length of years, does that not automatically include the days?

Commentators explain that the word "days" refers to the quality of the individual days that comprise the long years. A blessing for length of days means that each day will be satisfying. Years refer to a quantity of time, but days refer to the quality of that time and both are the reward for giving charity.

One of the few mitzvos for which the Torah promises long life is that of *"shilu'ach hakan,"* which is the mitzvah of sending away the mother bird before taking her young or her eggs. Fulfilling this commandment requires nothing more than a wave of the hand to shoo the mother bird away. The midrashic text, *Eliyahu Zuta*, comments that if the reward for this simple mitzvah is so great, how much greater must be the reward for giving charity, which requires the difficult sacrifice of parting with one's possessions.

The text continues: Those who give charity and study Torah are the only two categories of people about whom *Tehillim* (106:3) says, "How fortunate are they." The fortune they enjoy is a portion in the World to Come. One may ask why the Sages reveal the reward for these two mitzvos when it would become self-evident the instant one passes into the Next World. The answer is that it tells people who, because of some sin, are perhaps not deserving of a place in the World to Come, that there is a way to override this liability. The key to a long and joyful life in this world is also the key to the eternal joy of the World to Come.

Peace, which is called the vessel of all other blessings, is yet another reward for charity and Torah study. In regard to learning, the Torah (*Vayikra* 26:6) says: "I will provide peace in the land, and you will lie down with none to frighten you; I will cause wild beasts to withdraw from the land, and a sword will not cross your land." A similar promise is extended to those who give charity (*Yeshayah* 32:17-18), "The product of charity shall be peace, and the effect of charity, quiet and security forever. My people will live in a peaceful domain and in secure dwellings and in tranquil resting places." The experience of living in the Diaspora has taught every generation that, even in moments of relative quiet, the swords are being sharpened. Hashem has given His people a path that leads them unharmed past all the dangers, and it is paved with Torah learning, charity and kindness.

Step by **Step**

Today, when I give charity or learn, I will keep in mind the life-sustaining and life-enhancing results of these mitzvos.

לע"נ משה בן יוחנן קינרייך ז"ל — **6 Teves**
נלב"ע י"ח כסלו תשנ"ז

לזכות ישעיה בן שמסי ופלור בת אכדס — **7 Tammuz**
להפקד בזרע של קיימא

ז טבת
7 TEVES / CYCLE 1

December 12, 2002
January 1, 2004
December 19, 2004
January 7, 2006
December 28, 2006
December 16, 2007
January 3, 2009
December 24, 2009

ח תמוז
8 TAMMUZ / CYCLE 3

July 8, 2003
June 27, 2004
July 15, 2005
July 4, 2006
June 24, 2007
July 11, 2008
June 30, 2009
June 20, 2010

❧ *Feeling Right*

SEFER AHAVAS CHESED — Part II
Chapter XVII/XVII footnotes

*A*person who understands the benefits of giving is happy to give, and a person who is happy to give experiences even more of the benefits of giving. In many places within the Talmud, the Sages teach that one should give gladly, and that charity will always come back to the giver in some form. The Chofetz Chaim relates one story that illustrates the point in a most literal way.

The story (*Avos D' Rabbi Nassan* Chapter 3 Mishnah 9) is of a man who gave amply to charity throughout his life. That man was traveling on a ship, which was caught in a storm and plunged to the bottom of the sea. Rabbi Akiva, who witnessed the event, was sure that the man, along with everyone else on board, had perished. So sure was he of his observation that he agreed to testify before a rabbinical court so that the man's widow would be able to remarry. Just as he was getting ready to give his testimony, the man appeared.

"Who brought you up from the ocean?" asked Rabbi Akiva.

"The charity I gave brought me up," the man replied. He described the dispute he heard among the waves, arguing over which one would have the privilege of carrying the man to safety. Each wanted the privilege of saving the man who devoted his life to charity.

To this, Rabbi Akiva replied, "Blessed is Hashem, the G-d of Israel, Who chose for Himself the words of the Torah and the words of our Sages that live to eternity. Does not the verse say, 'Throw your bread on the face of the water, for in the course of time you shall find it,' and 'tzedakah saves a person from death'?"

These are the rewards of giving. Giving with joy brings further benefits. "You shall surely give him, and let your heart not feel bad when you give him, for in return for this matter, Hashem, your G-d, will bless you in all your deeds and in your every undertaking" (*Devarim* 15: 10).

And, therefore, a person should always be encouraged to continue to pursue this mitzvah, and it will bring blessing to his house. The words "give him" are expressed using two forms of the same word. This seeming redundancy actually conveys that a person's joy in giving should not diminish when someone needs his help a second, third, or even hundredth time.

A person may gladly offer help when a friend first loses his job, but a year later, when the friend has lost another job, and still cannot pay his bills, the person may begin to feel burdened. The Chofetz Chaim advises that the way to avoid feelings of resentment is to develop the understanding that the money is Hashem's, and the wealthy person has been blessed with the privilege of holding it in trust. The choice is set before the person; he can withhold the money, give it grudgingly, or give it happily, knowing that he is fulfilling his obligation to help the poor, and at the same time, bringing tremendous blessing upon his own household.

Step by **Step**

I will work on giving to others more enthusiastically.

לע"נ הרב דוד נח בן הרב יהודא זצ"ל — **7 Teves**
Dedicated by Yitzchok and Rivka Mashitz

8 Tammuz — Dedicated to the Chofetz Chaim Heritage Foundation
for all of their work on behalf of כלל ישראל

ח טבת
8 TEVES / CYCLE 1

December 13, 2002
January 2, 2004
December 20, 2004
January 8, 2006
December 29, 2006
December 17, 2007
January 4, 2009
December 25, 2009

ט תמוז
9 TAMMUZ / CYCLE 2

July 9, 2003
June 28, 2004
July 16, 2005
July 5, 2006
June 25, 2007
July 12, 2008
July 1, 2009
June 21, 2010

🐦 *His Best Hat*

SEFER AHAVAS CHESED — Part II Chapter XVII
footnotes

*W*hat a person holds in his possession, he holds for a time. What he gives away, he holds forever. With that in mind, he can release his possessions with joy, knowing that they will find him again, and remain with him forever, in the Next World. Whether he gives with joy or not, he is rewarded for his giving, the Chofetz Chaim reiterates, but if by performing the mitzvah with joy one can bring blessing into one's home, there is obviously much to be gained in developing a joyful perspective.

There are those individuals whose hearts are so deeply imbued with an understanding of the rewards charity brings that they are able to give without any sense of loss whatsoever. The Kapishnitzer Rebbe was one such individual. He spent his life gathering funds from those who could give, and searching every corner of the community to find those who needed the funds. He would not rest until every donated penny in his possession had found the place where it was needed.

In America, after World War II, a refugee came to see the Rebbe. The man was despondent over his tremendous losses. He had been a well-to-do man in Europe, and now he had nothing with which to start a family and establish a life. He was ashamed of his ragged appearance, especially the hand-me-down hat that sat upon his head like a symbol of all his travail. The Rebbe's heart went out to the man, whose own reflection in the mirror caused him such pain. The

Rebbe went to his closet and selected his finest wedding hat, and turned it over to the man. Later, his family questioned him: Why didn't he give away his weekday hat or his regular Shabbos hat?

"Which hat do you think I will be wearing in the World to Come?" he responded. "Of course it will be the hat I gave away. Aren't I entitled to sit in my finest hat in the World to Come? I gave away the hat I want to have forever."

With such a perspective, joy is a natural part of giving. There can be no reluctance to give when one can clearly imagine all that he has given surrounding his *neshamah*, glorifying it and testifying on its behalf in the World to Come. A person who trains himself to look at charity through this lens trains himself to enjoy giving, and he opens the doors of his household to all the blessings Heaven holds in store for him.

Step by Step

The next time I give away money or an item, I will keep in mind that it is being held for me on "layaway" in the World to Come.

ט טבת
9 TEVES / CYCLE 1

December 14, 2002
January 3, 2004
December 21, 2004
January 9, 2006
December 30, 2006
December 18, 2007
January 5, 2009
December 26, 2009

י תמוז
10 TAMMUZ / CYCLE 2

July 10, 2003
June 29, 2004
July 17, 2005
July 6, 2006
June 26, 2007
July 13, 2008
July 2, 2009
June 22, 2010

⚞ *Formula for Success*

SEFER AHAVAS CHESED — **Part II Chapter XVIII**

*I*f one loans all his money, it is not available to give someone in need of charity. By the same token, if one gives it all away, one has nothing to offer to the person in need of a loan. Tithing — giving one tenth of one's money to charity — is the formula the Torah provides for apportioning money for charity. Where, then, does one find the money with which to provide loans?

The Chofetz Chaim offers a halachic ruling that enables one to take loan money out of the money tithed for charity. His reasoning, which is discussed fully in a future chapter, is that money set aside so that it is available for use by the poor is in fact considered charity, even though one gives it with the expectation that it will be returned. The key is to keep the money in a separate fund, and restore the repaid money to that fund for further use by those in need.

To assure that tithed money is properly apportioned between charity and loans, the Chofetz Chaim offers a formula: One tenth of a person's income must be set aside for charity — that is simple tithing. Out of that amount, two-thirds should be given away to the needy. The other third should be set aside in a fund that is made available for those in need of a loan. The fact that it is being loaned rather than granted outright does not remove it from the category of charity, the Chofetz Chaim rules.

By allowing a certain portion of tithed money to be dedicated to loans, the Chofetz Chaim works along the grain of the human psyche, coaxing people to loosen their hold on their possessions. He understands that, even with the Torah's promise that tithing brings wealth, giving away one's money is an act of great faith. A person finds his way to that faith more easily if he is able to see that some of the money comes back to him. Even though he does not have use of it — it must remain in a separate, dedicated chesed fund — he has it in his possession. Little by little, watching the good that the chesed does for others and for oneself, one's faith in Hashem's promise is strengthened and one's grasp is loosened. Giving becomes not a difficulty, but a delight.

Today I will ascertain whether I have a methodical means for apportioning money specifically for chesed.

י טבת
10 TEVES / CYCLE 1

December 15, 2002
January 4, 2004
December 22, 2004
January 10, 2006
December 31, 2006
December 19, 2007
January 6, 2009
December 27, 2009

יא תמוז
II TAMMUZ / CYCLE 2

July 11, 2003
June 30, 2004
July 18, 2005
July 7, 2006
June 27, 2007
July 14, 2008
July 3, 2009
June 23, 2010

✎ Helping Yourself

SEFER AHAVAS CHESED — Part II Chapter XVIII

A Jew takes Hashem's promises on faith. There is one promise, however, that a person is allowed to put to the test. In only one instance is he allowed to say, "Hashem, I will do as You have commanded if You will deliver my promised reward." That instance is in the mitzvah of *"ma'aser,"* or tithing.

The promised reward is found in the words of the commandment itself — *"asser t'asser"* — which is simply translated as "tithe, you should tithe." The Sages explain the double wording with an alternative translation of the word *"asser."* The word is closely related to *"asher,"* which means to become wealthy. "Tithe so that you will become wealthy," the Sages expound.

The prophet Malachi (3:10) declares in Hashem's name, "Bring all of your tithes and test Me with this." Hashem promises here that if the Jewish people adhere to the commandment to tithe, they can expect Him to rain blessing down upon them. The verse speaks directly about the tithing of grain, but the Chofetz Chaim states that it applies equally to one's earnings.

The mechanism for tithing money is often misunderstood, the Chofetz Chaim says. The initial tithe must be taken from the principal — the lump sum that one receives through inheritance or other means. If the remainder of the principal is invested and continues to earn income, then 10 percent of the profits must be set aside as well. There are many who are careful to tithe their profits, but have never tithed the original principal.

Some omit this step out of ignorance of the requirement, but the *yetzer hara* plays a large role in preventing others, who know of the practice, from adhering to it. Quite simply, many people find it difficult to part with such a large sum, especially when they are counting upon it to produce their future income.

The Chofetz Chaim therefore offers advice to help people find a comfortable route toward fulfilling the mitzvah. Rather than giving the money away outright, he recommends setting it aside as a loan fund available to those in need. A person can even borrow from it himself as long as the money is repaid and he is willing to loan others amounts equal to what he has borrowed.

In the Chofetz Chaim's view, even though the person retains access to the money, it still qualifies as *tzedakah*. The Torah's goal is to build an understanding that a certain percentage of one's assets must be dedicated to the welfare of others, and setting aside a loan fund accomplishes this goal.

The Chofetz Chaim acknowledges that some halachic opinions hold that tithed money must be given away to be classified as charity. He therefore suggests a strategy that satisfies those opinions while still allowing people time to build up to the challenge of parting with their one tenth. That is, to set the money aside as a loan, but to do so with the intention that it will eventually be given to a worthy recipient.

However one satisfies the obligation to tithe, he is assured that it will be a source of real, tangible blessing to him. When a person prunes his wealth for the sake of giving charity, he can rely upon Hashem's promise that it will grow back more lush and healthier than ever.

Today I will review my system of tithing to make sure that it meets the requirements of the halachah.

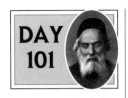
יא טבת
11 TEVES / CYCLE 1

December 16, 2002
January 5, 2004
December 23, 2004
January 11, 2006
January 1, 2007
December 20, 2007
January 7, 2009
December 28, 2009

יב תמוז
12 TAMMUZ / CYCLE 2

July 12, 2003
July 1, 2004
July 19, 2005
July 8, 2006
June 28, 2007
July 15, 2008
July 4, 2009
June 24, 2010

❧ *Making it Official*

SEFER AHAVAS CHESED — Part II Chapter XVIII

*E*very Friday afternoon, four poor Jews in one battered car go from neighborhood to neighborhood collecting money to aid in their individual plights. At most of the homes they visit, the donors rummage through their pockets and give the four whatever loose bills they happen to find. In some of those homes, the amount — whether it is a few quarters or a few dollars — is written down in a log. In other homes, the donor does not bother to keep track of such insignificant amounts.

One might consider the second attitude to be the more generous of the two. The Chofetz Chaim, however, urges people to write down every penny. Tithing must be done in a methodical, businesslike way if it is to be done correctly and consistently. Starting out, one should first declare that his commitment to tithe a certain amount is being undertaken *"bli neder,"* without a vow. In this way, there are no halachic complications if a person finds himself unable to keep his pledge, for a vow is a matter of great gravity in Jewish law. The second step is to start a log in which one records all his losses and gains. This is vital in calculating the amount of money that must be tithed. The person should set a time period — quarterly, semiannually, yearly — for assessing and paying his tithe. Through these steps, tithing becomes a defined mitzvah with a standard against which one can measure one's performance.

Besides its practical implications, keeping track of small donations plays an important psychological role as well. First of all, when a person writes down each small donation, he soon notices how quickly the amount grows. Knowing that this sum will be subtracted from his total obligation is ample encouragement for him to keep giving.

The Chofetz Chaim also observes that failing to keep a record of small amounts could eventually cause a person to give less than his obligatory amount. For instance, a person might find that the amount he has tithed is $400 less than he should have set aside. If he has been giving out small bills and change regularly without keeping any record, he is likely to assume that these amounts, over the course of time, have added up to the missing $400. Perhaps they have, but perhaps they only amounted to $300, or even $350. He may, because of his presumably generous spirit, find himself $50 shy of fulfilling the mitzvah. When a person is accurate for his own benefit — so as not to lose credit for money he has given away — his accuracy also benefits the people in need of those few stray dollars.

Today I will start a log in which I will record small cash donations.

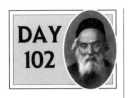
יב טבת
12 TEVES / CYCLE 1

December 17, 2002
January 6, 2004
December 24, 2004
January 12, 2006
January 2, 2007
December 21, 2007
January 8, 2009
December 29, 2009

יג תמוז
13 TAMMUZ / CYCLE 2

July 13, 2003
July 2, 2004
July 20, 2005
July 9, 2006
June 29, 2007
July 16, 2008
July 5, 2009
June 25, 2010

❧ *Taking Care of Business*

SEFER AHAVAS CHESED — Part II Chapter XVIII

*C*harity and business may seem to be polar opposites on the spectrum of dealings with money. One is about giving money away, the other about making it. One is about other people, the other is about oneself. Nevertheless, both operate most successfully on the same principles: a person must set realistic goals, commit to them, and keep a careful account of where he stands in relation to those goals.

The Chofetz Chaim recommends that even if there is no appropriate recipient for one's tithe money, one should separate it nonetheless and keep it available for a future opportunity. A person may even borrow from that money, as was mentioned on Day 100, as long as the money is available when a needy person requests it.

Ideally, a person should keep track of all his income and all his charitable contributions so that he will be sure he is meeting his obligations. For some people, however, record-keeping is difficult, either because of the nature of their business or the nature of their personality. If a person is unable to arrive at a definitive figure for his income and outlay, he should pledge his tithe based on an estimate and state at the outset that this is the case. As a last resort, one can work backwards, estimating one's income, subtracting what one has spent on family and household expenses, and extrapolating from there how much has gone to charity.

Just as careful record-keeping will reveal when a person has not fulfilled his obligation to tithe, it may also reveal that he has overpaid his due. For instance, a person might tithe based on expected income, only to find that some of it does not materialize. In that case, the Chofetz Chaim says, there is a question. The person may be able to redeem the extra amount from the next year's tithe; however, some opinions forbid this retroactive move. The best way to handle the situation is to preempt it by stating at the outset that one reserves the right to recoup any overpayment.

Another, more spiritually satisfying way of dealing with overpayment was demonstrated by Rabbi Yaakov Yosef Herman, a bastion of the American Torah world who lived most of his life on the Lower East Side of New York and later moved to Jerusalem. In his children's account of his life, they relate that his careful record-keeping of his *tzedakah* sometimes revealed that he had overpaid. "Hashem owes me $300," he would declare, and in due time, whatever amount he was owed would materialize. Because Hashem promises to repay and enrich those who give, Rabbi Herman knew he had not lost a penny.

Often, keeping track of *tzedakah* is simply a matter of putting in place a workable system. A person can make a special mark in his checkbook next to checks that count against his tithing obligation. He can record such checks in a separate section of his checkbook. The Chofetz Chaim urges every person to be systematic, no matter what system he chooses.

A person who treats the obligation with the seriousness of a business enjoys the rewards of a successful business — success, prosperity and the satisfaction that comes with knowing he is able to help others.

Step by **Step**

Today I will create a record-keeping system to assure that I fulfill my tzedakah obligations.

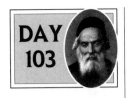
יג טבת
13 TEVES / CYCLE 1

December 18, 2002
January 7, 2004
December 25, 2004
January 13, 2006
January 3, 2007
December 22, 2007
January 9, 2009
December 30, 2009

יד תמוז
14 TAMMUZ / CYCLE 2

July 14, 2003
July 3, 2004
July 21, 2005
July 10, 2006
June 30, 2007
July 17, 2008
July 6, 2009
June 26, 2010

✑ *Priorities*

SEFER AHAVAS CHESED — **Part II**
Chapter XIX/XIX footnotes

A good businessman knows his target market. He does not just blindly assemble random merchandise in hopes that some of it will sell to someone. He aims precisely at the needs he is best suited to fill. In the business of *tzedakah*, the Torah defines the target market, assuring that each dollar given will go where it can do the most good. It sets priorities that allow an individual to use his *tzedakah* money wisely, helping those Hashem has positioned him to help.

The Chofetz Chaim reiterates at this point that there is no need that takes precedence over one's own family members. Even those one is obligated to support, such as an older child, can be given tithe money if he is in need. A person may also support his parents, if they are needy, with tithe money. If a person has other means through which to support his parents, however, he is obligated to do so. One may not give his tithe money to his parents when he has other assets to draw upon, and then count himself as having fulfilled his obligation to tithe. Beyond parents and children, one should look to his other family members — brothers and sisters, aunts and uncles, nieces, nephews and cousins. If they are in need, then they are the correct "target market" for the person's *tzedakah* enterprise.

When the family is not in need of *tzedakah*, the field of potential recipients appears to be wide open. The Chofetz Chaim helps narrow the choice by emphasizing the primacy of those sacrificing their material comfort to dedicate their time to learning Torah. The original purpose of tithing, in fact, reflects this priority. The prophet Malachi (3:10) says, "Bring your grain to the storage house and let it be food in My House [i.e., let the Levites and *Kohanim* have their food in order to serve Me], and test Me with this." This is the paradigm for the act of tithing in the present day. Those whose time is devoted to serving Hashem sincerely are the rightful recipients of one's tithe. Hashem promises abundance to those who support them.

Nonetheless, the poor still take precedence, even over a Torah scholar who is living very modestly but is not truly impoverished. If a person must choose which of these two individuals to help, he must choose the poor person. Providing a higher degree of material comfort to a struggling Torah scholar is not a priority over helping a person put food on the table, clothe his family or marry off his children.

Those who trim from their own assets to attend to the needs of others have Hashem's promise that their assets will grow back healthier and stronger, like a tree that is pruned. This fact indicates that one who tithes is protected from a reversal of fortunes, a situation which the Talmud (*Succah* 29b) says can occur overnight. The Chofetz Chaim advises a person to recount to himself the losses he could have sustained, but did not. If he has been careful to tithe and distribute the money properly, he can be sure that this merit protected him from the bad investment, the dishonest partner or any other factor that would have diminished his wealth. "Test Me with this," Hashem says. Giving is the one business venture in which success is Divinely guaranteed.

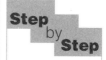

Today I will ascertain whether my tithe money is being properly distributed.

13 Teves — Joshua Fishman לע"נ יהושע בן יהודה ז"ל
Dedicated in loving memory by his children and grandchildren

14 Tammuz — May today's learning be a זכות for our משפחה.
Dedicated by Shimeon and Leah Weiner and family, Cleveland Heights, OH

יד טבת
14 TEVES / CYCLE I

December 19, 2002
January 8, 2004
December 26, 2004
January 14, 2006
January 4, 2007
December 23, 2007
January 10, 2009
December 31, 2009

טו תמוז
15 TAMMUZ / CYCLE 2

July 15, 2003
July 4, 2004
July 22, 2005
July 11, 2006
July 1, 2007
July 18, 2008
July 7, 2009
June 27, 2010

❧ *Ways to Give*

SEFER AHAVAS CHESED — **Part II Chapter XIX**

*A*nyone who has ever encountered a pile of charity solicitations in his mailbox knows that the world is a needy place. The Chofetz Chaim explains that some of these needs qualify for tithe money, and some do not. The clearest claim on tithe money comes from the poor, whether they are struggling Torah scholars or simply people who, for some reason, are unable to support themselves and their families. From that point, one enters into a vast gray area in which giving money may well fulfill a mitzvah, but not the mitzvah of tithing.

For instance, marrying off a young couple is a well-accepted facet of the mitzvah of chesed. When one considers this mitzvah as a destination for tithe money, however, questions arise. One is not giving money to put bread on a poor man's table. He is giving money to hire a band, pay a caterer, buy some flowers, liquor, perhaps a bridal gown. There are certainly happy, successful couples who have started life with a simple ceremony and a meal with close friends and family; a catered affair is obviously not a life-and-death necessity. The Chofetz Chaim, however, approves of using tithe money for this purpose. He reasons that the couple may endure embarrassment or grief if they cannot have a wedding that falls within the realm of "normal" for their community — although in the current age of excess, the word "normal" must be strictly defined. Helping a couple start out their life together in joy and optimism is a proper use for tithe money.

The same ruling holds for making a *bris* for another person's child. If the child's family would be unable to sponsor a basic *bris* on their own, one can use tithe money to cover the expenses.

In a more controversial ruling, the Chofetz Chaim states that one can use tithe money to write or purchase *sefarim* (holy books). There are a few conditions for this ruling, however. First of all, the books must be available for loan to others. Secondly, one must write on the book that it was purchased with tithe money. This ensures that when the owner passes away, the books will not be considered part of his estate. Instead, they would be donated to a synagogue or yeshivah where they would be available to the general public. Under these conditions the expenditure of tithe money on books becomes possible, for the money is actually going to benefit those who may not be able to purchase such books for themselves.

These opinions are by no means unanimously supported, the Chofetz Chaim himself points out. The Maharil and the Rema both maintain that tithe money is exclusively designated for alms for the poor. In the Chofetz Chaim's view, however, charity can take many forms. If someone cannot afford to make a wedding or *bris*, or purchase a *sefer*, one is greatly easing his financial burden by assuming these expenses. If the money helps someone in need, it is doing what Hashem wants it to do.

If I know someone needy who is encountering the expenses of a bris, wedding or other major event, I will offer some of my tithe money to alleviate the financial strain.

14 Teves — Rabbi Yakov D. Flaks לע"נ הרב יעקב דוד בן ר' אהרן פלקס ז"ל
Dedicated by wife, Dina, son, Mayer Mattis and grandson, Yonatan Flaks

15 Tammuz — May today's learning be a z'chus for our entire family.
Dedicated by Azriel Chaim and Batsheva Garfein

DAY 105

טו טבת
15 TEVES / CYCLE 1

December 20, 2002
January 9, 2004
December 27, 2004
January 15, 2006
January 5, 2007
December 24, 2007
January 11, 2009
January 1, 2010

טז תמוז
16 TAMMUZ / CYCLE 2

July 16, 2003
July 5, 2004
July 23, 2005
July 12, 2006
July 2, 2007
July 19, 2008
July 8, 2009
June 28, 2010

➤ Ask

SEFER AHAVAS CHESED — Part II Chapter XIX

*W*hen one thinks of the many occasions for giving that arise in Jewish life, one begins to comprehend the need for rabbinical guidance in meeting the obligation of tithing. "Purchasing" an *aliyah* in the synagogue, buying a raffle ticket from one's children's yeshivah, buying a raffle ticket from someone else's child's yeshivah, attending a charity dinner, participating in a Chinese auction, winning a trip for two to Israel from a Chinese auction—each of these instances provokes questions regarding the use of tithe money. For that reason one must have someone learned to whom one can turn for guidance.

The considerations are varied. For instance, in the case of someone who pays $150 for an *aliyah* in the synagogue — the honor of being called up to the Torah to recite a blessing — the money may count as tithe money only if the synagogue normally gives its earnings from *aliyos* to the poor. If it is earmarked for the synagogue's electric bill, the $150 may not qualify as tithe money.

A burning question for many Jewish families is whether the thousands spent each year on yeshivah tuitions may be counted as tithe money. There are many different perspectives on this question, and one cannot be sure of an answer without consulting a rabbi who knows his family's particular situation. Overall, however, the Chofetz Chaim says tuition money does not count against one's tithing obligation. His reason is that a person is obligated to teach his sons, and sending them to yeshivah is a fulfillment of that obligation, not a charitable endeavor. In the same way as one would not use tithe money to purchase an *esrog*, one cannot use tithe money to pay a yeshivah tuition. This is true, too, of tuition to a girl's school, even though the Torah does not specifically command a father to educate his daughter. There is still a personal obligation to raise one's children to a life of Torah and mitzvos, and in today's world, that is not possible without a solid Jewish education.

Despite the expense of educating children in the path of Torah, the Chofetz Chaim says that the expenditure does not erode one's wealth. This expense, like the money spent on Shabbos and Yom Tov expenses, is outside the "budget" one is allotted on Rosh Hashanah.

In all these instances and hundreds more, a person needs guidance to be sure he is giving what and where he should. Tithing may seem complicated, but in reality, it is only a lack of guidance that makes it so. The Kotzker Rebbe was once visited by a Chassid who complained of many problems. "Do you pray?" the Rebbe asked. The Chassid confessed, "I just can't pray." To that, the Rebbe replied, "That's your only real problem." In the same way, one can have many problems making tithing manageable and meaningful, but they all have one solution — a rabbi's listening ear.

Step by **Step**

When I am unsure of whether a certain contribution can come from tithed money, I will ask a rabbi.

15 Teves — Reb Meir Rosenbaum ז"ל לע"נ ר' מאיר בן ר' יעקב יהודה ז"ל
Dedicated by his children: Nockenofsky, Greenwald, Gluck, Rosenbaum and Katz families

16 Tammuz — R' Shmuli Teigman ז"ל לע"נ שמואל דן בן יוסף חיים ז"ל
Dedicated by Blake and Esther Reiser and family

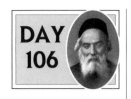

DAY 106

טז טבת
16 TEVES / CYCLE 1

December 21, 2002
January 10, 2004
December 28, 2004
January 16, 2006
January 6, 2007
December 25, 2007
January 12, 2009
January 2, 2010

יז תמוז
17 TAMMUZ / CYCLE 2

July 17, 2003
July 6, 2004
July 24, 2005
July 13, 2006
July 3, 2007
July 20, 2008
July 9, 2009
June 29, 2010

❧ *More and Less*

SEFER AHAVAS CHESED — **Part II Chapter XIX**

*I*f charity begins at home, a person might come to believe that his own financial needs ought to be considered an appropriate use of tithe money. The Chofetz Chaim discusses in particular someone who is in debt and unable to make a timely repayment. The obligation to repay a debt is one the Torah takes very seriously. *Tehillim* calls a person who refuses to pay debt, even though he is able, a *"rasha,"* an evil person.

In that light, it might seem that a person would be able to be "charitable" toward himself and pay his debt out of tithe money. However, the Chofetz Chaim rules against this use of tithe money. He maintains that paying a debt is a separate, personal obligation, and it takes precedence over giving tithe money. A person cannot give money to charity if it is owed to someone else. If there is no money left after paying the debt, the person can write down the amount he should have tithed, with intention of paying when he can. He cannot, however, count the money he used to pay the debt as tithe money.

On the other side of the spectrum is someone who is able to put more than 10 percent of his income into charity. The Torah puts forth the idea of tithing 20 percent through the words of Yaakov, who says: "And all that You give me, tithe, I will tithe." This "double language," using the word for tithe twice, is widely interpreted to mean tithing twice — giving 20 percent rather than 10 percent. The Chofetz Chaim says this is a commendable practice for those who can afford it. In practice, double tithing is done in the same manner as regular tithing; one sets aside the first 20 percent of his capital, and then 20 percent of all subsequent income.

The Chofetz Chaim recommends that the amount be treated not as a lump sum, but as two funds of 10 percent each. One half should be given to support those who are sacrificing their material comfort in order to devote their time to Torah learning. As was mentioned on Day 103, this use of tithe money reflects its original intent of supporting the *Kohanim* and Levites. The other 10 percent should be contributed to the general support and encouragement of mitzvos.

Because tithing — giving one tenth of one's income — carries with it specific blessings, one should be careful to calculate a tenth, whether once or twice. If one wishes to give more than a tenth but less than 20 percent, one should first give the tenth and then add to it to the extent that he can. He may ultimately be giving 12 percent or 16 percent, but he should be sure to first calculate his tenth. By making that calculation, he attaches himself to the blessings reserved for those who keep Hashem's trust, sharing the prescribed portion of the wealth Hashem has given them with those of His children in need of support.

Step by **Step**

Today I will make sure that, regardless of how much I give to charity, I am mindful of how much of it constitutes one tenth of my income.

יז טבת
17 TEVES / CYCLE 1

December 22, 2002
January 11, 2004
December 29, 2004
January 17, 2006
January 7, 2007
December 26, 2007
January 13, 2009
January 3, 2010

יח תמוז
18 TAMMUZ / CYCLE 2

July 18, 2003
July 7, 2004
July 25, 2005
July 14, 2006
July 4, 2007
July 21, 2008
July 10, 2009
June 30, 2010

❧ *Above and Beyond*

SEFER AHAVAS CHESED — Part II Chapter XX

*W*hile the Sages exhort the Jewish people to limit their charitable contributions to no more than 20 percent of their income, there are countless tales of righteous men who gave others all they had. The Sanzer *Rav* was one such man. He could not fall asleep at night if there was any money under his roof that had not been distributed. His son, a great scholar and leader in his own right, would sometimes debate with his father the validity of this practice, in light of the Sages' ruling. The Sanzer *Rav* told his son that he was forced to give all he had in order to counteract the tremendous load of sin on his shoulders. What sins did this holy man bear? They were the sins of the Jewish people; he lived his life as a representative of his people, and made their spiritual well-being his mission. He was therefore able to do what others, answering only for themselves, would not be permitted to do.

The average person is not permitted to give away more than 20 percent for very practical reasons. First of all, if such excessive giving were permitted, there would be those who compromise their financial health to the degree that ultimately, they would need help themselves. Secondly, the concept of giving charity would be transformed from one that most people can manage into one of great self-sacrifice, from which many might completely turn away. For the average individual, separating and donating 10 percent is enough of a challenge. Only when there is a crying need in the community is one actually obligated to give more — up to 20 percent. A person who goes beyond that is in spiritual danger. He is like someone wobbling on the top rung of a ladder he has never set firmly on the ground.

There is one time of life in which, according to some rabbinical opinions, a person may give away as much as he wishes. This is when death is imminent. The Chofetz Chaim is among those who put no limit upon how much a dying person can give away. There are others who limit the amount to a third or a half of the person's possessions, so that there will be an inheritance left for the heirs. The final decision on this matter must be made with the help of a rabbi familiar with a person's family situation. If, for instance, one's children are needy, giving the bulk of one's money away may not be permitted.

The Chofetz Chaim's perspective that a dying person cannot give too much away reflects a righteous person's clear focus on eternity. This was the vision of Mar Ukva, the great Talmudic Sage who, together with his wife, devoted his entire life to charity (see Day 88). In his final days in this world, he asked to see the records he kept of the charity he had given. He saw that he had accumulated 7,000 golden dinarim to leave to charity. "This is not enough," he said, and he gave more, for he knew that he needed as much as possible to sustain him on the journey from this world to the World of Truth.

Today I will make sure that my charitable contributions fall within the halachic guidelines of 10 to 20 percent.

יח טבת
18 TEVES / CYCLE 1

December 23, 2002
January 12, 2004
December 30, 2004
January 18, 2006
January 8, 2007
December 27, 2007
January 14, 2009
January 4, 2010

יט תמוז
19 TAMMUZ / CYCLE 2

July 19, 2003
July 8, 2004
July 26, 2005
July 15, 2006
July 5, 2007
July 22, 2008
July 11, 2009
July 1, 2010

➳ *Gift of a Lifetime*

SEFER AHAVAS CHESED — Part II
Chapter XX/XX footnotes

*C*harity, the Sages teach, has its limit, and that limit is 20 percent. Saving a life, however, has no such bounds. One does not need to limit his expenditure to 20 percent when money is needed to feed and clothe people who are starving, or redeem those who are in danger. While the Chofetz Chaim does not say that one is obligated to give more in such cases, he does clearly state that one is allowed to give whatever is needed to save a life.

The Talmud *(Bava Metzia* 62a) seems to indicate the opposite. It says that if a person is walking in the desert with a friend, and he has only enough water in his jug to save one of them, he has the right to keep the water for himself, because a person's own life takes precedence over the lives of others. The Chofetz Chaim clarifies this ruling, conceding that while one's own life comes first, one's wealth does not come before another person's life. Saving a life is a mitzvah of unparalleled value, equated with saving the world.

In the Talmud *(Bava Basra* 11a), Benjamin the Righteous, the administrator of a charity fund, was visited by a desperate woman in a time of famine. The charity box was empty, so he gave her money from his own account. Years later, Benjamin became deathly ill. The angels pleaded with Hashem to extend his life as a reward for having saved the woman and her sons. The death decree was overturned and Benjamin lived another 22 years. In the commentary *Iyun*

Yaakov, the 22 years are calculated as 272 months including leap years. That number corresponds to the numerology for *"ra'av,"* the Hebrew word for hunger. His reward was in direct proportion to the hunger from which he had saved a mother and her children.

In writing the pages of history, Hashem puts certain people in a position in which their willingness to love Hashem "with all your heart, with all your soul and with all your resources" (*Devarim* 6:5) is tested to its fullest extent. Such was the situation in America during World War II, when money meant the power to pay the bribes, purchase the visas and arrange the transports that could save European Jews from certain death. There were those who gave their $18, or their $180, or perhaps even their $1,800. There were also those, like the late Elimelech Gavriel (Mike) Tress, who could settle for nothing less than obeying the dictate to give "all your resources" out of love for Hashem's children.

Tress, a New York City-bred businessman, was ascending the ladder of financial success when, in 1939, he dove headfirst into the rescue activities of Agudath Israel of America. In the course of the war years, Tress donated every one of his assets to the cause of saving Jewish lives. First his money was transferred, month by month, into the Agudath Israel account. He then sold his stock portfolio block by block. When the stocks ran out, he took one, two and ultimately three mortgages on the apartment that was home to his growing family. Finally, he took personal loans to keep the life-saving funds flowing. As unimaginable as Tress's selflessness might be, he was not alone in rising to the terrible test of that generation. He and those like him understood that there is a time to calculate tithes, and there is a time to save lives.

When someone approaches me for money, I will take into account whether this is a life-and-death situation.

יט טבת
19 TEVES / CYCLE 1

December 24, 2002
January 13, 2004
December 31, 2004
January 19, 2006
January 9, 2007
December 28, 2007
January 15, 2009
January 5, 2010

כ תמוז
20 TAMMUZ / CYCLE 2

July 20, 2003
July 9, 2004
July 27, 2005
July 16, 2006
July 6, 2007
July 23, 2008
July 12, 2009
July 2, 2010

❧ *Holy Firewood*

SEFER AHAVAS CHESED — Part II Chapter XX

*T*here are rare individuals in this world whose hearts will not let them give less than their all to save another Jew from trouble. To such people, the Jewish people are like their own limbs; saving a Jew is no less urgent than saving their own right arm. The tales of such individuals sound like the otherworldly feats of angels, yet they are the deeds of human beings elevated by Torah and mitzvos to their highest spiritual level.

One such story is told about the Rachmistrivker Rebbe, from the dynasty of the Chernobyl Chassidim, who were descended from the Baal Shem Tov. One of the Rachmistrivker Rebbe's ancestors possessed an exquisite, hand-carved *succah* that had been made especially for him. The walls of the *succah* were carved with Kabbalistic formulas, names of Hashem and mystical designs that reflected the Heavenly realms revealed in the *Zohar*. This *succah*, which was known throughout Europe, was passed down through several generations, into the possession of the Rachmistrivker Rebbe. A time came when the Rebbe decided to travel to Israel, a journey over land and sea that was long, rough and dangerous. To everyone's amazement, the Rebbe took the boards of the *succah* with him.

On arriving in Israel, even the Arab dockworkers were astounded that anyone would take along such a cumbersome load. Nonetheless, the Rebbe had his holy *succah* to erect in the holy land. Year after year, people came from all over Israel to sit in this *succah*, kiss its walls, study its carvings and marvel at its beauty. One year, however, the *succah* disappeared, and in its place were the plain boards that everyone else used for their temporary dwelling. No one knew what had happened to the *succah*, and the Rebbe offered no explanation.

Ten years later, there was a wedding in Jerusalem. The father of the groom rose to speak, and the fate of the exquisite *succah* was revealed. Ten years earlier, the father related, his son, the groom, was a young boy stricken by an epidemic that was raging through the city. At the same time, World War I was raging throughout the continent; Turkey, which ruled Israel at the time, had confiscated all wood to use for fuel in its war effort. There was literally not a stick to be found. Unfortunately, the only treatment for the sick son was to soak in warm baths. The desperate father looked everywhere for some fuel with which to heat bathwater for his son, but nothing could be found. He turned to the Rachmistrivker Rebbe for help. Without a moment's hesitation, the Rebbe took the hand-carved boards of his *succah* and chopped them to pieces. "Here is fuel for your son's bathwater," he stated simply.

"That *succah* is why my son is here today standing under the *chuppah*," the grateful father said. To the Rebbe, there was no question. The *succah* had found its true purpose.

Step by **Step**

Today I will find some reading or learning material that will help me develop a stronger sense of Ahavas Yisrael, love for fellow Jews.

לע"נ זלמן חיים בן יעקב לייב ע"ה — **19 Teves**
לזכות יעקב בן גיטל נ"י — **20 Tammuz**

כ טבת
20 TEVES / CYCLE 1

December 25, 2002
January 14, 2004
January 1, 2005
January 20, 2006
January 10, 2007
December 29, 2007
January 16, 2009
January 6, 2010

כא תמוז
21 TAMMUZ / CYCLE 2

July 21, 2003
July 10, 2004
July 28, 2005
July 17, 2006
July 7, 2007
July 24, 2008
July 13, 2009
July 3, 2010

❧ *Partnership*

SEFER AHAVAS CHESED — **Part II Chapter XX**

*E*ver since Jacob brought the twelve tribes of Israel into the world, the Jewish people have utilized a division of labor in their service to Hashem. Each tribe received its own blessing, each was endowed with its own strength that, when combined with the strengths of the other tribes, encompassed Israel's total Divine mission. The relationship between the tribes of Issachar and Zebulun exemplifies this division of labor. Issachar was blessed with the wisdom to learn Torah. Zebulun was given the mercenary skills to travel the seas conducting trade. The money Zebulun earned had one purpose — to support Issachar in its learning. Earning money was one tribe's assignment in the overall mission; learning Torah was the other's.

The Torah demonstrates that because Zebulun's business dealings enabled Torah learning to take place, Zebulun shared equally in Issachar's honor and reward. When the princes of each tribe brought their gifts for the inauguration of the *Mishkan* — the Tent of Meeting erected during their wanderings in the desert — the tribe of Judah went first. Since Judah is the tribe designated for kingship, its primacy makes sense. The second prince was from Issachar, the tribe that produced those who learned Torah, served in the *Sanhedrin* and applied and established the foundations of Jewish law. The third tribe was Zebulun, the tribe of merchants. The Talmud explains that Zebulun came third, right behind the kings and scholars to illustrate that the reward destined for Torah scholars accrues equally to those who support them.

This is how the Jewish people operate — as a partnership, with each partner contributing according to his gifts and abilities, all toward the goal of sanctifying Hashem's name in this world. In that light, the Chofetz Chaim says, one does not have to adhere to a 20 percent limit in giving money to support Torah. Such support is not charity — it is one's share in a partnership. The profit is equally divided between the financial backer and the person who does the actual toil, and therefore, the money should be seen as a business investment. The *Shitah Mekubetzes (Kesubos 50)* upholds this view, ruling that the limit of 20 percent does not apply to money given to support Torah, whether the money is given to struggling families in *kollel*, or to a yeshivah, or one's own child who is dedicating his time to learning.

When a person views this money as his share in a lucrative partnership, he perceives requests for support in a different light. They are not outstretched hands looking for charity; they are potential partners willing to provide a person with a share in the immeasurable, eternal rewards that he may lack the opportunity to earn on his own.

Step by **Step**

When an opportunity arises to give money for the support of Torah learning, I will keep in mind that by virtue of my support, I am earning the reward of a Torah scholar.

כא טבת
21 TEVES / CYCLE 1

December 26, 2002
January 15, 2004
January 2, 2005
January 21, 2006
January 11, 2007
December 30, 2007
January 17, 2009
January 7, 2010

כב תמוז
22 TAMMUZ / CYCLE 2

July 22, 2003
July 11, 2004
July 29, 2005
July 18, 2006
July 8, 2007
July 25, 2008
July 14, 2009
July 4, 2010

❧ The Whole Job

SEFER AHAVAS CHESED — Part II Chapter XX

*G*reatness, from the Jewish perspective, lies in the pursuit of Torah learning. All the learning in the world, however, will not confirm greatness upon a person unless it instills within him a devotion to helping others. Only then is his service to Hashem complete. The most exalted figures in Jewish life are those whose wisdom is matched by their inexhaustible supply of compassion, and they teach their children this trait just as they teach them Torah.

A story of the Sanzer *Rav* illustrates how greatness in learning expresses itself in the highest levels of compassion: Over the course of time, the *Rav* had set aside money with which to marry off his daughter. Even the wedding gown had been purchased. One day, a poor man came to the *Rav* terribly distraught, for he had no money with which to pay for his daughter's upcoming wedding. The *Rav* gave him every item he had set aside for his daughter, including the gown. The daughter, who well understood her father's greatness, could not help but ask why everything — especially her gown — had to be given away. The *Rav* replied, "My dear daughter, don't you understand? For the Sanzer *Rav's* daughter, everyone will be fighting to contribute to the wedding. This family doesn't have any such advantage."

The zeal for helping others is the final ingredient that turns a person's Torah learning and mitzvah observance into a full-fledged source of blessing. The Chofetz Chaim illustrates this point through a *Midrash*: Rabbi

Acha, in the name of Rabbi Tanchum, speaks of a person who studies Torah, adheres to the mitzvos and teaches others. If that person has the ability to financially help others who are learning, but he neglects to do so, he falls within the purview of the words: "Cursed is the person who did not fulfill the words of this Torah." In contrast, the words "Blessed is the person who fulfills the words of this Torah" applies to someone who cannot spend time learning because he must struggle to support his family, and nonetheless does as much as he is able to help others who are learning.

The Chofetz Chaim points out that this person is blessed, even if the money he contributes amounts to more than the 20 percent allowed for tithing. The blessing is a bountiful one, for whenever the Torah curses those who lack a certain merit, its blessing vests tenfold in those who do all they can to bring that merit into their lives.

In a similar vein, the Skulener Rebbe, who stayed in Europe after World War II to look after the refugees, defied the Soviet government by keeping many Jewish orphans in his home and raising them in the path of Torah. The Rebbe struggled hard to find the resources to feed and clothe his hidden children. One cold night, the Rebbe could find no blanket with which to cover one of the orphans, so he removed the blanket from his own child's bed. The child assured his father that he did not mind relinquishing the blanket, but the Rebbe wanted to be sure that his son would not doubt his father's love. "My dear son, please understand," he said. "You have a father. You can at least warm yourself with that. That child has no one in the world; let him at least have a blanket."

Step by **Step**

Today I will think about whether my commitment to helping others is commensurate with my commitment to Torah learning and other mitzvos.

21 Teves — Jack Rabinowitz לע"נ יעקב בן ברוך חיים ז"ל
Dedicated by his children

22 Tammuz — Moshe Dembitzer לע"נ משה יהושע בן מרדכי אליעזר ז"ל
Dedicated in loving memory by his wife, children and grandchildren

כב טבת
22 TEVES / CYCLE 1

December 27, 2002
January 16, 2004
January 3, 2005
January 22, 2006
January 12, 2007
December 31, 2007
January 18, 2009
January 8, 2010

כג תמוז
23 TAMMUZ / CYCLE 2

July 23, 2003
July 12, 2004
July 30, 2005
July 19, 2006
July 9, 2007
July 26, 2008
July 15, 2009
July 5, 2010

✒ *High Maintenance*

SEFER AHAVAS CHESED — Part II Chapter XX

*I*f a person needs his money to cover his family's living expenses, he is obviously under no obligation to give it away. One need not force his own family into poverty in order to give to others. This concept, however, leaves a wide, wide berth for interpretation. What exactly constitutes proper support of one's family? The person who convinces himself that this obligation encompasses the best and latest model of everything does himself immeasurable damage. He establishes a lifestyle that drains his resources away from support of Torah and acts of chesed. His money becomes an instrument of worry, and sometimes, despair.

One of the key tasks faced by people living in prosperous times is to learn to distinguish desires from needs. A person who believes he "needs" a certain style of house, a certain brand of china, or a certain model of car is often led astray pursuing these objects. An ample income may begin to feel tight, simply because living expenses have been cranked up to their ultimate height. A person may take on debt in order to keep up the standard of living he has established. He may pursue shady business dealings, rationalizing that his family "needs" the money. In fact, the family does at that point need the money, simply to prop up the house of cards upon which it is built. Once people are accustomed to a luxurious lifestyle, anything less feels like deprivation.

There are those who look at this consumer mentality and declare it a vanity. Nonetheless, they pursue the same long shopping list of status symbols because, in their view, they must project a certain image of prosperity in order to retain their status in the business world. Were they to be perceived as people of lesser means, they imagine, others in business would be reluctant to extend credit to them. The Chofetz Chaim pierces this illusory logic, reasoning that others are not so easily deceived. A person will not find himself better able to sustain his business or obtain credit because of the elegance of his table setting. The idea that one must spend on luxuries in order to stay in business is simply a veil, hiding the same longing for status that animates the outright materialist. The results, too, are the same — a frenzied cycle of working and spending, with far too little left for the investments that bring real, lasting dividends.

The best protection against becoming caught in this cycle is foresight, says the Chofetz Chaim: "The wise man uses the eyes in his head" *(Koheles* 2:14). One must look ahead at the ripple effects of what he buys. He must consider what new "needs" will spring from this purchase, what new expenses will now become a part of his life, what impact this luxury will have on his children and their perception of a normal standard of living. If he looks ahead, he will see that his acquisition may actually be a terrible depletion — that by settling for less, he will ultimately reap so much more.

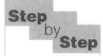

The next time I am about to make a discretionary purchase, I will consider spending less on the item and putting the difference toward charity.

22 Teves — Rochel Mashitz לע"נ הרבנית רחל בת ר' אהרן מאשיץ ז"ל
Dedicated in loving memory by her children and grandchildren, Monsey NY

23 Tammuz — May today's learning be a זכות for our משפחה.
Dedicated by Yonah and Dina Ruttenberg and family, Baltimore, MD

כג טבת
23 TEVES / CYCLE 1

December 28, 2002
January 17, 2004
January 4, 2005
January 23, 2006
January 13, 2007
January 1, 2008
January 19, 2009
January 9, 2010

כד תמוז
24 TAMMUZ / CYCLE 2

July 24, 2003
July 13, 2004
July 31, 2005
July 20, 2006
July 10, 2007
July 27, 2008
July 16, 2009
July 6, 2010

⌇ *Protecting the Business*

SEFER AHAVAS CHESED — Part II Chapter XX

*O*ne person takes 10 percent out of every dollar that comes to him. At the end of the year, these deductions amount to $5,000. Another person hears of a cause that moves him greatly, and writes a $5,000 check to support it. It so happens that this $5,000 is the correct amount to satisfy this second person's tithing obligation. The Chofetz Chaim looks at these two types of giving, and determines that the person who routinely takes 10 percent out of his income gains far more from his giving than does the person who is moved to write out the check to a worthy cause. The first person, who has made tithing a part of his life, is declaring through his act that Hashem has a portion in everything he does. He is making Hashem a partner in his enterprise and recognizing Hashem's hand in the other 90 percent that he keeps for himself.

Flowing from this perspective is a great sea of protection. A business partner does not extend his care and supervision only to his portion of the business, for he knows that the size of his portion depends on the size of the whole. When a person has Hashem as a partner, he invites His involvement in his entire enterprise. Because the person has aligned his goals with Hashem's goals, he has a guarantee that Hashem will help his business prosper and protect it from harm. He has Hashem's protection against fraud, misjudgment, overwhelming competition and the many other disasters that can throw a business into a tailspin.

That is the practical benefit of regularly turning 10 percent of one's income over to charity, but there is also a further, more spiritual aspect to this practice. If a person looks at each dollar that comes to him as the source of 10 cents for charity, he has in fact sanctified the entire dollar. The money for charity is the real fruit of this person's labor. Just as a person prunes, waters and cares for an apple tree solely to obtain the apples it yields, a person with this perspective works at his business — buying, stocking, selling, traveling, accounting, advertising, hiring — all to obtain the charitable contributions it yields. His effort toward earning money is sanctified because its purpose is to yield the tithe that will spread the light of Torah and alleviate the plight of those in need.

As I put aside money for tithing, I will make myself conscious of the idea that I am giving Hashem, my partner, His share.

כד טבת
24 TEVES / CYCLE 1

December 29, 2002
January 18, 2004
January 5, 2005
January 24, 2006
January 14, 2007
January 2, 2008
January 20, 2009
January 10, 2010

כה תמוז
25 TAMMUZ / CYCLE 2

July 25, 2003
July 14, 2004
August 1, 2005
July 21, 2006
July 11, 2007
July 28, 2008
July 17, 2009
July 7, 2010

⊰ 'Next to You'

SEFER AHAVAS CHESED — Part II Chapter XXI

*I*n the script of a person's life, there is a certain cast of characters, and each — from the stars of the show to the extras that filter on and off the stage — is integral to the drama. Each person is placed in one's life for a reason, and this is especially so of those who have needs that the "protagonist" has the ability to fill. The Torah charges each Jew with paying careful attention to those whom Hashem has cast in his personal script: "If your brother becomes impoverished and his means falter next to you, strengthen him—proselyte or resident—so that he can live next to you" (*Vayikra* 25:35).

The Chofetz Chaim examines interpretations of the phrase "next to you." He finds there a message based on the Talmud (*Temurah* 16a), which explains the meaning of a verse in *Mishlei* (22:2): "The rich man and the pauper meet; Hashem is the Maker of them all." When a person finds himself in the position of witnessing someone else's downfall, it is specifically because this poor man's circumstances are delivering a personal message to him: No one is immune to reversals, no one's fortune is guaranteed for life. One must therefore take the plight of another person to heart and make a sincere effort to restore him to stability and strength. That is why he is "next to you." One who loans money tc keep another person's business afloat performs the act of chesed in its ultimate form. He shows that he understands the source and purpose of his wealth, and Hashem therefore protects his position. If instead he looks upon the unfortunate person as someone suffering the results of his own bad judgment or bad luck, and thereby feels unmoved to help, he invites Hashem to show him firsthand the other person's perspective.

One famous story illustrates how a man was awakened to this understanding: The man was marrying off his son, and he and the bride's father had agreed upon all the financial arrangements. As the wedding approached, however, the bride's father suffered a major setback. He was left with a struggling business and only enough income to barely cover his family's immediate needs. He contacted the groom's father, explained the situation and regretfully backed out of the commitments he had made. The groom's father wanted to break the engagement, but first he sought advice from his rabbi, Rabbi Leib M'Kishenev.

"You'll be very glad you came to me with this problem," the rabbi told him upon hearing the details. "Give me a few days and I'll have a decision for you."

Based on the rabbi's comments, the groom's father felt certain that the rabbi agreed with his point of view. Upon returning to the rabbi for an answer, he was taken aback to hear, "The wedding should go ahead as planned, and if you can, you should help the bride's father rather than putting more pressure on him."

"But rabbi," the man protested, "why did you say I would be glad I had come to you with this problem?"

"You misunderstood me," Rabbi Leibish replied. "You should be grateful that you came to me with your problem, rather than the other man's problem."

Step by **Step**

If the opportunity presents itself to me, I will make an effort to use my chesed money to help someone weather a difficult period in business and thereby maintain his livelihood.

24 Teves — Joseph Klein לע"נ ר' יהושע בן פנחס ז"ל
Dedicated by Penina and David Klein and family

25 Tammuz — May today's learning be a זכות for our משפחה.
Dedicated by Moishe Leib Laufer

DAY 115

כה טבת
25 TEVES / CYCLE 1

December 30, 2002
January 19, 2004
January 6, 2005
January 25, 2006
January 15, 2007
January 3, 2008
January 21, 2009
January 11, 2010

כו תמוז
26 TAMMUZ / CYCLE 2

July 26, 2003
July 15, 2004
August 2, 2005
July 22, 2006
July 12, 2007
July 29, 2008
July 18, 2009
July 8, 2010

❧ *Win-Win*

**SEFER AHAVAS CHESED — Part II Chapter XXI
footnotes**

Giving a person a chance to redeem his business from the verge of bankruptcy is, in the Torah's measure, the equivalent of saving his life. When Hashem puts this mitzvah before a person, He is offering him an exceedingly precious merit. One must understand that the person who needs the help will be saved somehow, if salvation is what Hashem desires. The only question is who will have the golden opportunity to be the agent of salvation.

With the potential for such tremendous good, one would want to choose the most effective means possible for helping the person's business. An outright loan may have drawbacks. If the person's situation is dire enough, the loan may not be sufficient to solve the problem. Repayment may become just another drain on the business' dwindling resources. The recipient may come to dread meeting the creditor, even if he applies no pressure for repayment. Furthermore, the lender naturally would view the loan as a favor, and would tend to limit his involvement accordingly. A favor can only be expected to go so far.

An investment, in which both parties stand to gain, does not have such limitations. That is why the Chofetz Chaim recommends an investment in the struggling business as a superior vehicle for helping restore it to stability. If a lender also has potential to profit, he is willing to invest more money and effort. The Chofetz Chaim notes that the bare fact that the investor might gain from his investment does not in any way remove his money from the realm of chesed. Ultimately, the greater chesed is the strategy that will render the most benefit to the recipient. If one is able, within the confines of halachah, to profit from helping the other person, the help is likely to be more generous and consistent, and therefore of greater benefit to the recipient. The Torah's allowance for such an arrangement falls within the allowance of an *"iska"* (see Day 74 for detailed discussion), which differs from the prohibited practice of charging interest.

While the legal details of *iska* and interest are complicated, the underlying difference is not. When a person invests in a business, he only gains if the business gains. With interest, the lender gains even if the borrower loses; there is no kindness involved. In fact, such a transaction is among the worst of sins. The Chofetz Chaim relates that there is a chamber of Gehinnom reserved for those who capitalize upon another person's desperation.

There is a fine line between committing the terrible sin of exploiting someone's neediness and investing with him in his business venture. One's frame of mind forms part of the barrier between the two. If a person can tell himself, "I'm doing this to help him. I might gain from it, and I may not," he is on the correct side of the border. The Chofetz Chaim is actually recommending that a person hold two contradicting thoughts at once. He must look for ways to make his investment profitable — for that is what the recipient most needs — while disassociating himself from any real concern about his own gain. The person who can succeed with this strategy can help restore another person's business while shielding the recipient from any sense of shame or obligation. He may or may not gain financially, but spiritually, he will have hit the jackpot.

Step by **Step**

If I am called upon to help someone stabilize his business, I will carefully consider the best way to help.

25 Teves — Ralph S. Gindi ז"ל לע"נ רפאל בן רחל ז"ל
Dedicated in loving memory by his wife and children — נלב"ע ד' שבט

26 Tammuz —

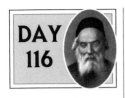

כו טבת
26 TEVES / CYCLE 1

December 31, 2002
January 20, 2004
January 7, 2005
January 26, 2006
January 16, 2007
January 4, 2008
January 22, 2009
January 12, 2010

כז תמוז
27 TAMMUZ / CYCLE 2

July 27, 2003
July 16, 2004
August 3, 2005
July 23, 2006
July 13, 2007
July 30, 2008
July 19, 2009
July 9, 2010

✦ *Breaking the Fall*

SEFER AHAVAS CHESED — Part II Chapter XXI

*O*ne who applies insight to his act of chesed applies a fine polish to the crown that chesed earns him. As mentioned previously, an outright loan may not be the best answer for someone whose means of support is crumbling beneath him. Investment in his business is one alternative the Chofetz Chaim suggests. Other situations may best be ameliorated by finding the person a job, helping him develop a marketable skill or connecting him with other people.

Certainly, one facing a desperate situation will benefit from having someone looking out for his welfare so that he will not become mired in loans that he will be unable to repay. One should help arrange payments that are as small as possible, stretched out over the longest possible duration of time. The lender of chesed money is wise to consider the overall sustainability of the debtor's business; if the debtor is pushed into bankruptcy by onerous repayment terms, neither party benefits.

Keeping a person from falling into poverty is a chesed of the highest order. The Chofetz Chaim presents the example of the man who sustains his family with a cow. When the cow dies, the greatest chesed one can do is to help him purchase a new one. In today's context, the same chesed might be done by helping someone replace his computer, his musical instrument, his taxicab, or any other item upon which his livelihood depends.

"Fortunate is the person who tends wisely to the poor," says *Tehillim* (41:2). "On the day of evil,

Hashem will save him." The blessing comes not just from offering help, but from offering wise, sensitive, appropriate help.

The Chofetz Chaim supports this concept with the words of Rabbi Elazar (*Succah* 49b): "The reward for charity is based on the amount of kindness within it."

In one story that illustrates this concept, there was a woman who lost her husband in a terrible car accident. A member of the community came to the widow and asked for permission to go through her husband's financial records. He removed all the bills and statements and told the woman, "I'm going to take care of this. You just take care of your children." The man organized all the information, arranged payment schedules, raised money and lifted a terrible burden from the grieving family. Following this experience, he did the same for other widows, and soon became known as the person to contact for this type of help.

One day, his young daughter stepped out between two parked cars and was hit. She hovered between life and death as the doctors offered only the dimmest prognosis. Miraculously, she recovered. She described to her father a dream that had occurred in her near-death state. In it, there was a man she did not recognize, who told her, "Don't worry, you're going to live." She described the man, who was to her a stranger. To her father, however, the description was quite familiar. It was the neighbor whose widow he had helped — the first of his many such endeavors. The man's chesed was a crown, but the sensitivity in his chesed was the crown's jewel — a jewel as precious as his daughter's young life.

Step by **Step**

If there are people in my life who are suffering through difficult times, I will try to find a practical, effective way to help.

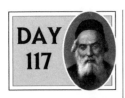

כז טבת
27 TEVES / CYCLE 1

January 1, 2003
January 21, 2004
January 8, 2005
January 27, 2006
January 17, 2007
January 5, 2008
January 23, 2009
January 13, 2010

כח תמוז
28 TAMMUZ / CYCLE 2

July 28, 2003
July 17, 2004
August 4, 2005
July 24, 2006
July 14, 2007
July 31, 2008
July 20, 2009
July 10, 2010

⊷ *A Good Job*

SEFER AHAVAS CHESED — Part II Chapter XXI

To strengthen a businessman who is faltering takes savvy, and it takes money. Not everyone is positioned to be of real help in such situations. That does not mean, however, that the commandment to strengthen one's faltering brother is out of reach for the average person. There are many situations in which even a middle-class person with no money to invest has the opportunity to perform — and reap the rewards — of this life-giving mitzvah.

The Chofetz Chaim points out that those on the middle and lower rungs of the economic scale often live in constant danger of falling into dire straits. A car-service driver, a handyman, a woman who helps with housekeeping or baby-sitting, the owner of a small store — any of these individuals may be one job or one bad business week away from disaster. Patronizing their businesses, employing them and using their services fulfills the commandment to strengthen one's brother just as completely as does the act of investing in someone's thousand-man factory. Even a person who has the wherewithal to be of help to a large business enterprise is obligated to help the simple, struggling worker to stay afloat as well. He is not relieved of the burden of looking around him at the everyday people who cross his path, simply because he is putting a large sum into saving his neighbor's business empire.

Even if using the services of a struggling fellow Jew will cost a person additional money, the Chofetz Chaim says, one should do it nonetheless. The additional cost is simply money spent on the mitzvah, money which Hashem promises to recompense at some point, in some way. Whatever a person seeks to accomplish, Divine assistance is the essential component for success. One who chooses his employees or contractors with attention to their need for the income channels Hashem's help into the endeavor. Conversely, saving money at the expense of a Jew in need will not, in most cases, save any money at the bottom line.

Helping people who are locked permanently into a financial struggle can be a discouraging experience. People who have few assets with which to cushion their setbacks may find themselves in need again and again, creating a sense of futility for those who help them. The Chofetz Chaim sees this factor as no reason to cut off one's help or support. As many times as a person stumbles, one is obligated to step in and prevent his downfall. Even if one saves the same person's life a hundred times, each and every time he acts, he is saving a life.

I will try to use people whom I know need the income when I am in a position to hire help or patronize a business.

DAY 118

כח טבת
28 TEVES / CYCLE 1

January 2, 2003
January 22, 2004
January 9, 2005
January 28, 2006
January 18, 2007
January 6, 2008
January 24, 2009
January 14, 2010

כט תמוז
29 TAMMUZ / CYCLE 2

July 29, 2003
July 18, 2004
August 5, 2005
July 25, 2006
July 15, 2007
August 1, 2008
July 21, 2009
July 11, 2010

ᵅ Right Place, Right Time

SEFER AHAVAS CHESED — Part II Chapter XXII

*W*ith one hour to go until the children stream hungrily through the front door in need of lunch, the housewife sets about making her *cholent* — a special Shabbos stew prepared on Friday. Potatoes are an essential ingredient, and she finds that somehow, she has run out of them. She calls one neighbor, then another, and finally, on the third call, locates some extra potatoes she can borrow. A few potatoes seems like a small favor to the lender, yet to the borrower, they are a minor salvation. She will not have to waste her last hour of preparation time driving to the supermarket, plying the aisles and waiting in the check-out line. She will not feel the tension of rushing home to beat the school bus. She will be more likely to enter Shabbos with a feeling of serenity, a feeling that will spread to her husband and children. All of this will have come from a few potatoes.

While charity is limited to money, the Talmud says (*Succah* 49b), chesed includes physical acts of kindness as well. The Chofetz Chaim urges every Jew to appreciate the value of acts such as lending someone a needed utensil. When a person takes time out of his own activities and inconveniences himself even slightly to provide an item to someone else, he is performing a chesed of great value, simply because the other person needs the item. To the lender, it may be something unused in a drawer or closet, but to the person who needs it, it is the key to accomplishing what that person has set out to achieve. Lending someone a needed object satisfies the mitzvah of strengthening one who is falling, especially when the item enables a person to earn a livelihood.

The Chofetz Chaim urges every Jew to recognize the value of lending. He maintains that in the World to Come, issues involving the loan of seemingly insignificant items may become, for some people, very significant indeed. If one is asked, "Why did you refuse to loan your neighbor $50,000?" one may have a perfectly justifiable reason: a lack of resources. If, however, the person is questioned about his refusal to lend his lawn mower, or take ten minutes to give someone's car a boost, his answer is not as likely to be acceptable.

These are favors most anyone has the time and resources to provide. In such instances, the poor man may find himself on the giving end; he may be the one with the booster cables while the luxury-car owner waits stranded on the road. If such is the case, the poor man is obligated to help the rich man. In the reverse situation, where the rich man has what is needed, there is an even stronger obligation to help. This is because the poor person may be embarrassed to ask, and a refusal would have a more devastating effect. Life is filled with instances in which a person finds himself in the position to fill someone else's need. Each of his reactions to these situations is a tiny, imperceptible stroke in a painting — the landscape that will surround him in the World to Come.

Today I will gear myself to say "yes" to a favor whenever possible.

כט טבת
29 TEVES / CYCLE 1

January 3, 2003
January 23, 2004
January 10, 2005
January 29, 2006
January 19, 2007
January 7, 2008
January 25, 2009
January 15, 2010

א אב
1 AV / CYCLE 2

July 30, 2003
July 19, 2004
August 6, 2005
July 26, 2006
July 16, 2007
August 2, 2008
July 22, 2009
July 12, 2010

⨳ *Why Not?*

SEFER AHAVAS CHESED — Part II Chapter XXII

*I*f there were a bank that promised: "Invest $100 and earn interest on $1 million," there is no doubt that the line of customers would wrap around the block. No one would be heard complaining that going to his room, searching through his drawer and digging out the $100 was too much trouble. There are, however, those who find a trip to the basement to find a hammer for a neighbor far too arduous to undertake, even though the reward for this simple task is far beyond the effort it requires.

Following through on the bank analogy, one would be even less likely to hear someone say, "It's my $100. Why should I let the bank have it? What if they lose it?" The abundant gains would clearly make the minimal risk seem meaningless. The Chofetz Chaim states that in the case of chesed, minor inconvenience and risk are meaningless compared to the benefits. One who allows himself these excuses is excusing himself from a spiritual windfall, and at the same time, setting himself up for a harsh judgment when, at the end of his days, he must account for his failure to help those he could have helped. A little exertion, a little generosity of spirit can make a tremendous impact on another person's day — sometimes even his life. The Chofetz Chaim urges people not to let small obstacles stand in the way of an immense mitzvah and the rewards it brings.

Of all the objects one can loan someone, a *sefer* with which the other person can learn Torah stands apart from the rest. This is an act of chesed whose benefits reach beyond this world, bringing the borrower both a tangible tool for the here and now, and an eternal merit forever after. *Tehillim* (112:3) refers to this particular act of kindness when it says, "Wealth and riches are in his house and his charity endures forever." The person possessing these "great riches" is one who authors *sefarim* and lends them to others. Lending a *sefer* rises to the level of supporting Torah learning, a potent mitzvah that opens the door to a vast storehouse of reward and blessing.

The Chofetz Chaim examines yet another reason people resist loaning their possessions to others, and that is animosity. If the person at the door is someone toward whom one harbors ill feelings, the temptation to deny his request is great. "I don't owe him anything" is often the phrase echoing in one's mind. To this, the Torah (*Vayikra* 19:18) replies: "You shall not take revenge and you shall not bear a grudge against the members of your people; you shall love your fellow as yourself—I am Hashem."

The final phrase, "I am Hashem," is the explanation for the verse. Each person fails sometimes to live up to the expectations Hashem has expressed for His people. Yet Hashem continues, through chesed, to sustain all living creatures, including His flawed and erring human creatures. There is no doubt that Hashem judges man with perfect accuracy, yet even in that blazingly clear light, He still finds room for chesed. Man, whose understanding of others is far from perfect, has no excuse to punish perceived slights with the withdrawal of kindness. A Jew learns from Hashem: Kindness must flow in a steady stream, not in premeasured drops.

Step by **Step**

The next time a person toward whom I harbor some ill feelings is in need of help, I will try to offer whatever help I can.

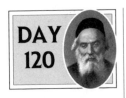

DAY 120

א שבט
1 SHEVAT / CYCLE 1

January 4, 2003
January 24, 2004
January 11, 2005
January 30, 2006
January 20, 2007
January 8, 2008
January 26, 2009
January 16, 2010

ב אב
2 AV / CYCLE 2

July 31, 2003
July 20, 2004
August 7, 2005
July 27, 2006
July 17, 2007
August 3, 2008
July 23, 2009
July 13, 2010

❧ *The Borrower*

SEFER AHAVAS CHESED — **Part II Chapter XXII**

*I*n the dynamics between lender and borrower, the obligations run in both directions. The Chofetz Chaim has made a strong case for accepting upon oneself the risks and inconveniences of lending, yet the borrower, by taking someone else's possession, places a great weight of responsibility upon his own shoulders as well. A borrower who does not treat the item he has borrowed in accordance with halachah may place himself in the category of a robber.

Such is the case for someone who treats an item harshly or uses it in a way it was not intended to be used. Even if the lender does not specify verbally or in writing that the item must be treated in a certain way, the borrower is responsible for keeping his usage within normal expectations. The term "robber" also applies to someone who takes an item without permission, even if he believes the owner will not mind. It applies to someone who damages or destroys a borrowed item and refuses to replace it. A borrower is also prohibited from loaning the item to a third party, even if it will still be returned to the owner on time.

The Chofetz Chaim points out another common transgression among people borrowing an item from others — laxity in returning it. The urgency with which one is consumed when the item is needed dissipates quickly once the need has been fulfilled. At that point, many people will find themselves too busy to bring the item back to its owner. When the need is pressing, the borrower finds the time to pick up the item; it is uppermost on his mind. The Chofetz Chaim says one should feel the same urgency about returning it, so that the owner will have use of the item and no unintended harm will come to it while it is in the borrower's domain. One should remember that if he damages what he borrows — even if it happens through events completely outside his control — he must compensate the owner. Every moment the item stays in the borrower's possession puts him at risk of having to replace or repair it. If he is properly aware of the responsibility he bears for the other person's possession, he should be burning to relieve himself of the burden.

Rabbi Yisrael Salanter demonstrated this powerful sense of obligation in an episode that has become legendary. He had traveled to another town to deliver a lecture. As he walked to the synagogue where the lecture was to take place, a downpour struck. One of his escorts opened an umbrella and handed it to him. The Rabbi carried it with him into the synagogue. It stayed at his side throughout the lecture, and for a long time after as people came to greet and speak to him. Finally, his hosts suggested that he retire to the home where he was staying, but he refused. First, he wanted to return the umbrella. He would not turn it over to his hosts so that they could find the owner and return it. He would not leave it in the synagogue to be reclaimed. He stood in his place for nearly an hour until the owner of the umbrella was located and the item was returned. The words of his lecture were lost to history, but his deed and the lesson within it assumed their place in posterity.

I will become more conscientious about returning borrowed items as soon as I have finished with them.

1 Shevat — Bella Elfant Heiman — נלב"ע ב' שבט — לע"נ בילא בת וועלוול ע"ה
Dedicated lovingly by her daughter and son-in-law, Ruth Linda and Lewis Weisfeld

2 Av — Moishe Horn ע"ה לע"נ משה מניס בן יעקב יצחק ע"ה
Dedicated by Devorah, Dov, Moishe, Ariella and Eli Elias

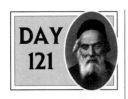
ב שבט
2 SHEVAT / CYCLE 1

January 5, 2003
January 25, 2004
January 12, 2005
January 31, 2006
January 21, 2007
January 9, 2008
January 27, 2009
January 17, 2010

ג אב
3 AV / CYCLE 2

August 1, 2003
July 21, 2004
August 8, 2005
July 28, 2006
July 18, 2007
August 4, 2008
July 24, 2009
July 14, 2010

~ Giving All

SEFER AHAVAS CHESED — Part II Chapter XXIII

*T*he value of the loan or charity is not defined by the dollar amount. The Chofetz Chaim cites the words of *Avos D'Rabbi Nassan* Chapter 13: ".... If a person gives his friends all the gifts in the world, but his face is angry, it is as if he has given him nothing." The attitude with which the charity or loan is given determines its true value. Citing the same source further, the Chofetz Chaim adds, "One who receives a friend with a pleasant expression, even if he does not give him anything, it is as if he has given him all the best gifts in the world." From these two quotes, it is apparent that money given with scorn can do no good. It is also clear that if one must refuse a request, he can still give a priceless gift by treating the petitioner with compassion.

The secret to developing this attitude, says the Chofetz Chaim, is to reexamine the verse in the Torah (*Shemos* 22:24) "When you lend money to My people, to the poor person who is with you ..." The words "with you" can be interpreted to mean that one must imagine the plight of the poor person as he comes to ask for help. One must imagine how he hesitates before knocking, how he rehearses his words hoping to find a tone that is convincing but not demanding, how he watches the potential donor's face, looking for signs of sympathy or scorn, as he waits nervously for the answer upon which so much depends. By keeping the poor "with you," a person naturally comes to the correct attitude in giving.

To ask for help is to lay one's self-esteem at someone else's feet. If the giver is wise, he will lift the needy person up. If he is arrogant or unfeeling, he may, G-d forbid, trample another person's spirit. There is a story of a bride in Israel whose father was forced to go door-to-door collecting money for the wedding. When the ceremony reached the ritual called the *badekken*, when the groom places a veil over the bride's face, the bride burst into tears. Her mother asked her why, and she replied: "I'm thinking as my face is covered, how many times did my father want to cover his face when he went door-to-door asking people to help marry me off."

A pleasant demeanor and warm words are a Jew's obligation to every person who crosses his path. Rabbi Isser Zalman Meltzer was once sitting in his apartment in Jerusalem when one of his students excitedly reported, "The Brisker *Rav* is coming up the stairs!" Rabbi Isser Zalman ran out the door to greet him, only to find that the visitor was someone else — albeit someone who bore a resemblance to the Brisker *Rav*. He escorted the guest into the house with great fanfare and asked his wife to set out a special table of refreshments. When the guest had gone, the puzzled students asked the Rabbi why he had treated him with such great honor. "I went running out of the house thinking it was the Brisker *Rav*," said Rabbi Isser Zalman. "I was wearing my biggest smile and thinking about how I would honor this great man. Then I saw it wasn't him. But don't I owe every person my best smile and my greatest honor?"

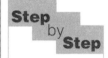

When someone comes to me for a favor or charity, I will make sure to greet the person with a smile and a pleasant demeanor.

2 Shevat — Samuel Weiner לע"נ שלום בן לוי ז"ל
Dedicated in loving memory by his grandchildren, Aki and Daniel Fleshler

3 Av — May today's learning be a z'chus for Klal Yisrael.

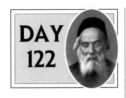

ג שבט
3 SHEVAT / CYCLE 1

January 6, 2003
January 26, 2004
January 13, 2005
February 1, 2006
January 22, 2007
January 10, 2008
January 28, 2009
January 18, 2010

ד אב
4 AV / CYCLE 2

August 2, 2003
July 22, 2004
August 9, 2005
July 29, 2006
July 19, 2007
August 5, 2008
July 25, 2009
July 15, 2010

✎ *The Best Intentions*

SEFER AHAVAS CHESED — Part II Chapter XXIII

$\mathcal{S}$ome people give charity just because they are supposed to do so. Most people, however, have other motives as well. It brings honor and recognition, protects one's family, acts as a merit for recovery from illness, brings forgiveness for sins and provides many other tangible and spiritual benefits. The fact that a person has one or more of these motives in mind when he gives charity does not in any way diminish the value of the mitzvah. Even if the person's primary goal is to impress the world with his wealth, his act of giving still stands.

According to *Pesachim* (8a),"One who says, 'I am giving this coin for *tzedakah* so that my son will live,' or so that 'I will merit the World to Come,' he is completely righteous."

There are two reasons for this. First of all, for most Jews, the fact that charity is a mitzvah plays at least some part in the decision to give. A Jew wants to fulfill Hashem's will, even if there are other benefits he hopes to receive from his act of giving. Secondly, the recipient of the charity or chesed benefits regardless of the giver's motivation.

The story is told of a wealthy man in Russia who maintained a guesthouse, free of charge, for passersby. The Baal HaTanya, Rabbi Shneur Zalman of Liadi, passed by this house one day. He sought out the owner and praised him for his tremendous act of kindness. The owner replied hesitantly, "I don't know how much of a chesed this really is. Maybe I'm doing it just for the merit or the honor. I can't be sure I'm doing it sincerely." The Baal HaTanya assured him, "Don't worry about whether you're doing it sincerely, because the people who are eating here are eating sincerely."

The quest to give altruistically can backfire if it restrains one from giving. The needy person is not affected by the giver's motives. All he needs is some help, provided in a way that does not assault his dignity and perhaps even lifts his spirits. The giver's imperative is to do the mitzvah, no matter what thoughts are behind it. The Talmud (*Pesachim* 50b) urges a Jew to "always engage in Torah and mitzvos, even if it is not purely for the sake of Heaven, for out of ulterior motives will emerge sincere motives." If a person refrains from the mitzvah out of concern for the purity of his motives, he is putting more distance between himself and his spiritual goals.

One who has reached a level at which he gives charity solely to fulfill the will of Hashem does achieve benefits that a person with mixed motivations cannot. The Talmud (*Pesachim* 50b) discusses what appears to be a contradiction in the description of the rewards for charity. One source says charity generates kindness as far as the Heavens, and another source says it generates kindness even above the Heavens. The Talmud reconciles the difference, explaining that in the first case, charity is given with personal motives, and in the second case, it is given solely for Hashem's sake. In either case, an act of kindness toward one individual is an act of kindness toward the world. No matter what one's motivations may be, there is every reason to act.

Step by **Step**

If an opportunity for charity arises that involves some honor or personal gain, I will make my decision based on the benefits for the recipient.

DAY
123

ד שבט
4 SHEVAT / CYCLE 1

January 7, 2003
January 27, 2004
January 14, 2005
February 2, 2006
January 23, 2007
January 11, 2008
January 29, 2009
January 19, 2010

ה אב
5 AV / CYCLE 2

August 3, 2003
July 23, 2004
August 10, 2005
July 30, 2006
July 20, 2007
August 6, 2008
July 26, 2009
July 16, 2010

✒ *Three Sacrifices*

SEFER AHAVAS CHESED — **Part II Chapter XXIII**

A person who studies the Torah sees that it is clearly the work of man's Creator, for no other document so insightfully penetrates the inner workings of man. The Torah recognizes that there are different types of individuals and different circumstances; therefore, it lays out different paths upon which to approach Hashem. These variations are expressed in the three different types of sacrifices prescribed for service in the *Beis HaMikdash.*

The *Midrash Tadshei* Chapter 12 compares these sacrifices to types of righteousness.

The first sacrifice, the *"korban olah,"* is a burnt offering that is completely consumed on the altar. The person who brings this sacrifice takes nothing back from it, not even a bit of meat. This compares to those who serve Hashem purely out of love. They are thoroughly imbued with a sense of gratitude toward Hashem, and will do all they can to express their love, even when there is no personal benefit to be attained.

The second type of sacrifice is the *"korban shlomim,"* or peace offering, in which the greater part of the sacrifice is to be eaten by the person who brought it. Part of the meat goes to the *Kohanim* and part of it is consumed on the altar, but most of it benefits the giver. The Chofetz Chaim compares this sacrifice to one who approaches Hashem with a *"bakashah"* — a request. He is also ardent in his service to Hashem, but as he serves, he hopes to earn merit that will bring him a good, righteous life. He hopes for the intellectual ability to learn Torah, for long life, a cure for illness, a good wife and children — all that he needs to maintain a life of Torah and mitzvos.

The Chofetz Chaim stresses that this, too, is a beautiful path of spirituality. The fact that there is yet a higher road does not turn this into a negative way of approaching Hashem. It suits many more people than the first way, and provides a stepping stone for those who will eventually serve Hashem purely out of love. The biggest mistake would be to eschew any service at all because one cannot perform at the loftiest level.

The third type of sacrifice is the *"korban chattas,"* which is a sin offering brought as an atonement. The individual who corresponds to this type of offering is the one who serves Hashem out of *"yirah,"* or fear. He seeks protection from punishment in this world and in the World to Come. He hopes for merit to avoid the repercussions that the Torah reserves for those who do not keep its precepts. He, too, serves Hashem wholeheartedly, but his motivation is the avoidance of suffering in this life and retribution thereafter.

The *Midrash Tadshei* stresses the fact that all three types of sacrifice are brought to the same *Beis HaMikdash* and received by the same *Kohen*. They all engender the benefits of a sacrifice, and all are valid ways of accomplishing valid spiritual goals, even though their underlying motivations differ. This concept, extended to the mitzvah of charity, teaches that no matter what motivation drives a person to give, his giving is still viewed by Heaven as a holy sacrifice. There are only high roads and still higher roads in the performance of this mitzvah; all of them lead upward.

Today I will commit myself not to second-guess my motivations for giving, but to simply give when the opportunity arises.

4 Shevat — Mary Pearlman ה"ע יעקב בת מרים נ"לע
Dedicated in loving memory by her sons, Moshe, Avrohom and Dovid Pearlman

5 Av —

ה שבט
5 SHEVAT / CYCLE 1

January 8, 2003
January 28, 2004
January 15, 2005
February 3, 2006
January 24, 2007
January 12, 2008
January 30, 2009
January 20, 2010

ו אב
6 AV / CYCLE 2

August 4, 2003
July 24, 2004
August 11, 2005
July 31, 2006
July 21, 2007
August 7, 2008
July 27, 2009
July 17, 2010

✑ *The Wrong Reason*

SEFER AHAVAS CHESED — Part II Chapter XXIII

*G*ive for the wrong reasons and the right reasons will come, the Chofetz Chaim has clearly stated. There is, however, one motivation for giving that sets the act upon negative terrain. This motivation expresses itself in an internal monologue: "I gave so much. What's wrong with my neighbor? He makes millions yet he hasn't donated half as much as I have. I can't believe he can be so stingy."

Using one's own generosity — whether driven by pride, hope for reward or a simple sense of obligation — to denigrate those who have given less envelops a radiant mitzvah in a shroud of negativity. Other motivations, such as the desire to maintain one's status in the community, can be stepping stones toward purer acts of giving. Regarding these types of ulterior motives, the Chofetz Chaim says the mitzvah of *tzedakah* still stands undiminished. When the subtext of one's charity is to show oneself how inferior other people are, however, the mitzvah loses its exalted status.

A person who finds his mind engaging in this type of thinking can stop himself, the Chofetz Chaim says, by remembering the source of the money he is giving. He must bring himself to realize that the money has been granted to him by Hashem out of kindness, and not because of any innate superiority he believes himself to possess. His duty is to disburse the money as Hashem has commanded; in this way, he makes himself deserving of further gifts. Someone who takes this view cannot possibly spend time judging others for what they have or have not given. It is of no consequence to one's own situation.

In the Chofetz Chaim's days in Poland, anti-Semitism was tightening its grip. It was no longer safe for Jews to enter the local hospitals, and Jewish doctors were being pushed out of the profession. The Chofetz Chaim, along with other leaders of the time, organized a meeting to start a Jewish hospital that would fill the community's need. The leaders estimated an amount per bed that would be necessary to run the 250-bed hospital, and opened up the floor for pledges. One of the town's wealthiest men rose to his feet and announced, "I donate ten beds." The cheers that greeted his announcement were not quite enough for him, however. He then pointed to a young Torah scholar who lived in dire poverty in order to dedicate his time to learning: "And how many beds is he going to give?" the wealthy man scoffed.

The Chofetz Chaim answered for the young man. "Your donation of so many beds was very generous and much appreciated," he said. "But it is because of this young man that ten times the number of beds will not be necessary." One can be proud of his money, and proud of what his money can accomplish. He cannot, however, forget the reason there is any money, any sustenance at all in this world.

Step by **Step**

If I am in a situation in which people are making public pledges, I will clear my mind of any negative thoughts about those who seem to be giving less than they could.

5 Shevat —

6 Av — Isaac Flohr לע"נ ר' יצחק בן ר' אהרן ז"ל
Dedicated by Flohr's Gifts and Judaica

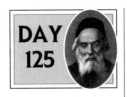
ו שבט
6 SHEVAT / CYCLE 1

January 9, 2003
January 29, 2004
January 16, 2005
February 4, 2006
January 25, 2007
January 13, 2008
January 31, 2009
January 21, 2010

ז אב
7 AV / CYCLE 2

August 5, 2003
July 25, 2004
August 12, 2005
August 1, 2006
July 22, 2007
August 8, 2008
July 28, 2009
July 18, 2010

✌ *Payback*

SEFER AHAVAS CHESED — Part II Chapter XXIV

The person who borrows money takes upon himself an ironclad commitment to repay. If a creditor cannot obtain repayment and takes a borrower to *beis din* — rabbinical court — the court is not permitted to waive the debt. Instead, it must seek assets the borrower owns that can be sold to satisfy the obligation. There are guidelines to protect the borrower's barest necessities, and there are individual circumstances that must be considered, but the simple letter of the law is that whatever the debtor owes, he must pay.

This is especially true if the borrower has the money but refuses to part with it. If he is a strong, physically imposing man, he may believe that the creditor will be afraid to confront him to redeem the money. This violates the Torah prohibition (*Vayikra* 19:13): "You shall not cheat your fellow." This is true whether the money in question is a loan or a payment for services. In either case, one who uses this type of intimidation to hold onto money that is owed to someone else is in violation of a Torah law.

The Talmud uses the term "*rasha*," or evil one, very sparingly, reserving it for only four categories of miscreant. One of those is the person who does not repay a loan when he is able to do so. "*Rasha*" is a shameful designation for a person to bear, certainly one with which he would take issue were it applied by a neighbor or associate. A person who is recalcitrant regarding his debts applies this designation to himself.

This is not the way a Jew is meant to define himself. "Do not consider yourself a wicked one," says *Avos* (2:13). The Chofetz Chaim interprets this verse to mean that a person should refrain from acts that categorize him as a *"rasha."* This applies especially to a Torah scholar, for his actions are judged by others to be a reflection of the Torah and Hashem Himself. Even if such a person is within his rights in his utilization of someone else's money, he must pay attention to the impression others may have of his action.

The term *"rasha"* also applies to someone who uses borrowed money for an unintended purpose. The lender gives the money with a certain understanding of the risks involved. If the borrower changes the rules of the game by using the money for some other purpose, he is misusing the loan. If the money is lost, he is responsible. The Chofetz Chaim warns that there are no lasting gains from misusing someone else's money. He quotes from *Derech Eretz Zuta* (3:2): "If you take what is not yours, what is yours will be taken from you."

There is for every curse an even greater blessing, and that applies to this situation as well. Even though the person who conducts himself properly is merely doing what is required, the fact that he is refraining from prohibited behavior makes him worthy of great blessing: "One who guards himself, to conduct himself in a way of justice, becomes one of those who are bringing closer Hashem's salvation of the Jewish people," says the Chofetz Chaim. He bases this quote on *Yeshayah* 56:1 which states, "Observe justice and perform righteousness (charity), for My salvation is soon to come and My righteousness to be revealed." Just one person, doing nothing more heroic than honoring his debts, has the power to bring redemption.

Step by **Step**

Today I will be sure I am up to date on any loans others have provided to me.

6 Shevat — In honor of my mother, Dorothy Coventon, for all that she has done for me. Dedicated by Chana Coventon

7 Av — Jack Fogel לע"נ יעקב זאב בן יהודה ארי' ז"ל
Dedicated by Nussie & Esther Fogel and family and Shalom & Ettie Fogel and family

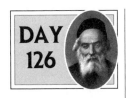
ז שבט
7 SHEVAT / CYCLE 1

January 10, 2003
January 30, 2004
January 17, 2005
February 5, 2006
January 26, 2007
January 14, 2008
February 1, 2009
January 22, 2010

ח אב
8 AV / CYCLE 2

August 6, 2003
July 26, 2004
August 13, 2005
August 2, 2006
July 23, 2007
August 9, 2008
July 29, 2009
July 19, 2010

✑ Abraham's Tent

SEFER AHAVAS CHESED — Part III Chapter I

*U*p until this point, the Chofetz Chaim has been enlightening the Jewish people with a deeper understanding of all the good they can accomplish with their financial assets. Chesed, however, is not just money. One reason the Talmud declares chesed to be superior to charity is because with charity, one gives only money; with chesed, one may give his physical effort as well. Of all the areas in which one may extend oneself in chesed, hospitality to guests — *hachnasas orchim* — is considered the "crown jewel."

Hospitality is so essential a foundation of the Jewish way of life that the Torah devotes an entire *parashah* — *Parashas Vayeira* — to illustrating its principles. Abraham is the protagonist in the *parashah,* and Abraham is also the ancestor most closely identified with the trait of chesed. It is his hospitality, above all else, that exemplifies his excellence in this trait. Every Jewish pre-schooler learns about *Parashas Vayeira* by building a replica of Abraham's tent with its four doors open to each direction of the desert, so that wanderers coming from anywhere would find a welcome.

One particularly instructive episode in this *parashah* is when Hashem "visits" Abraham as he recovers from his *bris*. Three visitors — angels disguised as men — come upon Abraham's tent, whereupon he leaves Hashem's Presence to tend to their needs. In that one action, the exalted status of hospitality is conveyed with unmistakable clarity: Better to rush to a guest's aid than tarry longer with Hashem.

The Torah's detailed description of Abraham's hospitality serves, according to the Chofetz Chaim, as "a sign to us, that we should strengthen ourselves in this regard." The mitzvah of *hachnasas orchim* is not a one-shot act. It is a way of life — a focus on the door, rather than the walls, of one's home. One learns further from *Parashas Vayeira* that this mitzvah is an essential element in the raising of children: "Command your children in this regard," Hashem tells Abraham immediately after his interaction with his guests. Children who grow up with a flow of fellow Jews into their home and around their table grow up understanding that a Jewish home is not a private fortress; it is a miniature power plant, producing warmth and light for the world.

Step by **Step**

Today I will invite a guest for a Shabbos meal.

7 Shevat — Yosef Asseraf ז"ל לע"נ יוסף בן עזיזה ז"ל
הונצח על ידי בתו, מרים סטקר וילדיה, דוד ומרים ומשפחתה

8 Av — Jack Glicker ז"ל לע"נ ישעי' יצחק בן שלמה ז"ל
Dedicated in loving memory by his children, Rabbi & Mrs. Moshe Gottesman and family

DAY 127

ח שבט
8 SHEVAT / CYCLE 1

January 11, 2003
January 31, 2004
January 18, 2005
February 6, 2006
January 27, 2007
January 15, 2008
February 2, 2009
January 23, 2010

ט אב
9 AV / CYCLE 2

August 7, 2003
July 27, 2004
August 14, 2005
August 3, 2006
July 24, 2007
August 10, 2008
July 30, 2009
July 20, 2010

⁂ *Shifting the Odds*

SEFER AHAVAS CHESED — **Part III Chapter I**

*E*veryone hopes for a good match for the young men and women in their families. The Chofetz Chaim relates an ancient story that illustrates the important role *hachnasas orchim* can play in fulfilling these hopes: There was a young woman named Rivkah who came from a family of thieves and liars. Her prospects for marriage appeared to be limited to other thieves and liars, for whom her pedigree would be more an asset than a drawback. The odds of her establishing a family with a righteous young man seemed dim indeed.

For Rivkah, one of the four mothers of the Jewish people, however, the odds did not matter. So great was she in the trait of *hachnasas orchim* that Hashem shifted the odds in her favor and gave her Isaac as a husband. The Torah set the stage for this shift when Eliezer, Abraham's servant, designed the method by which he would be able to faithfully fulfill the task Abraham has given him — to find a wife of Isaac. Eliezer wanted to be sure that he would choose the correct woman, so he established a sign by which he would know he had found her: "The maiden that will come and offer me a drink, and my camels to drink, she is the one for Isaac."

The sign that Eliezer chose was based on his understanding that the legacy of Abraham's household was hospitality. Choosing a mother for the next and all succeeding generations meant choosing a woman who would run her home in accordance with

278 ☐ CHOFETZ CHAIM

this legacy so that it could be passed along undiluted. Because Rivkah met this test, she was lifted from her unseemly surroundings and placed in a position of spiritual royalty. Despite the fact that she was the daughter of the disreputable Bethuel and the sister of the dishonest Laban, she became the wife of Isaac, the very paradigm of righteousness.

The Chofetz Chaim invites a deeper look at this simple story. Rivkah saw Eliezer and ran to his assistance, stating — just as Eliezer had stipulated — that she would bring Eliezer a drink and water his camels as well. She took notice of a traveler passing into her line of vision — her eyes were open to the opportunity for chesed that came before her. She did not leave the task to someone else, but took it upon herself. When she acted, it was with a zealousness for helping, a desire to offer above and beyond the minimum expected. She exhibited not only the trait of chesed, but the trait of *ahavas chesed*, a trait with the power to permeate a marriage, a home and a new generation. Because she proved that she was the one to continue Abraham's legacy of *hachnasas orchim*, she succeeded in finding the best possible marriage partner. The message, says the Chofetz Chaim, is that if it worked for the grandmother of the Jewish people, it can work for the grandchildren as well. A child trained to reach out to others with hospitality arrives at maturity equipped with the essential building blocks of a faithful Jewish home.

Step by **Step**

The next time I have a guest in my home, I will go one extra step to make him or her comfortable.

ט שבט
9 SHEVAT / CYCLE 1

January 12, 2003
February 1, 2004
January 19, 2005
February 7, 2006
January 28, 2007
January 16, 2008
February 3, 2009
January 24, 2010

י אב
10 AV / CYCLE 2

August 8, 2003
July 28, 2004
August 15, 2005
August 4, 2006
July 25, 2007
August 11, 2008
July 31, 2009
July 21, 2010

❧ *Mining the Mitzvah*

SEFER AHAVAS CHESED — **Part III Chapter I**

achnasas orchim is a mitzvah from which many treasures flow, like a mine that produces a wide array of jewels. *Parashas Vayeira* yields yet another of these treasures — the blessing of children. As the *parashah* unfolds, Abraham runs out to meet his three visitors despite his physical pain and the oppressive heat of the day. He gives them a royal welcome, although they appear to him as nothing more than wayfarers. Following this, they inform him: "Sarah, your wife, is going to have a son." The connection is clear to see. Abraham showed the angels the richness of his soul, and they in turn promised him an heir for his treasure. The Chofetz Chaim stresses that the Torah's implications go far beyond the specific instances it records and the specific people it names. Its lessons extend to every individual in every era.

One who performs *hachnasas orchim* does not have to limit his kindness to those who are needy. Providing hospitality to a wealthy person is every bit as much of a mitzvah, as the Maharil points out in *Sefer Yesh Nochlin*. He cites a scenario in which a prominent person arrives at the door, and the host treats him with due honor. This simple act validates his sense of himself as a person of accomplishment and stature. The host has the power, by virtue of the honor he gives this guest, to bolster this person's spirit. The guest's feeling of well-being is the host's mitzvah. This principle is in force to an even greater extent when the man at the door is poor. In giving the poor man money, one performs the mitzvah of *tzedakah*. In addition, the greeting and smile that comes with the donation is an act of *hachnasas orchim*.

It is not surprising, then, that one's inclination runs in just the opposite direction. The wealthy, important friend receives one's brightest smile and finest welcome. The bedraggled man standing hopefully at the door receives, at best, the wan greeting reserved for the uninvited guest. The *yetzer hara* succeeds in masking the potential treasure hidden in the interaction with the poor man. He makes him appear a nuisance, when in fact he is the key to tremendous spiritual riches. One can defeat the *yetzer hara*'s strategy, however, by realizing that the irritation one feels at the knock on the door is the surest sign that an opportunity lies on the other side of it. A person who manages to bypass his initial annoyance and greet the guest with a warm smile will be recompensed. He will find a smile on a stranger's face when he needs to see one.

As much as *hachnasas orchim* defines a Jew, it defines a Jewish community. In the *Shulchan Aruch* (*Yoreh De'ah Siman* 256, *Se'if Katan* 1, in the name of the Mordechai), the principle is established that *hachnasas orchim* is essential to the infrastructure of any Jewish community. If there is no unofficial network of homes that take in guests, the community leaders are obligated to establish a system and mandate the participation of its members. A Jewish community in which a stranger cannot find a meal, a place to rest and a roof over his head does not qualify as a Jewish community. Abraham's children know how to treat a stranger.

Step by **Step**

If I am equipped to do so, I will find opportunities to offer my home to out-of-town guests in my community.

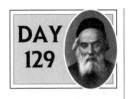
י שבט
10 SHEVAT / CYCLE 1

January 13, 2003
February 2, 2004
January 20, 2005
February 8, 2006
January 29, 2007
January 17, 2008
February 4, 2009
January 25, 2010

יא אב
11 AV / CYCLE 2

August 9, 2003
July 29, 2004
August 16, 2005
August 5, 2006
July 26, 2007
August 12, 2008
August 1, 2009
July 22, 2010

✑ *Hospitality Perfected*

SEFER AHAVAS CHESED — Part III Chapter I

*B*ecause people are not always cooperative and pleasant, bringing people into one's home is not always pleasant. It is in the most difficult situations, however, that the greatest potential for spiritual gain often lies, as this story illustrates.

During the pogroms of the Chmielnicki rebellion in 1647 and 1648, a Jew named Reb Leiber escaped with his family and some money to a small village. There he helped establish a tent camp for his fellow refugees. One day, while praying alone in the woods, he was accosted and beaten by the son of a local nobleman. That night, the young man became desperately ill. His father begged the holy Reb Leiber to forgive his son's vicious deed, but Reb Leiber would agree only on the condition that the nobleman build housing for the Jewish refugees.

The houses were built, and the village grew. Reb Leiber built a guest house to accommodate wayfarers passing through the area, and offered first-class treatment to everyone from the famous to the ragged. One day, however, his pride in his endeavor overstepped appropriate bounds: "My *hachnasas orchim* can even rival that of our forefather, Abraham," he said. This one comment spelled months of suffering for Reb Leiber, for as the Sages say, Hashem holds the righteous man to the very strictest levels of judgment. This is in order to prevent any stain on his soul that would interfere with his full Heavenly reward.

The test began one day when an utterly repulsive individual banged on the guest house door screaming, "Let me in!" The man gluttonously ate his way through Shabbos, constantly demanding service and attention, which Reb Leiber patiently provided. When Shabbos was over, Reb Leiber went to the man's room and found that the rude brute had been transformed into an angelic presence. He was Elijah the prophet, who had come to test Reb Leiber. In passing the test, Reb Leiber was rewarded, not with absolution for his prideful comment, but with the opportunity to wander in exile for a year to earn his absolution.

Reb Leiber accepted the prophet's offer and set out for a year of wandering, learning firsthand how one feels when he must depend on the kindness of others. In one town, he was directed by the president of the community to spend Shabbos at the home of the cemetery guard. In that community, each member was required to take a turn providing hospitality to travelers. Upon arriving at his host's house, Reb Leiber discovered an impoverished, angry couple resentful that their meager Shabbos meal would have to be shared. They hid none of their outrage from their guest, who did his best to placate them.

Finally, they drove him out of the house, and he wandered back to the synagogue for the night. There, the rabbi greeted him by name. "It has been revealed to me that the difficulty you endured today is the equivalent of an entire year in exile. Please spend the rest of Shabbos at my home, and then you can go home. Your soul is perfectly pure."

On arriving home, Reb Leiber doubled the size of his guest house. If his hospitality was outstanding before his experience, afterward it was — like his soul — utterly perfected.

> **Step** by **Step**
>
> *The next time I have a guest who seems to me to be difficult, I will view it as a test and try to rise to the occasion.*

10 Shevat — L'zichron olam our father, Luzer Wolbrom ז"ל ואלבראם ונחמיה בן דוב אלעזר ר' לע"נ
Dedicated by Moshe and Rita Laufer

11 Av — Yakov Menachem Paneth יבלח"ט ישעי'-ל יחזקא בן ע"ה מנחם יעקב לע"נ
Dedicated by his loving grandparents, Yisroel & Shoshana Lefkowitz

DAY
130

יא שבט
II SHEVAT / CYCLE 1

January 14, 2003
February 3, 2004
January 21, 2005
February 9, 2006
January 30, 2007
January 18, 2008
February 5, 2009
January 26, 2010

יב אב
12 AV / CYCLE 2

August 10, 2003
July 30, 2004
August 17, 2005
August 6, 2006
July 27, 2007
August 13, 2008
August 2, 2009
July 23, 2010

❧ *The Holy Altar*

SEFER AHAVAS CHESED — Part III Chapter I

*A*mong the many terrible voids left by the destruction of the Temple is the inability of a Jew to bring a sacrifice to atone for his sins. *Hachnasas orchim* provides another medium for accomplishing this vital task. The Talmud (*Chagigah* 27a) quotes Rabbi Yochanan and Reish Lakish explaining that in the days since the destruction of the Temple, "a person's table is an atonement for him." In fact, the act of welcoming a hungry person to one's table does more than atone for a particular sin — it actually places that person in the category of a *"tzaddik,"* a righteous man. "One who has mercy on others and gives food to the hungry is a *tzaddik*," says *Derech Eretz Rabbah*, Chapter 2.

The value of sharing a meal with someone increases dramatically when the guest is a Torah scholar, for providing sustenance or assistance to a Torah scholar is a special brand of chesed that encompasses both the act of kindness and the great mitzvah of supporting Torah study. A person who provides food and hospitality to a Torah scholar, in the Talmud's words (*Berachos* 10:b), is compared to one who brings the continual sacrifices — the *"korban tamid"* to the altar. The continual sacrifices were brought at the outset and the close of each day's service, and they served a special purpose. In the merit of these sacrifices, the walls of the Temple could not be penetrated by enemies of the Jewish people.

Hospitality extended to a Torah scholar in one's home similarly envelops one's home in Divine protection. The prophet Elisha had once been given shelter in the attic of a woman's house. In the words she used to express her gratitude for having the opportunity to host Elisha, she used the expression *"tamid,"* which means always (*Malachim II* 4:9). The Talmud sees in the use of that word the link between providing hospitality to a *tzaddik* and bringing the *korban tamid*.

When one's home is open to Torah scholars, one's spiritual level is gradually elevated by their presence. By extending *hachnasas orchim* to the learned and the wise, a tremendous wellspring of positive influence flows into the home. One should not, of course, limit one's hospitality to this caliber of guest; as the story of Reb Leiber illustrated (Day 129), much can be gained by offering a warm welcome to even the most difficult guest. The essential point is to view one's resources as a potential source of assistance to those who learn Torah. One who fails to do so, according to the Talmud (*Sanhedrin* 92a), robs himself of blessing.

If there are rabbis, teachers, lecturers or other learned people who travel to my community, I will make an effort to offer them hospitality.

11 Shevat — Aaron Rothwachs לע״נ אהרן ע״ה בן ירמיהו הלוי יבלחט״א
Dedicated by his loving family

12 Av — May today's learning be a זכות for all the חולים of כלל ישראל.

יב שבט
12 SHEVAT / CYCLE 1

January 15, 2003
February 4, 2004
January 22, 2005
February 10, 2006
January 31, 2007
January 19, 2008
February 6, 2009
January 27, 2010

יג אב
13 AV / CYCLE 2

August 11, 2003
July 31, 2004
August 18, 2005
August 7, 2006
July 28, 2007
August 14, 2008
August 3, 2009
July 24, 2010

❧ *Dramatic Effects*

SEFER AHAVAS CHESED — Part III Chapter I

Hachnasas orchim is a mitzvah with the strength to revise reality, turning friends into strangers and strangers into friends. The Chofetz Chaim cites the passage in the Talmud (*Sanhedrin* 103) that poses the dramatic reversals effected by those in Jewish history who performed, or failed to perform, this mitzvah. "How great is the principle of providing food for guests. It distances those who are close, and brings close those who are distant; it shields the eyes from the wicked and brings to rest the Divine Presence, even upon the prophets of *Baal;* and it renders the inadvertent as intentional."

To understand this elliptical passage, one must identify its specific references. The first part of the verse, distancing those who are close, refers to the nations of Ammon and Moab. They are blood relatives of the Jewish people, descended from Abraham's nephew Lot. They made their mark in history, however, through their drastic departure from the ways of Abraham's family, for it was these two nations that failed to provide hospitality to the Jewish people as they traveled to Eretz Yisrael through the wilderness. Rather than running to greet their cousins with food and drink, they warned them to stay off their territory. For this egregious failure, these nations that exhibited no concern for the wayfarer were forever banned from joining the ranks of the Jewish people.

The verse further indicates that *hachnasas orchim* has the effect of drawing close someone who was a complete stranger to the Jewish people. This part of the passage refers to Jethro, Moses' father-in-law. Jethro had no common lineage with the Jewish people. Nevertheless, when Moses arrived in Jethro's land of Midian, Jethro's instant response was: "Bring that man and let him eat." The simple translation of the verse is that Jethro called for and provided him with bread. As a reward for this, the Talmud says, Jethro's descendants rose to become members of the *Sanhedrin*, the final arbiters of Jewish law. Not only were they permitted to join the Jewish people; they were elevated to a role in which they held the responsibility for the entire nation's proper observance of the Torah.

Hachnasas orchim in these two historical instances is the cement that binds the relationship. Where it is missing, a close relationship dissolves into enmity. Where it is present, it creates a new closeness strong enough to span generations.

When I invite guests to my home, I will include those neighbors or acquaintances with whom I would like to have a closer bond.

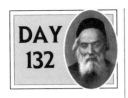
יג שבט
13 SHEVAT / CYCLE 1

January 16, 2003
February 5, 2004
January 23, 2005
February 11, 2006
February 1, 2007
January 20, 2008
February 7, 2009
January 28, 2010

יד אב
14 AV / CYCLE 2

August 12, 2003
August 1, 2004
August 19, 2005
August 8, 2006
July 29, 2007
August 15, 2008
August 4, 2009
July 25, 2010

✑ *A Disastrous Omission*

SEFER AHAVAS CHESED — Part III Chapter I

*D*avid was being pursued by jealous, wrathful King Saul. He was forced to flee, but before he did so, he had a final, good-bye encounter with his beloved friend, King Saul's son Jonathan. This extraordinarily righteous man, who should have been heir to the throne, was David's loyal companion. Their bond was so deep that it is widely acknowledged as the all-time exemplar of true friendship. Vowing continued loyalty to each other regardless of the outcome of the conflict, they bid each other farewell, and then, Jonathan made a fateful omission. He neglected to provide David with food for the road. Through this mistake, the Chofetz Chaim relates, one can see the devastating effect — even on a righteous man — of failing to provide for the wayfarer.

David's travels brought him to Nob, a city of priests. On arrival, his gnawing hunger drove him to request that the priests provide him with the special bread reserved only for them. Under normal circumstances, a nonpriest who partakes of this bread is liable for death. In this special situation, however, the priests provided David with the bread he needed to regain his strength. Events then surged forward along an unpredictable path of destruction. Saul's general, Do'eg the Edomite, had witnessed the priests' concession to David. He conveyed the information to Saul in a way that suggested that the priests were in league with David against the king. Saul ordered Do'eg to wipe out the entire city of Nob – its priests and their families. Ultimately Saul was left with no allies, and both he and Jonathan were killed by the Philistines.

The Talmud comments that there were many steps leading to this tragic result, many pivots upon which the story turned. In the final analysis, however, it was Jonathan's neglect of *hachnasas orchim*, in just this one instance, that paved the path to the bitter end.

"From all of this," says the Chofetz Chaim, "we learn how great one's caution must be that he does not turn a blind eye to the mitzvah of *hachnasas orchim*, and as a reward for this, Hashem will save him and all his children from the difficulties of this world." This blessing is the natural outgrowth of the principle that the reward is always greater than the punishment. If the result of neglecting *hachnasas orchim* was the extinguishing of Saul's line, the reward for performing the mitzvah is a promise of a long, thriving line of future generations.

The next time a guest comes to my house, even for a relatively short visit, I will make sure to offer some food and drink.

יד שבט
14 SHEVAT / CYCLE 1

January 17, 2003
February 6, 2004
January 24, 2005
February 12, 2006
February 2, 2007
January 21, 2008
February 8, 2009
January 29, 2010

טו אב
15 AV / CYCLE 2

August 13, 2003
August 2, 2004
August 20, 2005
August 9, 2006
July 30, 2007
August 16, 2008
August 5, 2009
July 26, 2010

✎ *Abraham's Way*

SEFER AHAVAS CHESED — Part III Chapter II

*A*braham did not need the scrolls of the Torah to tell him how to fulfill Hashem's will. Generations before Mount Sinai, he was already living a Divinely directed life: "You hear My voice and keep My observances, My commandments, My laws and My Torah" (*Bereishis* 26:5). That one short verse is all the information provided regarding Abraham's adherence to a plethora of commandments and all of their accompanying details. Of all these commandments, however, there is one that the Torah singles out for a full, detailed exploration — the mitzvah of *hachnasas orchim*. It is this mitzvah that is revealed in detail and nuance through the narrative in *Parashas Vayeira*.

The Chofetz Chaim observes that Abraham's actions in this story set a template for the development of the Jewish people. If the Torah goes to such lengths to spell out the details, says the Chofetz Chaim, surely one is obligated to study these details and acquire the understanding that they are there to impart. The first of these details is Abraham's willingness to sacrifice personal comfort for the sake of providing a welcome to guests. At the time of this narrative, he was in the painful third day of recovery from his *bris*, which he had undergone at the age of 99. If anyone would have had reason to say, "I've proven my devotion to Hashem. Now I need to rest," it would have been Abraham at that moment. Nevertheless, he positioned himself at the door of his tent, hoping that he would have the opportunity to serve a wayfarer that happened by.

The second detail is that he awaited no one in particular. There were no sultans or sheiks expected in the desert that day. He made himself available, despite his pain, to whomever Hashem would send his way. When his visitors appeared, it mattered not in the least that they seemed to be simple, dusty desert travelers. He rose quickly, ran to greet them and bowed before them as if they were royalty. He pleaded with them for the opportunity to serve them, as if they were doing him the kindness. At this point, the Chofetz Chaim turns away from the Torah's narrative toward modern-day reality and he asks, how can one even attempt to live up to this level of hospitality? Few people have the opportunity or inclination to sit by the door all day waiting for guests. Fewer still would feel the urge to bow down to a stranger at the door.

Bowing, the Chofetz Chaim explains, is not always a physical act. It can be expressed in a tone of voice, in the manner in which one receives a guest, in the little extras one provides for the guest's comfort. Everyone knows how to receive a guest wholeheartedly; it is a response usually reserved for those who mean the most to one's life. In detailing Abraham's reception of his guests, the Torah teaches that one's best face should not be kept for special occasions. Everyone who comes to the door deserves to see it.

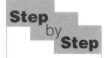

The next time someone arrives at my home, I will put a little extra effort into making him feel that he is important to me.

14 Shevat — Meyer E. Fink לע"נ ר' מאיר יהודה בן ר' אליהו ז"ל
Dedicated by the Fink, Friedman, Mayerfeld and Wolf families

15 Av — Dedicated to my spouse, Yvonne, for her love, kindness and striving for harmony

טו שבט
15 SHEVAT / CYCLE 1

January 18, 2003
February 7, 2004
January 25, 2005
February 13, 2006
February 3, 2007
January 22, 2008
February 9, 2009
January 30, 2010

טז אב
16 AV / CYCLE 2

August 14, 2003
August 3, 2004
August 21, 2005
August 10, 2006
July 31, 2007
August 17, 2008
August 6, 2009
July 27, 2010

❧ *Kindness*

SEFER AHAVAS CHESED — Part III Chapter II

The Shabbos guest enjoyed a lavish meal, sumptuous desert, uplifting singing, enlightening conversation and, finally, he longed quietly for his traditional Shabbos afternoon nap. For some reason, however, the hosts were making no motions toward ending the meal. The fifth child embarked upon his explanation of the week's *parashah*. The preschooler stood on her chair and performed several songs. The master of the house brought out some nuts and fruit, along with a thick anthology of Torah commentaries and a volume of Talmud. There was more conversation, more eating, more singing. At that point, the host had finished reviewing his texts, and he began a lengthy discourse on the week's Torah portion. The younger children had gone off to play. The wife got up to clear the dishes, but the guest sat dutifully in his seat, praying that his eyelids would somehow remain open. The guest began to feel a bit ungrateful, but he had to admit to himself that he just wanted to go home.

Had these hosts studied the example set by Abraham when he tended to his guests in *Parashas Vayeira*, the Shabbos guest might have been spared this well-intentioned detainment. What one learns from Abraham's deeds is to place the guest's comfort above all else. Upon greeting his guests, Abraham brought them water and invited them to wash their feet. In modern-day custom, this might translate into offering road-weary travelers a shower or a chance to wash up. Although a host might be eager to lay out his elaborate spread upon the table right away, Abraham teaches that first one must make sure the guest is physically comfortable. "Lean under the tree," he invited his guests. In today's circumstances, the visitor might appreciate the offer of a comfortable seat, a chance to cool down or warm up, a light snack to whet the appetite. The message to the guest is: "Welcome to my household. Make yourself at home."

Abraham did not immediately invite his guests for a full meal. First, he offered them some bread. The Chofetz Chaim points out two lessons from this. One is to allow guests a chance to leave quickly if they are pressed for time. As the example above illustrates, there is no kindness in keeping people within one's home longer than they wish to be there. Abraham invited his visitors to eat some bread, letting them know right away that after they had eaten, they were free to continue on their way. The other lesson is to avoid making a guest feel that he is causing great exertion on his host's part. In the way of all the righteous of the Jewish people, Abraham's deeds far outshone his words. He offered bread, but produced a feast. "Say little and do much" (*Avos* 1:15) is the best description of a proper host's attitude.

In all these details, one overall principle emerges. The host's task is to sensitize himself to his guest's needs. He should not push his own agenda upon the guest, but rather concentrate on making the guest feel welcome and comfortable. *Hachnasas orchim* is, after all, an act of kindness.

15 Shevat — May today's learning be a זכות for דוד בן חנה נ"י.

16 Av — In honor of Norman and Marcia Hoppenstein

טו שבט
16 SHEVAT / CYCLE 1

January 19, 2003
February 8, 2004
January 26, 2005
February 14, 2006
February 4, 2007
January 23, 2008
February 10, 2009
January 31, 2010

יז אב
17 AV / CYCLE 2

August 15, 2003
August 4, 2004
August 22, 2005
August 11, 2006
August 1, 2007
August 18, 2008
August 7, 2009
July 28, 2010

❧ *Every Step*

SEFER AHAVAS CHESED — Part III Chapter II
footnotes

*B*esides its value as an instructive guide on the mitzvah of *hachnasas orchim*, the details of Abraham's kindness related in *Parashas Vayeira* serve another purpose as well. Each deed he performed for his guests is a separate fountainhead of merit that produced a distinct gift for the Jewish people. The Talmud (*Bava Metzia* 86b) elaborates: Whatever Abraham did for his guests himself, Hashem Himself did for the Jewish people as they wandered through the wilderness. Whatever Abraham sent others to do, Hashem did for His children through a messenger.

The Torah relates that "Abraham ran to the cattle," to choose a calf for his guests. In turn, when the Jews in the desert longed for meat, Hashem directed the wind to bring the birds directly to them so that they could satisfy their appetite. In regard to Abraham's hospitality, the Torah says, "And he took butter and milk" to serve. His personal attention was recompensed when Hashem sent manna from Heaven to feed the Jews. Abraham stood over his guests and personally served them. In turn, Hashem said, "Behold, I stand before you at the rock" (*Shemos* 17:6). To provide water for his visitors, Abraham ordered his servants, "Let some water be brought" (*Vayeira* 18:4). In the same manner, Hashem appointed an agent to provide the Jews with water in the wilderness; He commanded Moses to strike a stone, initiating a flow of water that became known as the Well of Miriam. This served the Jews throughout their journey.

The Chofetz Chaim points out the vast bounty built into Hashem's system of rewards. Because of this one instance in which Abraham provided water for his three guests, Hashem provided water for 600,000 men, along with their wives and children, for 40 years. Because of this one time that Abraham fed his guests butter and milk, Hashem took upon Himself the obligation to provide miraculous sustenance to His children for their entire journey.

While one cannot attempt to measure the reward for a mitzvah, in this case the Talmud's equation seems so far out of balance as to be unfathomable. How could these deeds, perfect as they were, give rise to 40 years of Hashem's miraculous nurturing of an entire nation?

The answer, the Chofetz Chaim explains, is that Abraham's acts were by no means one-time deeds. He had devoted his life to bringing passersby into his home, teaching them to see Hashem's kindness in the food he gave them, instructing them to recite the blessing after meals, instilling in them whatever awareness of Hashem they were capable of absorbing. He set up his enterprise at the crossroads of idol-worshipping tribes, knowing the caliber of guest he could expect. Finally, after all his sustained effort, he merited an opportunity to feed angels, and that was the act that opened Heaven's storehouse to millions of his children generations later.

One can learn from this, says the Chofetz Chaim, the inestimable value of every act of *tzedakah*, no matter how futile it may seem. "One who pursues

(Continued on page 383)

Step by **Step**

I will try to pay attention to each element of the hospitality I provide to my guests.

---

16 Shevat — May the learning in this sefer be a z'chus and עלי' for the neshamah of
אהרן בן ישראל, נלב"ע ט"ז בשבט תשס"א

17 Av — Rabbi Yehoshua Kreindler ז"ל לע"נ יהושע בן יהודה ז"ל
הונצח ע"י משפחתו לזכרון עולם

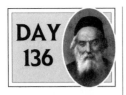

DAY 136

יז שבט

17 SHEVAT / CYCLE 1

January 20, 2003
February 9, 2004
January 27, 2005
February 15, 2006
February 5, 2007
January 24, 2008
February 11, 2009
February 1, 2010

יח אב

18 AV / CYCLE 2

August 16, 2003
August 5, 2004
August 23, 2005
August 12, 2006
August 2, 2007
August 19, 2008
August 8, 2009
July 29, 2010

❧ The Last Act

SEFER AHAVAS CHESED — Part III Chapter II

*A*fter the guests have been greeted, after they have been made comfortable, given food and drink and rest, an important juncture of the visit is reached. How a guest leaves one's home can be the defining moment for the entire visit. A guest can be treated royally throughout his visit, but if he is left to wander out the door alone with a vague "good-bye" issued from another room, he will not walk away with the feeling that his presence was valued. He might feel that the hosts are relieved to have discharged their obligations — that "good-bye" was really "good riddance." The taste left in his mouth will not be that of the delicious meal, but rather that of the shabby send-off. On the other hand, if he is walked out the door with warmth and friendliness, with sincere thanks for his presence and hopes for his return, the aftertaste of the visit will be sweet.

Escorting a guest out of one's home and down the block or to his car tells him that the host wishes to prolong the visit. It imparts the sense that the guest is valued as a person, and is not just the object of one's mitzvah. His thoughts, his conversation and company are being sought out, even pursued, past the threshold of the home. This, the Torah teaches, is capable of restoring a person's spirit, of literally giving him life.

The Torah relates that Abraham established an *"eishel,"* which means an inn. The Talmud (*Sotah* 10a) expounds on the word *"eishel"* to provide an acronym for the essential elements of *hachnasas orchim*. The first letter in the Hebrew word — "*alef*" — stands for "*achilah*," meaning food. The second letter — "*shin*" — stands for "*shesiyah*," meaning drink. The final letter — "*lamed*" — in some opinions stands for "*linah*," meaning a place to sleep, and in other opinions, stands for "*levayah*," meaning escort. Even without this mnemonic device, the Torah teaches the importance of escorting one's guests simply by presenting in detail Abraham's interaction with his angelic guests. As the Chofetz Chaim has been pointing out throughout this section on *hachnasas orchim*, every element of Abraham's performance stands as an eternal guide for the Jewish people in the proper treatment of guests.

From that narrative emerges the true importance of the manner in which a person sends off his guests. Abraham's hospitality was flawless in every way. There was no need he failed to notice, no amenity he failed to provide. His *hachnasas orchim* was a perfect diamond, but it took the final polish of "*levayah*" to bring it to its full value, to give it a luster that would shine through the generations.

Step by **Step**

The next time I see a guest off, I will make sure to do so in a way that makes him feel valued.

17 Shevat — Chaim Herman לע"נ חיים בן ר' יהודה לייב ז"ל
Dedicated by Ruth and Fishel Kipust

18 Av — לע"נ משה גרשון בן ירמי-הו צבי ז"ל
Dedicated by his wife, Marilyn Berkovits and daughters

יח שבט
18 SHEVAT / CYCLE 1

January 21, 2003
February 10, 2004
January 28, 2005
February 16, 2006
February 6, 2007
January 25, 2008
February 12, 2009
February 2, 2010

יט אב
19 AV / CYCLE 2

August 17, 2003
August 6, 2004
August 24, 2005
August 13, 2006
August 3, 2007
August 20, 2008
August 9, 2009
July 30, 2010

❧ *Protection*

SEFER AHAVAS CHESED — **Part III Chapter II**
footnotes

*P*roviding a wayfarer food and water is obviously a lifesaving gesture. Surprisingly, offering him an escort can be every bit as important to pre-
serving his life, and failure to see to this final detail of
hachnasas orchim can have dire results for both the
host and the visitor. The story is told of a man who
established a large guest house for travelers on the
road. One day, a terrible fire broke out and destroyed
his entire enterprise. He went to the Kotzker Rebbe
and asked, "How could Hashem let this happen when
the whole purpose of the house was *hachnasas
orchim*?" The Rebbe pointed out the fatal flaw in the
operation of the guest house. The man provided food
and drink to his guests, but he never escorted them on
their way. This meant that in the acronym of *"eishel"*
(see Day 136) the letter *"lamed,"* for *"levayah,"* was
missing. The letters remaining — *"alef"* and *"shin"* —
spell *"eish,"* meaning fire.

Failing to escort a guest is not the simple omission of
a detail; it is a potential source of tragedy. The Torah
presents a discussion of the *"eglah arufah,"* the axed calf,
which deals with the halachah regarding a dead body
that is found between two towns. The procedure in such
an event is that the rabbinical court is summoned to the
site and required to atone, saying: "We did not spill this
blood. Our eyes did not see who did it." This procedure
immediately raises a question: Why would the sages of
the community be required to answer for a murder? The

underlying meaning of this statement is a confession that they did not see to this wayfarer's needs. He was not sent off properly with an escort and food for the road. Rather, he was left to wander off by himself, vulnerable to the dangers of the journey.

The Sages teach that one who accompanies a guest even the minimum distance of four amos along a city street provides a protection for that person en route. Conversely, of one who neglects this duty it is said: "It is as if he is spilling blood."

In practical terms, an escort can direct the traveler to the right road and warn him against dangerous areas. On another level, Kabbalah teaches that when a person escorts someone, part of his presence accompanies the traveler as he continues on his way.

The principle at work in the case of the *"eglah arufah"* is grounded in human psychology as well. The Elder of Navardok explained that a friendly send-off provides a person with a sense of well-being, and that can be his best weapon in fending off an assailant. A person who feels valued has the will to live and the optimism to struggle for his survival. One who feels that no one cares about his comings or goings feels depressed, and is thus robbed of the strength to run away or mount a struggle against an assailant on the road.

One further aspect of Abraham's *hachnasas orchim* deserves note; he enlisted the help of his son Ishmael in tending to his guests, despite the presence of numerous servants. This detail, like all the others, is an instruction to the Jewish people. Families that involve their children in greeting, serving and escorting their guests are forming, brick by brick, the foundation of the homes their children will eventually build for themselves.

The next time I have guests in my home, I will involve my children in some aspects of hachnasas orchim.

18 Shevat — In memory of our parents
Dedicated in loving memory, by Yehudit and Israel Preminger

19 Av —

DAY
138

יט שבט
19 SHEVAT / CYCLE 1

January 22, 2003
February 11, 2004
January 29, 2005
February 17, 2006
February 7, 2007
January 26, 2008
February 13, 2009
February 3, 2010

כ אב
20 AV / CYCLE 2

August 18, 2003
August 7, 2004
August 25, 2005
August 14, 2006
August 4, 2007
August 21, 2008
August 10, 2009
July 31, 2010

✒ *Heaven's Help*

SEFER AHAVAS CHESED — Part III
Chapter II/II footnotes

*S*ince *hachnasas orchim* involves divining the needs of another person, successfully fulfilling the mitzvah is not in the host's hands alone. He must rely upon the visitor to let him know what is needed, and upon his own common sense to hear the requests that are unspoken. In other words, he must depend upon Hashem's help, for only through His assistance can one know that his chesed will be appropriate and complete. The Chofetz Chaim advises that the mitzvah can at least start off on the right road if the host makes sure to greet his visitor warmly, with a pleasant expression. The next step is to provide food and drink, whether or not the guest requests it. Often a guest will refrain from asking, and even refuse refreshments when offered, simply to avoid burdening the host. This is an area in which many people err. In one story, a group of boys were lost on a field trip, and an acquaintance living nearby took them into his house. He treated them kindly and arranged transportation for them to get back to their destination. "Is anyone hungry?" he asked them. Politely, they all said "no" as their empty stomachs rumbled. "Does anyone want a drink?" Again, they all declined, despite their thirst. While the host congratulated himself on his chesed and the boys congratulated themselves on their politeness, a major portion of a beautiful mitzvah fell away from the picture.

In a similar story, a rebbe brought several lost boys into his house and, understanding that they would be embarrassed to ask, he put snacks and drinks on the table for them. He stood by them watching, and no one partook of the food. After a while, the rebbe put the snacks away. Years later, recalling the incident, one of the boys disclosed that they had not eaten because they were ashamed to do so with their rebbe standing over them. With just a bit more sensitivity, the rebbe would have known to walk away from the table, but the idea had not occurred to him.

These instances might seem to indicate that only a mind reader can fulfill the mitzvah of *hachnasas orchim*. In reality, the Chofetz Chaim says, such situations prove that one needs *"Siyata di'Shmaya,"* Divine Assistance, to properly care for one's guests. The means to acquire this assistance is to first do one's best to fulfill the mitzvah, and then to pray that Hashem will fill in the gaps. When one is preparing for a guest or when a visitor comes to the door unexpectedly, one can and should ask Hashem to guide his steps so that his efforts will succeed in bringing to a fellow Jew a sense of welcome and well-being.

When a guest comes into my house, I will put out food and drink regardless of whether the guest indicates a desire for it.

19 Shevat — May today's learning be a z'chus for us.
Dedicated by the Spitz and Bauer families

20 Av — Gustave Stern ז״ל לע״נ מרדכי בן אברהם ז״ל
Dedicated by his family

כ שבט
20 SHEVAT / CYCLE 1

January 23, 2003
February 12, 2004
January 30, 2005
February 18, 2006
February 8, 2007
January 27, 2008
February 14, 2009
February 4, 2010

כא אב
21 AV / CYCLE 2

August 19, 2003
August 8, 2004
August 26, 2005
August 15, 2006
August 5, 2007
August 22, 2008
August 11, 2009
August 1, 2010

✑ *With a Smile*

SEFER AHAVAS CHESED — **Part III Chapter II**

*O*ne person provides an open door to his home, fine food and drink on his table and a soft bed to sleep in, constituting the perfect fulfillment of the mitzvah of *hachnasas orchim*. Another person offers all the same amenities — the same quality food, drink and bed — and the result is an assault on the guest's spirit, a terrible transgression of the prohibition against embarrassing a fellow Jew. The only difference between the two scenarios is the expression on the host's face.

Whatever a person's private thoughts, whatever his financial or emotional state, his duty as a host is to smile. That is because the guest will automatically feel embarrassed if he detects unhappiness in his host's demeanor. He will automatically assume that it is his presence that is causing — or at least exacerbating — the problem, even if the host explicitly tells him otherwise. Smiling through distress is a heroic act, a deed of self-sacrifice and self-control that elevates the emotional well-being of others above one's own need to indulge in one's worries. The person who takes it upon himself to make others feel good, even while he himself is suffering, earns great blessing. Conversely, the person who makes a guest worry and suffer, demonstrating through his expression that the visit is an imposition, thoroughly depletes the merit of his hospitality.

Ordinarily, the Jewish philosophy is to avoid flaunting one's wealth. When a person brings a guest into his home, however, he is justified in projecting an image of affluence if in doing so, the host assures the guest that he is not usurping food or other assets that are in short supply. A host must never allow his guest to feel uncomfortable about indulging in whatever is being offered. He should not stare at the guest as he eats, and should certainly not complain that there is not enough food to go around. Making the food appear plentiful — even if it is not — is part of the mitzvah. "Break up your bread for the hungry," says *Yeshayah* 48:10. The *Zohar* (*Vayakhel*) explains that this verse instructs the host to break the bread into large slices, so that the guest will feel comfortable taking an ample portion. Were he to slice it himself, he might feel constrained from taking as much as he desires.

Expressing interest in the guest as a person is also an essential to making him comfortable. Often the best policy is to sit with the guest and eat, so that a conversation can flow more easily and the guest is not too busy answering questions to partake of his meal.

For the overnight guest, the host must provide the best accommodations he has to offer. Putting someone in an uncomfortable bed or a noisy, cold or overheated room will certainly destroy his night's sleep, and may make him feel like an unwelcome burden on the household as well. The guest who wakes up rested is one who leaves feeling physically and emotionally strengthened by his stay in his host's home.

Step by **Step**

I will pay attention to my facial expression when I serve my guests and try to overcome any fatigue or irritation I might be feeling.

20 Shevat — Selma Eisenberg ע"ה לע"נ סלמא בת משה יעקב ע"ה
Dedicated by her children, Rochel Boland, Michael Eisenberg and Debbie Stein
21 Av — לזכות ברכה מלכה בת אליהו שלום שתחי"

כא שבט
21 SHEVAT / CYCLE 1

January 24, 2003
February 13, 2004
January 31, 2005
February 19, 2006
February 9, 2007
January 28, 2008
February 15, 2009
February 5, 2010

כב אב
22 AV / CYCLE 2

August 20, 2003
August 9, 2004
August 27, 2005
August 16, 2006
August 6, 2007
August 23, 2008
August 12, 2009
August 2, 2010

☙ In His Shoes

SEFER AHAVAS CHESED — **Part III Chapter II**

*A*s in every aspect of chesed, the best way for a person to determine what is really needed is to put himself in the other man's shoes. Most people can project how they would feel entering into someone else's home under various conditions. They can imagine how a traveler feels after a long journey; his deepest desire may be a shower and a change of clothes. A mother coming into a strange house with an entourage of small children may want nothing more than some cookies and apple juice on the table and place for the children to run and play. A charity collector in the midst of a long day of knocking on doors is most likely in need of some encouragement, refreshment and a place to rest his feet for awhile. By using one's power of empathy, one can target the needs of the guest more precisely and avoid making errors that would detract from the mitzvah.

In doing so, a person also protects his own interests. At the present time, he may be in the position of the giver, the host, the source of food and shelter, but he should realize in the cyclical turnings of the world, the situation could reverse. No asset comes to a person with a guarantee of permanence; today's giver may be tomorrow's recipient. How a person treats those who come to him for help determines whether or not he will keep the assets he has been granted. It also influences how he and his offspring will be treated when their time of need arises.

In the Talmud (*Shabbos* 151b) Rabbi Chia says to his wife, "Give to the guest, because our children may need from him." She responded, "Are you cursing us?" He denied that his comment was a curse: "When you curse, you suggest that something out of the ordinary should happen. This is ordinary."

Even a person whose assets remain with him will find he needs others at some juncture in his life. Even a wealthy man can be lost on the road, fall ill while away from home or find himself stranded in transit as Shabbos approaches. In any of these cases, he needs the caring hospitality of others. If he has made the effort in his dealings with guests to protect their dignity and provide for them with graciousness, these are the attitudes that will greet him when he finds himself reliant upon the compassion of others.

The Chofetz Chaim warns against a common mistake people make regarding *hachnasas orchim* — refraining from inviting someone who needs a place because one feels his home is inadequate for receiving this particular guest. If there is no better option for the guest, one should issue the invitation and let the guest decide whether he wishes to accept. One cannot dishonor someone by offering him the best he has — whatever it is.

In my future dealings with guests, I will utilize the technique of projecting myself into their situation so that I can accurately gauge their needs.

לע"נ אמי מורתי בדרה בת הרב סעדי-ה ז"ל — **21 Shevat**
נלב"ע כ"א טבת תשס"א — הונצח ע"י אהובה ופנחס מוסר (בתה וחתנה)

22 Av — Wendy זעלדה בת יוסף ע"ה לע"נ
Dedicated by her sister, Nechama Sarah

כב שבט
22 SHEVAT / CYCLE 1

January 25, 2003
February 14, 2004
February 1, 2005
February 20, 2006
February 10, 2007
January 29, 2008
February 16, 2009
February 6, 2010

כג אב
23 AV / CYCLE 2

August 21, 2003
August 10, 2004
August 28, 2005
August 17, 2006
August 7, 2007
August 24, 2008
August 13, 2009
August 3, 2010

❧ Life-Saving

SEFER AHAVAS CHESED — Part III Chapter II
footnotes

*I*n the simple act of escorting a guest out the door and on his way, a person performs an act of kindness whose reward, according to the Rambam, surpasses that of every other form of chesed. The Rambam's conclusion is supported by many statements throughout the Talmud, but the truth of the concept emerges easily when one studies the other side of the coin. A person who is not escorted — someone who is left to drift out the door and find his own way — feels like a non-entity. His vital spirit is crushed. The send-off a person receives is what forms his lasting impression of his value in his host's eyes, and by extension, in his own eyes.

So essential is the practice of escorting a visitor that the Rambam relates that the rabbinical courts had the custom of appointing agents to accompany people in their travels. If the court was lax in this duty and harm to a traveler resulted, those who failed to fulfill the duty were considered to have spilled his blood. On the other hand, the act of escorting a guest even four *amos* — about eight feet — carries tremendous reward.

There are specific guidelines as to what qualifies as fulfillment of the mitzvah of escorting a guest. In times when cities were smaller and roads were more dangerous, the guidelines were upheld with greater stringency. At the very least, however, the host should walk the guest to the door and eight feet beyond.

Rabbi Elchonon Wasserman, the renowned student of the Chofetz Chaim, visited America in the early 1930's to raise money for his yeshivah. During his stay, he resided in an apartment building that had an elevator. Each of the many individuals that came to see him there was escorted personally by Rabbi Wasserman to the elevator, where he waited with them until their departure. This, in Rabbi Wasserman's view, was the escort that he owed each of his guests.

The Chofetz Chaim holds that a guest cannot waive his right to the minimal level of escort. That is because failing to provide any escort at all is compared to spilling the guest's blood; one cannot say to a fellow Jew, "I give you the right to spill my blood."

The distance one should escort a guest is therefore dependent on the situation. If the city streets are generally safe, the requirement is less. If they are dangerous, the host must do all he can to assure his guest's safe passage. If the route is well marked and easy to follow, the host need not worry about pointing out the way. If it is confusing and poorly lit, however, the host must make sure that the guest sets off in the right direction. In an area where there are dangerous neighborhoods nearby, the host must do his best to prevent the visitor from wandering into them accidentally.

Even if a guest only has to walk across a quiet suburban street, the host still has an obligation to escort him the minimal distance. As mentioned earlier, the guest's personal safety is not the only issue. Equally important is the opportunity to send the guest off buoyed by the feeling that "My presence counts."

When guests depart from my home, I will make sure they have accurate directions to their next destination.

22 Shevat — Scott Michael Kaufman ט"חלבי ,רעב רשא 'ר ןב ל"ז לכימ המלש נ"על
Dedicated by his brother, Gedaliah Yerachmiel & Rochelle Kaufman and family

23 Av —

DAY 142

כג שבט
23 SHEVAT / CYCLE 1

January 26, 2003
February 15, 2004
February 2, 2005
February 21, 2006
February 11, 2007
January 30, 2008
February 17, 2009
February 7, 2010

כד אב
24 AV / CYCLE 2

August 22, 2003
August 11, 2004
August 29, 2005
August 18, 2006
August 8, 2007
August 25, 2008
August 14, 2009
August 4, 2010

✑ *Safe Passage*

SEFER AHAVAS CHESED — **Part III Chapter II**

A man is rushing down the sidewalk of a city street, hoping that he has not missed his bus. Suddenly he becomes aware of a voice calling in his direction. At the curb, a car stands idling while the driver shouts, "Excuse me, sir! Can you give me some directions?" A mitzvah has now presented itself to the pedestrian. He can pretend he does not hear the request and walk on. He can give a few vague instructions that might get the man somewhat closer to his destination; or, he can provide the driver with accurate directions and stick with the task until he feels sure that he has been understood.

The demands of *hachnasas orchim* make the last option the only option. Although the driver is not a guest in the man's home, he is a wayfarer in need of help, and this pedestrian is the one he has chosen — Hashem has chosen — to have the opportunity to provide that help. If the pedestrian walks away, his purpose in being at that place at that time will have been defeated. If he offers uselessly vague instructions, he will be accountable if the driver, in his confusion, has an accident or strays into a bad neighborhood.

Certainly when someone is a guest in a person's home, the host bears responsibility for getting him to his next destination safely. If the neighborhood is a dangerous one, the guest must be provided with an escort. One common situation arises when a babysitter comes to the home to care for a child. Even if one feels there is no danger and the babysitter is willing to walk alone, she should be escorted safely home.

Another common situation is when one encounters someone outside a wedding hall, lecture or other gathering place, who asks, "Are you heading in my direction?" If the person inquiring will otherwise take an unsafe route home — such as a subway late at night or a dangerous walk — the answer to his question should be, "As a matter of fact, I am going through that neighborhood." One should offer the ride, even if it is out of one's way.

Even if a guest has a car parked right outside the host's house, the host must not allow him to drive it if, for any reason, he is unable to do so safely. If the guest is overtired, not feeling well, or intoxicated on Purim, the host should drive him or find him a taxi or other means to get home.

When a person travels, he also bears some responsibility for reassuring those who might be worried about his safety. If a person knows he will be late, he should take the few minutes to call those who are waiting for him so that they will not spend one unnecessary moment contemplating the many frightening possibilities associated with travel. Even if the traveler feels that the worries are overblown or unjustified, he should respond to the reality of the situation; people worry, and he should not agitate them when he could, with a two-minute investment of time, provide peace of mind.

Step by **Step**

When someone asks me for directions, I will make it my responsibility to make sure they understand where to go.

23 Shevat — Celia Kurzman ה"ע צבי 'ר בת טשרנא נ"לע
Dedicated by Debbie and Shloimi Kopolovics and family

24 Av —

כד שבט
24 SHEVAT / CYCLE I

January 27, 2003
February 16, 2004
February 3, 2005
February 22, 2006
February 12, 2007
January 31, 2008
February 18, 2009
February 8, 2010

כה אב
25 AV / CYCLE 2

August 23, 2003
August 12, 2004
August 30, 2005
August 19, 2006
August 9, 2007
August 26, 2008
August 15, 2009
August 5, 2010

✣ *Eternal Wages*

SEFER AHAVAS CHESED — Part III Chapter II

*T*he wages one earns by helping a guest are inestimable, as is illustrated in an episode from the Book of Judges. During the time in history that is recorded there, the Jews were in the process of conquering the Canaanite cities in the land of Israel. A group of Jewish spies waited outside one such city until a Canaanite man emerged from the gate. They asked the man for directions: How could they enter the city, and where could they hide? They promised that neither he nor his family would be harmed when the Jews came to conquer. The man saw their vulnerability in their current situation, and gave them the information they needed. He and his family were protected in the bloody conquest that ensued, and the man then went on to found a city, which he named Luz.

Luz is a city synonymous with the concept of eternity. The Angel of Death had no dominion there; people who reached an age at which they were satiated with life on earth had to leave the city limits to embark on their journey to the Next World. Earthly conquerors had no power in Luz either — neither Sennacherib nor Nebuchadnezzer were able to destroy the city. The Chofetz Chaim points to this story as the Torah's illustration of the everlasting rewards that can result from just one instance of helping a traveler in need. There are many ways of providing this help — directions, shelter, food, use of a cell phone, assistance with a flat tire or a dead battery — and all have the potential to bring immeasurable reward, for they remove the traveler from his vulnerable position and prevent any harm that might have come to him.

The Chofetz Chaim introduces another concept in the realm of receiving guests — including a guest room in the construction of one's house. The person who includes in his blueprint for construction a place for the car, a place for the toys, a place for the computer and so forth may well have the resources to include a place for guests as well. Such a room, which offers guests an added degree of comfort and privacy, can become the wellspring of great blessing for the entire household. One should remember to preserve this blessing by sending the guest off in the right way — well prepared and safely escorted. As the story of Jonathan and David (see Day 132) illustrated, the entire mitzvah can be turned toward tragedy by failing to provide food for the road.

In one final instruction on *hachnasas orchim*, the Chofetz Chaim reiterates that this mitzvah is a communal responsibility. Any upstanding Jewish community should be sure that it has an organized method of taking care of guests who enter its precincts. There should be an official group of designated people whose task is *hachnasas orchim*. "Those that strengthen themselves in this mitzvah," says the Chofetz Chaim, "how happy is their lot."

If my synagogue or community does not have an official hospitality committee, I will try to initiate the organization of one.

כה שבט
25 SHEVAT / CYCLE 1

January 28, 2003
February 17, 2004
February 4, 2005
February 23, 2006
February 13, 2007
February 1, 2008
February 19, 2009
February 9, 2010

כו אב
26 AV / CYCLE 2

August 24, 2003
August 13, 2004
August 31, 2005
August 20, 2006
August 10, 2007
August 27, 2008
August 16, 2009
August 6, 2010

~ *Facing Fate*

SEFER AHAVAS CHESED — **Part III Chapter III**

*M*ost people would rather think about pleasant things, and man's vulnerability to sickness, his pain, struggle and mortality are not pleasant things. For this reason, the Torah singles out the mitzvah of visiting the sick — *bikur cholim* — as a special brand of chesed. It is among the mitzvos listed in the Mishnah (*Shabbos* 127a) regarding which: "one eats their fruits in this world and the principal remains in the World to Come."

The Talmud (*Sotah* 14a) presents a paradox: The Torah (*Devarim* 13:5) declares, "You should follow after Hashem." Another verse, however, makes that demand seemingly impossible to obey, for "Hashem is a fire that consumes" (*Devarim* 4:24). The Talmud seeks to reconcile these verses: How does one follow Hashem without being consumed? One who seeks to elevate himself to the level of prophet or messiah most certainly will feel Hashem's heat. One who follows in His ways, however, will be drawn closer to Him. The Talmud (*Bava Metzia* 30b), quoting *Shemos* (18:20), explains: "Teach them the way they should travel in." "The way" refers to chesed in general. "That they should travel in" refers specifically to *bikur cholim*.

The discussion in this portion of the Talmud relates to visiting a person who is a *"ben gilo,"* which means someone born under one's *"mazal,"* or astrological sign. To a certain extent, two people born in the same period share a similar fate, and the Talmud states that when a person visits a *ben gilo* who is sick, he takes upon himself one-sixtieth of the illness. That amount in halachah is often viewed as nullified by the other 59 parts. If a drop of milk falls into a pot of meat, a rabbi will under most circumstances declare the meat still edible if there is 60 times more meat than milk in the pot. Such situations, of course, require the opinion of a rabbi who understands the specific case. As a general principle, however, one-sixtieth represents an amount of adulteration that is neutralized by the whole. In the case of *bikur cholim*, the point is that the visitor is affected by his contact with the sick *ben gilo*, but he is not made sick himself.

The fact that the Talmud frames its *bikur cholim* discussion in terms of a *ben gilo* may reflect a certain facet of human psychology. The *ben gilo* is someone whose fate one shares. When a person hears that an acquaintance is ill with a type of disease that strikes frequently, the person is saddened for two reasons. First of all, he is pained by his friend's suffering. In addition, he understands that he might someday share his friend's fate. Visiting his friend requires the courage to come face-to-face with his own mortality and constant dependency upon Hashem's kindness.

This does not mean that a person should actually expose himself to a dangerous disease. If such exposure seems called for, one must consult with a rabbi for the proper guidelines. In circumstances where danger is not an issue, the Chofetz Chaim acknowledges that for many people, the emotional toll may be an issue. To this, he responds that the merit of the mitzvah itself carries tremendous protective powers. Visiting someone who is ill, in fact, often strengthens the visitor, giving him the faith and optimism to overcome the fears that lurk in the corner of every human heart.

Even if I am not comfortable doing so, I will try to visit or call someone I know who is sick.

DAY 145

כו שבט
26 SHEVAT / CYCLE 1

January 29, 2003
February 18, 2004
February 5, 2005
February 24, 2006
February 14, 2007
February 2, 2008
February 20, 2009
February 10, 2010

כז אב
27 AV / CYCLE 2

August 25, 2003
August 14, 2004
September 1, 2005
August 21, 2006
August 11, 2007
August 28, 2008
August 17, 2009
August 7, 2010

❧ *Everyone's Mitzvah*

SEFER AHAVAS CHESED — Part III
Chapter III/III footnotes

There is no one too great, nor anyone too ordinary, to perform the mitzvah of visiting the sick. Everyone is eligible to earn the merit of this deed, and everyone is obligated to perform it when the opportunity arises. Even the most revered Torah scholar has a responsibility to visit his neighbor or acquaintance who is lying sick in bed. He has no right to think, "I have nothing in common with him. I'll leave it to his circle of friends and family to take care of him." On the other hand, an ordinary individual should not excuse himself from visiting the great man, thinking, "Why would he want to see someone like me?"

The effect of another person's concern and attention is immeasurable, as is illustrated by an incident from the life of Rabbi Abraham Pam. In the back of the synagogue where Rabbi Pam regularly prayed, there was an old man who could be found day after day in his customary seat. One day, he was missing, and Rabbi Pam's inquiries elicited the news that the man was sick in the hospital. Although Rabbi Pam wished to visit the man, he could not, because the rabbi was a Kohen. (A Kohen is someone descended from the Priests of the Jewish people. Kohanim are in some circumstances forbidden to enter a hospital.) Instead, Rabbi Pam wrote the man a letter saying that his presence in synagogue was missed, that he prayed for his recovery every day, and that he would love to visit but was unable to because he was a Kohen.

The old man was ecstatic with his mail. The great Rabbi Pam, the head of the famous Yeshivah Torah Vodaath, had written to him. He prayed for him. He would even have come to visit him if only he could. The man showed the letter to everyone who entered the room. His elated spirits soon boosted his physical strength as well, and a full recovery ensued. When Rabbi Pam heard of the impact his letter had made, he cried: "What did it take to write that letter? Nothing. A pen and a piece of paper. I jotted a couple of lines and sent it over."

With that quick gesture, he restored a person to life. That is the power of a moment of thoughtfulness — a ten-minute phone call, a half-hour visit, a get-well card, a small gift. What, then, is the cost of the many such opportunities missed? If extending oneself a little bit has the potential to renew someone's spirit, what justification can one have when, in the World to Come, all the lost opportunities are laid out before one's eyes?

Obviously, not every act of *bikur cholim* will result in totally restored good health, but even if one can make that day — or just that hour— more bearable, one has accomplished a deed of heroic proportions. The Chofetz Chaim adds a note of caution to this discussion; a person should be attentive to the patient's needs, visiting as much — but no more than — is appreciated and beneficial.

Step by **Step**

I will try to extend myself to those in my community who are sick, even if they are not within my immediate circle.

26 Shevat — David Lacob לע"נ דוד אלחנן בן פישל ז"ל
Dedicated by his family: Adele, Brynie, Steven and Risa

27 Av —

כז שבט
27 SHEVAT / CYCLE 1

January 30, 2003
February 19, 2004
February 6, 2005
February 25, 2006
February 15, 2007
February 3, 2008
February 21, 2009
February 11, 2010

כח אב
28 AV / CYCLE 2

August 26, 2003
August 15, 2004
September 2, 2005
August 22, 2006
August 12, 2007
August 29, 2008
August 18, 2009
August 8, 2010

✤ *Doing Good*

SEFER AHAVAS CHESED — **Part III Chapter III**

*W*hen a person's health is compromised, well-meaning gestures can sometimes do more harm than good. To prevent this result, the Chofetz Chaim offers guidelines for *bikur cholim*. He cites *Shulchan Aruch Yoreh De'ah* (*Siman* 335), which permits only relatives and close friends to visit the patient within the first few days of his taking ill. Casual friends and distant acquaintances should wait three days, so that the situation has a chance to stabilize. If the patient becomes critically ill immediately, however, everyone should visit as soon as possible. There is no obligation to wait.

When a person takes ill, much is occurring on the physical plane. Much more, however, is occurring on the spiritual plane, and the visitor must take this into account also when he makes his visit. The Torah teaches that the *Shechinah* — the Divine Presence — rests at the head of a sick person. The visitor is therefore prohibited from sitting at a level significantly above the patient. If he is lying on the ground for some reason, one may not sit next to him. It is not necessary, however, to measure the height of the bed relative to the height of the chair. One may sit on a chair next to the bed, even if it happens to be slightly higher.

Equally important to understanding the obligation to visit the sick is understanding the obligation to leave the patient alone if that is better for him. The Chofetz Chaim enumerates certain types of illness in which the patient may be better off without personal visits.

Someone with digestive problems who is unable to control his elimination processes is one such case because of the embarrassment he may have. Someone with severe headaches or eye problems, or someone for whom speaking is difficult, may also in some cases be better off without personal visits.

This does not mean, however, that such people should be left alone. The Chofetz Chaim recommends visiting outside the patient's room, inquiring of his relatives or caretakers about his condition so that he knows someone is concerned. The message should be conveyed to the patient that his friend has come and asked for him, is praying for him and willing to help in any way that is appropriate. Even when a person is in no condition to accept visitors, the knowledge that others care about his well-being is as vital as ever. A person may not want others to see him in his weakened state. He may not want to feel obligated to carry on a conversation. He may not want company, but more than anything else, he does not want to be forgotten.

If I know someone who is not in a condition to receive visitors, I will try to make sure my concern is conveyed to him in some other way.

DAY 147

כח שבט
28 SHEVAT / CYCLE 1

January 31, 2003
February 20, 2004
February 7, 2005
February 26, 2006
February 16, 2007
February 4, 2008
February 22, 2009
February 12, 2010

כט אב
29 AV / CYCLE 2

August 27, 2003
August 16, 2004
September 3, 2005
August 23, 2006
August 13, 2007
August 30, 2008
August 19, 2009
August 9, 2010

❧ *Behind the Scenes*

SEFER AHAVAS CHESED — Part III Chapter III

*B*ikur cholim is a deed that can take place on center stage — at the side of the sick person — or, when necessary, completely behind the scenes. Sometimes, the recipient of this act of kindness is not even aware of it. There is no grateful smile to reward the doer; there is only the knowledge that he has fulfilled his obligation to emulate Hashem by caring for someone in pain.

The Sadivner Rav, the saintly leader of a small synagogue in Brooklyn, lived up to this obligation with a combination of overflowing compassion and stubborn persistence. In one instance, an elderly member of the synagogue took ill and was placed in the hospital. For many weeks, the Sadivner Rav made a long daily trek on foot to the hospital to inquire after the man, even though the patient was not permitted any visitors. The rabbi would seek out the doctor and ask about the man's condition, treatment and prognosis. "I'll be back tomorrow," he would conclude.

Finally, a nurse asked him, "Why are you coming here every day? You know you can't go in to see him." The Sadivner Rav replied, "I come for two reasons. You know, the man has no family. I want him to know that I care about him and I'm thinking about him. Secondly, I want the doctors and nurses to know that there is someone who cares about him and is thinking about him."

The rabbi well understood that in the high-pressure, high-speed world of a city hospital, the patients who had friends and relatives expressing interest in their cases would be tended to first. Their needs would be cast constantly in the forefront of the doctors' and nurses' field of vision. He made it his mission to be the voice for those who had no voice. Even without ever laying eyes upon the patient, he performed the mitzvah of *bikur cholim* to its fullest extent, keeping a place in his heart and a place on his daily agenda for a fellow Jew in his time of need.

The lesson here should not be misconstrued. *Bikur cholim* does not mean harassing already overworked doctors and nurses. In fact, an aggressive, argumentative attitude will often elicit a backlash that could cause the patient and his advocates to be avoided as much as possible. The point is that when one shows that the patient is someone who is valued, that impression has an impact on those who care for him. Human nature is such that if the patient were, for instance, the king of a foreign country, his needs would be assiduously attended to. By visiting someone regularly and inquiring after his condition, one confers a degree of importance upon that person, and this inevitably has an impact on his treatment.

In practical terms, going to the hospital even when one cannot see the patient enables one to find out firsthand what the patient needs. Anything that will make the patient more comfortable, whether or not the patient is aware of one's intervention, is part of the fulfillment of this mitzvah. In the end, every element of this act of kindness is a means to convey one's concern for the patient, to deliver the encouragement and support that are the essential spiritual ingredient in every cure.

If I have occasion to visit someone in the hospital, I will inquire whether there are other patients who have no visitors, and pay one of them a visit as well.

כט שבט
29 SHEVAT / CYCLE 1

February 1, 2003
February 21, 2004
February 8, 2005
February 27, 2006
February 17, 2007
February 5, 2008
February 23, 2009
February 13, 2010

ל אב
30 AV / CYCLE 2

August 28, 2003
August 17, 2004
September 4, 2005
August 24, 2006
August 14, 2007
August 31, 2008
August 20, 2009
August 10, 2010

✑ *With a Prayer*

SEFER AHAVAS CHESED — Part III Chapter III

A person setting out to visit someone who is sick might wonder what he should bring him. The Chofetz Chaim answers conclusively: Bring a prayer. The essence of *bikur cholim* is praying to Hashem to grant a complete recovery to the patient, and without that element, the mitzvah is incomplete. One should not, however, make his prayers apparent to the patient, who may interpret the act as an indication of the severity of his illness. Rather, one should pause momentarily while in conversation or while performing some task for the patient, and speak quietly from the heart, saying: "Hashem, please heal him/her."

To pray with the correct intensity, it is important to perceive the patient's real situation. One should allow him to express his pain and fear. In addition, halachah dictates that one should not visit during the first three hours or the last three hours of the day. This rule relates directly to the efficacy of one's prayers. If a person visits in the early part of the day, he will usually see the patient at his best and may not take the situation seriously enough to pray with the necessary fervor. On the other hand, in the last part of the day the visitor will usually see the patient at his worst. This may cause him to give up hope for a cure, and he may not pray with the belief that his prayers can be answered. Nevertheless, if one has no choice but to visit during the first or last three hours of the day, he may do so.

When praying at the bedside of the sick, one can pray in any language. Because the Divine Presence rests at the head of the sick person, the words of prayer are being received directly. When one prays in another location, one should pray in Hebrew. Although Hashem obviously understands every language, the holy language fuels the prayers' ascent. Because the words are not being uttered directly before the Divine Presence, they are in most cases being conveyed by Hashem's messengers to the Heavens, a task more efficiently fulfilled when the prayers are in Hebrew. In any case, the sincerity of the prayer is more important than the language. A hollow prayer in Hebrew will not ascend faster than a heartfelt prayer in one's native tongue.

Prayers for the sick should not focus exclusively on the patient one is visiting. Instead, one prays for the recovery of the specific person among all the sick people of Israel. This turns the private prayer into a petition for the benefit of the entire nation, and gives it a vastly greater impact. It harnesses the merit of all those who are ill in Jewish communities throughout the world, and casts their lot together, creating an infinitely more powerful draw upon Hashem's stores of mercy.

When one prays for the sick on Shabbos, the wording is different: "Shabbos prohibits us from crying out and may a recovery come speedily." Shabbos itself is a curative force. A person once posed a question to the Skverer Rebbe debating this proposition. In this person's experience, illnesses seemed to have always worsened on Shabbos. The Rebbe explained that Hashem brought out the peak of the illness on Shabbos precisely because Shabbos carries the power to contain it. The person who experiences his worst symptoms on Shabbos is in a certain way fortunate; at his moment of crisis, he is in the hands of the Supreme Source of healing.

Whenever I visit a sick person, I will find an opportunity to say a short prayer on his behalf.

29 Shevat — In honor of George Burnett שלום בן שיינדל נ"י
Dedicated by Keith and Judy Burnett and family

30 Av — Michael Lee לע"נ מאיר חיים בן יצחק הלוי ז"ל
Dedicated by Mr. & Mrs. Yaakov Lee and family

DAY 149

❧ *Just Rewards*

SEFER AHAVAS CHESED — **Part III Chapter III**

The benefits of *bikur cholim* to the person suffering from ill health are clear to see. The benefits to the person who performs the mitzvah may not be as patently obvious to the casual observer, but they are indeed a tangible reality in this world, as well as an everlasting spiritual treasure in the World to Come. The Chofetz Chaim first provides a glimpse of the spiritual reward, quoting from the Talmud (*Nedarim* 40a): "One who visits a sick person is saved from Gehinnom, as the verse [*Tehillim* 41:2] says, 'Fortunate is he who cares wisely for the needy, for on the day of evil, Hashem will save him.'" The day of evil is the Day of Judgment, which every person must eventually face at the end of his time on earth. The evil from which Hashem saves him is the fire of Gehinnom.

The Talmudic verse continues with a description of the rewards granted in this world to one who cares for the sick. "Hashem will protect him and give him life and make him prosper in the land." The protection to which the verse refers is protection against the *yetzer hara*. The blessing of "life" is protection from suffering and pain. The prosperity in the land is material wealth that will cause the person to be honored by those among whom he lives.

Citing the *Sefer Keren Orah*, the Chofetz Chaim explains how these three earthly rewards correspond, measure for measure, to the benefits one bestows upon the sick person through *bikur cholim*: One who visits the sick has three objectives. First, he seeks to enhance the patient's physical comfort. In return, he earns Hashem's protection from physical suffering. Secondly, where it is possible and appropriate, the visitor is obliged to gently guide the person toward a spiritual view of his situation. He should encourage him to consider avenues of self-improvement that would bring merit for his recovery, since Hashem is the source of both forgiveness and healing. In return for his efforts in building the patient's spiritual strength, Hashem protects him from the corrosive effects of his own *yetzer hara*. The visitor's third objective is to build up the patient's will to live, letting him know that he is valued, and that his well-being is of concern to others. As reward for the honor and dignity the visitor bestows upon the patient, Hashem grants him wealth and the honor that accompanies it.

In these three ways, the person who sets out to benefit those suffering through illness benefits himself most of all. He creates a well-endowed fund of merit that will protect and support him as he continues in his holy endeavors throughout a long and fruitful life.

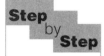

When I tend to someone who is ill, I will keep in mind that all I am giving is ultimately to my own benefit.

לע"נ פסח בן משה אהרן ז"ל — **30 Shevat**
Dedicated by the Goldstein grandchildren and great-grandchildren

1 Elul — In honor of my parents, Manny and Sylvia Danzer
Dedicated by Rabbi David Danzer

א אדר
1 ADAR / CYCLE 1

February 3, 2003
February 23, 2004
February 10, 2005
March 1, 2006
February 19, 2007
February 7, 2008
February 25, 2009
February 15, 2010

1 ADAR II

During Hebrew leap
years, a thirteenth month
called Adar Sheni is
added to the calendar.
During those years, the
lessons for the days of
Adar should be studied
during each of the Adars.

March 5, 2003
March 12, 2005
March 8, 2008

ב אלול
2 ELUL / CYCLE 2

August 30, 2003
August 19, 2004
September 6, 2005
August 26, 2006
August 16, 2007
September 2, 2008
August 22, 2009
August 12, 2010

❧ *Someone Else*

SEFER AHAVAS CHESED — **Part III Chapter III**

---

*T*here is a job that needs to be done — a job that strikes most people as unpleasant, time consuming, upsetting and awkward. If there is a long line of other people who are likely to take on this task, the average person is more than happy to leave it to them. The job is *bikur cholim*, and this is the *yetzer hara*-induced reasoning that causes otherwise compassionate, well-meaning people to overlook the mitzvah.

No one is immune from the sin of complacency in this regard. The Talmud (*Nedarim* 41a) records a story of a student of Rabbi Akiva who became ill. Rabbi Akiva had thousands of students, representing the cream of the generation's Torah scholars. Not one of them, however, took it upon himself to visit this sick colleague, for each was sure that others were doing so. The students were all too busy, but their teacher — Rabbi Akiva — was not. He went to visit his student and was shocked to find him alone and untended. Rabbi Akiva swept his room, washed the floor and spent some time with his student. "Rabbi," the student told him, "you gave me life." When Rabbi Akiva returned to the learning hall, he delivered to his students the stark admonition that "one who does not visit the sick, it is as if he is shedding blood."

The comparison is more than metaphorical. One visitor might be the person who knows the right doctor for the patient's illness. He might have experience with an effective medication or treatment. He might have access to something or someone the patient needs. One person can make a life-and-death difference.

The Chofetz Chaim criticizes his generation for laxity in the mitzvah of *bikur cholim*, especially in regard to the poor of the community. The obligation to visit the sick extends to everyone, he states, and applies especially to the poor, for in the case of the poor, the accusation of "bloodshed" is even more likely to reflect reality. The poor person may not be able to afford a good doctor and proper medication. He may not have household help to clean his surroundings and prepare his meals. He may lack adequate heat and a warm blanket to keep him comfortable. While the beloved rebbe or respected community leader is showered with attention in his moment of need, the poor man might suffer alone. Without visitors, he could lie in his bed for days unheeded, feeling as if he simply does not exist. The despair alone could rob him of his will to recover.

The Talmud (*Kesubos* 68a) compares one who averts his eyes from the needs of others to one who engages in idol worship. Following the *yetzer hara*'s advice in this matter is like casting oneself upon a strong tide that pulls inexorably away from Torah and mitzvos. Averting one's eyes — not looking — means not seeing. Not seeing means remaining unaware of someone's pain, emotional stress and material deprivation. The *yetzer hara* understands that once a person sees all this, he will feel compelled to help and a flood of chesed will result. The person may raise money to help the poor, sick man. He may offer advice, assistance, comfort. He may find that in the end, he is credited with saving someone's life.

Step by **Step**

I will fight off the urge to leave bikur cholim to others whom I perceive as being more obligated or qualified to help.

ב אדר
2 ADAR / CYCLE 1

February 4, 2003
February 24, 2004
February 11, 2005
March 2, 2006
February 20, 2007
February 8, 2008
February 26, 2009
February 16, 2010

2 ADAR II

During Hebrew leap
years, a thirteenth month
called Adar Sheni is
added to the calendar.
During those years, the
lessons for the days of
Adar should be studied
during each of the Adars.

March 6, 2003
March 13, 2005
March 9, 2008

ג אלול
3 ELUL / CYCLE 2

August 31, 2003
August 20, 2004
September 7, 2005
August 27, 2006
August 17, 2007
September 3, 2008
August 23, 2009
August 13, 2010

✃ *Heroes*

SEFER AHAVAS CHESED — **Part III Chapter III**

---

*C*aring for the sick is not just a personal obligation, says the Chofetz Chaim. Every community should have an organization dedicated to this mitzvah, for it is a source of essential help to those in need and a source of great blessing for the entire community. Such a society should have one central mission, and that is to supply whatever is needed by the patient and his family. A *bikur cholim* organization has to step into the sick person's home and assess the situation. One person may need a doctor. Another may need someone to care for the children. Another may need meals for the family. A *bikur cholim* society's concerns extend to any assistance required to weather the crisis.

"How good and beautiful it would be," says the Chofetz Chaim, "if every city had such an organization." This is especially so because the absence of these services can violate the Torah prohibition "You shall not stand aside while your fellow's blood is shed" (*Vayikra* 19:16). In other words, one is not permitted to stand idly by as another person's life ebbs away. In its simplest sense, this law means that one must stop and help a person who is ill or injured. This, most people instinctively understand; they are willing to step up to the role of hero to rescue a person in distress. The blood of one's fellow, however, may not be spilling in an action-packed episode requiring heroic intervention. The old woman in the attic apartment who feels too ill to take herself to the doctor is also "your fellow." Her blood — her life — may also be ebbing away, and one easily might be lulled into standing by idly. "I'm sure her children are looking in on her," one might think, or "Her landlady must check in on her." Knocking on her door might not seem like a heroic lifesaving gesture, yet it is. For such a deed, one earns the Torah's promised reward: "Fortunate is he who cares wisely for the needy. On the day of evil, Hashem will save him"(*Tehillim* 41:2).

Those who project themselves into the lives of neighbors who are suffering with illness can conceive of acts of kindness nearly boundless in their merit. The Chofetz Chaim refers to one city in which a group of people took turns sitting through the night at the bedside of a sick man. Their chesed sprouted hundreds of offshoots. They tended to the patient, they comforted him, they gave the patient's family a chance to sleep, which enabled them to care for him and keep his business going, which in turn enabled the household to function. All this could be attributed to this one service the community provided.

Although the mission of *bikur cholim* is to ease the plight of the needy sick, its services can be of value to the wealthy as well. Even when someone can hire help, he cannot always hire reliable, compassionate help. Those who step in to offer their assistance provide a resource money cannot buy. They give the patient tangible help combined with the priceless intangible of knowing his neighbors care about him. A city populated by individuals willing to help each other in this way, says the Chofetz Chaim, is a city blessed.

If it is realistic for me, I will find out what I can do for my local bikur cholim organization. If there is no such group, I will try to initiate formation of one.

2 Adar — Menachem Shlomo Senderovits לע"נ מנחם שלמה בן בנימין ז"ל
Dedicated by Yankie & Mindy Amsel and family

3 Elul — לע"נ העענטישא בת מלך ע"ה
Dedicated in loving memory by Adam and Elisheva Rabinowitz

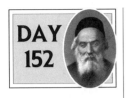

ג אדר
3 ADAR / CYCLE 1

February 5, 2003
February 25, 2004
February 12, 2005
March 3, 2006
February 21, 2007
February 9, 2008
February 27, 2009
February 17, 2010

3 ADAR II

During Hebrew leap
years, a thirteenth month
called Adar Sheni is
added to the calendar.
During those years, the
lessons for the days of
Adar should be studied
during each of the Adars.

March 7, 2003
March 14, 2005
March 10, 2008

ד אלול
4 ELUL / CYCLE 2

September 1, 2003
August 21, 2004
September 8, 2005
August 28, 2006
August 18, 2007
September 4, 2008
August 24, 2009
August 14, 2010

✒ *Delicate Matters*

SEFER AHAVAS CHESED — Part III Chapter III

*O*ne of the three purposes of visiting the sick (see Day 153) is to gently guide them toward settling their material as well as spiritual accounts. When a person's health is compromised, the possibility arises that the details of his financial dealings may become lost or misconstrued. One is obligated, according to the *Shulchan Aruch*, to help him put his dealings into writing if necessary, and to verify matters such as loans, credit and consignments.

There is a significant problem in meeting this obligation, the Chofetz Chaim acknowledges, and that is the possibility of causing the patient alarm. If his friends are trying to settle his affairs, he may reason, they must be expecting his imminent departure.

The Chofetz Chaim recommends a custom outlined in the *Chochmas HaAdam* which overcomes this obstacle: Certain communities had a rule that on the third day of a person's illness, the synagogue's administrator would visit the patient and discuss writing or updating his will. Because the practice was established and uniformly applied, there was no implication of doom in it.

In the area of spiritual accounting, the obligations and obstacles are similar. It is entirely possible to frighten a patient to near-death by telling him it is time to repent for his sins. Nonetheless, one of the goals in the act of *bikur cholim* is to guide the patient to repentance and to the recitation of *"Viduy,"* the confession that is recited before one passes into the Next World. The Chofetz Chaim points out that *Viduy* need not be seen as a frightening event. Repentance is a standard feature of a Jew's spiritual life, and when a person is ill, one may be able to encourage him to see it as a merit for recovery rather than a last rite.

Despite the importance of this aspect of *bikur cholim*, the Chofetz Chaim acknowledges it may sometimes be impossible to introduce the topic without alarming the patient. In that case, silence is the best policy.

If it is clear that the sick person knows that his life is ebbing, one should discuss with a rabbi the appropriate way to proceed with *Viduy*. In the event that one is advised to say *Viduy* with the person, great tact is essential to avoid robbing the person of hope. Relatives who may become tearful should be asked politely to leave the room. The patient should be assured that repentance and confession are a powerful merit for a long life.

If the patient is unable to recite the words, he should be encouraged to let his heart do the speaking. If necessary, one can read the words to him and he can listen. If he is unable to do that much, he can say or think the words, "May it be Hashem's will that my passing should atone for my sins." No matter what the outcome of the illness, repentance can only do good. If this does turn out to be the person's last days, his confession provides him with an eternal asset, for anyone who recites it automatically receives a portion in the World to Come. If he recovers, the *Viduy* has certainly not been wasted, for it sends him forward into life endowed with a pure, cleansed soul.

In appropriate situations, I will try to assist those I visit with settling their affairs, or ascertain that someone is taking on this responsibility.

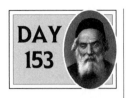
ד אדר
4 ADAR / CYCLE 1

February 6, 2003
February 26, 2004
February 13, 2005
March 4, 2006
February 22, 2007
February 10, 2008
February 28, 2009
February 18, 2010

4 ADAR II

During Hebrew leap
years, a thirteenth month
called Adar Sheni is
added to the calendar.
During those years, the
lessons for the days of
Adar should be studied
during each of the Adars.

March 8, 2003
March 15, 2005
March 11, 2008

ה אלול
5 ELUL / CYCLE 2

September 2, 2003
August 22, 2004
September 9, 2005
August 29, 2006
August 19, 2007
September 5, 2008
August 25, 2009
August 15, 2010

✎ *Taking Care*

SEFER AHAVAS CHESED — Part III Chapter III/IV

*P*reparing for the Next World is not an activity most people wish to face. It is, however, the prime example of an activity that ought not be put off until tomorrow. One who can help an ill person close his financial and spiritual accounts performs an act of profound and everlasting kindness. He essentially helps to guarantee the sick man's World to Come. "One who guides the sick person and does his best to bring him to *teshuvah*, he is like an angel that promotes his good and he causes him to be saved from strict judgment" (*Zohar, Parashas Pekudei*).

Because of the delicacy of these topics and their potential to upset the ill person, one must seek advice before undertaking this aspect of *bikur cholim*. The Chofetz Chaim stresses that there is great merit in putting one's affairs in order. Settling accounts and repenting for sins are a potent protection at any stage of life, and the ill person can take heart in the fact that these are powerful steps for bringing about a recovery. If the patient is wealthy and has not given adequate charity during his life, he may be very willing to commit himself to remedying the situation should he recover. That commitment alone could be the merit he needs for recovery.

Dealing with these issues ultimately replaces anxiety with a feeling of tranquillity that allows one to either go forward in life with a clean slate, or pass into the Next World prepared for the journey. On the other hand, if one does not settle these matters, the opportunity may be lost forever. The Chofetz Chaim looks to King Solomon to express the wise approach to preparing well for the Next World. First, one must pay close attention to how he spends his days on earth: "See life with the wife you love" (*Koheles* 9:9), the simple translation says, but Rashi explains that this means to share one's life with Torah — to see one's mundane affairs through Torah's prism.

The Chofetz Chaim summarizes the three most important elements in a person's life: First is Torah study, then the concept of repentance and finally, the pursuit of mitzvos and kind acts. Torah study is the cornerstone of this edifice, says the Chofetz Chaim, because the other two concepts are built upon it. One who is immersed in Torah will become sensitized to sin and to the needs of others.

This hierarchy can lead to a misconception, however. A person might believe that if he has no time to learn Torah, he has nothing to gain by pursuing the other two ideals. The Chofetz Chaim answers once again through King Solomon; "All that your hand finds to do that is within your power, do" (*Koheles* 9:10).

One should not leave it to his offspring to create the merit that will assure his position in the World to Come. A person who tells himself, "I'm too busy to get involved in spiritual matters, but my children will do better than I did," may find himself waiting an eternity for his descendant's merits to accrue. They, too, might find themselves too busy. Even Hillel, whose children were of unquestionable holiness, declared, "If I am not for myself, who is for me?" A person must take care of all he can, while he can.

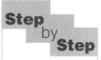

When I have the urge to put off an act of kindness, I will remember that the opportunity may never be available again.

4 Adar — In honor of my parents, Renee Molko and Mr. & Mrs. Shelton and Carol Gorelick
Dedicated by P'nina Miriam Gorelick

5 Elul — May today's learning be in honor of Bethy Guttman.
Dedicated by Mayer Guttman and children

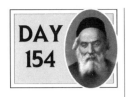

DAY 154

ה אדר
5 ADAR / CYCLE 1

February 7, 2003
February 27, 2004
February 14, 2005
March 5, 2006
February 23, 2007
February 11, 2008
March 1, 2009
February 19, 2010

5 ADAR II

During Hebrew leap years, a thirteenth month called Adar Sheni is added to the calendar. During those years, the lessons for the days of Adar should be studied during each of the Adars.

March 9, 2003
March 16, 2005
March 12, 2008

ו אלול
6 ELUL / CYCLE 2

September 3, 2003
August 23, 2004
September 10, 2005
August 30, 2006
August 20, 2007
September 6, 2008
August 26, 2009
August 16, 2010

❧ *No Better Time*

SEFER AHAVAS CHESED — Part III Chapter IV

A businessman with no time to spare suddenly finds himself lying in the hospital fighting a mystery ailment. He thinks to himself: "If this turns out to be something serious, I'm going to make sure I leave behind enough money to build that new classroom wing of my grandchildren's yeshivah. I'll give a nice amount to my synagogue, and I'll make sure that *Hatzalah* gets a new ambulance, too. I'd better think about anyone I need to ask forgiveness from, and anyone I owe ... and what I want to tell my children and grandchildren. Maybe I should write an ethical will ..."

The man's medical tests all come back negative, he is released from the hospital, and by the end of the week, whatever had afflicted him is gone — and so are his resolutions. To his mind, they are for another time, a time when his journey to the World to Come is really imminent. The Chofetz Chaim counters this reasoning with a question: How can one know that, when the time is at hand, he will be able to speak to his children? How does one know he will have the presence of mind to settle his affairs? How can one be sure that he will even know that his time is at hand? This type of gentle passage is a blessing that not everyone receives. A more sensible approach, therefore, is to tend to these matters while one is able.

The Chofetz Chaim suggests that during a person's lifetime he can establish some form of trust with a principal that will produce dividends for a charitable organization. He stresses that such a plan must be pursued carefully, with professional advice. There are guidelines on how one's money should be divided among the causes of Torah, places of prayer and charitable endeavors, and these, the Chofetz Chaim says, are outlined in *Sefer Yesh Nochlin*.

Most importantly, in establishing a charitable trust, one must avoid trespassing the prohibition against charging interest, or any other halachic requirement, for a mitzvah performed with tainted money is not acceptable to Hashem. Even in the days of the *Beis HaMikdash*, the *"korban olah"* or burnt sacrifice that was completely consumed by flames was not considered kosher if it was purchased with tainted money. The person who brought the sacrifice took absolutely nothing from it, yet it was still null and void if it came from misbegotten money.

Done correctly, a fund that supports a charitable cause provides the benefactor with a unique and eternal benefit. Such a fund serves many people in the community. Among them may be someone from whom the benefactor had once borrowed an item or some money, which he had failed to return in his lifetime. Through the service he has established, he is in effect making his repayment to that person, enabling him to rectify a sin even after his passing. He thereby has the merit to become an exception to the iron-clad rule that one can only repent while one is alive, all because he heeded King Solomon's words: "All that your hand finds to do that is in your power, do."

If I have the funds available to me, I will consider establishing a trust to benefit a charitable cause.

ו אדר
6 ADAR / CYCLE 1

February 8, 2003
February 28, 2004
February 15, 2005
March 6, 2006
February 24, 2007
February 12, 2008
March 2, 2009
February 20, 2010

6 ADAR II

During Hebrew leap
years, a thirteenth month
called Adar Sheni is
added to the calendar.
During those years, the
lessons for the days of
Adar should be studied
during each of the Adars.

March 10, 2003
March 17, 2005
March 13, 2008

ז אלול
7 ELUL / CYCLE 2

September 4, 2003
August 24, 2004
September 11, 2005
August 31, 2006
August 21, 2007
September 7, 2008
August 27, 2009
August 17, 2010

❧ True Friend

SEFER AHAVAS CHESED — **Part III Chapter IV**

*T*he time comes, and a person wishes to leave instructions for the handling of his estate. He understands that the money he leaves for charity is the only bequest with the power to deliver riches to his door in the World to Come. The instructions he gives, the Chofetz Chaim says, should be given before witnesses, and these witnesses should not be limited to his children. He observes that children have a general tendency to revise their parent's wishes once the parent has passed on. They tend to focus upon what the money could accomplish for the living, without considering the priceless merit it brings their parent as his soul struggles to rise to higher realms in the World to Come.

The Chofetz Chaim presents an allegory from *Pirkei D'Rabbi Eliezer* (Ch. 34) that helps explain this seemingly hardheaded assessment: A man receives a summons from the king. He knows this could mean trouble for him, and he is filled with fear. He finds his best friend and begs him, "Please, come with me to the king and vouch for my character." The friend politely declines. He then tries another, more casual friend. This person offers to accompany him en route to the palace. Standing before the king with him, however, is out of the question. He would rather not risk the possible implications of being identified as the man's friend. Finally, the man turns to a casual acquaintance, a man he converses with only occasionally. "I will come with you," the man says steadfastly. "I will stand with you before the king and tell him what a fine, upstanding man you are."

The first friend is a person's money — his beloved money that he spends so much time cultivating, that he treasures and pursues with all his energy. The moment one leaves this world, the money and honor can do him no good. The second friend is his family. They will accompany him, but only up to his grave. At that point, they must turn back to their own lives and concerns. The third friend is a person's mitzvos, repentance and good deeds: "Your righteous deeds will precede you" (*Yeshayah* 58:8). These are the only true friends a person has in the Next World. They testify on his behalf, telling the King of kings that this is a person who had compassion upon others. They plead for forgiveness for his sins and demand that, measure for measure, he receive Hashem's compassionate judgment. Each mitzvah a person fulfilled in life creates an angel that comes to his defense. The many temporal pleasures that seemed so precious in life not only abandon the person, they turn against him to accuse him.

Everyone needs a true friend with whom to face the King, and as the allegory illustrates, that friend's importance is often not perceived in life. The "friend" is the instance in which a person forces himself to give a smile and a dollar to a man who has knocked at the door a little too late in the evening. It's the prayer a person pushes himself through, constantly rechanneling his distracted mind back into the words. It's the fund-raising project he takes on when there is no time to spare. These acts are not pursued and treasured in their time. Only when, at the moment of truth, they alone appear at one's side, does their true value shine.

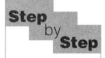

I will turn more of my time, attention and energy toward activities that will create "true friends" for me.

לע"נ ברוך בן אלי' ז"ל — **6 Adar**
Dedicated by Dianne Ghelman and family

7 Elul — לע"נ פני בת אורי ומיכא-ל (המכונה מישל) בן יעקב ע"ה
Dedicated by the Guzelgul family

✑ *Financial Security*

SEFER AHAVAS CHESED — Part III Chapter IV

A person's need for material security sits on a seesaw, balanced on the other side by the person's faith. The more one sees his possessions as a means of enriching his eternity, the less he needs to hold onto them tightly in this world. He knows that his children's future cannot be guaranteed by the inheritance he leaves them — Hashem alone controls the account book. From this point of view, he sees that his real security — his well-being in the eternal, spiritual realm — depends not on what he amasses for his family, but on what he gives away to those in need.

The Torah expresses this concept in its directive to support the Kohanim: "What a man gives the Kohen belongs to him" (*Bamidbar* 5:10). On the surface, the verse reflects the simple idea that the donations given to the Kohen become the Kohen's possession. The Chofetz Chaim, however, offers another interpretation: That which a man gives the Kohen belongs to the man — the giver. The Kohen is the Torah's prime example of someone who does not possess his own assets. Every tribe was given a portion of the land of Israel, with the exception of the tribe of Levi, which was to serve in the *Beis HaMikdash*. Kohanim, a special branch of Levi, served as the Priests. In order to free this select tribe for its holy duties, the rest of the Jewish people were given the responsibility to support them. The Chofetz Chaim illuminates the internal workings of this system: What a person gives to those in need is the only possession he keeps forever. To the extent that one supports the Kohen — or anyone dependent upon others for sustenance — one acquires his permanent wealth.

For someone who has internalized this truth, the idea of bequeathing money to charity is not frightening — it is the most secure feeling he can imagine. He is like someone who has shipped his possessions in advance of his journey; he knows he will arrive to find everything there and waiting for him. The Talmud (*Bava Basra* 11a) discusses a king named Munbaz, whose kindness and generosity were legendary. His vast treasury was in his eyes a bottomless well from which to draw plentiful amounts of charity to ease the plight of his subjects. Once he was asked, "Your parents added to the treasures of their forefathers and you waste it by giving it away?" He answered: "My forefathers gathered all these treasures, and traditionally, as kings do, they hid them in the ground. I gather treasures and I hide them up there [in Heaven]." In his wisdom he understood that what his forefathers had left behind on earth, he would possess forever.

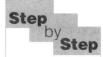

I will try to rely less on material possessions for my sense of security.

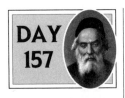
ח אדר
8 ADAR / CYCLE 1

February 10, 2003
March 1, 2004
February 17, 2005
March 8, 2006
February 26, 2007
February 14, 2008
March 4, 2009
February 22, 2010

8 ADAR II

During Hebrew leap
years, a thirteenth month
called Adar Sheni is
added to the calendar.
During those years, the
lessons for the days of
Adar should be studied
during each of the Adars.

March 12, 2003
March 19, 2005
March 15, 2008

ט אלול
9 ELUL / CYCLE 2

September 6, 2003
August 26, 2004
September 13, 2005
September 2, 2006
August 23, 2007
September 9, 2008
August 29, 2009
August 19, 2010

❧ True Chesed

SEFER AHAVAS CHESED — Part III Chapter V

*O*ut of all the acts of kindness that spring from a Jew's emulation of Hashem, only one receives the designation *"chesed shel emes,"* meaning "true chesed." That is the care one provides for the deceased — seeing to his purification, funeral and burial. Undertaking these tasks is "true" kindness because, unlike any other favor or loan one provides, these deeds have no chance of being repaid by the recipient in this world. What a person does for the deceased, he does without any earthly, material incentive.

The Torah's prototype for one's duties toward the deceased derives from *Parashas Chayei Sarah* (Chapter 23). Abraham eulogizes his wife and sees to her burial. Later, in *Parashas Vayechi*, Jacob asks that he be accorded the same final dignity.

The Sages highlight just how strong an obligation rests upon the Jewish community to see to the proper burial of its members. The Talmud (*Moed Katan* 27b) states that when someone passes away in a city, nobody in the city is permitted to engage in work until the person is buried. This rule is not seen in practice today only because most cities now have a *"chevra kadisha,"* a burial society, that tends to the deceased.

This prohibition against work applies no matter what the status of the deceased — whether learned or ignorant, rich or poor. Even if the person has relatives who will take care of his arrangements, the obligation still rests upon the community. Those who are involved in learning, however, are permitted to continue their pursuits until the deceased is brought out for burial. At that point, if the deceased was someone who learned or tried to learn, even the greatest scholar is required to leave the study hall and attend to the mitzvah at hand. The thought that "there will be enough people there without me" is voided by the Sages' ruling as to how many people constitute "enough" people at a burial. That number is 600,000 — an attendance unlikely to be reached at the funeral of even the most revered figure.

Of great importance in tending to the deceased, regardless of his stature, is to be sure that there is a *minyan* at the gravesite so that mourners can recite the prayers of *Kaddish* and *Birchas Aveilim*. It is incumbent upon all the people of the city, the Chofetz Chaim says, to be sure there is a *minyan* at the burial site. If necessary, a lottery system can be established to obtain the necessary participation.

Furthermore, if possible, the deceased should be buried on the day of his passing. The Chofetz Chaim quotes the *Zohar* that spending the night in this world causes pain to the soul, therefore every effort should be made to assure a prompt burial. He notes, however, that there are valid justifications for breaking with this rule. For instance, in the case of a venerated Torah leader, time might be necessary to allow people to travel to the funeral so that the proceedings will reflect his stature. There are many other reasons as well. The community must make sure, however, that the main reason is not simple laziness. In this truest form of chesed, in which the recipient can no longer advocate for himself, his needs must be treated with the utmost loving care.

I will make an effort to attend the funerals of people in my community — even those with whom I did not have a close personal tie.

לע"נ גיטל ע"ה בת אליהו יצחק שליט"א — **8 Adar**
Dedicated by her family

9 Elul — Rabbi Daniel Lewin לע"נ דניאל בן ר' יהודה ע"ה
Dedicated by Lewin, Lewis and Fishfeld families

ט אדר
9 ADAR / CYCLE 1

February 11, 2003
March 2, 2004
February 18, 2005
March 9, 2006
February 27, 2007
February 15, 2008
March 5, 2009
February 23, 2010

9 ADAR II

During Hebrew leap
years, a thirteenth month
called Adar Sheni is
added to the calendar.
During those years, the
lessons for the days of
Adar should be studied
during each of the Adars.

March 13, 2003
March 20, 2005
March 16, 2008

י אלול
10 ELUL / CYCLE 2

September 7, 2003
August 27, 2004
September 14, 2005
September 3, 2006
August 24, 2007
September 10, 2008
August 30, 2009
August 20, 2010

✑ *Final Words*

SEFER AHAVAS CHESED — Part III Chapter V

*T*he words spoken about the deceased at his funeral — the eulogy — are a significant part of the *"chesed shel emes"* performed on his behalf. "It is a great mitzvah to properly eulogize the deceased," the Chofetz Chaim says. "Properly" is not necessarily dramatically or eloquently. It does not involve oratorical flourishes or comic relief—only sincerity—for words that come from the heart enter the heart. A chilling story was told about a man who had eulogized his wife. His father-in-law, bereft at the loss of his daughter, critiqued the man's speech with these words: "It was too good." In other words, if the husband could prepare so well and speak so eloquently, he could not have been speaking from a broken heart.

There are several purposes to the eulogy, and none of those purposes include impressing the audience. Primarily, the aim is to draw out the tears of those present. For the family of the deceased, who most acutely feel the pain of the loss, the eulogy provides a release. It allows the sadness to flow outward, helping the healing process to begin. For others, the words of the eulogy are meant to penetrate the heart with a sharper sense that the loss of this life, unique in the world, is their loss too. There is one less source of prayer, kindness and holiness in this world, and the Jewish people have one less source of merit. "One who cries for a loss of a good person, Hashem forgives all his sins," says the Talmud (*Shabbos* 105b). These tears are so precious to

Hashem that "He counts them and stores them in His hidden storehouse."

All of this applies to the loss of a person of any stature. In the case of a Torah scholar, an even greater level of care is required to make sure that the community understands and cries for the loss of one of its generation's luminaries.

Rabbi Abraham Pam, *zt'l*, once described the ability of people in this world to reach their loved ones in the Next World with gifts of real value. When a person says *Kaddish* for someone, he said, the soul of the deceased knows he has been remembered. It is like a postcard from his loved one. If people learn Mishnayos on his behalf, he feels an even stronger level of love and concern — as if he has received a letter. Best of all, said Rabbi Pam, is when one undertakes an act of kindness as a merit for the departed. That is like sending to Heaven a package filled to capacity with the kind of riches that only a soul in the World of Truth can fully enjoy.

Step by **Step**

If I hear news of someone's passing or I am present at a eulogy, I will try to bring into focus the full meaning of the loss.

9 Adar — Mr. Mendel Senderovits לע״נ ר׳ מנחם שלמה בן ר׳ בנימין ז״ל סענדעראוויטש
Dedicated by his wife, Mrs. Esther Senderovits, and children

10 Elul — שרה רחל בת קונה שתחי׳ שתזכה לרפואה שלמה בתושח״י
Dedicated by Jeanette and Menachem Weinschel and family

≈ *To Give Comfort*

SEFER AHAVAS CHESED — **Part III Chapter V**

A Jew who has just lost a loved one does not have to weather his grief alone. "And you will walk after Hashem, your G-d," the Torah states. Hashem is seen throughout the Torah bringing comfort to the bereft, and so — walking after Him — His people bring comfort to each other. "*Nichum aveilim*," the mitzvah of comforting mourners, is also a powerful expression of the commandment to "love your neighbor as yourself," for who, in a time of intense grief, does not wish for someone to come and soothe him? *Nichum aveilim* is not only chesed, it is one of the categories of chesed from which one derives benefit in this world without detracting from the reward that awaits in the World to Come.

One who visits a mourner must attune himself to what is needed in the given situation. Sometimes there are practical matters that need attention, since the mourner is forbidden from engaging in most mundane activities during the first week of mourning. Visitors may help to care for the mourner's children, answer the telephone, bring in food, straighten up the room or anything else that is needed. Most often, however, it is company a person needs most. The company of others allows the mourner to express his grief to a listening ear, share memories of the deceased and, most of all, feel that others care about his loss. The prevalent custom is to offer the mourner a blessing upon one's departure: "May Hashem comfort you amid the rest of the mourners of Zion and

Jerusalem." Reciting that verse, however, is not the main point of the visit. Providing support and comfort — easing the mourner's pain — is the point.

The Chofetz Chaim observes that in some communities, the mitzvah of *nichum aveilim* is taken lightly, especially when the mourner is a poor person who lacks status. The correlation between a paucity of money and a paucity of friends puzzles the Chofetz Chaim, but he postulates that phenomenon might be explained by looking at the opposite side of the coin. The rich often find themselves with many more friends and relatives than they realized they had. Everyone wants to claim friendship or kinship to the rich. For the poor person, however, the visit is all the more important, because his sources of support and joy are so much more limited.

In real terms, however, the poor person has good reason to take heart, for while his neighbors may keep their distance, Hashem draws close. "Hashem is close to the brokenhearted" (*Tehillim* 34:19). One who goes to comfort a person who is not receiving many visits, therefore, is doing an act of kindness for someone who is especially precious to Hashem. The reward for that person's mitzvah, therefore, will also be especially precious.

I will try to make time to perform the mitzvah of nichum aveilim, comforting mourners, whenever it arises.

יא אדר
II ADAR / CYCLE 1

February 13, 2003
March 4, 2004
February 20, 2005
March 11, 2006
March 1, 2007
February 17, 2008
March 7, 2009
February 25, 2010

II ADAR II

During Hebrew leap
years, a thirteenth month
called Adar Sheni is
added to the calendar.
During those years, the
lessons for the days of
Adar should be studied
during each of the Adars.

March 15, 2003
March 22, 2005
March 18, 2008

יב אלול
12 ELUL / CYCLE 2

September 9, 2003
August 29, 2004
September 16, 2005
September 5, 2006
August 26, 2007
September 12, 2008
September 1, 2009
August 22, 2010

❧ *Heavenly Dancing*

SEFER AHAVAS CHESED — Part III Chapter VI

*D*ancing at a wedding might seem, at first glance, to be somewhat of a frivolous mitzvah, but as the Torah and Talmud prove, it is an act befitting the greatest of people. The chesed is especially worthy when the bride and groom are from a poor family, or from a wealthy family that has suffered a loss of its fortune. In any case, joy and liveliness are a wedding's most important features.

The Chofetz Chaim stresses that this rejoicing must reflect the essential element of modesty. Without it, there may be hundreds of guests, music and dancing, but the most important presence, the Divine Presence, will be absent, leaving the new couple to set out without the gift they most need to succeed in their life together.

Within the confines of modesty, rejoicing at a wedding is the source of many rewards. One who performs this act of chesed merits a life of Torah. His act is viewed as the equivalent of bringing a thanksgiving offering to the altar of the *Beis HaMikdash*. He is credited, as well, with helping to rebuild the ruins of Jerusalem. A story of the *chassidic* leader Rabbi Moshe Leib of Sassov conveys the everlasting joy this mitzvah confers upon the doer.

Rabbi Moshe Leib once encountered a ragged family traveling by wagon toward another city. He discovered that the sad-looking group was the groom's wedding party en route to the bride's town. Wasting no time, he curtailed their journey long enough to buy them proper clothes and a few items for the couple. He then rushed to the bride's town, only to discover an equally dire situation. The rabbi settled himself in the town's study hall and railed at all present, "Don't you know that a poor boy and a poor girl are being married here tonight? Why hasn't anything been done?" He did not cease until everyone had taken on some responsibility for the upcoming affair.

It turned out to be a gala celebration. Toward the end, as the bride and groom were getting ready to leave, the band began playing a tune, and Rabbi Moshe Leib started dancing with all his heart. His exuberance took hold, and soon the whole crowd was caught up in the joyous melody. "Hashem, when my time comes," cried Rabbi Moshe Leib, "I wish to enter Heaven with this tune!"

Many years later Rabbi Moshe Leib of Sassov passed away. As the mournful procession carried his holy body to its final resting-place, a group of runaway horses pulling wagons of musicians swept into the crowd. The musicians, who had been entertaining at another event, were still playing their song. "Get out of here! Don't you see this is a funeral?" the onlookers cried. The band members, however, were completely puzzled. "We're sorry," they replied. "We don't know what happened. The horses just took off."

Suddenly, one of the mourners understood. "That song! Isn't it the melody from the wedding that Rabbi Moshe Leib remembered with such joy? Isn't that the song he said he wanted to accompany his journey to the Next World?"

A quick rabbinical conference ensued, and it was decided that, despite the irregularity of the measure, the music would be played as Rabbi Moshe Leib of Sassov was laid to rest. With the exuberant melody soaring through the air, his soul soared to its reward, just as he had wanted.

Step by *Step*

The next time I attend a wedding, I will keep in mind the tremendous value of dancing and bringing joy to the couple.

לע"נ אברהם יעקב בן שלמה יהודה ז"ל — **11 Adar**
לע"נ רפאל דוד בן מנחם נחום הכהן ז"ל — **12 Elul**
תנצב"ה — יהא זכרו ברוך

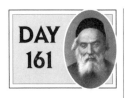
יב אדר
12 ADAR / CYCLE 1

February 14, 2003
March 5, 2004
February 21, 2005
March 12, 2006
March 2, 2007
February 18, 2008
March 8, 2009
February 26, 2010

12 ADAR II

During Hebrew leap
years, a thirteenth month
called Adar Sheni is
added to the calendar.
During those years, the
lessons for the days of
Adar should be studied
during each of the Adars.

March 16, 2003
March 23, 2005
March 19, 2008

יג אלול
13 ELUL / CYCLE 2

September 10, 2003
August 30, 2004
September 17, 2005
September 6, 2006
August 27, 2007
September 13, 2008
September 2, 2009
August 23, 2010

❧ *Paying the Way*

SEFER AHAVAS CHESED — Part III Chapter VI

*D*ancing at a wedding is sometimes the second step in the mitzvah of bringing joy to the bride and bridegroom. Making the wedding is, in some cases, the essential first step. The Chofetz Chaim, citing the *Shulchan Aruch Yoreh De'ah* (*Siman* 256:15), says that if the treasurer of a charity has money that is not earmarked for a particular cause, his first priority should be to provide for the wedding needs of a poor or orphaned girl; there is no greater charity. It might seem contrary to common sense that, above all the other important uses to which a charitable fund could be put, outfitting a girl in a wedding gown and bridal jewelry should take precedence. The priority is established, says the Chofetz Chaim, for the simple purpose of averting the pain and embarrassment the bride would feel if she were forced to walk down the aisle looking like a pauper, rather than the queen she should be on her wedding day. The bride's feelings are what turn apparently superfluous outward trappings into an important and valid use of the money.

The mitzvah of helping a poor girl make a wedding is all the more weighty when one considers the fact that in many venues throughout Jewish history, a girl who had no one to provide a wedding for her often remained unmarried. In such a case, the community that neglected her needs would bear responsibility for all the troubles her unmarried status brought upon her throughout her life. To avoid such situations, many cities have a "*hachnasas kallah*" committee which takes upon itself the task of alleviating the plight of orphaned or impoverished girls.

Those who give or raise money for this mitzvah set into motion a powerful positive chain reaction. For the needy young women, they provide the means to embark on a new life with joy and dignity. In doing so, they lay a solid foundation for a new generation. For the bride's parents, they provide a solution to one of life's most heartbreaking situations — the inability to marry off one's children. For such parents, as children arrive at marriageable age, the satisfactions of raising a family can turn into a mounting sense of despair. Those who see to this mitzvah help erase that despair and transform it into its exact opposite — the indescribable joy of bringing a child to his or her *chuppah*, marriage canopy. The One Who gives the ability to perform an act of kindness will pay a reward for all the goodness that ensues.

When people are approached by someone collecting money to marry off a child, there is a tendency to see the person's need as a sign of his own irresponsibility or an unfair social system. A man once asked Rabbi Abraham Pam, *zt'l*, the head of Yeshivah Torah Vodaath, why he should give wedding money to the many large families from Jerusalem whose economic problems were, in his opinion, the result of a social system that made no sense. Rabbi Pam answered the question by honing in on the only truly relevant fact: For the person standing at the door, his heart churning with pain and hope, politics and economics are utterly beside the point. One must respond to him by doing what one can to help a fellow Jew walk his daughter down the aisle and into her future.

Step by **Step**

When I have spare money designated for charity, I will keep in mind that marrying off poor brides takes precedence over other needs.

---

12 Adar — May today's learning be a זכות for our משפחה.
Dedicated by Adena and Dov Goldman

13 Elul — לע"נ משה אלימלך בן שמואל אברהם סימקאוויטש ז"ל
Dedicated by his children — נלב"ע י"ד אלול

יג אדר
13 ADAR / CYCLE 1

February 15, 2003
March 6, 2004
February 22, 2005
March 13, 2006
March 3, 2007
February 19, 2008
March 9, 2009
February 27, 2010

13 ADAR II

During Hebrew leap
years, a thirteenth month
called Adar Sheni is
added to the calendar.
During those years, the
lessons for the days of
Adar should be studied
during each of the Adars.

March 17, 2003
March 24, 2005
March 20, 2008

יד אלול
14 ELUL / CYCLE 2

September 11, 2003
August 31, 2004
September 18, 2005
September 7, 2006
August 28, 2007
September 14, 2008
September 3, 2009
August 24, 2010

❧ *The Right Niche*

SEFER AHAVAS CHESED — Part III Chapter VII

*I*f a person wants to be successful in his profession, he must pick a profession for which he has some aptitude. A man with a poor sense of direction would not succeed as a pilot. A man with a shaky grasp of mathematics should probably stay out of accounting. Each person has certain gifts and the obligation to discover how to use them to their best advantage.

In one's chesed career, the same principle holds true: A wealthy man and his wagon driver were traveling together to a distant town when a snowstorm blocked any further progress. The two men — who were amiable companions after all their years together — realized that they would have to make Shabbos in the nearest town. When they arrived, the rich man gave his driver some extra money to buy himself a large, freshly baked challah. He then found himself an elegant inn, purchased a bountiful hot meal and readied himself for Shabbos. Once dressed in his finest clothing, he decided that, as long as he was stuck, he might as well do something helpful. He stationed himself outside the town on the snowy road with the intention of helping other travelers whose wagons became bogged down in the snow. Of course, he had no real knowledge of how to manipulate a wagon, and his meddling only caused travelers to dig themselves deeper into the slippery ruts in the road.

The driver, too, decided to take this opportunity to do some good. With his extra-large challah awaiting him in his meager room, he felt magnanimous and invited other wayfarers to join him for the meal. Normally, these wayfarers would be invited by the wealthy people of the town, who would provide them with what was often their only hot meal of the week. Nonetheless, they followed the wagon driver to his room, believing that he, too, would present them with a filling Shabbos meal. When they found that all he had to offer was part of his challah, they reacted with angry disbelief. "What's wrong?" the driver asked. "I have so much more than I usually do, I just wanted to share it!" The disappointed guests explained that they had lost their chance for a full meal. "And now it's too late!" they despaired.

The story points out the folly of taking upon oneself a chesed that is beyond one's means, and neglecting the chesed one is well prepared to do. Had the wagon driver stationed himself on the road to help the travelers, he could have been of real help. Had the wealthy man invited the wayfarers to share his meal, he would have been able to provide them with a real, satisfying taste of Shabbos. A person has to understand what he has to offer, and then offer it where it will do the most good.

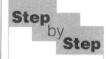

Today I will assess what strengths and assets I have and how I can apply them to chesed.

13 Adar — Oscar Arthur Tannenbaum ז"ל לע"נ אשר בן מאיר ז"ל
Dedicated by his daughter, son-in-law and family, Joan Devorah & Yehudah Aryeh Bersin
לזכות אברהם קלונימוס בן גיטל נ"י — **14 Elul**

Loving Kindness □ 349

DAY 163

יד אדר
14 ADAR / CYCLE 1

February 16, 2003
March 7, 2004
February 23, 2005
March 14, 2006
March 4, 2007
February 20, 2008
March 10, 2009
February 28, 2010

14 ADAR II

During Hebrew leap years, a thirteenth month called Adar Sheni is added to the calendar. During those years, the lessons for the days of Adar should be studied during each of the Adars.

March 18, 2003
March 25, 2005
March 21, 2008

טו אלול
15 ELUL / CYCLE 2

September 12, 2003
September 1, 2004
September 19, 2005
September 8, 2006
August 29, 2007
September 15, 2008
September 4, 2009
August 25, 2010

≈ *Thoughtful*

SEFER AHAVAS CHESED — Part III Chapter VII

*O*f all the gifts a person utilizes in performing an act of kindness, intelligence is perhaps the most important. "How fortunate is the person who cares wisely for the needy," says *Tehillim* (41:2). This is an umbrella statement that covers every form of chesed performed for every person in need. The verse continues, promising that "on the difficult day, Hashem will save him." As mentioned previously, the "difficult day" is widely interpreted to mean the Day of Judgment. Hashem's salvation is the reward to someone not just for helping someone, but for doing so with wisdom.

The word used in the verse, "*maskil*," is connected to the word "*sechel*," which means common sense. The use of this word qualifies the kind of help one should provide, requiring a person to give serious thought to the needy individual's situation. For instance, if a poor woman has just given birth, one may wish to give her money to hire some household help. If she has many other bills, however, that money might end up helping to cover them, leaving her without the rest she needs to regain her strength. A better strategy, in that case, might be to hire and pay a housekeeper for her. Realizing that a person is needy is the first step. Considering the consequences of his poverty and finding ways to alleviate them are the steps that bring chesed into the realm of "*maskil*."

The Chofetz Chaim, relating to the circumstances of his time, offered some suggestions that indicate the type of thinking that is needed. For instance, he recommended that if one is going to loan money to a poor person for food, he should try to give the money at a time when the prices are low, or staple items are on sale, or fruit is in season — the time when the person can get the most for his money.

The Talmud (*Succah* 49a) stresses that the essence of charity is chesed. One provides for another person not just to discharge an obligation, but to do an act of kindness. Charity is only valid to the degree that it actually helps the recipient. The giver must not only consider the recipient's material situation, but his emotional one as well. He cannot do good by giving in a way that causes the recipient embarrassment. In most cases, he should try to keep the act of giving private, or if possible, completely anonymous. By giving careful thought to what a person needs and how to most effectively provide for those needs, a person animates his act of charity with the life-giving force of chesed. "On his difficult day," Hashem will repay his deed, giving him the reward of eternal life.

Step by **Step**

When I am involved in helping a needy individual, I will give more consideration to that person's various needs and ways to meet them.

14 Adar — Shirley Goldman לע"נ שפרה בת קלונמוס קלמן ע"ה
Dedicated in loving memory by her children and grandchildren

15 Elul — לע"נ מלכה ריזל בת ברכה ע"ה — נלב"ע י"ט אלול
Dedicated by Leah & Shmuel Tarter and children

טו אדר
15 ADAR / CYCLE 1

February 17, 2003
March 8, 2004
February 24, 2005
March 15, 2006
March 5, 2007
February 21, 2008
March 11, 2009
March 1, 2010

15 ADAR II

*During Hebrew leap
years, a thirteenth month
called Adar Sheni is
added to the calendar.
During those years, the
lessons for the days of
Adar should be studied
during each of the Adars.*

March 19, 2003
March 26, 2005
March 22, 2008

טו אלול
16 ELUL / CYCLE 2

September 13, 2003
September 2, 2004
September 20, 2005
September 9, 2006
August 30, 2007
September 16, 2008
September 5, 2009
August 26, 2010

❧ *Wearing Kindness*

SEFER AHAVAS CHESED — Part III Chapter VII

*S*ensitivity to the poor person's needs is the hall-mark of chesed and the key to reaping chesed's full reward. Sometimes, more than food, money or any other type of help, a person needs clothing. A new school year, a family simchah, Yomim Tovim, a job interview — any of these events might severely strain the clothing budget of a family living close to the financial edge. Hashem performed this mitzvah when he provided clothes for Adam and Eve; it therefore stands as one of the ways in which a human being can emulate Hashem.

The Talmud (*Sotah* 14a) specifies providing clothes as a fulfillment of the verse, "Open your hands and provide for the poor person whatever he needs." This mitzvah is singled out because it best expresses one of the underlying concepts of chesed: One must tend to people's needs, regardless of their circumstances. A person who needs clothing may not necessarily be poor. For instance, someone's luggage might have been lost en route to a foreign city. He may arrive with nothing but the clothes on his back, and even though he might be a very wealthy individual, in this situation, he is needy. One might feel there is no obligation to help the man — perhaps he could easily afford to go to a store and purchase himself a whole new wardrobe. Wealth is not a relevant factor, says the Chofetz Chaim, just as it is not relevant to whether one is obliged to visit a sick person. If he is sick, one is obligated to visit him. The responsibility rests on each person to undertake acts of chesed, even where the recipient seems to have adequate resources already.

This point emerges clearly through the circumstances under which Hashem first clothed Adam and Eve. They were in no way needy; all the earth and its every resource belonged to them. They were, however, confused and frightened by their sin and its consequences. Hashem recognized that while, theoretically, they could easily fashion their own clothing, realistically at that point in time they needed help — and so, Hashem helped them. The Chofetz Chaim translates the message conveyed in the Adam and Eve scenario: Even if a person's wealth and power arouse the envy of all who know him, when his time of need arises, one is obligated to help.

The Chofetz Chaim invests much time in convincing his readers that the rich, too, deserve chesed, and concludes that for the poor, the imperative is far greater. When those who cannot afford clothing are provided for, the mitzvah doubles to incorporate *tzedakah* as well. At times, it can rise to the level of saving a life, for inadequate clothing in cold weather can destroy the health of a poor person.

In the Chofetz Chaim's time, well-organized communities would set aside money specifically to purchase winter clothes for the needy. In current times, many organizations have been established to collect used clothes and coats in good condition; these are redistributed to the poor. Regarding people engaged in these endeavors, the Chofetz Chaim proclaims, "How fortunate is their lot!" They are among those who faithfully seek to emulate Hashem's kindness, providing clothing — and dignity — to the poor.

Step by **Step**

Today I will sort through some of the clothing in my house and find items of good quality and good condition to donate. They could go to an organization, a large family in my neighborhood, or a relative.

15 Adar — Saul Leiser לע"נ שאול ארי' אליעזר בן ישראל יעקב
Dedicated in loving memory by his daughter, Chanie Walfish

16 Elul — Pola Stolowicz לע"נ פעשא בת יהושע ע"ה
Dedicated by the Stolowicz and Rosenblum families

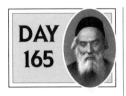
טז אדר
16 ADAR / CYCLE 1

February 18, 2003
March 9, 2004
February 25, 2005
March 16, 2006
March 6, 2007
February 22, 2008
March 12, 2009
March 2, 2010

16 ADAR II

During Hebrew leap
years, a thirteenth month
called Adar Sheni is
added to the calendar.
During those years, the
lessons for the days of
Adar should be studied
during each of the Adars.

March 20, 2003
March 27, 2005
March 23, 2008

יז אלול
17 ELUL / CYCLE 2

September 14, 2003
September 3, 2004
September 21, 2005
September 10, 2006
August 31, 2007
September 17, 2008
September 6, 2009
August 27, 2010

❧ *Clothes of Honor*

SEFER AHAVAS CHESED — Part III Chapter VII

*G*iving a person clothing accomplishes more than simply protecting him from the elements. It restores the recipient's self-respect, saving him from the disgrace of appearing in ragged, ill-fitting garb that telegraph his poverty to all who see him. Unlike a donation of food or money, a donation of clothing feeds the recipient's dignity. A gift of clothing may enable someone who has fallen on hard financial times to maintain his status within his community. It may allow his children to go to school and mix with their peers without shame. Because the giver has acted to protect the honor of another person, Hashem rewards him by upholding his financial status, guaranteeing that he will never be in a position to need clothing from others. That is the blessing, says the Chofetz Chaim, that comes with providing clothing.

The reward is by no means limited to this world, however. In the World to Come, the reward is also a garment — a radiant, glorious garment woven of the person's mitzvos. These are clothes that confer upon their wearer the kind of status and honor that cannot be purchased for any amount of money on the earth below. As the prophet Zachariah proclaims (3:4): "I will remove from you your sins, and I will dress you with clothes of honor."

One's wardrobe in the World to Come is a reflection of one's activities on earth. In his commentary on the Talmud, the Maharatz tells of a dream he had about his saintly father, who had passed away. His father appeared in the dream dressed in regal robes with a golden crown upon his head. The Maharatz noticed, however, that in contrast to all this grandeur, his father's feet were bare. His father explained to him that his Heavenly attire was the reward for the many mitzvos and acts of kindness he had performed throughout his life. His bare feet represented his one deficiency; although he had given much charity from his own pocket, he had been reluctant to walk around collecting for those in need. In a rare Heavenly occurrence, he had been allowed to come to his son in a dream to ask that he remedy the situation. If he would walk the streets in his father's stead, collecting charity for the poor, he could earn himself and his father a pair of eternal shoes.

I will keep in mind that a simple chesed — giving good quality hand-me-downs to someone who can use them — carries with it great reward.

16 Adar — Reb Dovid Dachs ז"ל לע"נ הרב דוד בן הרב חיים יצחק ז"ל
Dedicated in loving memory by his grandchildren, Shlomie & Libby Dachs and family

17 Elul — Shulamis Atkin ע"ה לע"נ פריידע שולמית בת חיים צבי ע"ה
Dedicated in loving memory by Penina and Jay Orlinsky

יז אדר
17 ADAR / CYCLE 1

February 19, 2003
March 10, 2004
February 26, 2005
March 17, 2006
March 7, 2007
February 23, 2008
March 13, 2009
March 3, 2010

17 ADAR II

During Hebrew leap years, a thirteenth month called Adar Sheni is added to the calendar. During those years, the lessons for the days of Adar should be studied during each of the Adars.

March 21, 2003
March 28, 2005
March 24, 2008

יח אלול
18 ELUL / CYCLE 2

September 15, 2003
September 4, 2004
September 22, 2005
September 11, 2006
September 1, 2007
September 18, 2008
September 7, 2009
August 28, 2010

✎ *A Little Foresight*

SEFER AHAVAS CHESED — Part III Chapter VII

*W*ith the right outlook, life presents constant opportunities to help other people with barely any extra effort or expense. A person who orients his vision toward those opportunities can generate countless blessings for himself and his family, simply by being aware and proactive. The Chofetz Chaim offers an example that illustrates how one who applies his "*sechel*," his intelligence, to the needs of others can do much good at little cost to himself.

In Russian Lithuania, where the Chofetz Chaim lived, the winters were long and frigid. Firewood was scarce. Often, the snow made the roads impassable and shipments of wood simply did not arrive. What came was usually moist and always very expensive. The cost of heating even a small home was enough to send a middle-class family plunging toward poverty. For a poor family, there was a real question of living through the winter. The wealthy, however, were able to capitalize on the abundance of wood available in the summer. They would buy a plentiful supply of dry wood at low prices and store it for later use. The poor, with no cash to spare, could not take advantage of the summer bargains.

The Chofetz Chaim sees in this dire situation the perfect example of chesed with "*sechel*." The wealthy man could well afford to purchase more wood than his own household would need. If he bought an extra hundred wagonloads or more during the summer, and stored it on his property, he could sell it at summer prices to the poor families in the community. By buying the wood at a fair market price, they would be spared the embarrassment of taking charity. The rich man would get back his financial investment while immeasurable dividends mounted in the World to Come. The warmth and comfort of the families he helped, the lives of those who might have perished from the cold, the financial stability he allowed families to maintain — all these and their ever-growing aftereffects would accrue to his Heavenly account. In addition, he would have enough wood to give to those who could not afford to buy, even at summer prices. For those people, his chesed would amount to saving a life.

The precise details of this example are obviously not applicable today, but the details of the scheme are not at the heart of the Chofetz Chaim's message. It is the outlook on life that he wishes to impart. There are many other opportunities that a person may be equipped to capitalize upon. The Chofetz Chaim urges each person to be on the lookout for his unique assets and the most beneficial ways to use them.

I will try to incorporate a chesed into something I do for myself or my family.

DAY 167

יח אדר

18 ADAR / CYCLE 1

February 20, 2003
March 11, 2004
February 27, 2005
March 18, 2006
March 8, 2007
February 24, 2008
March 14, 2009
March 4, 2010

18 ADAR II

*During Hebrew leap
years, a thirteenth month
called Adar Sheni is
added to the calendar.
During those years, the
lessons for the days of
Adar should be studied
during each of the Adars.*

March 22, 2003
March 29, 2005
March 25, 2008

יט אלול

19 ELUL / CYCLE 2

September 16, 2003
September 5, 2004
September 23, 2005
September 12, 2006
September 2, 2007
September 19, 2008
September 8, 2009
August 29, 2010

✋ *The Value of Wood*

SEFER AHAVAS CHESED — Part III Chapter VII

Those who see a need and devise an efficient chesed to fulfill it are accomplishing far more than is apparent on the surface. In Day 166, the Chofetz Chaim presents a scheme by which wealthy people can assure that poor people have firewood for the winter. He mentions that there are communities that have organized just such a system, bringing great blessing upon themselves and illustrating the power of the Jewish people working together to solve seemingly intractable problems.

The Talmud (*Taanis* 28a) relates another scheme in which the Jews coordinated their efforts to gather wood for another fire — the sacred fire of the *Beis HaMikdash*. In the days of the Second *Beis HaMikdash*, people considered themselves privileged to donate wood for the fire of the altar. During one period, however, the Romans issued a decree forbidding the delivery of wood to the *Beis HaMikdash*. The Jews would not accept the loss of the altar's fire, and so they devised a plan. They assembled wooden ladders and carried them along, explaining to officers at various checkpoints that they were on their way to do repairs that required a ladder. Their ruse was successful. When they reached the *Beis HaMikdash*, they disassembled the ladders and left the wood. For their dedication, the Talmud lauds these men with the words "of sainted memory." The firewood brought by these men long ago in Jerusalem had a counterpart in the firewood brought in the Chofetz Chaim's time to help to heat the homes of the poor. Those who donated wood to the altar enjoyed the honor of knowing that their effort brought cleansing for the Jewish people's sins, for it was that fire that consumed the sacrifices. In the times since then, there has been no comparable means of purification. The Chofetz Chaim, however, says that the man who goes door to door collecting money for firewood for his poor neighbors — an effort undertaken with little fanfare and no glory — has no less merit than the men in the Talmud's narrative.

The Talmud emphasizes that chesed is Hashem's preferred vehicle for effecting forgiveness. This is illustrated in a conversation in which Rabbi Yehoshua ben Chananyah laments, "Woe is to us! The Temple, the source of forgiveness for our sins, has been destroyed." Rabbi Yochanan ben Zakkai replies "My son, do not despair. We have another atonement, and that is acts of kindness. For Hashem says 'For I desire kindness, not a sacrifice'" (*Hoshea* 6:6). Hashem's desire is that his people use their physical being — their hands and feet, their arms and legs, their eyes, ears and brains — as a vehicle to perceive the needs of others and get the job done. For those who see the world this way and dedicate their physical abilities to this purpose, each day of life opens a new door to blessing.

Step by **Step**

I will get together with a few other people and try, even on a small scale, to organize some chesed needed by my community.

18 Adar — Simmy Richman יבלח"ט לע"נ רוחמה מרים סימא ע"ה בת אברהם שמחה
Who personified the teachings of this sefer

19 Elul — In memory of Elisabeth Feick
Dedicated by Robert Cabral, Ursula Heppner and Elfriede Hicks

יט אדר
19 ADAR / CYCLE 1

February 21, 2003
March 12, 2004
February 28, 2005
March 19, 2006
March 9, 2007
February 25, 2008
March 15, 2009
March 5, 2010

19 ADAR II

During Hebrew leap
years, a thirteenth month
called Adar Sheni is
added to the calendar.
During those years, the
lessons for the days of
Adar should be studied
during each of the Adars.

March 23, 2003
March 30, 2005
March 26, 2008

כ אלול
20 ELUL / CYCLE 2

September 17, 2003
September 6, 2004
September 24, 2005
September 13, 2006
September 3, 2007
September 20, 2008
September 9, 2009
August 30, 2010

◆ *Disaster Insurance*

SEFER AHAVAS CHESED — Part III Chapter VII

A person needs a sense of security, and to an extent, he can buy it. Fire insurance can protect a person's house. Medical insurance can protect him from the cost of illness. Car insurance can limit the expenses incurred through an accident. Insurance cannot, however, prevent the fire, the illness or the accident. Security can go only so far; faith in Hashem must do the rest. The Chofetz Chaim, however, presents an insurance policy offered by Hashem Himself, to cover just the kind of disasters a person dreads. It is the verse from *Tehillim* upon which so much of the philosophy of chesed is built: "Fortunate is the man who cares wisely for the poor. On the difficult day, Hashem will save him."

Every person on earth can expect to have difficult days. The Talmud (*Arachin* 16b) goes so far as to state that a person should worry if forty days elapse without some kind of vexation. Difficulties and challenges are signs of Hashem's maintenance — an adjustment here, a cleansing there — fine-tuning the soul so that it will eventually merit its full reward. One who does not experience these adjustments should fear that either he is consuming his reward in this world, or that he is beyond repair.

The Chofetz Chaim, therefore, does not offer a blanket guarantee against all of life's troubles. He focuses on the verse's phrase "the difficult day." This is the worst day of a person's life, the day he cannot possibly face alone. On that day, when he feels that he is at the edge of the abyss, Hashem will catch him. Hashem will stand by his side and strengthen him to do what needs to be done. One purchases this insurance by caring for others with wisdom.

Forethought and planning are the keys to accomplishing chesed at its highest level — in a way that preserves the recipient's dignity. In some cases, this means presenting a gift as a loan, with the provision that it can be paid back, "whenever you're able." Optimally, one can find someone a job that will lift him out of poverty. Even if the person is not qualified for the jobs that are available, there are ways to allow him to feel he is earning his bread. If he is trying to sell something that no one wants to buy, the highest form of chesed is to purchase it, claiming it is "just what I was looking for." If he is offering a service — even one that people do not generally need — it is a chesed to hire him with a relieved exclamation that "I've been trying to find someone to do this for so long." The Chofetz Chaim, citing the words of the *Sefer Chassidim*, describes the perfect beauty Hashem sees in these "invisible" acts of kindness: "There is charity that does not look like charity; however, it appears before Hashem as the greatest charity."

If I know someone in need of financial help, I will try to help him in a way that he does not perceive as charity.

לע"נ ר' יוסף אריה לייב בן ר' אלימלך יצחק ז"ל — **19 Adar**
נלב"ע ט' אדר תשנ"ד

20 Elul — In honor of Dr. Hylton Lightman
Dedicated by his family, Lawrence NY

כ אדר
20 ADAR / CYCLE 1

February 22, 2003
March 13, 2004
March 1, 2005
March 20, 2006
March 10, 2007
February 26, 2008
March 16, 2009
March 6, 2010

20 ADAR II

During Hebrew leap
years, a thirteenth month
called Adar Sheni is
added to the calendar.
During those years, the
lessons for the days of
Adar should be studied
during each of the Adars.

March 24, 2003
March 31, 2005
March 27, 2008

כא אלול
21 ELUL / CYCLE 2

September 18, 2003
September 7, 2004
September 25, 2005
September 14, 2006
September 4, 2007
September 21, 2008
September 10, 2009
August 31, 2010

❧ *Kinds of Poverty*

SEFER AHAVAS CHESED — **Part III Chapter VII**

A person in need is not always a person in need of money. There are many other types of needs, and all of them can be addressed with the same strategy one employs to help the financially poor — using one's head. The Chofetz Chaim describes some other types of deficiencies that place a person in the category of *"dal,"* or needy. For instance, someone may lack physical strength, either because of age or infirmity. One must think about that person's situation: What errands or chores does he need done? What type of care does he require? Dealing wisely with such a person means perceiving his needs so that he can avoid the discomfort of asking for favors.

"Dal" may also include someone who carries grave worries in his heart. If one has the ability to do something practical to alleviate his worry, one should do so. If there is nothing a person can do, he can still offer a listening ear and a dose of encouragement. Others are considered *"dal"* because they are poor in knowledge. The Sages say (*Nedarim* 41a), "There is no poverty except in knowledge," and indeed, a lack of knowledge can lead one to every other form of poverty. If a person's lack of knowledge is causing him to veer from the path of Torah, one must certainly use wisdom and sensitivity to find a way to steer him in the right direction. Drawing someone back into a life of Torah and mitzvos, according to the *Zohar* (*Chadash Parashas Lech Lecha*), is the greatest form of helping

the poor person, for this deed averts not just a lifetime of spiritual poverty, but an impoverished eternity.

There are also those whose spiritual life is working well, but whose ignorance of worldly matters keeps them locked in a financial struggle. For such people, enlightened help consists of some guidance and education in wise investing. This not only helps the person maximize whatever capital he has remaining to him, it also allows him to preserve his status in his family and community.

Helping others make their way in this world, helping them overcome their deficiencies so that their lives can function smoothly, is an act that is treasured in Heaven. The Chofetz Chaim offers this allegory: A man has a son, an inexperienced young man who has moved to a distant city. There he finds a mentor — a kind, knowledgeable individual who is willing to help him navigate his new environment. The father's gratitude is not difficult to imagine. He can stop worrying, knowing that his son has the support of a good, capable person. Just as that father would want to reward his son's mentor, so does Hashem overflow with reward for those who, out of love for their fellow Jew, protect and guide His children.

Step by **Step**

I will be more aware of other kinds of needs around me, and try to offer wise assistance where I can.

לזכות יהודה דוד בן ריבה פיגא נ"י — **20 Adar**

21 Elul — Mrs. Rana Frankel לזכות רנה פיגא בת חיים זאב שתחי'
Dedicated by the Frankel family

DAY 170

כא אדר
21 ADAR / CYCLE 1

February 23, 2003
March 14, 2004
March 2, 2005
March 21, 2006
March 11, 2007
February 27, 2008
March 17, 2009
March 7, 2010

21 ADAR II

During Hebrew leap years, a thirteenth month called Adar Sheni is added to the calendar. During those years, the lessons for the days of Adar should be studied during each of the Adars.

March 25, 2003
April 1, 2005
March 28, 2008

כב אלול
22 ELUL / CYCLE 2

September 19, 2003
September 8, 2004
September 26, 2005
September 15, 2006
September 5, 2007
September 22, 2008
September 11, 2009
September 1, 2010

❧ *Sharing the Wealth*

SEFER AHAVAS CHESED — Part III Chapter VII

A person's whose poverty is in Torah learning may not appear poor at all. It takes acuity of vision to see that person's poverty. Material poverty is plain to see. If one were to encounter someone standing in the winter cold without a coat, he would drop everything and find the person something with which to cover himself, lest he freeze to death. When one sees a Jew without Torah, he must also see the urgency of the situation, for this person is also dangerously exposed. He risks arriving in the Next World devoid of the garment that only Torah can create for him.

Teaching Torah to the person who is poor in knowledge elevates a person to a level beyond that which he merits on his own. The Talmud (*Bava Metzia*, 85a) states in the name of Rabbi Shmuel bar Nachmani, who cites Rabbi Yonasan: "Anyone who teaches his friend's son Torah merits to dwell in the Heavenly Academy." This is the place reserved for the saints and sages of the generations; an ordinary individual would have scant hope of ever experiencing its splendor. The Talmud is saying that just such ordinary individuals — people who work for a living, raise their families and struggle through daily life — earn the right to bask in Heaven's most exalted realm, simply by teaching Torah to another man's child. Reish Lakish (*Sanhedrin* 99b) states that one who teaches his friend's son Torah receives credit for giving him life: "It is as if you made him." Furthermore, the Chofetz Chaim, citing the

Talmud (*Bava Metzia* 85a), says, "One who teaches Torah to the son of someone who is ignorant, even if Hashem has issued as a decree against him, He will annul that decree only in this merit."

Teaching Torah is more than a chesed. According to *Avos D'Rabbi Nassan*, it is the fulfillment of a commandment contained in the Mishnah (*Avos* 1:12): "Love people and bring them close to Torah." Based on *Tanna D'Vei Eliyahu Rabbah* (Ch. 27), the Chofetz Chaim recommends that the teacher use a slow, consistent method to gradually bring Torah within reach of the student. He should teach him one verse of the *Shema* each day; teach one halachah each day; guide him to perform one mitzvah each day. In this way, he will gradually weave his coat, thread by thread, for the World to Come.

I will become more aware of ways in which I can, formally or informally, share Torah learning with other people.

Sharing one's learning with someone requires great sensitivity. A person must not be perceived to be imposing his beliefs on someone else. Rather, he should present himself as someone who has something valuable to share — someone who respects and cares for the other person and simply wishes to help him develop a relationship to Hashem. With this approach, entire families and their subsequent generations have been reconnected to their source of spiritual sustenance.

If the void in Torah learning is allowed to remain vacant, the evil inclination is guaranteed to rush into the vacuum. Helping to steer someone's child into a yeshivah steers him away from every temptation and falsehood the secular world has to offer. It is an endeavor blessed with a propensity for success. The Sages say, "Be especially careful with the children of the poor, for the Torah will come forth from them" (*Nedarim* 81a).

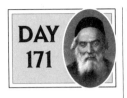
כב אדר
22 ADAR / CYCLE 1

February 24, 2003
March 15, 2004
March 3, 2005
March 22, 2006
March 12, 2007
February 28, 2008
March 18, 2009
March 8, 2010

22 ADAR II

During Hebrew leap
years, a thirteenth month
called Adar Sheni is
added to the calendar.
During those years, the
lessons for the days of
Adar should be studied
during each of the Adars.

March 26, 2003
April 2, 2005
March 29, 2008

כג אלול
23 ELUL / CYCLE 2

September 20, 2003
September 9, 2004
September 27, 2005
September 16, 2006
September 6, 2007
September 23, 2008
September 12, 2009
September 2, 2010

❧ *The Torah of Kindness*

SEFER AHAVAS CHESED — **Part III Chapter VIII**

*S*ometimes, no matter how much thought one puts into helping another person through a difficult situation, no solution appears. Even then, however, one is not powerless — not as long as one still possesses the power of speech. Words have been known to move people from sickness to recovery, from despair to hope, from confusion to clarity.

There is a story that is told about Rabbi Moshe Leib of Sassover, and also of Rabbi Meir of Premishlan. The story may well be true of both men, and of other rebbes as well, for all were keenly attuned to the pain of their fellow Jew. In this story, a man came to the Rebbe seeking advice for his terrible situation. He detailed his woes, and much to his dismay, the Rebbe had to agree that the circumstances were bleak. "I don't know what to tell you," the Rebbe told the unfortunate man. "All I can do is give you a blessing."

The man received his blessing and left, still feeling downcast. Moments later, the Rebbe ran after him. "Wait!" he called. "There is one more thing I can do. I can cry with you." The two men sat and cried together until there were no more tears. Upon preparing to leave, the man told his Rebbe, "I've never felt better." Chesed done with words is a unique category of kindness, with unique power to salve the pain of others.

One of the most powerful acts of kindness one can effect through speech is teaching. A verse in *"Aishes Chayil"* ("A Woman of Valor") [*Mishlei* 31:26], which is recited at the Friday night Sabbath meal, states "Her mouth opens with wisdom, and the Torah of kindness is on her tongue." The Talmud (*Succah* 49) explains that "the Torah of kindness" is Torah learned for the purpose of teaching others. It might appear then that the Chofetz Chaim is suggesting that all of one's chesed be geared toward the spiritual needs of others. This is not, however, a complete mitzvah. Chesed still requires a person to use his material assets and physical abilities to help people in a practical, material way.

The Talmud (*Rosh Hashanah* 18a) relates a story that delineates the proper balance between spiritual and practical pursuits. Abaye and Rava, two of the Talmud's Sages, were descended from Eli, a High Priest, upon whom Hashem proclaimed a curse. The curse was that no descendant would live to old age. Rava and Abaye differed in their approaches to Torah learning and chesed. Rava dedicated himself totally to Torah study, assuming that if he were needed for an act of chesed, he would be approached and would then respond. This was his interpretation of the principle that one who is engaged in learning should only leave it if nobody else can perform the chesed.

Abaye, in contrast, dedicated some of his considerable talents to performing acts of chesed. He reasoned that, because of his superior skills and enthusiasm for chesed, he was required to become involved, for although others might be able to perform the task, no one could do it with the same degree of efficiency and success. Rava lived for just 40 years. Abaye lived to 60, the age past which one is considered an elder. The extra 20 years compensated for the learning he had missed in pursuit of chesed. Thus, he lacked nothing in the end.

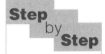

Today I will examine the balance of chesed and learning in my life.

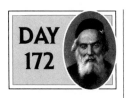

כג אדר
23 ADAR / CYCLE 1

February 25, 2003
March 16, 2004
March 4, 2005
March 23, 2006
March 13, 2007
February 29, 2008
March 19, 2009
March 9, 2010

23 ADAR II

During Hebrew leap
years, a thirteenth month
called Adar Sheni is
added to the calendar.
During those years, the
lessons for the days of
Adar should be studied
during each of the Adars.

March 27, 2003
April 3, 2005
March 30, 2008

כד אלול
24 ELUL / CYCLE 2

September 21, 2003
September 10, 2004
September 28, 2005
September 17, 2006
September 7, 2007
September 24, 2008
September 13, 2009
September 3, 2010

❧ *With a Word*

SEFER AHAVAS CHESED — Part III Chapter VIII

*T*o give money requires having it — and not everyone does. Neither does everyone have time and energy to apply to others' needs. One asset almost every person does have, however, is an endless supply of words. This is a nondepletable resource that can accomplish tremendous good every single day of one's life.

The Chofetz Chaim offers a few general ideas of how to maximize the power of chesed inherent in the power of speech: Someone might be aware of a grudge that a friend or family member is holding against another person. If he has the trust of that friend or relative, he might be able to find the words that will remove the anger from his heart.

One can also use words to avert someone else's suffering. The Chofetz Chaim sets up a scenario in which someone knows that certain people are thieves. He hears them discussing another man's great wealth with the obvious goal of making him their next mark. It is a mitzvah of chesed to add to the conversation: "Oh, him? Poor man, I heard he lost everything." The information is not true, but it is chesed. Sarah, Abraham's wife, is said to have done a chesed when she told Pharaoh that she was Abraham's sister. This piece of misinformation protected Abraham from the harm that would have come to him as a result of Pharaoh's desire for Sarah.

The greatest level of this type of verbal chesed is to directly approach someone who is slated to be victimized and advise him on how to protect himself. A person who has the ability to do this for another person is obligated to speak.

Through words a person may have the power to help a person get a job, find a marriage match, get into a certain school, receive credit, earn a second chance; there are countless ways in which a few positive words can help. When one uses his words for this purpose, *Tosefta Pe'ah* (Chapter 3) explains, "Because of this thing, Hashem will bless you" (*Devarim* 15:10.) The term *"divar,"* meaning "thing," can also mean "word." Because of just a few "good words" one expends to help another person, a special blessing is bestowed upon him.

The Vilna Gaon's wife spent many hours each week with a friend, going door-to-door-collecting money for the poor. The two women agreed that the first of them to pass into the Next World would let the other know what awaited on the other side. The friend passed away first, and after some time, she came to the Vilna Gaon's wife in a dream. "I can only reveal to you one small thing," she said. "Once we knocked on a door, but the person wasn't home. As we walked away, you noticed him and lifted one finger to point him out. We approached him and got our donation, with which someone was helped. You cannot imagine what reward Heaven has destined for you, for just that one little gesture."

The lifting of a finger, the uttering of a sentence or two, a smile, a handshake — no chesed goes unnoticed.

Step by **Step**

I will be more aware of opportunities to put in a "good word" for someone.

23 Adar — To Lee, Alex, Adam, Dina and Levi
Dedicated by Shimon and Lynne Kushner

24 Elul — May today's learning be a זכות for our משפחה.
Dedicated by Moishe and Malka Schreiber

כד אדר
24 ADAR / CYCLE 1

February 26, 2003
March 17, 2004
March 5, 2005
March 24, 2006
March 14, 2007
March 1, 2008
March 20, 2009
March 10, 2010

24 ADAR II

During Hebrew leap
years, a thirteenth month
called Adar Sheni is
added to the calendar.
During those years, the
lessons for the days of
Adar should be studied
during each of the Adars.

March 28, 2003
April 4, 2005
March 31, 2008

כה אלול
25 ELUL / CYCLE 2

September 22, 2003
September 11, 2004
September 29, 2005
September 18, 2006
September 8, 2007
September 25, 2008
September 14, 2009
September 4, 2010

❧ *The Soundingboard*

SEFER AHAVAS CHESED — **Part III Chapter VIII**

*T*he adage that "talk is cheap" stands at the opposite end of the Torah's view of words. Talk is powerful. The harm it can do is well known, but the Chofetz Chaim is now elaborating on its even greater potential to do good. Talk is the medium through which a person can impart to others the benefits of his experience. There is a time in every person's life when he needs advice. He faces a situation that is new or confusing to him, and he needs someone else to help him find the right direction. Offering someone good advice can change the course of his life; it might repair his marriage, improve his relationship with his children, make his business successful, steer him toward the right neighborhood or rabbi. Even a wealthy person, who may appear to be in control of his universe, sometimes needs the perspective of others, and providing advice to him is a chesed as well.

Talk is so valuable because it contains a priceless element. Words are manufactured by the body, but the raw material for them comes from the soul. They therefore have a unique power to soothe another person's soul. Words can do more than provide protection, direction and advice — they can provide succor. When one sees a person who is in a state of depression, there might be nothing practical one can do to help. In that case, the chesed at hand is to sit with the person and speak to him, to let him speak, and try to remove some of the worry from his heart.

In his *Igeres HaTeshuvah*, Rabbeinu Yonah states that this form of chesed is within everyone's reach. The Talmud (*Bava Basra* 9b) says that if someone gives a perutah—a coin of little value – to a poor person, he receives six blessings. Someone who takes time to sit with the poor person and hear his woes receives eleven blessings.

The Chofetz Chaim adds that someone who tries to brighten another person's darkness can expect the same kindness from Hashem in his time of need. He explains exactly how this mitzvah is to be done: A person must set aside his own agenda for a time and focus on someone else's troubles with the same intensity he would apply to his own.

The Talmud (*Taanis* 22a) relates that Rav Broika once stood with the prophet Elijah in a crowded marketplace. Rav Broika asked Elijah to point out, of all these people passing by, who was guaranteed to merit direct passage into the World to Come. Elijah selected two rather nondescript men, prompting Rav Broika to investigate. He asked them, "What do you do all day?" They replied, "When we see someone who is unhappy, we go to him and we talk to him until he's happy. Then we go to the next person." The men did not have magic words that they used to repair these despairing souls. They just had patience; they let the recipients of their chesed know that at that moment in time, nothing else and no one else was important.

Step by **Step**

The next time someone comes to me with a problem, I will try to focus fully on what they are saying and how they are feeling.

כה אדר
25 ADAR / CYCLE 1

February 27, 2003
March 18, 2004
March 6, 2005
March 25, 2006
March 15, 2007
March 2, 2008
March 21, 2009
March 11, 2010

25 ADAR II

During Hebrew leap
years, a thirteenth month
called Adar Sheni is
added to the calendar.
During those years, the
lessons for the days of
Adar should be studied
during each of the Adars.

March 29, 2003
April 5, 2005
April 1, 2008

כו אלול
26 ELUL / CYCLE 2

September 23, 2003
September 12, 2004
September 30, 2005
September 19, 2006
September 9, 2007
September 26, 2008
September 15, 2009
September 5, 2010

✒ *Rallying the Troops*

SEFER AHAVAS CHESED — Part III Chapter VIII

*T*he telephone rings, and on the other end is the principal of the local yeshivah. The man who answers the phone knows that there is only one reason the principal calls — to ask a favor. The principal is perceptive enough to detect a vague note of dread in the man's voice. He is also wise enough to know that, in drawing this individual into an act of chesed, he is doing a mitzvah for which both the man and he will be rewarded.

Rabbeinu Yonah (*Taanis* Chapter 3) exhorts: "Teach the masses how to do *tzedakah* and chesed." One who does so has a share in the reward earned by those he has encouraged. In a sense, getting others to give is more difficult than giving from one's own pocket because there is an element of embarrassment involved. One who willingly subjects himself to this feeling in order to raise money for a worthy cause is demonstrating a true love of kindness that motivates him to reach beyond his own financial means to fill a need.

Returning to his discussion of words as an instrument of chesed, the Chofetz Chaim offers one more powerful application of this concept: praying for others. As was mentioned in the discussion of *bikur cholim*, prayer is an essential element of the chesed done for those who are ill. Even if the patient does not know others are praying for him (such knowledge might, in some cases, alarm the patient), putting someone else's well-being into one's personal prayers is an act of profound kindness. The same applies whenever one knows of a person facing difficulties, whether the problem is in the area of marriage, children, a livelihood, spirituality, health or any other area of life.

Praying for a person, says the Chofetz Chaim, should be a Jew's automatic response when he hears of another's troubles. "Hashem, please help him," is all that is required. One can insert these prayers into the proper places of *Shemoneh Esrei*, or utter them quietly, then and there, as the person's woes are being reported. Some people might feel comforted knowing that others are praying for them, and there is an element of chesed in providing that comfort. The real chesed, however, is in the concrete help one renders — the Divine Assistance one draws from Heaven — when praying for someone's salvation or recovery.

Abraham prayed for the people of Sodom, a fact unknown to and unappreciated by them. It was, nonetheless, an act of chesed. The chassidic giant, Rabbi Tzadok HaKohen, notes that Abraham's prayer for Sodom is the longest prayer recorded in the Torah, and it failed to save anyone except for Lot. Following the sequence of events further, however, reveals the real value of that prayer: From Lot came the people of Moab, and from Moab came Ruth. From Ruth came King David, and from King David came *Sefer Tehillim*, the eternally eloquent medium through which Jews throughout the ages have found the voice to petition Hashem.

Praying for others is a kindness for which repayment is guaranteed. The Sages say (*Bava Kamma* 92a): "The one who prays for a friend, even though he needs the same thing, he will be answered first." By taking someone else's concerns into his heart and making them part of his prayers, a person reveals his own compassion. With compassion he is then answered.

The next time I hear of someone's difficulties, I will pray to Hashem for help.

25 Adar — Moshe Asiag לע"נ משה בן דוד ז"ל
Dedicated in loving memory by his family

26 Elul — May today's learning be a z'chus for my family.
Dedicated by Stacy Weissenberger, Beverley Hills, CA

כו אדר
26 ADAR / CYCLE 1

February 28, 2003
March 19, 2004
March 7, 2005
March 26, 2006
March 16, 2007
March 3, 2008
March 22, 2009
March 12, 2010

26 ADAR II

During Hebrew leap years, a thirteenth month called Adar Sheni is added to the calendar. During those years, the lessons for the days of Adar should be studied during each of the Adars.

March 30, 2003
April 6, 2005
April 2, 2008

כז אלול
27 ELUL / CYCLE 2

September 24, 2003
September 13, 2004
October 1, 2005
September 20, 2006
September 10, 2007
September 27, 2008
September 16, 2009
September 6, 2010

❧ *Neglected Treasure*

SEFER AHAVAS CHESED — **Part III Chapter VIII**

*K*nowing that each person has a purpose in the world, some people spend their lives waiting for their moment. The Chofetz Chaim urges every person to view every day as a constellation of moments, an endless horizon containing a billion chances to shine. By grasping as many of these opportunities as possible — the simple favor, the "how are you," the phone call, the offer of a seat on the bus or a lift into town — one can be sure he will not miss his moment while he is waiting for it to happen.

One might wonder why human nature seems to lean away from these simple, ever-accessible sources of merit. The Chofetz Chaim cites an elucidating *Midrash Aggadah* related in *Sefer Lev David:* The prophet Elijah was traveling with Rabbi Yehoshua ben Levi when they came upon a throng of crazed customers pressing forward into the door of a crowded shop. The two men arduously made their way inside, and were shocked to discover that the shop's coveted merchandise was rotten dog meat. Furthermore, this putrid fare was being sold at an exorbitant price. Down the road, there stood an empty shop. Through the window the storekeeper could be seen waiting longingly for a customer. Upon entering his shop, Elijah and Rabbi Yehoshua discovered rich, fresh calf meat, selling for a rock-bottom price.

Rabbi Yehoshua was perplexed by the irony. "What you have seen is an allegory," Elijah explained. The purveyor of putrid dog meat was the "yetzer hara" — the evil inclination — whose worthless wares always seem so wildly attractive to the public. People are willing to expend endless amounts of time and money and to have experiences and possessions whose illusory appeal evaporates in moments. The *yetzer tov* — the good inclination— who sells his wholesome fare of Torah and mitzvos finds few takers. His merchandise is a source of lasting nourishment that anyone can afford, and yet it goes unnoticed.

The Chofetz Chaim presents an up-to-date example of this phenomenon. The *yetzer hara* sometimes expresses itself in the need to score an absolute victory in every disagreement. A person who operates in this mode may spend vast amounts of money to win his point. He is quick to enter into litigation, quick to hire "the best lawyer money can buy," all so he can win what he has convinced himself is a battle of principle. For all this expenditure of emotional energy and money, nothing has been gained from the Divine perspective, "Because He desires kindness" (*Micah* 7:18).

The Chofetz Chaim explains this seemingly insane rush to destruction, and equally insane indifference to an easy source of spiritual wealth: People are simply too busy, too swept up in the rat race, to think. The *yetzer hara* fills a person's mind to capacity with worries about what may or may not occur in an hour, in a day or in ten years, distracting him from the opportunities standing right before him.

The cure to this form of madness is to focus, says the Chofetz Chaim. When a person reminds himself of

Step by **Step**

Today I will try to be less pre-occupied so that I can be more aware of opportunities for small, simple acts of kindness.

(Continued on page 383)

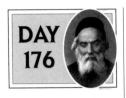

DAY 176

כז אדר
27 ADAR / CYCLE 1

March 1, 2003
March 20, 2004
March 8, 2005
March 27, 2006
March 17, 2007
March 4, 2008
March 23, 2009
March 13, 2010

27 ADAR II

During Hebrew leap years, a thirteenth month called Adar Sheni is added to the calendar. During those years, the lessons for the days of Adar should be studied during each of the Adars.

March 31, 2003
April 7, 2005
April 3, 2008

כח אלול
28 ELUL / CYCLE 2

September 25, 2003
September 14, 2004
October 2, 2005
September 21, 2006
September 11, 2007
September 28, 2008
September 17, 2009
September 7, 2010

✂ *The Final Analysis*

SEFER AHAVAS CHESED — **Part III Chapter VIII**

*A*fter closely examining the mitzvah of chesed and exploring the beauty of each of its hundreds of facets, the Chofetz Chaim binds the entire contents of his book with one all-encompassing ideal — the fear of Heaven. Every reward that chesed brings the doer, and every ray of light it brings the world, is only enduring if the chesed springs from this root. If a person accepts upon himself Hashem's dominion and follows the ways of the Torah, then the chesed he performs will be worthy of the myriad blessings that the Torah promises.

The reason for this is simple. "Doing good" is a meaningful term only if "good" can be defined. When one does "good" as the Torah defines it, one creates positive forces in the world. If one defines good according to some other standard or one's own subjective standard, the outcome cannot have a lasting positive influence, and very often, the "good" will result ultimately in evil. For instance, a person might start an organization to help families pay medical expenses. Without a perspective rooted in the Torah, his good can produce much evil: He might skim money from the donations, reasoning that it is "fair compensation" for his efforts. He might steer money toward less needy friends and relatives reasoning that "charity begins at home." He might keep dishonest records or take money from unsavory sources, reasoning that since saving a life supersedes almost every other mitzvah, his cheating is justified.

To avoid poisoning his chesed he must keep it rooted in the laws of the Torah, ask for and accept rabbinical guidance and, most of all, know that Hashem sees all he does. Otherwise, his effort to do good could spawn misery, hardship and, worst of all, a desecration of Hashem's name.

Heading far off-track is not only a danger with major chesed endeavors. It can pollute even the simplest acts. For instance, someone who scoffs at or is ignorant of Torah might believe he is helping a mourner by taking him out to socialize with friends a few days after he suffers the loss of a parent. The "helper" sees only the immediate result — perhaps the mourner is able to smile for a short while — but the Torah knows that in the long-term, a period of focused grief enables one to experience real happiness in its proper time.

In *Parashas Ha'azinu*, the Chofetz Chaim finds support for his contention that only fear of Heaven can lay a sound foundation for chesed. The verse declares: "If they were wise they would understand this; they would comprehend what takes place at the end" (*Devarim* 32:29). The Sifri explains this verse: "Had the Jewish people concentrated on the words of Torah, no evil could have ever had any effect on them. What did I say to them? 'Accept upon yourself the yoke of Heaven, and convince each other to have fear of Heaven, and lead each other to acts of chesed.'" Of one who follows this formula, says the Chofetz Chaim, "How fortunate is he, and how good it will be for him."

Whenever I engage in an act of kindness, I will let the Torah guide my actions and decisions.

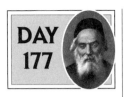
❧ An Evolving Mitzvah

SEFER AHAVAS CHESED — Conclusion

*I*n an age when Jewish communities are blessed with long lists of chesed organizations — everything from a volunteer ambulance corps to crisis hotlines to free hot meals for the sick — a volume elaborating upon this mitzvah might seem superfluous. In the Chofetz Chaim's day, too, European communities were well organized with *bikur cholim* organizations, guest houses, burial societies and charity funds. "I know, I know," says the Chofetz Chaim in the concluding essay of this volume, "that many are saying that we are talking about chesed as if it were not already being performed."

Chesed is being performed, but it is also being transformed, by the particular circumstances of each new generation. This fluidity is borne in the verse "You shall open your hand unto him, and surely lend him enough for his needs" (*Devarim* 15:8). The last three words of the verse turn chesed into a continually evolving mitzvah, for the needs of a Jew change as society changes. The verse teaches that one must endeavor to give or find for a person the help he needs in order to live at a standard that is normal for him. In the days when Jews lived in tents, all one had to do was provide a tent. In times when a simple apartment costs $1,000 a month, the obligation to meet another person's needs becomes far more complicated. Taking care of one's own needs becomes far more complicated, and the tension between giving to others and taking care of oneself becomes complicated as well. For instance, should one forgo a late-model car in order to help someone else put food on the table? Should one spend thousands of dollars for a Succos in Israel, or give the thousands to his local charity so that the city's poor can buy *lulavim* and *esrogim*? Does a poor person "need" a phone? A cell phone? A computer? A dishwasher?

The Chofetz Chaim experienced this phenomenon even in his relatively nontechnological times. He therefore contended that the obligations involved in doing chesed need constant review. One must constantly adjust one's idea of how much help other people require to be sure that their real needs are being met. It does not suffice in current times to declare that a telephone, for instance, is not a real need, since people lived quite well without them for thousands of years.

A person can be quite accurate in assessing what other people need, and still fall short of properly fulfilling his obligations in chesed, simply because he is inaccurate in assessing what he himself is capable of giving. Every person must give in proportion to the resources Hashem has granted him. One who gives less than he can may find that by undernourishing his chesed, he brings upon himself difficulty rather than blessing. A middle-class man's contribution of $50 may stand as praise to his name, while a rich man's contribution in the same amount may stand as an eternal rebuke. Chesed is a powerful vehicle of blessing, but one can only navigate it successfully by constantly reviewing the map and rechecking the directions. The road is ever changing.

I will try to set aside time to review the laws of chesed on a regular basis.

28 Adar — May the Ahavas Yisrael engendered by today's learning be a זכות for our משפחה.
Dedicated by Shlomo & Esther Pomerantz, Chicago, IL

29 Elul — לזכות משפחתנו
Kenneth Ephraim and Julie Pinczower

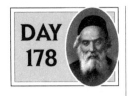

כט אדר
29 ADAR / CYCLE 1

March 3, 2003
March 22, 2004
March 10, 2005
March 29, 2006
March 19, 2007
March 6, 2008
March 25, 2009
March 15, 2010

---

29 ADAR II

During Hebrew leap
years, a thirteenth month
called Adar Sheni is
added to the calendar.
During those years, the
lessons for the days of
Adar should be studied
during each of the Adars.

April 2, 2003
April 9, 2005
April 5, 2008

ל אדר*
30 ADAR / CYCLE 2

March 4, 2003
March 11, 2005
March 7, 2008

* During Hebrew leap
years, Adar I has 30 days.
During those years, the les-
son for 29 Adar should be
learned again today.

❧ *Who Is Rich?*

SEFER AHAVAS CHESED — Conclusion

*H*alachah will answer a person's specific questions about when and how much to give others. The right questions, however, can only arise out of the right perspective, and in present times, that perspective is often warped by the high heat of consumer culture. In previous generations, most people spent their money on basic necessities and gave a portion of their budget to charity. Today, millions of dollars go to neither necessities nor charities. They go instead to luxury, the definition of which must be left to each individual. The Chofetz Chaim warns, however, that a person who treats himself to only the best will have a difficult time justifying tightfistedness toward others.

The balance between giving and self-indulgence often tips when people hit difficult economic times. Indeed, they have less to give, but they often make a brave attempt to maintain their standard of living despite the decreased cash flow, going into debt to keep the same vacation plans and household staff that graced better days. "When things turn around," they reason, "we'll be able to pay off the debts." The bravery falters, however, when they are asked to maintain their level of support for charity: "I can't do it this year. Times are hard." The Chofetz Chaim thus concludes that, no matter how much chesed is being done, it is never a closed subject.

The final words of his volume are a plea to every Jew — and a prophetic plea to his pre-Holocaust generation — to gather close to Hashem under chesed's protective cover: "It is known that the power of *tzedakah* and chesed weakens the attribute of justice ... And today, we see ... that this attribute of justice is becoming so strong in the world from one day to the other —how many sicknesses and terrible deaths through horrible, unimaginable accidents — and the ammunition of the Heaven of blessing seems in our eyes deficient. We have no day whose curse is not greater than that of the day before it. How much more are we obligated to increase our acts of charity and kindness! Perhaps through this we will merit to curtail the attribute of justice and the entire world will be filled with mercy."

A young man once came to enroll in the Chofetz Chaim's yeshivah. The Chofetz Chaim perceived that he would exert a negative influence, and rejected his application. Nonetheless, he offered the boy hospitality for the night, until he could catch the morning train home. That night, the elderly Chofetz Chaim climbed the stairs to the chilly attic, removed his coat and covered the boy. Years later, that boy became an important member of the Communist party. Legislation came across his desk that would effectively kill the yeshivos of the region, and contrary to all his beliefs, he could not bring himself to sign it. His comrades did not understand his reluctance, but he knew what was stilling his hand. "That coat that the old rabbi laid upon me still warms me to this day," he explained.

I will cultivate ahavas chesed in my life, so that I may come to love giving to others as much as I love giving to myself and my family.

The Chofetz Chaim's love of every Jew created the warmth of that coat, and that warmth emerges still through the pages of his *sefer Ahavas Chesed*. He reaches through the generations and lovingly passes down this coat — this mitzvah of chesed — enwrapping his children in the only garment that can protect them against life's harsh winds.

29 Adar — May today's learning be a זכות for כלל ישראל.

30 Adar —

Continuations...

CONTINUED FROM DAY 11 — PAGE 47

by which they are rewarded. The keys are in Hashem's hand, but the extent to which chesed comes into play is in the hand of each individual. In this regard, one receives precisely what one gives to others.

CONTINUED FROM DAY 54 — PAGE 133

In contrast, the person who trains himself in giving will not only get a larger return for his investment, says the Chofetz Chaim. Ultimately, he will most likely give more as well. His constant, disciplined giving will add up to a greater sum when the final figures are tallied. Every dollar he has loaned, every dollar he has contributed, every bit of time and effort he has given will create a "nest egg" of riches that will support him eternally.

CONTINUED FROM DAY 60 — PAGE 145

— has its corollary in giving away time. People fear that even the few shreds of time left to them will evaporate, leaving them utterly depleted. The answer to this fear also has its corollary in the monetary form of chesed: One cannot lose. Every minute a person gives enriches and energizes every other moment of his day.

CONTINUED FROM DAY 65 — PAGE 155

When he does an act of chesed in his parent's name, it is as if he is sending a big, beautifully wrapped package. Every Jew wants *"nachas"* — spiritual pleasure — from his children. Raising them in the ways of chesed is the surest path to achieving that goal in this world and forever after.

CONTINUED FROM DAY 82 — PAGE 189

Jews. His efforts, and the cooperation, talent and courage he demanded of others, were instrumental in saving tens of thousands of Jews from the fires of the Holocaust. One cannot begin to count the Jewish lives, the words of learning, the *tefillos* and mitzvos that were spawned by Rabbi Wasserman's one piece of advice.

CONTINUED FROM DAY 135 — PAGE 295

charity and kindness will receive life and charity and honor" (*Mishlei* 21:21). In what way is charity rewarded by charity? From all the unworthy recipients and questionable situations emerges real charity. Only one who persists in giving through whatever means he can, whenever he can, will ever have the chance to feed the angels.

CONTINUED FROM DAY 175 — PAGE 375

Hashem's infinite kindness, he naturally longs to come closer to Him. He innately understands that the way to accomplish that goal is to engage himself in acts of kindness. His eyes are open to the value of the neglected "merchandise" down the block, and he takes home all he can.

Chesed Connections
Step by Step to a Chesed Revolution

Chesed Connections

Many people have adopted one special chesed or even one element of a chesed as their own. This list has been assembled to capture your imagination and help you find your niche.

▶ ## Bereavement Services

Bereavement lasts much longer than the week-long shivah. Your life experience may make you particularly suited to help.

- Provide meals, money, tutoring, babysitting, counseling.
- Organize a group of volunteers to provide these services to the community.

▶ ## Bikur Cholim — Visiting and Assisting the Sick

Bikur cholim is much more than visiting a nursing home or someone who is ill.

- Take a wheelchair-bound person/elderly individual for a walk.
- Call someone who is ill.
- Volunteer to feed patients who cannot feed themselves.
- Drive someone to the doctor or hospital.
- Cook for someone (and/or the person's family) who is ill.
- Shop for someone who is homebound.
- Take care of the child/children of someone who is ill.
- Blow shofar or read the Megillah for someone who is homebound or in the hospital.
- Set up a network of volunteers to provide these services community-wide.
- Start a fund to help cover medical expenses.
- Pray for those who are ill.
- Collect surplus medical equipment and make it available to those in need.

- Organize a community bus to area hospitals.
- Create a hot line to inform the sick about resources available to them.
- Help someone who is ill put his personal papers, finances, will, etc. in order.
- Create a group of knowledgeable volunteers to help with this sensitive matter.

▶ Car

- Offer a ride to someone whose destination is along your regular route.
- Deliver or pick up a package for an individual or nonprofit organization.

▶ Chevra Kaddisha — Burial Preparations in Accordance with Jewish Law

- Find out from local nursing homes if Jewish patients have proper burial arrangements and work to put such arrangements in place.
- Where necessary, raise money for this purpose.
- Join a *Chevra Kaddisha* and help in the preparation of deceased individuals.
- Volunteer weekly or monthly for a phone line that is contacted when burial services are needed.
- Volunteer to provide a graveside *minyan* for those who do not have family.
- If you are in a position to do so, volunteer to say *Kaddish* for someone who has no one else to say it.

▶ Food for the Needy

- Start a fund to help needy families with food expenses.
- Collect, package or distribute food to the needy.
- Start an organization in your community to provide food for the needy.
- Solicit "gift certificates" from local groceries to give to the needy.

▶ Hachnassas Orchim — Inviting Guests

- Invite new neighbors for a meal.
- Network with friends and neighbors to invite singles or travelers for a Shabbos or holiday meal.

- Offer lodging in your home for out-of-town visitors and fundraisers.
- Create a list of time schedules and directions to all area shuls, kosher restaurants, etc. in your neighborhood.
- Giving directions is a chesed. They should be given clearly and in detail.

▶ Hatzolah — Volunteer Ambulance Corps

- Take Emergency Medical Technician training.
- Financially support your local Hatzolah organization.
- Organize such a group in your community.
- Donate a garage or driveway for a Hatzolah ambulance or equipment.
- Donate medical equipment in memory or merit of a loved one.

▶ Homework Help

- Volunteer an hour a week to help someone with homework.
- Set up a hot line to help with homework.

▶ Jobs

- Offer to serve as a reference for someone who had done satisfactory work for you.
- Take an active role in finding someone a job.
- Network within your work and social circle to find jobs for people in your community.
- Circulate resumes of people seeking employment.
- Set up an organization within your community to help people find jobs.
- Help someone polish his/her resume.
- Give someone in need of a job an opportunity to work for you when possible.

▶ Language

- If you speak a second language, help people communicate with household help, workers, doctors, etc.

▶ Lost and Found

- Take the time to return an object that you find.
- Hang posters or take out a classified ad to find the owner of a

lost object.

- Set up a hot line to facilitate the return of lost objects.

▶ Mentor

- Get trained to be a mentor to a child in need of special attention.
- Spend time with a child/teen on a regular basis.
- Organize a hotline and volunteers to spend time with children in need of such attention.

▶ Mothers — Postpartum Assistance

- Take care of other child/children.
- Cook for the family.
- Organize and or pay for household help.
- Organize a hotline for those in need of such services.
- Organize a list of volunteers to help the family.

▶ Shidduchim — Assisting Singles in Finding Their Mates

- Invite a single for a meal.
- Make or suggest an introduction.
- Listen to a single's concerns.
- Network with others to find *shidduchim*.
- Start a group in your neighborhood to meet once a month to work on *shidduchim*.

▶ Shomrim - Community Watch

- Volunteer your time to help your community watch group.
- Organize such a patrol in your community.
- Support such a patrol in your community.

▶ Simchas Chassan Kallah — Bringing Joy to Bride and Groom

Creating a lively atmosphere at a wedding is a chesed for the chassan and kallah.

- Dance at a wedding.
- Attend a wedding—even without an invitation—specifically for

the purpose of dancing and enlivening the atmosphere.

- Organize a group to dance at a wedding.
- Make a wedding or *Sheva Berachos* for a couple that is needy or without family.

▶ Tehillim

- Pray for those facing difficult times.
- Organize a group in your neighborhood to complete *Sefer Tehillim* daily or weekly as a merit for someone in need.
- Create a *Tehillim* chain-call list to engender widespread prayers for urgent medical situations.

▶ Telephone

There are many telephone services that are designed to help people in different situations. It is a chesed to inform people of these resources.

- Work to bring such programs to your community.
- Volunteer for a program that is already in place.
- Support such programs in your community.

Chazak Line:

Free inspirational Torah shiurim available round the clock

- Call Chofetz Chaim Heritage Foundation at 845-352-3505 to promote Chazak in your community.

Crisis Hot Line

Telephone help for many different life crises such as domestic or emotional issues

There are too many services to list. Therefore,we are providing the number to one central service, Yitty Liebel Helpline, (718 HELP NOW), which will refer you further.

Shmiras Halashon Shailah Hot Line:

For free anonymous halachic answers to questions regarding the laws of proper speech, call 718 951 3696.

Halachah Hot Line:

Answers to halachic questions provided over the phone

▶ Torah

- Teach someone Torah for a set time each day/week especially a child/adult who does not have a comprehensive Jewish education.
- Learn with someone over the phone.
- To be connected with a learning partner, call Partners in Torah at 212-227-1000 or 800-788-3942
- Start a five-minute learning session with a colleague or neighbor using one of the many books set up for daily learning. Call Chofetz Chaim Heritage Foundation at (800) 867-2482 to order learning materials.

▶ Tutoring

- Volunteer to tutor in a subject in which you are proficient.
- Set up a free tutoring service for children who cannot afford a tutor.

▶ Words

- Greet people with a friendly word and a smile — even those who are not your friends.
- Send a note to someone who is down.
- Compliment those around you.
- Acknowledge other people's acts on your behalf with a thank-you note or call.
- Where appropriate, try to mediate a dispute.

▶ Gemach – Acronym for *Gemilas Chassodim* (free loans)

Audio-Visual Equipment Gemach

Equipment to enable a bedridden family member to participate in a simchah through live transmission

Baby Items Gemach

- Furniture — high chair, portacrib, pack 'n play, swing, scale, bassinet, etc.
- Car seats
- Carriages

* Breast pumps
* Formula
* Mother's milk

Books Gemach

The average home has many books that are no longer in active use. A lending library can be started by gathering these surplus books and organizing them in a central location.

* Donate books to a shul or school.

Bris Gemach

* Money for *bris* expenses
* Baby outfit
* *Bris* pillow, pillowcase
* Food for the *bris* meal

Clothing Gemach

* Coats
* General clothes for men, women, children
* Preemie clothes and special items
* Dresses for bride and bridal party
* Collect or help sort clothing

Computers Gemach

* Donate used, functioning computers to a person or organization.
* Volunteer to help maintain, repair and upgrade computer for a charity organization.
* Do data entry for a *gemach* or nonprofit organization.
* Organize a computer exchange to collect and distribute used computers in good condition.
* Teach someone the basics of using a computer

Furniture Gemach

* Organize volunteers to pick up and sort donated furniture.
* Create a hot line for people in need of furniture.
* Donate good-quality used furniture.

Mezuzos Gemach

- Purchase a *mezuzah* for someone who cannot afford one or is just learning about its significance.
- Have several *mezuzos* on hand to lend to those in need until they can purchase their own.

Money Gemach

- Loans for specific purposes: buying a home, making a *simchah*, paying tuition, paying medical bills, business loans, etc.

Nichum Aveilim Gemach– Helping Mourners

- Chairs for those sitting *shivah*
- Torah for house of mourning
- *Siddurim/mishnayos* for *aveilim*
- Food for *aveilim*
- Household help for *aveilim*

Pidyon Haben Gemach

- *Pidyon haben* tray

Purim Gemach

- Costumes
- Mishloach Manos to those who are ill, alone or without family

Sewing Patterns Gemach

- Save any pattern you use and pass it on to someone.
- Organize a central location for people in your community to exchange and donate patterns.

Simchah Gemach

- Centerpieces
- Tablecloths
- Liquor and wine
- Sound equipment
- Clothing

Weddings, Bar Mitzvahs:

- Gowns, wigs, headpiece for bride

- Coat for bride if *chuppah* is outdoors
- Make-up for bride on wedding day
- Gowns and dresses for wedding party
- Formal maternity wear
- Candlesticks, tablecloths, runners, table skirts
- Silver cup for ceremony
- Props for dancing — streamers, archway, umbrellas, etc.
- Centerpieces
- Tables
- Chairs
- Folding beds for out-of-town guests
- *Bentchers*
- *Bentcher* baskets
- *Challah* covers
- Microphone
- *Siddurim/chumashim*
- Trays
- Give leftover cake and untouched food to the needy.

Shalom Zachor Gemach

- Donate chickpeas, candies and beer, the traditional foods for a *shalom zachor*.

Tefillin Gemach

- Sponsor the purchase for someone in need.
- Have an extra pair made to keep in shul for anyone in need.
- Organize a community collection of *tefillin* to be checked and given /loaned to those in need.

Torah Tapes Gemach

- Lend someone a Torah tape.
- Give someone a Torah tape.
- Organize a Torah-tape library in your community.

Toy Gemach — games, books, bicycles

- Organize a collection of toys in good condition to be given to those in need

- Donate toys in good condition to a school, day care center, or pediatric ward

Transportation Gemach

Specially equipped van to transport the disabled to doctors, simchas, etc.

....

Do **you** have a unique chesed project in which you or your community is involved?

Please share it with us, and help us create a Chesed Revolution.

Send suggestions to:

Loving Kindness

Chofetz Chaim Heritage Foundation
Att: Shaindy Appelbaum
6 Melnick Drive
Monsey, NY 10952

Fax: 845-352-3505 Attention: Shaindy Appelbaum
Email: lovingkindness@chofetzchaimusa.org

Chesed Planning Calendar

Week of _____

Rabbi Paysach Krohn, the well-known speaker and author suggested the "chesed planner" as a way to grow in chesed. Writing down the chesed you do each day encourages you to keep up your momentum.

USE THIS PLANNER TO CREATE YOUR OWN RECORD OF KINDNESS!
PHOTOCOPY THIS PAGE AND STAPLE TOGETHER AS A BOOKLET.

Sunday:

❑ Done   ❑ Was unable to do, reschedule for _____.

Monday:

❑ Done   ❑ Was unable to do, reschedule for _____.

Tuesday:

❑ Done   ❑ Was unable to do, reschedule for _____.

Wednesday:

❑ Done   ❑ Was unable to do, reschedule for _____.

Thursday:

❑ Done   ❑ Was unable to do, reschedule for _____.

Friday:

❑ Done   ❑ Was unable to do, reschedule for _____.

Shabbos:

❑ Done   ❑ Was unable to do, reschedule for _____.

The Chofetz Chaim Heritage Foundation

Since 1989, the Chofetz Chaim Heritage Foundation has successfully launched innovative methods of promoting the Torah's wisdom on human relations and personal development. The foundation utilizes a vast array of effective communication tools including books, tapes, video seminars, telephone classes and a newsletter, designed to heighten one's awareness of such essential values as judging others favorably, speaking with restraint and integrity, and acting with sensitivity and respect. The Chofetz Chaim Heritage Foundation's programs reassert the Torah's timeless recipe for building a world of compassion and harmony.

The following opportunities for learning and personal growth are available through our offices.

BOOKS

Chofetz Chaim: A Lesson A Day and **Chofetz Chaim: A Daily Companion** can be used to participate in Shmiras Halashon Yomi. Learning the laws of proper speech every day, in small portions, is the method that the Chofetz Chaim recommended for observing this crucial mitzvah. The Torah tells us that Shmiras Halashon is a limitless source of blessing for ourselves, an essential element in our prayers being accepted, and the most effective way to merit Hashem's mercy.

Chofetz Chaim: Lessons in Truth brings to life the Chofetz Chaim's inspiring words on the topics of honesty and faith. This valuable addition to any Torah library is perfect for reading aloud to family, students and study groups and can be used as a springboard to discussions on how to bring its message into practice.

Daily Learning Calendar

This free daily learning calendar created by the Manchester Rosh Yeshivah, *zt'l,* is already used by thousands to participate in the program by learning the Chofetz Chaim's work, ***Sefer Chofetz Chaim***, in the original Hebrew or ***Guard Your Tongue*** in English.

TELEPHONE CLASSES

Our **Chazak Inspiration Line** offers easy-to-listen-to, 10-minute lectures on a wide range of topics such as Shalom Bayis, Shmiras Halashon, Inspiration for Difficult Times and Attaining Happiness. Callers have the opportunity to be inspired by some of today's most dynamic speakers, including Rabbi Yissocher Frand, Rabbi Ezriel Tauber, Rabbi Fishel Schachter and others. This free service is available 24 hours a day at:

Brooklyn: 718-258-2008 pin # 1234, **Monsey: 845-356-6665** pin # 3100 and **Toronto: 416-227-1070 ext. 222** pin #5100.

E-MAIL

Our email products offer subscribers a daily dose of inspiration. [Email editorial@chofetzchaimusa.org.]

Shmiras Halashon Yomi is a daily email, taken from the highly popular **Chofetz Chaim: A Lesson A Day.**

Inspiration Online offers quotes from the Torah's timeless wisdom that will motivate and inspire.

THE SHMIRAS HALASHON SHAILAH HOTLINE

This telephone hotline puts callers in contact with expert rabbanim who can answer your halachic questions concerning proper speech. This free service is available at:

718-951-3696 from 9:00 to 10:30 p.m. Monday thru Thursday and Saturday nights.

CHOSEN WORDS NEWSLETTER

This unique biweekly publication is devoted entirely to providing inspiration and practical ways to grow in Avodas Hashem. Available for synagogues and schools and in an email version for individuals, it is filled with advice on effective prayer, better relationships and personal growth. Each issue provides engaging questions for Shabbos-table discussions that make self-improvement in Avodas Hashem a lively and important family topic. Call to bring this newsletter to your school or shul. **845-352-3505 ext. 103.**

MACHSOM L'FI

While Shmiras Halashon is a requirement every day and at all times, focusing specifically on this mitzvah for a set period each day is a proven way to bolster your overall observance. Those who undertake a Machsom L'fi, commit themselves, in conjunction with others, to avoid speaking or hearing lashon hara during a two-hour period each day. This can be done as a powerful merit for someone who is ill, or for anyone that needs Divine mercy. Our office has everything needed to start a Machsom L'fi.

MISHMERES

This program brings 11,000 high-school girls throughout the country exciting programs and learning on Shmiras Halashon and character development. For information on how your school can join, call **732-905-9909.**

B'DRACHOV

The elementary school division of our organization is devoted to creating teaching tools, resource material and programs for making character development an integral part of the classroom. To join our programs or for curriculum materials contact B'Drachov, at **732-905-9909.**

For more information about these or any of our other programs, please call us at **845-352-3505.**

Chofetz Chaim Heritage Foundation
6 Melnick Drive
Monsey, NY 10952